AF560397

77

HUMAN VALUES

Principles and Practices

BOOKS BY THE SAME AUTHOR

1. Advanced Public Administration
2. Public Administration: Theory and Practice
3. Public Financial Administration
4. Public Health Policy and Administration
5. Public Personnel Administration: Theory and Practice
6. Administration and Management of NGOs: Text and Case Studies
7. Panchayati Raj in India: Theory and Practice
8. Urban Development and Management
9. Management Techniques: Principles and Practices
10. Encyclopaedia of Disaster Management (Set in 3 Vols.)
11. Management of Hospitals: Hospital Administration in the 21st Century (Set in 4 Vols.)
12. Hospital Core Services
13. Hospital Managerial Services
14. Hospital Preventive and Promotive Services
15. Hospital Supportive Services
16. Health Care System and Management (Set in 4 Vols.)
17. Health Care Management and Administration
18. Primary Health Care Management
19. Health Care Organisation and Structure
20. Health Care, Policies and Programmes
21. Nursing Services: Management and Administration
22. Distance Education in 21st Century
23. Encyclopaedia of Higher Education in 21st Century
24. Human Values and Education
25. Stress Management
26. Population Policy and Family Welfare Administration
27. International Administration
28. International Civil Service: Principles, Practice and Prospects
29. Social Welfare Administration (2 Volumes)
30. Family Planning Programme and Beyond
31. Education Policy and Administration
32. Human Resource Development in 21st Century
33. Disaster Management
34. Slum Improvement through Participatory Urban Based Community Structures
35. Development Planning and Administration
36. Public Health Administration
37. Hospital Administration: Theory and Practice
38. Principles, Problems and Prospects of Co-operative Administration
39. Personnel Administration in Co-operatives
40. Public Personnel Administration and Management
41. Right to Information and Good Governance
42. Health Education: Theory and Practice
43. School Health Education
44. Good Governance: An Integral Approach
45. Disaster Administration and Management

IN PRESS

46. Education of Lifestyle and Lifetime Diseases
47. Health Education of Communicable and Non-Communicable Disease
48. Health Education Administration: From International Level to Village Level
49. Education for Healthy Urban Cities
50. Environment and Value Education
51. Women Health Education
52. Rural Health Education

HUMAN VALUES

Principles and Practices

DR. ARUNA GOEL
Professor of Sanskrit, Panjab University, Chandigarh,
Member, University Grants Commission,
Member, Indian Institute of Advanced Study, Shimla,
Member, Sahitya Academy, (Sanskrit Board), Government of India,
New Delhi

DR. S.L. GOEL
Editor, The Indian Journal of Public Administration, New Delhi
Vice-President, Executive Council,
Indian Institute of Public Administration, New Delhi
Professor of Public Administration (Retd.)
Panjab University, Chandigarh
Emeritus Fellow, University Grants Commission
Director, State Bank of India (Local Board), Chandigarh
Director, National Horticulture Board, Ministry of Horticulture,
Government of India, New Delhi
Formerly Member UGC, Member Distance Education Council
and Member All India Board of Management, AICTE

DEEP & DEEP PUBLICATIONS PVT. LTD.
F-159, Rajouri Garden, New Delhi-110027

HUMAN VALUES
Principles and Practices

ISBN 978-81-8450-095-0

Typeset by S.S. COMPOSERS,
3190, Mohindra Park, Shakur Basti, Delhi-110034.

Printed in India at MAYUR ENTERPRISES,
WZ Plot No. 3, Gujjar Market, Tihar Village, New Delhi - 110 018.

Published by DEEP & DEEP PUBLICATIONS PVT. LTD.
F-159, Rajouri Garden, New Delhi-110027.
Phones: 25435369, 25440916
E-mail: ddpbooks@yahoo.co.in • ddpubs@gmail.com
Showroom:
2/13, Ansari Road, Daryaganj, New Delhi-110002 • Telefax: 23245122

Contents

Preface

Principles and Practice of Value Education are of paramount significance to make individuals, society and Universe a fit place to lead a peaceful and prosperous life.

Values are neither easy to define nor to measure yet education is normative enterprise where value plays a vital role for determining the quality of life. Values can be defined as objectives and states of affairs that are designed by an individual. Value is something which pervades everything. It determines the meaning of the world as a whole as well as the meaning of every person, every action, even the smallest change introduced into the world by an agent has a value (Losskey and Marshall, 1935).

Value education involves social education but extends beyond it in so far as it covers the way the individual deals with his own powers and potentialities as well how he behaves in his relationship with other people and the community at large. It is as much concerned with striving for personal wholeness as with generating a responsible attitude towards others and an understanding of right and wrong behaviour.

S.B. Chawan Committee Report presented to the Rajya Sabha on February 26, 1999 states: Values are principles which direct our actions and activities, they are in-built in our society common to not only all the communities but also to all religions at all times. These values, if deteriorated will hasten or accelerate the breakdown of family, society and nation as a whole, India has an age-old tradition of values interwoven in the national fabric. Although there has been advancement in science and technology, there has been general erosion of values, which is reflected in day-to-day life of large section of present society, our young generation under the growing influence of negative aspects of western culture is stranded on the crossroads, not able to decide which way to take.

The philosophy about value is that value should help anyone to the real knowledge and goal of life in a righteous manner. It is equally important to ensure that the youth are equipped with core values needed to live as responsible citizens in complex democratic societies.

Pt. Jawaharlal Nehru said: "Let us pursue our path to industrial progress with all over strength and vigour and at the same time remember that material riches without tolerance and compassion and wisdom may turn to dust and ashes." There is growing recognition that many adolescents are not sufficiently prepared to deal with the demands of modern society. Traditional mechanisms for passing on lifeskills, (e.g. family, community role models, cultural traditions) may no longer be adequate in many communities. The reasons given for this include the weakening of traditional support structures as urbanization breaks up the extended family. There is also the power of the media in shaping the development of youth and the rapid social changes that make the lives of young people, their expectations, values and opportunities so different from that of their parents. In addition, adolescents face increasing risks to their health and development, such as HIV/AIDS, drug abuse, stress, violence and suicides.

How can we overcome these problems of 21st century. The answer is the imparting of lifeskills education with values as the most important ingredient. Lifeskills education is a unified and developmental approach to help children and adolescents learn how to deal with difficulties of daily life. growing up and risk situations.

The main thrust of Value Education should be to ensure practice of values by all. We have seen that all religions agree on important values and therefore, if we follow these values, we can usher an era of peace, progress and development.

The present book "Human Values: Principles and Practices" has been divided into ten chapters. Chapter-1 deals with meaning, significance and scope of value education. Chapter-2 suggests the role of family in injecting values among the members of the family. Family is first and basic unit and a suitable institution where children can imbibe human values by imitation unconsciously. From family, one moves to the society. Chapter-3 deals with the methods, procedures and role of society in moulding the individual in social culture and values. Social values can keep the individual imbued with value system. Chapter-4 deals with role of education from primary school to higher education level in making students learn good values and practice them. Education is the real instrument to create good values among students. In this the author has discussed the role of teacher, curriculum development, educational environment and educational facilities as well. Chapter-5 examines the role of Yoga in promoting a value system which is perfect and can make society worth living. Chapter-6 suggests the role of religious scriptures in encouraging their followers to practice values. The emphasis has been laid on the need of integration of the value from all religions as the ultimate aim of all religions is the same. Chapters 7, 8, 9 examine the role of legislature, executive and judiciary in promoting good values through practice in these forums by their members.

Suma Varughesse in her article on Spirituality in Life Plus, July and Sept. 2004 beautifully explains that: Our ancient Values can transform the existing values system. To quote her:

"Let us begin by considering the concept of interconnection. One of the Buddha's great truth . . . as also the central truth of the Upanishads, interconnection means my welfare is linked with yours. I cannot harm you without harming myself. I cannot despoil the earth or pollute the rivers without endangering myself. I cannot exterminate species without forging my own extinction. I cannot cheat, harm or manipulate another without making the world less safe for myself. Conversely, if I spread love and goodness, goodness and love will impinge on me. The concept of interconnection has the potential to change our outlook and therefore society radically. Politics will become a means to serve the society rather than be a naked chase for power.

Economics will be guided by concern for the environment rather than for profit-making. The conflicts, whether at the level of nations, community or within the family or even with one's own self, will melt away once we experience the fact that we are all one. It all boils down to a great heaving shift in the world culture, giving birth unquestionably to the New Age."

At the conference, *"Dialogue among civilizations quest for new perspectives"*, July 9-10, 2000 the concept of values was elaborated as: Values may be defined as those desirable ideals and goals which are intrinsic in themselves and which, when achieved or attempted to be achieved, evoke a deep sense of fulfilment to one or many or all parts of what we consider to be the highest elements of our nature. Values are norms, which hold and sustain life and society and establish a symbiotic and interdependent relationship between humankind and ecosystem. Values denote a fundamental category; in a common understanding they correspond to what we mean when it is said that Truth, Beauty and Goodness are the Supreme value of life. They occur to us whenever we try to conceive all those states of our being or becoming in which we are likely to find some kind of ultimate fulfilment.

An article in *Hindu*, "Ethics of Life" dated 30th June, 2007 suggests that an honest attempt to probe the root cause of happiness would gradually reveal that it is within the self and not in external sources—wealth, power, fame, name, success, etc. This truth is the basis of all spiritual teaching that advocates the practice of dharma. It also implies a disciplined life that gives peace, mental strength and inner happiness. Virtues such as patience, forgiveness, piety, honesty, sanctity, control of senses, learning, truthfulness, etc. benefit both the individual and society."

It is hoped that the book "Human Values: Principles and Practices" would be useful to all to ensure peace and bliss on this earth. All of us agree about good values in theory. But when it comes to practice, we either of our own benefit or compulsions from other well known personalities deviate from following the values. It becomes all the more serious when this is committed by persons holding high office in the Executive, Legislature and Judiciary. When common man observes all this happening, he also joins the race and looses faith in values.

To quote Gita in Sloka 21, Chapter III:

यद्यदाचरति श्रेण्ठस्तत्तदेवेतरो जनः ।
स यत्प्रमाणं कुरुते लोकस्तदनुवर्तति ॥ 3/21

'For whatever a great man does, that very thing other men also do; whatever standard he sets up, the generality of men follow the same'.

The common run of men begin to follow whatever the great man establishes by his precept and practice as the standard of morality, and perform their duties exactly on the lines laid down by the great man. This is meant by the statement that "whatever standard is set-up by the great man, is followed by the generality of men." Therefore, the great and noble man of knowledge, holding a position of honour in society, should in the interest of the world order very carefully perform his own duties and thus all men will perform their duties.

ARUNA GOEL
S.L. GOEL

1

Meaning, Significance and Scope of Values

> Since the Observance of Moral Principles Yields spiritual excellence, it ought to be guarded as more important than preservation of one's life.
>
> —*Thikkural*

Indeed, India can make a powerful contribution to the evolution of a truly universal human civilization of the future based on this pious ethos of reason and morality. That alone will build-up a world order where development is not bereft of humane and spiritual values, where development is guided by a value-based system following the path of righteousness and virtue, character and morality, and where development is measured not just in terms of GDP but in terms of overall content of happiness, character and value orientation of the humanity at large. It is this ethos that we need to build up, promote and propagate; it is this learning environment that we should establish in our educational institutions."

The modern world is marked by a widespread explosion of knowledge and tremendous achievements in Science and Technology, coupled with a general decline and reversal of human values as well as an alarming deterioration

CHART 1.1

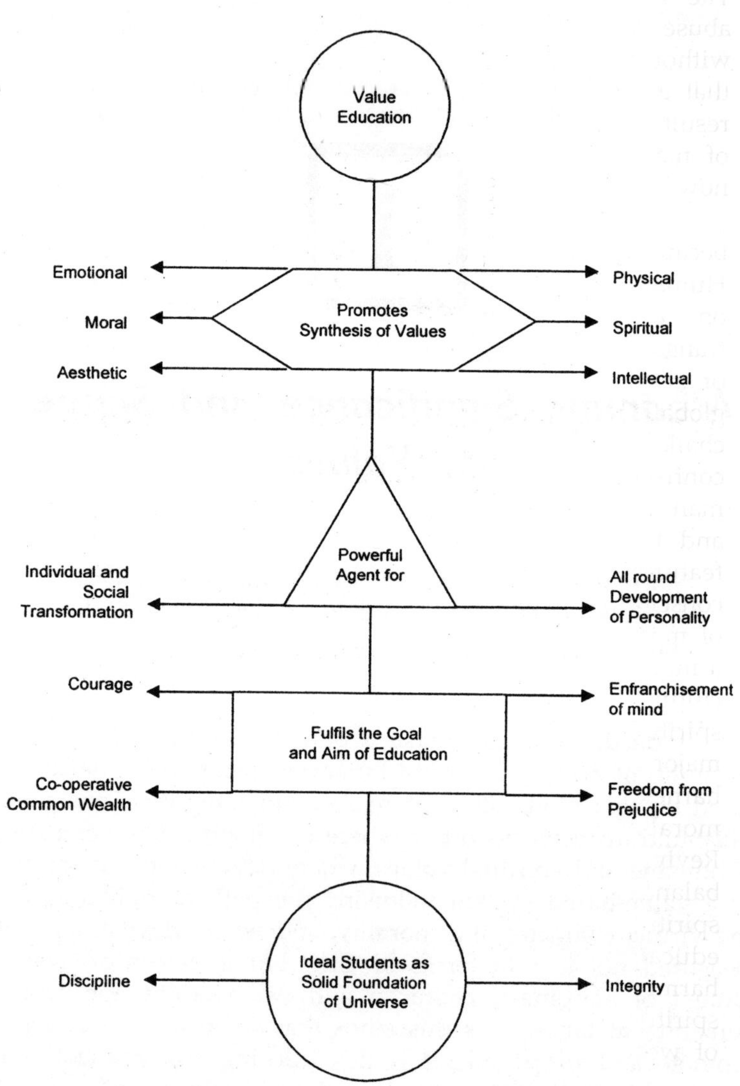
Value Education
Emotional
Moral
Aesthetic
Promotes Synthesis of Values
Physical
Spiritual
Intellectual
Individual and Social Transformation
Powerful Agent for
All round Development of Personality
Courage
Co-operative Common Wealth
Fulfils the Goal and Aim of Education
Enfranchisement of mind
Freedom from Prejudice
Discipline
Ideal Students as Solid Foundation of Universe
Integrity

of moral and mental health both of individuals and societies. The recent spate of crimes, violence, terrorism, and drug abuse makes us aware of the significance of human values, without which human life loses all meaning. It is also evident that a mere economic prosperity and material wealth cannot result in a lasting well-being of mankind. The inner strength of mankind springs from within, which seems ill-nourished now.[1]

Dhokalia feels that today humanity binds us together because the global society has created oneness of mankind. Human rights and their co-relative human duties are founded on eternal and universal human values and ideals transcending all man-made boundaries—civilization, cultural or geographic. In our times of social, political and economic globalization, additional values are being questioned and challenged and so education as a social institution is confronted with new challenges in respect to the view of man, one's perception of knowledge and the educational aims and the vision of good life and values and its substantive features. The goal of elevation of man's awareness and consciousness, and of enlightenment of his soul with a view of making a new harmonious multi-cultural world order and a more humane civilization requires a synthesis of varieties of cultural and religious diversities of materialism with spiritualism and of the values, ideals and the spirit of all major religions of the world. This further underlines harnessing of every branch of knowledge and the union of moral and secular values with constitutional and legal norms. Revival of the duty-oriented society, a spiritual basis and balancing of human rights and duties as co-relatives and spiritual regeneration of the entire human life through education in a wider sense, can pave the way for a harmonious, just and peaceful global order. Moral and spiritual source of rights and duties enjoins tenacious pursuit of worthy ideals and human values.[2]

Swami Vivekananda Observes: To be happy is the universal urge of all beings and at all times. One has to be at peace with oneself to be happy. There can be no peace for a turbulent mind. Vasanas, desires, take away the peace of mind. It is only when we follow a value system that we can have a serene, contemplative mind. When mind is calm, we can turn it within to 'see' the treasure of pure consciousness. No treasure on earth is equal to a slice of that tattva. Mind has to be loosened from durvyapara (misdeeds and engaged in acquiring sadgunas (virtues). In Gita, Krsna talks about the developing human values and says that a mind which has daivisampatti (divine qualities) has santi (PEACE). These values make us introspective and correct our personality.

The philosophy about value is that value should help anyone to seek the real knowledge and goal of life in a righteous manner. It is equally important to ensure that the youth are equipped with core values needed to live as responsible citizens in complex democratic societies.

However, under the lust of materialism, the people in the world became selfish and exploited their brethren causing disequilibrium in world economic and social order. People of India with a rich heritage of co-operative living succumbed to these temptations causing social and economic imbalances. What is the way-out to come out of this chaos? How can we create a social and economic order based on equity and justice? How can we serve the millions who are suffering under the weight of the present socio-economic order? The answer is plain and simple that is following all types of values which are common world over and are basic and relevant for all times, Einstein, the greatest scientists of our times expressed strongly in favour of values to strengthen the social fabric of the society. He said: "A positive aspiration and effort for an ethical and moral configuration of our common life is of overriding importance. Here, no science can save us. I believe, indeed, solely the practical and factual in our education has led directly to the importance of ethical values."

Yoga is special skill in the performance of activities. The skill consists in maintaining the uniformity of mind in success and failure. The person who maintains this skill performs all the works as his duty. He dedicates his mind to God.

Samacittatva is unfailing equanimity—or evenness of mind in all situations—favorable or unfavourable. The person is not elated when good things happen nor gets angry when misfortune betides. This unwavering evenness of mind is true knowledge.

Yoga is knowledge, understanding of things like the self, acquired from the scriptures and the Preceptors. The single-pointed and striking realization of these truths, by controlling the sense organs is Yoga.

Here in this present human life the Self must be known. This is the injunction. How? If the Self is known in this birth the life's goal is achieved. This is the supreme truth. His life is fruitful. If the Self is not known in this life, that would become useless.

Tapah, the concentration of the physical body, the sense organs and the mind; **damah,** discontinuance from sense objects, Karma, Agnihotra, rituals, etc. One who attains holiness by means of purification of the heart through these things can get the knowledge of Brahman.

Don't Speak Untruth

Not that there ever was or is in them any falsehood. Contrary to that speaking untruth is the behaviour of bad people. Can any body become free from death? and decrepitude by his falsehood. For which reason (martyah), man (sasyam iva) like corn, (Pacyate), tatters and dies and after death (punah) again; sasyam iva ajavate, (reborns like conr). Thus what one can gain in this impermanent human world by breaking his own words?

Classification of Values

Values have been classified differently by different educationists and philosophers. Mascarend has classified them as professional values, operational values and dynamic values. National Education Policy (1986) classified all the values into three main categories—Personal values, social values and National values. All the three supplement one another. Adherence to personal values would promote better social and national values:

All these three aspects if practiced would make students value conscious. The need for value education has been stressed by all the commissions set-up for educational development from time to time,

Values can be classified in different ways under different categories. For example, they can be either intrinsic or instrumental, depending on whether they are desires for their own sake or are meant to be means to achieve something. Values like truthfulness, happiness, spirituality and knowledge are intrinsic while desire for money and power is an instrumental value. Values can also be classified as moral and aesthetic. Moral values deal with perceptions of right and wrong while aesthetic values reflect beauty and ugliness. Values can again be classified as positive or negative depending on the what a person wants and those he would like to avoid. They could also be considered as higher or lower. Higher values are intellectual, aesthetic, moral and spiritual in character while lower values are for material or physical gains.

Value can also be classified as theoretical, economic, aesthetic, social, political and religious. Theoretical value means having dominant interest in the discovery of truth and is empirical, critical, rational and intellectual in approach. Economical value means that an object commands a money price. People value money or material things not for their own sake but for the pleasure and enjoyment that they provide. Economic values are instrumental rather than intrinsic they are values of commodities in exchange and arise out of production and use of material goods.

Aesthetic value refers to the experience that a person has when he perceives an object as beautiful or conversely ugly. One realizes an aesthetic value when one perceives an object as a unified expression of meaningful feelings. The aesthetic experience is a special kind of experience and is an interaction between an object and a subject. The subject that is the person contributes sense organs and also depends on his past experiences for appreciation or dislike of objects. One gets social values from friendship, love, family and participation in good activities. Political values represent interest in political matters and/or having alliance with a particular political party. Lastly, if a person considers an object divine, it is aid to have a religious value and its experience is called religious experience, which may be spiritual or divine.[3]

Meaning

Let us discuss the meaning as given by various commissions and experts.

The Oxford English Dictionary defines ethics as the science of morals or moral principles. Values, norms, standards, morality like expressions are also considered synonyms to this expression and recently "social responsibility" has also been used. It has, but to me, something to do with the sense of right or wrong—what is permissible and what is done.[4]

Before founding BHU, Malviya had said: "To revitalize India as a Nation, it is necessary to feed her youth with old spiritual and moral values and religion must be made a part of education based on Indian ideals."[5]

To achieve real happiness you have to imbibe ideals, values and principles, acquire the right qualities and adopt the right attitude. Primacy must be accorded to character and morality. Aim high in life and regard failures as pillars of success. Be optimistic and ever smiling. Your constant endeavour in life should be to become a good person. This can be achieved by thinking good, speaking good and doing good. Goodness implies quality of caring, compassion, kindness, benevolence, sacrifice, love of truth, humanism, tolerance, harmony, non-violence and morality. Virtue always follows goodness; cultivate good habit and make goodness a habit; for man without goodness is not better than a beast. The truly great are not those who have more money or brains or higher status or position. What really matters is whether you have been kind and helpful to others. This can be achieved when you expand your capacity to love and not to hate others. Love begins when we care for others and take trouble to bring comfort to those in pain and suffering. This is the best way to be happy and this is the best way to be great.[6]

The three most important things I have learned in my life and I want to share with you, are:

- first, from my father, that there is dignity in every kind of work;
- second, from Massachusetts Institute of

Technology, which is where I graduated, always to strive for excellence;

- third, from Indira Gandhi, never to abandon hope; and
- While my own experience has taught me that hard work and integrity have no equal.

You must always search for excellence. This quest is something that must guide you. Compromise on standards of integrity has been a source of national disaster that we have lived with too long. Your generation must restore the faith that the founding fathers of modern India held—faith that we must aspire only for the best.[7]

In the UNESCO Report "Learning to be", the true meaning and content of education has been explained as follows: "The physical, emotional and ethical integration of the individual into a complete man is a broad definition of the fundamental aim of education."

An ideal system of education would enable individuals to know and develop to the fullest extent their intellectual potentialities, and promote their awareness of social and human values, so that they can develop a strong character and live better lives and function as responsible members of society. It is by transforming the human being that social transformation can be brought about. The future of the human race is dependent exclusively upon a radical transformation of human consciousness and one of the most important means of affecting this transformation is an integral and value-oriented education. In the context of educational philosophy, they refer to those desirable ideals and goals, which are intrinsic in themselves and which when achieved or attempted to be achieved, evoke a deep sense of fulfilment. The ultimate values, which are characteristically Indian, are "Satyam, Shivam, Sundaram"—'Truth, beauty, and goodness": which inspire one to know the truth, to seek the beautiful and do the good. These are the ultimate values that have to be cultivated though education."[8]

Values are neither easy to define nor to measure yet education is normative enterprise where value plays a vital role for determining the quality of life. Values can be defined as objectives and states of affairs that are designed by an individual. Value is something which pervades everything. It determines the meaning of the world as a whole as well as the meaning of every person, every action, even the smallest change introduced into the world by an agent has a value. (Losskey and Marshall, 1935).[9]

Dr. A.P.J. Abdul Kalam, said, "If you want to leave your footprints on the sands of time, do not drag your feet. According to John F. Emling, "Values are those aspects of anything which, when re-organised and understood, encourage, induce or incline to use them for the purpose."

Jai Chand Chandel (2002) observes that "Values are those standards which we use to influence the attitudes, values and actions of others. It is a yardstick that is used to guide the actions, attitudes, comparisons, evaluations, and justifications of others and self. These are the guiding principles of life and help in all round development of the individual."

D.H. Parker says, "Values belong wholly to the inner world of mind. The satisfaction of desire is that real value; the thing that serves is only an instrument. A value is always an experience, never a thing or an object."

Elizabeth B. Hurlock observes that "Values are concepts heavily weighted with emotions. They are concepts of the desirable, which influence the child's selection from available modes, means and ends of action. Because they are primarily subjective, they are stronger predispositions of behaviour than concepts with less heavy emotional weighting are."

According to M.P. Hung, (1975) Values as a judgement concerning the worth of an object, persons, group or situation. Value judgment contains evaluating rating terms, such as good, moral, immoral, beautiful, ugly, etc."

T. Parson (1960) says that "Values is an element of a shared symbolic system which serves a criterion or standard for selection among the alternatives of orientation which are intrinsically open in a situation."

Radhakrishnan Commission (1948)

"If we exclude spiritual training in our institutions we would be untrue to our whole historical development."

Sri Prakasa Committee on Religious and Moral Instruction

"Every effort must, therefore, be made to teach students true moral values from the earliest stages of their educational life."

Kothari Commission (1964-66)

"A serious defect in the education system is the absence of provision for education in social, moral and spiritual values. A national system of education that is related to life, needs and aspirations of the people cannot afford to ignore this purposeful force."

National Policy on Education (1986)

"The growing concern over the erosion of essential values and an increasing cynicism in society has brought to focus the need for readjustments in the curriculum in order to make education a forceful tool for the cultivation of social and moral values."

Programme of Action NPE (1992)

"The framework emphasized value education as an integral part of school curriculum. It highlighted the values drawn from national goals, universal perception, ethical considerations and character building. It stressed the role of education in combating obscurantism, religious fanaticism, exploitation and injustice as well as the inculcation of values"[10].

In addition to the emphasis of commissions on moral education, persons of eminence have also advocated the cause of moral education for all round development of the youth.

Education is a powerful and pervasive agent for all round development, individual and social transformation. This alone can sustain culture and civilization. A balanced development of mind and body in harmony with the spirit is the key to the enrichment of human personality and also the key to 'true education,' which must in the ultimate analysis help humanity to rise to a higher level of consciousness. Gandhiji said: "Unless the development of mind and body goes hand in hand with a corresponding awakening of the soul, the former alone would prove to be a poor lopsided affair. By spiritual training, I mean education of the heart. A proper and all round development of the mind, therefore, can take place only when it proceeds *paripassu* with the education of the physical and spiritual faculties of the child. . . . Our children must from their infancy be taught the 'dignity of labour'. Thus the true meaning of education is harmonious development of head, heart and hand, i.e. enlighment of mind, compassion and dignity of labour." Such qualities would automatically promote the development of youth.

Sarvepalli Radhakrishnan said: "The three things—vital dynamism, intellectual efficiency and spiritual direction together constitute the proper aim of education. Moral and spiritual training is an essential part of education. Enfranchisement of the mind, freedom from prejudice and fanaticism, and courage are essential. What we need today is the education of the whole man—physical, vital, mental, intellectual and spiritual. . . . If education is to help us to meet the moral challenge of the age and play its part in the life of the community, it should be liberating and life giving. It must give a basic meaning to personality and existence and equip us with the power to overcome spiritual inertia and foster spiritual sensitivity. . . . Seat of learning should produce men and women who will move together to develop common ideals and purposes, love each other and co-exist to create a co-operative common wealth."

Swami Vivekananda had proclaimed: "We must have life-building, man-making, character building-education." Shanker Dayal Sharma, former president of India, the scholar-educationalist had said, "The aim and objective of all education is to maintain, sustain and develop a healthy mind in a healthy body. Co-curricular and extra-curricular activities have as much place in our system as the curriculum and the syllabus. The lack of such activities is the reason for the growing evils of habitual smoking, drinking and drug-addiction fast growing amidst our student community. . . . Education is not injection or injunction. It is not indoctrination of views and ideas or just an imposition of one's views upon others. In short, education should not be an infliction. The moment education becomes such an infliction, the consequence will be student indiscipline, strikes and agitations within the campus." Pandit Nehru rightly said: "A vast responsibility . . . rests on our universities and educational institutions and those who guide their destinies. They have to keep their lights burning and must not stray from the right path even when passion convulses the multitude and blinds many amongst those whose duty is to set an example to others."

Gurudev Rabindranath Tagore had a vision for such an education: "Education must aim at the development of moral, spiritual and ethical values and we should seek them in our own heritage as well as in other cultures and civilizations . . . It should be such that Indians do not lose sight of their rich heritage—their thought must be rooted to the ideals set forth in the great writings and works of our sages, poets and philosophers. The noble goals and high values set forth in our precious culture must be adhered to."

Shanker Dayal Sharma had said: "Thus a teacher must succeed in conveying the larger ideals of service to the community, virtues of tolerance and respect for all faiths, the importance of character, integrity and discipline and the value of humanism to his pupils. They should also be made aware of our heritage and culture." He was a great advocate of 'developing a mature attitude towards religion'. To quote him again. . . "Acquaintance with prayers of different religion and hymns and songs of various faiths could also, surely, help our youth to recognize the intrinsic purity, beauty and practical usefulness of different religious thoughts."[11]

Value is a "conception explicit or implicit, distinctive of an individual or characteristic of a group of those desirable traits which influence the selection from available modes and ends of action." (Wuchohn, 1957). (Rokeach, 1973) defined values as "enduring belief, a specific mode of conduct and state existence along a continuum of relative importance." Values are the criteria for determining levels of goodness, worth or beauty.

Values in our education is a hotly debated subject nowadays. This is because of the chaotic conditions observed in almost all spheres of our national life. It is conjectured, not without reason, that this chaos is mainly due to *lack of values* in the education being imparted in India. This was formulated, as is well-known, by Macaulay in 1836 more to enslave the Indian mind than to liberate it, so that Indians would remain loyal to British Raj, being alienated from their native Vedic culture, education and Sanskrit language. As planned, this gradually weaned our intellectuals away from our classical heritage and from the Sanskrit language, in which lay all our spiritual, cultural, social, and political traditions. We lost our indigenous system of education in which hearing, chanting and memorizing played a great part, assimilation of ideas took place through a well-planned life of service to teacher, contemplation and meditation, all under his guidance. Thus the educated ones in that system were men who had not only knowledge but also character. Knowledge had become a part of their life, influencing their thoughts, emotions and actions.

The Sanskrit for values is Dharma or Sadâcâra. Dharma is described as 'the set of values that sustains the creation without which the very existence of it would be threatened.' Sankaracharya defined Dharma as the values that sustained human beings and helped them to enjoy happiness both in this as well as in the spiritual world.

Thus education in India meant not merely intellectual cramming of information into the brain but the application of them into one's life so that life became better at individual, social, secular, spiritual levels. Education was a life-transformer. That is real education which liberates.[12]

Eminent Journalist, Mr. V.N. Narayanan, Editor, *The Hindustan Times,* delivered the Convocation Address at the XV and XVI convocation of the Nagarjuna University. He said, "When we face problems of ethics, we tend to solve them by research, by statistics, by the use of instruments and resources rather than by moral energy. The Victorian society in Britain, the pre-Independence Congress party under Mahatma Gandhi, Abraham Lincoln's era in U.S. politics displayed this moral energy. This is not to be confused with excessive Puritanism or moralism. All it demanded of the people was the feeling that they were put on this earth in order to leave it a better place than you found it."[13]

R. Satya Raju in his Article, "Human Values in University Management" suggests the following:

(a) Value education means a positive effort for bringing about a synthesis of physical, intellectual, emotional, aesthetic, moral and spiritual values in a human being;

(b) Due to total neglect in the last six decades after independence, the present focus is on revival of moral and spiritual values in education; and

(c) The government should have no reservation in introducing and funding universal religion of human values in the form, in the contents and in the methodology of education at all levels.

Let us understand three areas of education and our values; viz.

(a) "Truth" seeking through scientific and objective processes which are followed by the scientists;

(b) "beauty" creates appreciation through the processes of artistic and unique expression followed by artists; and

(c) "goodness" constructed through the processes of subjective and meaningful contracting followed by social scientists. There is danger in trespassing the boundaries of sciences to arts-to-social sciences without transforming our own respective perspective and amending the tools of analysis used by our own discipline areas. This has implications of prioritizing values in various disciplines and their scholars. These scholars in turn influence the value substance and methodology prescribed for institutions in a centralized model of education.[14]

All these three aspects if practiced would make students value conscious. The need for value education has been stressed by all the commissions set-up for educational development from time to time,

Maslow says , "If we want to know the possibilities of spiritual growth value growth or moral development in human beings then I maintain that we can learn most by studying our most moral, ethical or saintly people."

Rationale and Philosophy of Values

A recent conference, "Dialogue among civilizations quest for new perspectives", July 9-10, 2000 elaborated the concept of values as:

Values may be defined as those desirable ideals and goals which are intrinsic in themselves and which, when achieved or attempted to be achieved, evoke a deep sense of fulfilment to one or many or all parts of what we consider to be the highest elements of our nature. Values are norms, which hold and sustain life and society and establish a symbiotic and interdependent relationship between humankind and ecosystem. Values denote a fundamental category; in a common understanding they correspond to what we mean when it is said that Truth, Beauty and Goodness are the Supreme value of life. They occur to us whenever we try to conceive all those states of our being or becoming in which we are likely to find some kind of ultimate fulfilment.

There are, indeed, values of physical life, values of emotional life, values of mental life, but these values constantly point towards certain basic and ultimate values, which are moral and spiritual in character.

Moral and spiritual values are the foundations of the highest peaks of civilization, and since they emancipate humanity from narrow grooves of thought, they deserve to be understood more and more clearly and more and more meaningfully. Moral and spiritual values appear to be the common elements of various religions promoting everlasting peace and universal harmony; we look up to the ethical and spiritual values in our effort to rise above differences among religions. In recent times, a vast effort has been made to discover the pursuit of those values—moral and spiritual—which are to be found among all religions. And it has been rightly argued that what is most important in religions is the pursuit of ethical and spiritual values, which transcend the externalities of religious institutions.

Science, morality and spirituality are intimately intertwined and they should not be viewed as antagonistic to each other. Indeed, the survival of human race at the present

CHART 1.2

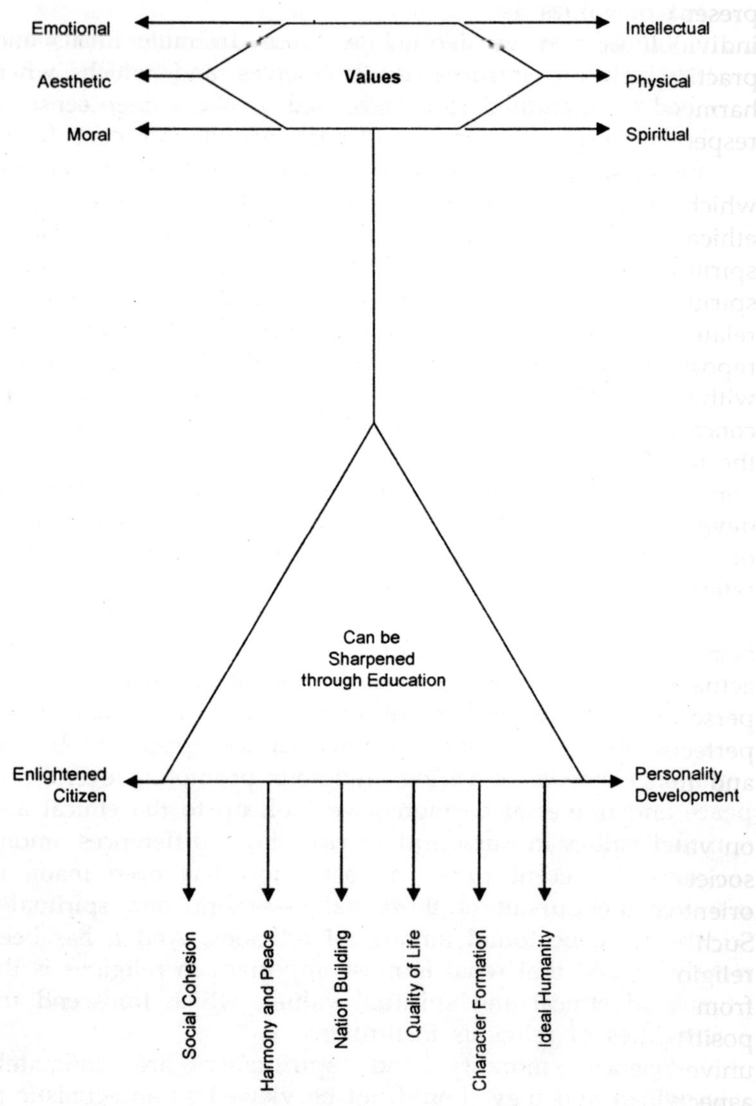
Emotional
Aesthetic
Moral
Values
Intellectual
Physical
Spiritual
Can be
Sharpened
through Education
Enlightened
Citizen
Personality
Development
Social Cohesion
Harmony and Peace
Nation Building
Quality of Life
Character Formation
Ideal Humanity

critical juncture of human history will depend upon the pursuit of ethical and spiritual values. It has been rightly contended that peace is a most desirable objects of the present world and that peace cannot be achieved unless individuals and increasing masses of people contemplate and practice ethical and spiritual values such as those of unity, harmony, mutuality, friendship, faithfulness, sincerity and respect for diversity.

Spirituality is premised on universal consciousness, which can serve as the basis of the unity of humankind, and ethical systems derive their force and sustaining power from spiritual consciousness. In the field of education, ethical and spiritual values need to be encouraged, since they are directly related to the character development of students. In the latest reports of UNESCO, "learning to be" and "Learning: Treasure within", the highest ideals have been put forward. The concept of "To Be" is so defined as to mean development of the fullness of personality in all richness. And this fullness of personality involves fullness of ethical and spiritual development. The ideal of "To Be" is distinct from the ideal of "To Acquire" and "To Possess." The ideal of "To Be" refers to that direction of effort which leads the individual to look deeply within oneself and to find in his or her inner being the source and treasure of his or her potentialities and actualities, the source of a harmony of the complexity of personality, and the source of fulfilment in some kind of perfection that transcends egoism and which rests in a vast and integrated self-hood.

The National Policy on Education has laid special stress on value-education. It has been said, "In our culturally plural society education should foster universal and eternal values, oriented towards the unity and integration of our people. Such value education should help eliminate obscurantism, religious fanaticism, violence, superstition and fatalism. Apart from the combative role, value education has a profound positive context based on our heritage, national goals, universal perceptions. It should lay primary emphasis on this aspect."

R. Natarajan, Former Chairman AICTE has rightly said in his convocation address at Triputi:

When we say that a person has 'values', we imply that he has certain fundamental beliefs about what is desirable or good, and that he attempts to use these in directing his life. For beliefs of this kind to be called values, two conditions are generally had to apply.

- Values are formed as a result of reflection and judgment; this they are different from desires.
- A person's values are beliefs which he sees as applicable not only to himself, but also to others; essential to the idea of value is the function of commanding.
- A person's values are beliefs which he sees as applicable not only to himself, but also to others: essential to the idea of value is the function of commanding.[15]

The Seven Sins, according to Mahatma Gandhi, are:

Politics without Principle.
Wealth without Work.
Pleasure without Conscience.
Knowledge without Character.
Commerce without Morality.
Science without Humanity.
Worship without Sacrifice.

To quote Anita Shetty: Values are those standards or codes of conduct conditioned by one's cultural tenets, guided by conscience, according to which one is supposed to conduct himself and shape his life pattern by integrating his benefits, ideas and attitudes to realize the cherished ideals and aims of life. By values we mean the criterion or basis for choosing between alternative courses of action. High values lead to objective, fair, correct decisions and actions and ensure the welfare of all concerned. Low values do exactly the opposite. Therefore, what we need more today is moral leadership focused on courage, intellectual integrity and sense of values. There is no substitute for a sense of value.

Sir Aurobindo says: In the right view both of life and of yoga all life is either consciously or subconsciously a yoga. For we mean by this term a methodized effort towards self-perfection by the expression of the potentialities latent in the being and a union of the human individual with the universal and transcendent existence we see partially expressed in man and in the cosmos."[16]

To quote Anita Shetty, "value is a conception, explicit or implicit, distinctive of an individual or characteristics which influences the selection, from available modes and ends of action" Wuchohn (1957). Rokeach (1973) defines values "as an enduring belief, a specific mode of conduct or end state existence along a continuum of relative importance."

Values maybe described as a system of personality traits which are in harmony with the inner nature of an individual and which are in accordance with the values approved by the society. The process of valuing is what we go through when we make judgment about things, events and people that we encounter in our day-to-day life.

Adisankaracarya has given many values implicit in Yoga which can make life beautiful. Let us mention some of them, Yoga is special skill in the performance of activities. The skill consists in maintaining the uniformity of mind in success and failure. The person who maintains this skill performs all the works as his duty. He dedicates his mind to God.

Essentials for Value Education

1. Creating a Congenial Environment

Universities can play great role in imparting value education. L.P. Singh in a Document, "Morality in Public Affairs" has rightly stressed the role of universities in this direction. To quote him: A university has the unique opportunity of imparting its values and disciplines to the youth, who are potentially the most creative part of a society, and who are at the stage when the mind is most capable of imbuing the right ideas and principles. The number of boys and girls passing out of our universities every year runs into

CHART 1.3

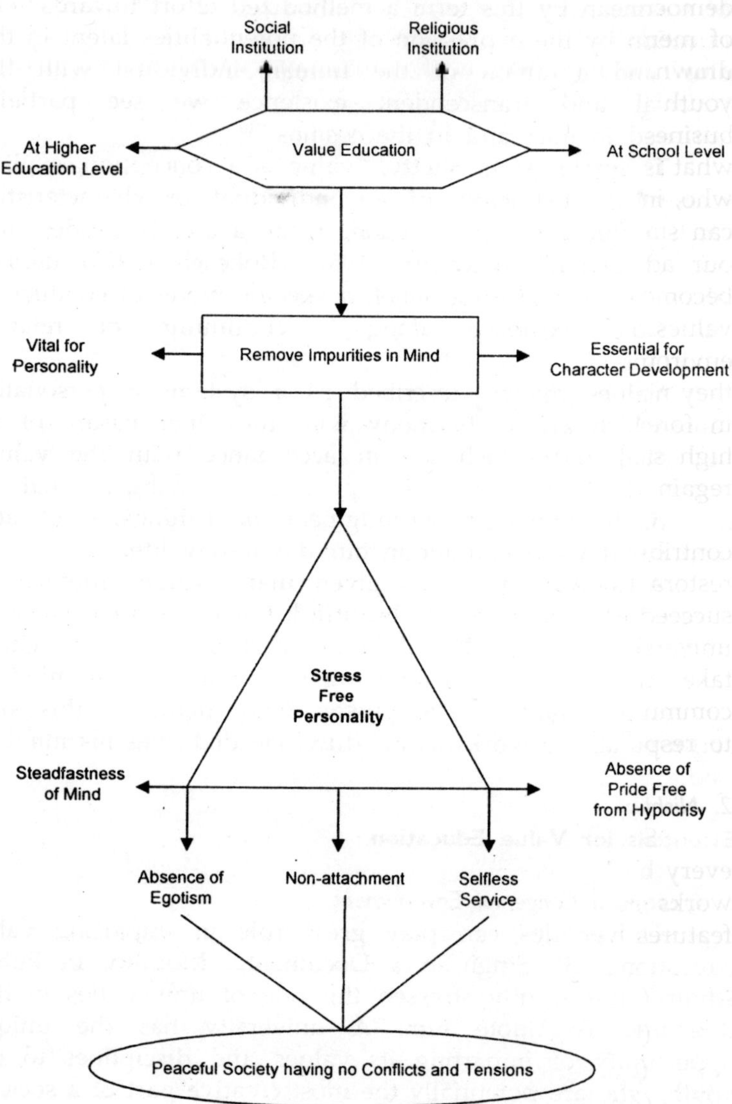

Social Institution
Religious Institution
At Higher Education Level
Value Education
At School Level
Vital for Personality
Remove Impurities in Mind
Essential for Character Development
Stress Free Personality
Steadfastness of Mind
Absence of Pride Free from Hypocrisy
Absence of Egotism
Non-attachment
Selfless Service
Peaceful Society having no Conflicts and Tensions

several lakhs, and it is from these that our ministers and most of our legislators (compared to legislature of many democratic countries the Lok Sabha has a higher percentage of members who are graduates or have higher degrees) are drawn. It is from the annually enlarging pool of educated youth that our civil services, learned professions, and business and industries at the higher levels, are manned. And what is of immense importance, it is graduates of universities who, in vast numbers, become teachers in schools, where they can start the process of molding the minds and character of our adolescents. The universities have been and can again become radiating centers not only of knowledge, but also values. They can provide to our talented scholars an environment in which they can realize creative potentialities; they now do so in most cases only when they go out to work in foreign universities where they earn great distinction. A high standard of creative work can help our universities to regain their soul.

Our universities can, over a period, make decisive contribution to the enlightenment of the public mind, and restoration of ethical standards. He believes that if we succeed in taking care of standards and values in our universities, the moral problems of the rest of society will take care of themselves. You members of universities community have great challenge before you, and it is for you to respond to it.

2. *Nishkam Karma (Selfless Service)*

S.K. Chakraborthy has suggested work ethics where every body is motivated by the ethical and moral values and works with the doctrine of Nishkam-karma. The salient features of Nishkam-karma have been identified as under:

(a) Psychological energy conservation,
(b) Reactionless steady action,
(c) Perfection (as the aim),
(d) Inner autonomy,
(e) Freedom (Swaadheen),
(f) Socio-Economically appropriate,

(g) Work Commitment,
(h) Work as Worship for excellence,
(i) Mind Enrichment, and
(j) Leads to yoga with the transcendent/higher self.

Nishkam-karma will bring holistic transformation in the work and will culminate in the following results:

(a) a stress free mind at work,
(b) a feeling for works as acts of consecration,
(c) a pure, transparent mind,
(d) an abiding instinct for ethical rectitude,
(e) an inner sanctuary of fullness, and
(f) an all embracing, other related mind.

The idea of Ethics is beautifully enunciated in Rig Veda. To quote: Veda and Vedanta inspire and encourage modern man to have common aims, common mind, common purpose, common thoughts, so that our hearts are united, so that all may live happily together. (R.V. 10.191-3-4). Human Resource Development should aim at inculcating moral and spiritual values among students which are the essence of life. Without them human behaviour is rudderless and they can never decide what is false, what is ugly, and what is beautiful. Without such power, students may be incapable to solve potential and emerging problems. Hence real education of moral and spiritual values is essential to make human resource development a reality.

3. *Teachers at all Levels of Education should be Embodiment of Ethical Values*

University faculty should be the embodiment of ethical values since they're considered nation builders through their students. They must follow a code of ethics which may be designed and followed by them. There should be total transparency. University can be eye opener to people in politics and administration. It is high time that the higher education institutions should set example of following ethical values in letter and spirit. Higher education has to play this extension role to make the country develop and the benefits of development pass on to millions of common men suffering from poverty, and ill-health, unemployment, illiteracy, etc.

Prashant Bhushan feels that the prevailing environment is full of corrupt practices at all levels. "Corruption has steeped into every part of this country's public life. From top to bottom, Prime Minister to a peon, cutting across almost every office or organisation of all Governments, Central, State or local, the vast majority of public officials in this country has become corrupt."[17] S.R. Maheshwari suggests immediate measures to root out this growing menace of unethical practices to save the nation. To quote him:

Low ethics, today, is no doubt a world-wide phenomenon but its effects are most pernicious in developing countries, like India, characterised as these are by vulnerable economies. The country's policy-makers must realise that its economic and social costs are virtually devastating: it demoralises the civil service and adversely affects its performance. It must be fought. Otherwise, the society will be forced to resort to extraordinary measures, like violence, to deal with the evil. [18]

O.P. Dwivedi, an eminent scholar, suggests the need of moral base for the Government to save the country from further degradation. To quote him:[19]

No country is immune from the moral disarray which we have seen recently. Even in the People's Republic of China, which was hailed as a paragon of public virtue and morality, however due to some cases of public service unethical activities and corruption have been reported. In many nations, a widespread sense of moral disarray exists, neither industrial nor Third World countries are exempt from this disarray. Everywhere, instances are on the rise detailing the collapse of standard and quality of service. This has contributed to the public cynicism; but at the same time, public is clamouring for a new set of bases for public morality and decent moral standards. Because, if we don't wish to be swallowed by the sea of amorality and self-centered hedonism, there will have to be some agreement (or consensus) about the behaviour of individuals, particularly those holding public offices.

The vacuum created because of traditional and 'old-fashioned' values drawn from religious sources and based on common sense being discarded in favour of materialism and selfish individualism, clearly points to the need for a code of ethics. As a matter of fact, no specific standards were left sacred against which the conduct of public officials (as well as business people) could be measured. And as clergy and religious leaders were told to keep out of the state affairs, the protective layer of public morality was left exposed to the onslaught of corruption, dishonesty, sleaziness, deception and selfish individualism. That protective layer in the body politic is needed back. For no nation or a society, irrespective of its political and religious orientation, can live in a moral vacuum. There have to be some articles of faith (drawn from the societal culture, traditions, and religions) governing our lives, which must be resurrected and strengthened. We already know that one cannot legislate honesty and good behaviour; these have to come from within. For that, one has to look to our religions where such attributes are considered sacred. But, one does not acquire such attributes by thinking alone; these have to be drilled in the thinking process of the officials. But that could be possible if their moral consciousness is raised so that they are able to fight against the forces of corruption, favouritism, and malpractice. Otherwise, they will continue to be adrift in the sea of amoralism, of which the prevailing administrative culture has come to symbolise. It is to prevent further decay that they ought to think in terms of drawing on their priceless of spiritual and cultural heritage. Thus, there is a need within the secular domain of the administrative culture to seek the spiritual guidance. Only by demonstrating high standards of personal integrity, fairness, justice, and by regarding their work as Dharma, public officials may be able to arrest those insidious forces which have penetrated the foundation as well as the structure of India's administration. Such is the requisite of a moral government.[20]

Ethical values, in simple terms, are the values that tell us what is the right, proper and acceptable way of behaving. Ethical values are indispensable for good governance. An efficient and technologically sound administrative machinery, unless it stands on high ethical pedestal, does not serve the public, but it services a self-perpetuating and exploitative system.

4. Values in Practice

Col. D.S. Cheema in his article, "Ethics in Management: The Indian Scene"[21] in *The Tribune*, dated 11.9.2000 stated that since a manager is expected to get desired and specified results from and through people, the focus of attention of management and that of the managers is on results. There is no doubt that the manager should be result-oriented, yet it appears that almost exclusive emphasis is laid on results and results alone. Many a management thinkers believe that the solution to the problems of managerial obsession with results and its undesirable effects lies in our heritage, traditions and ethos. It is relevant to mention here the concept of "Karma-yoga" and "Sthitha Pragnya" as propounded in the Bhagwad Gita. It is well known that 'Karmayoga' calls for action without expecting the results and "Sthitha Pragnya" denotes equanimity whether the results are achieved or not. A manager should aim at professional commitment when it is action and emotional detachment when it is the result.

> Karmanye Vaadhikaraste maa phaleshu kadachan;
> Maa karmaphalaheturnbhoorma te sangostwakarmini
>
> (Your right is to work only, but never to its fruits; Let not the fruit of action be thy motive, nor let thy attachment be to inaction).
>
> —*Bhagavad Geeta*

5. Need of Code of Values

"The document prepared by Deptt. of Administrative Reforms and public grievances has chalked out a Code of Ethics which need implementation. The objective of Code is to prescribe standards of integrity and conduct that are to apply in the public services. The principles stated below underlie and supplement the rules and laws to regulate the public and private conduct of various public services.

Selflessness: Holders of public office should take

decisions solely in terms of the public interest. They should not do so in order to gain financial or other material benefits for themselves/their family, or their friends.

Integrity: Holders of public office should not place themselves under any financial or other obligation to outside individuals or organisations that might influence them in the performance of their official duties.

Objective: In carrying out public business, including making public appointments, awarding contracts, or recommending individuals for rewards and benefits, holders of public office should make choice on merit.

Accountability: Holders of public office are accountable for their decisions and actions to the public and must submit themselves to whatever scrutiny is appropriate to their office.

Openness: Holders of public office should be as open as possible about all the decisions and actions that they take. They should give reasons for their decisions and restrict information only when the wider public interest clearly demands.

Honesty: Holders of public office have a duty to declare any private interest relating to their public duties and to take steps to resolve any conflicts arising in a way that protects the public interest.

Leadership: Holders of public office should promote and support these principles by leadership and example. .

These principles apply to all aspects of public life especially universities. The Committee has set them out here for the benefits of all who serve the public in any way.

6. *Create Enlightened System based on Ethical Values: Jaideep Singh feels*[22]

The Enlightened Organisation would be intensely imbued with a sense of spiritual mission. Take the case of a company producing, say, shoes. It would experience itself not merely in the business of manufacturing and selling shoes, but, simultaneously, in the spiritual mission of protecting and taking care of human feet. The degree to which members of the organisation feel themselves involved in a spiritual mission will bring to them the deep psychic experience of living a worthwhile, meaningful life and will be reflected directly in their level of motivation and cooperation. This is so because the deeper biological layers of man, as Professor Abraham Maslow has identified in his Theory of the Hierarchy of Human Needs, are Biological, Security Social, Self-respect and Self-Actualization, i.e., the needs for Truth, Goodness, Beauty, Justice, Perfection, Completeness, Unity, Uniqueness, meaningfulness, etc., and it is precisely these propulsion that we have traditionally called the spiritual thirst of man.

Role of Values in Education

I Building of Human beings with strength and power based upon our Ancient Values

Even during the last century Swami Vivekananda had issued the following warning, "All political and social system and organizations basically depend upon the goodness of man. Men cannot be made virtuous by an Act of Parliament. It cannot be taken for granted that if the Parliament enacts good legislation a nation becomes automatically strong. But if the people of a country become good and great, that country becomes automatically good and great. Of all forms of wealth in the world man is the most valuable.

"Acts of Parliament, Government, political administration", all these are indeed means, but they are not our final goal. Beyond them there is a goal, which is not governed by any of these factors. Christ discovered that moral fervour and purity of heart are true sources of strength. Our sages proclaimed the same truth. It is thus that religion strikes at the root of the problem, it moulds man's character.

"So every improvement in India requires first of all an upheaval in religion. Before flooding India with socialistic or political ideas, first deluge the land with spiritual ideas. The first work that demands our attention is that the most wonderful truths confined in our Upanishads, in our scriptures, in our Puranas must be brought out from the books, brought out from the monasteries, brought out from the forests, brought out from the possession of selected bodies of people, and scattered broadcast all over the land. . . .

CHART 1.4

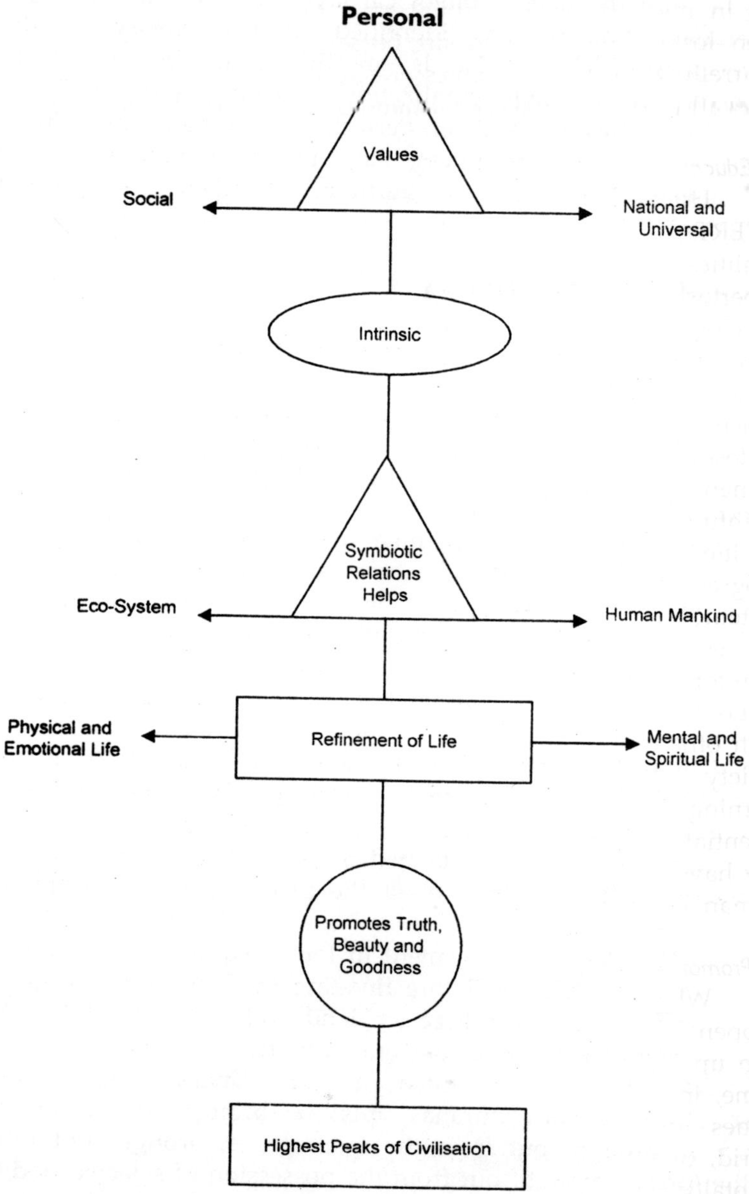

Personal

Values

Social

National and Universal

Intrinsic

Symbiotic Relations Helps

Eco-System

Human Mankind

Physical and Emotional Life

Refinement of Life

Mental and Spiritual Life

Promotes Truth, Beauty and Goodness

Highest Peaks of Civilisation

"The secret of achieving national spirit in our country lies in regaining our spiritual strength, which seem to have been lost. If we have to lift ourselves up, we should stop quarrelling among ourselves. Keep the motto before you—"Elevation of the masses without injuring their religion."[23]

2. Education for Peace: Values for Co-operation

His Holiness The Dalai Lama in his extension lecture at NCERT spoke of the exceptional intellectual abilities and qualities possessed by human beings, which make them superior to all other species. These qualities could be developed and nurtured through education to help man achieve higher levels of development. He referred to the rich legacy of Indian tradition, its ancient system of education, which promoted spirituality and produced great thinkers, philosophers and spiritual leaders. The inculcation of good human qualities like compassion, respect and sense of truthfulness, caring, etc. have been a part of the Indian way of life. But now when India has achieved tremendous progress, there is a decline in human values. The modern system has no place for spirituality whereas human values are essential for leading a happy life. Human values, therefore, have to be brought in the education system but without attaching them to any religion. Friendly relationships with others according to him are essential for peace. Modern society is becoming increasingly interdependent hence learning to live together in the family, with neighbours is essential for national and world peace. Children from young age have to be made aware of the interdependence between human beings.[24]

3. Promotes Efficiency through Ethical Values

When the mind is concentrated efficiency is found to happen. Swami Purananda rightly states[25]: The right values step up one's efficiency. In order to manage our own life at home, in the world and in our professional field, the higher values are necessary, so that our reaction to the outside world, our judgement of the situation that is around us—all is totally changed. And, we will be able to, not only face the challenges in front of us, but also still discover in our minds a lot of mental energy left, which we can apply for our planning the future.

Ethical virtues are the intelligent ways of reviving man's exhausted energies and fatigued spirit to live. By living these healthy values of righteous living, the individual unshackles his psychological personality from its self-made entanglements. As a contrast to this, the negative tendencies cultivated by the 'diabolically fallen' are self-made shackles that chain a man to a realm of confusions and sorrows forbidding him to grow into the ampler fields of his own inner possibility.

4. Co-ordial Relations between the teacher and students: Values of Respect, Love and Affection

Swami Lokeswarananda observes that according to the Indian tradition, a teacher is like a lighted lamp from which other lamps may be lighted. This underlines the fact that a teacher must himself be a highly educated man, otherwise he is not entitled to teach. Can a blind man lead another blind man?

But it will be a mistake to think that academic qualification is the only criterion of a teacher. He may have encyclopaedic knowledge, but to this must be added moral excellence of the highest order. He need not teach high moral principles, he has to live them. A teacher should be an example of what is best in man. He can inspire by what he is and not by what he knows. 'To know is to be'—runs a popular dictum in India. Knowledge is useless if it does not make a man perfect—perfect not merely in skills and abilities, but also in character.

The teacher's task is to impart knowledge but to do this, he must first enkindle in the pupil a thirst for knowledge. He must also train his pupil's body and mind, train his faculties, so that the pupil can use them to his best advantage. Mind is man's most powerful organ. A healthy mind under control is man's best friend and guide. Given such a mind and a desire to learn, a student can learn by his own efforts, with the assistance of the teacher or even without. In fact, one learns best when one learns by one's own efforts, for how much knowledge can a teacher pass on to his pupil? Also, the knowledge that the teacher imparts may turn out to be outdated, if not also wrong. The most a teacher can do is to give his pupil a sense of direction, that is, tell him what to learn and how to learn it and also how to apply that knowledge for his own good and the good of his community.

The relationship between the teacher and the taught is exactly like the relationship of the gardener and the flowers on the bush. The gardener does not create the flowers from the soil and the manure; the flowers must themselves come from the bush. The gardener can only tend its roots, water it, protect it, see that it has the correct amount of sunlight and shade—all these externals he can provide. But no more gardener can guarantee the blossom; it can come only from the bush itself.

Similarly, the teacher's job is to nurture the student with right thoughts. The student must be given a conductive and protective environment where he or she need not overstrain to live. But the blossoming—the real fragrance and beauty of the personality—must come from within.[26]

If contemporary education is to be value-based, it can never be done without the teachers themselves understanding, appreciating and upholding the life-sustaining moral values. The teachers cannot have any excuse whatsoever. If one cannot practise these values, one should not dream of teaching as a job. In fact, teaching is not a job. It is a mission and vision for life and for posterity. Swami Vivekananda established the Ramakrishna Mission order in 1897. Now there are a number of educational institutions, administered by Ramakrishna Mission throughout the country. They are transmitting the universal values of austerity, brotherhood, compassion, dedication, empathy, faithfulness, grace, hardwork, integrity, justice, kindness, liberty, mercy, non-violence, obedience, perseverance, fortitude, rationality, selflessness, truth, unity, virtue, wisdom, yoga and zest. A unique enterprise in educational endeavour is Sri Sathya Sai Baba Institute of Higher Learning, a deemed university, for the promotion of value-based education. It is situated at Prasanti Nilayam (AP), the headquarters of Sri Sai

Baba mission. There are similar institutions, run by other missions in the country. If these educational institutions can be strengthened further, of course, within the secular framework of the Indian Constitution, India will ably meet the challenges of the twenty first century.

K. Muralidharan in his article Value in Education: A changing concept" in *University News*, January 7-13, 2002 strongly feels that:

The Indian culture is deeply rooted in spiritual values and unless these values find their way into the life of students, education will lose its significance and will not fulfil its function of endowing the students with a vision to live by and with the ideals to work for. Therefore, in deference to the cherished goals of democracy, socialism, humanism and secularism, it is very essential that our education system should evolve a new positive morality, which could effectively be built into the school curriculum.

It is essential that, the teachers also should be exposed to the traditional values and ethics of education through training programs from time to time. They should not confine to their job to a mere matter of completing syllabus and following the curriculum. There should be a platform for teachers to deliberate on any sensitive issues or topics as and when the need arises. They should also explore the ideas of accepting modernisation, globalisation and liberalisation from the academic point of view. They should also learn while imparting their duties for which they are meant. By creating a conductive atmosphere for intellectual rigor and freedom of expression and thought, one can practice values in education.[27]

The National Commission on Teachers (1852), also known as Chattopadhyay Commission, observed:

"There has been a feeling of grievance on the part of the teachers that they do not receive the status and respect from society that their profession and role demand. . . It may be recalled that the Guru never demanded reverence by the Shishya, his parents and the adult community gladly and gratefully proffered it to the teacher. So must the teacher earn status through achievements. The closer the teacher the more he is able to link himself and his vocation with the mission for the nation, the more relevant he will become and more revered by students, parents and society. We underscore that the primary task of the teacher is concerned with man-making namely the making of the Indian of tomorrow. The Universal; the Guru (Teacher) is personal in relationship. The illustrious poet, Kalidasa, speaks of the Guru in the following words: "He converts darkness into light and makes the invisible God visible."

5. Value Education Promotes Personality Development and Social Cohesion

Value education helps oneself and one's relation to society. Value education makes one peaceful and by his personality, he adds peace to the society. Individual and society supplement each other.

Education is a personality building process. It has always been linked with society. It has both a personal and social dimension, and like the two sides of the same coin, these are inseparable. According to Gandhiji, real education did not consist in packing the brain with information, facts and figures, or in passing examinations by reading the prescribed number of books, but by developing the right character. At present, our education system is largely involved in preparing the younger generation for developing their cognitive domain. It is mainly based on the preponderance of public examination and excessive competitive spirit at the cost of developing the more important affective domain. Today, what is being done is to educate the heads and hands and not the hearts. Essential education must lead to internalisation of the obligation on the part of each human being to be value-conscious in word, thought and deed. Lack of value education has been an important factor in the global scenario of growing violence and terrorism, pollution and ecological imbalances. The Education Commission (1964-66) and the National Policy on Education (NPE-1986) stressed the importance of value-oriented education in our country. The Rammurthy Committee Report (1990) recommended that the imparting of value education should be an integral part of the entire educational process.[28]

6. An integral 'Vision' for National Regeneration: National Values

Value education makes the youth powerful. They contribute a great deal to the national reconstruction and national development.

An old Jewish proverb says that 'a man without a dream and a nation without a vision shall perish'. We need a great vision to build a great nation. In the multi-religious context of India, this vision has to be an inclusive one. It must be deeply rooted in the truth, goodness and beauty of our ancient culture and tradition and at the same time, it must also be in harmony with the scientific developments of the era. We are fortunate that our Constitution has been able to capture and embody this spirit of unity and harmony of cultures and religions and the scientific temperament of the modern world.

I am inspired to present to you here a vision of a great India firmly rooted in her own rich spiritual and cultural heritage and at the same time fully open to the scientific development of humankind. I have termed this great India of our vision Bharatiya Dharma Rajya or Dharma Bharathi in short.

Bhartiya Dharma Rajya is the vision of an India of love, unity and peace built on the integral concept of Dharma and on the ensuring Bhartiya Dharma as embodied in the Preamble and Article 51(A) of the Indian Constitution. This is the vision of an awakened India of political stability, social harmony and economic prosperity built on an integral vision of life and reality. It is the vision of a disciple nation of God on earth where all religions and cultures will be respected for their unique insights into Truth and valuable contributions towards human welfare, an India where all living beings will live in harmony and peace with one another as the fulfilment of our age-old dream of a Vasudhaiva Kutumbakam. This is our vision of the great India of the third millennium that will be a land and light of Dharma in humanity's quest for a culture of life, unity and peace on earth.

'Peace and Value Education for Schools/Colleges' should present and promote this noble and inter-religious vision of Bhartiya Dharma Rajya in our intuitions of learning and among our youth if it is to lead to the much needed national regeneration of India. This is a religious task more than a political task that can only be achieved through inter-religious cooperative action. It will be difficult for political parties and governments to take up this task on their own, they can only support and collaborate with religious-minded and peace-loving patriotic citizens of India in this divine mission.[29]

7. *Value Education will Build Character*

At present, the Government of this country is striving to bring about universal education. In this context, it will be useful to consider what the purpose of education is. Great men of this land have declared that education should foster character, help the acquisition of good qualities, or seela, and eradicate vices, knowledge should also enable us to understand the truth about things. Saivite and Vaishnavite saints have proclaimed that God alone is Truth, and the rest is maya or illusion. These sages and saints endeavored to realise Truth, that is God. In Him they found their supreme joy. They looked at everything else as the sources of evil and suffering. In the Vedas, the Paramatman is spoken of as Truth. When it is declared that everything connected with this world is mithya, or false, it to so much to condemn the world as to affirm that the Paramatman alone is true.[30]

Right education should make us know that God is the Truth. Knowledge must fill one with good qualities through which alone one can realize the Truth, that is God. Therefore, the goal of knowledge is the understanding of the Ultimate Truth. The first fruit of education must be humility and self-control. Education that does not produce these qualities is useless. We find that people in countries where modern education has spread are not as virtuous as they should be. Unsophisticated illiterates, like those slaving in the tribal areas of South African jungles, are found to be more honest than those who have received the doubtful benefits of modern education. It is sad to note that in our own schools and colleges, indiscipline is rampant now-a-days. Even girls, who are by nature docile, have caught this infection of indiscipline. All these developments give rise to the question whether this kind of education is after all necessary or useful. Such education is the cause of stress among students.

From time immemorial, the necessity to acquire knowledge is being emphasized and he who has had no education is considered an animal. Vidyaa viheenah pasuh says Bhartruhari. But what is the type of education our ancients had in mind when they said Vidyaa vinaya sampanna? A thing can be done either in the dharmic way or in the adharmic way. Good results will flow when a thing is done in the right way.[31]

8. Study of the life of Great men to learn from their practice in life

We must train our people from an early age to study the lives of great men who led an unattached life, free from debasing passions like lust, anger, greed and fear and, following their example, develop faith in God. This will help them to grow up into dutiful and honest citizens, disciplined to lead a moral and ethical life. If the government also takes sufficient interest in making provision for teaching moral and spiritual values to children, it stands to gain much. For one thing, expenditure on police and law courts will get reduced. They will also be free from the troubles arising from strikes and other forms of student indiscipline.

"The Inculcation of moral and spiritual values in the minds of the people from the early years is most desirable that provision should be made for the teaching of moral and spiritual values in educational institutions.[32]

9. Nation building and promotion of peaceful world order

In the words of Sri Sathya Sai Baba, education is for man-making, nation-building and promotion of peaceful world order. At the dawn of the new millennium and in the changed policy framework of the Government, there is an urgent need among teachers to inculcate values among students so that they develop into integrated personalities blossoming mentally, emotionally, intellectually, ethically and spiritually (Khandelval, 2001). Teachers in higher education have to act as a role model to bring back values among students, educational institutions and in the society as a whole. They have to act as role models in terms of their honesty, sincerity, hard work and determination towards their duties and responsibilities in order to create an example before their students. The students at this stage are at the cross-road of their career and life. At this stage, normally students seek to identify with some role models for their life. Therefore, the role of teacher at this level of education is to create and recreate the values among students, in educational institutions and the society as a whole. They have a greater responsibility in shaping the destiny of future generation and the country as well. They should also come forward catering to the educational needs at primary and secondary levels in the society. They should be conscious about their social responsibilities. No external force should be required to inculcate in them a sense of dedication and responsibility. The role of teacher at the higher level is different from their counterparts at other stages on account of these teachers' greater involvement with activities related to research, publications, training and administrative responsibilities.[33]

10. Core Values-based Education Promotes Ideal Humanity

The Parliamentary Standing Committee on Human Resource Development in its Eighty-first Report on Value-based Education (1999) has highlighted that Truth (Satya), Righteous Conduct (Dharma), Peace (Shanti), Love (Prema) and Non-violence (Ahimsa) as the Core universal values, which need to be identified as the foundation stone on which the value-based education programme can be built up. All the religions of the world have also emphasized that non-violence, tolerance and peace are the fundamental components of humanity. Great philosophers and social thinkers of East as well as West have seen education as a process leading ultimately to spiritual development. UNESCO in the context of peace, refers education not only to general education acquiring cognitive capital but ability to live together.[34]

11. External and Internal Values must act in harmony

The wonderful development of science during the past three hundred years concerns the external nature and the world outside. The study of the nature and potentialities of the human mind is of more recent origin – it has a history of about hundred years. It is true that with the help of scientific equipment, like the microscope and telescope, the scientist has understood innumerable minute details of the exterior world. But many of the scientists are realizing, though belatedly, that the nature of the mind, its constant tendency to flow outward, prevents it from getting an insight into many other aspects of the mind which can be achieved only by the practice of meditation.

Scientists have provided us with various kinds of conveniences and comforts by discovering innumerable natural laws and thus uncovering the secrets of nature. It has to be admitted that the human power of investigation has reached an all-time high; man has displayed the peak of his intellectual ability. But is it not within his power to create a beautiful world full of honesty, justice, brotherhood, mutual understanding, cooperation, peace and tolerance? Why has he not succeeded in creating such a world?

The following voice of a poet reflects the present predicament of mankind:

People fear people
Doubt reigns everywhere
Behind the curtain of peace
Martial moves the revolution
Meanness yet unheard of
Devilishness in patriotic garb
Tuskers among nations crush life apace
Not to speak of the bloody flame
Rising high on the West
Bullets are at play
Mad after martial joy

The scientist can make the five elements dance to his tune, he can transverse land, water and space at a marvelous speed, and he can drive away terrible epidemics, which threaten the human race. Can't he instill in the hearts of men, who live and thrive now, but who are liable to decay and die, a sense of brotherhood and friendship? Can't he quench the primordial fire of hatred by pouring forth the ambrosia of love?

The following is the answer to the question:

Progress is to take place in two fields. It relates to the

two faces of nature: The one is the physical nature, the nature of the external world. The other is the inner nature of man. The one is related to the world that we see. The other one is related to the inner-self of man with whose help he is able to see the world outside and investigate.

If man is able to increase his power to free himself from the hold of the surrounding world or environment, if he increases his freedom, if he gains control over nature, we may say that the change we call development leads to progress. In this respect, the innumerable discoveries of scientists have helped us gain control over the outside nature. Undoubtedly, we are moving on the path of outward development and progress. But is there a comparable development in the regions of the mind?[35] Upon this understanding depends the solution of educational problems.

12. Ethical and Moral Values: The Foundation of the Quality of Life

Ethical and moral values are the basis of good life as ethical culture indeed ennobles human life. Ethics, religion and spirituality have become synonymous terms in common parlance as they co-exist in the development of moral culture and of righteous and virtuous life. Moral living starts through dedication to ideal principles, maxims and human values. A righteous and virtuous life and a clear conscience provide the backbone of spiritual as well as a humane material progress of the civilized man and his society.

No ideal, ideology, institution or religion is self-operative. It is through human agency alone that ideals and institutions established for their realization are made operational. History bears witness to perversions, distortions and abuse or misuse of ideals and institutions for the reason that human being is essentially imperfect though he seeks perfection. It is true that perfection is not attainable by imperfect beings, however it is always worthwhile attempting and this depends largely upon a meaningful education of man with a view to fertilizing the soil within so that the vessel may bear rich, juicy and truthful fruits. Sustenance of human values, ethics and morals in human society and spiritual enlightenment of man seem to be decidedly more effective and meaningful goals of educational philosophy to follow. It is principally inadequate appreciation of the essentially spiritual nature of man and prevailing disrespectful attitude towards the role of true religion or spiritualism in protecting and promoting the spiritual core of human beings which accounts for the crisis of our times.

Ever since the dawn of human civilization, conscious efforts have been made by man to cultivate values in order to humanize himself by conquering his animal instincts and ennobling his life by harmonious development of all the faculties. When one realizes that one's actions affect the entire society, the value system that we live by and the choices that we make acquire paramount importance. Living a life based on noble values enables human beings to refine their character which is called culture. The culture of a people or a nation is based upon the values that those constituting it live and uphold in their lives. When the cultural values deteriorate, civilization declines but when these are promoted civilization flourishes. Whenever higher ideals are abandoned and fundamental cultural values of the society are totally ignored, civilizations have disappeared. If perversions of man's desires and natural urges transgress the control and limits set by nature, it results in the loss of culture which is his internal aspect. When his culture declines, it eventually results in withering away of civilization which essentially manifests external aspect of man's social life.

The modern world is marked by a widespread explosion of knowledge and tremendous achievements in Science and Technology, coupled with a general decline and reversal of human values as well as an alarming deterioration of moral and mental health both of individuals and societies. The recent spate of crimes, violence, terrorism, and drug abuse make us aware of the significance of human values, without which human life loses all meaning. It is also evident that a mere economic prosperity and material wealth cannot result in a lasting well-being of mankind. The inner strength of mankind springs from within, which seems ill-nourished now. To fill up the void regarding human values, the richest resources are available in the texts and scriptures of all the religions of the world which have guided people in their thoughts, feelings and actions for ages. Human virtues have been propounded and preached by many great sages, Prophets and teachers who had perceived subtle truths of human life, for the benefit of their adherents and for those who would derive benefits by studying their sayings and advices. Some of their sayings were understood by people in letter and spirit, enriching and elevating them, but some others were not understood well, ending up as mere outward rituals, blind faiths, intolerance with others and hatred for other faiths. More than a century ago, Swami Vivekananda had said: "We want to lead mankind to the place where there is neither the Vedas, nor the Bible, nor the Koran, yet this has to be done by harmonizing the Vedas, the Bible and the Koran. Man ought to be taught that religions are but the varied expression of the religion, which is oneness, so that each may choose the path that suits him best."[36]

13. Growth in Spiritual Values

One of our noblest duties in life is to grow. This is the screaming cry of all evolution. Growth in the biological apparatus was the command in the lower stages of evolution. After having attained manhood, the demand is to grow our moral stature, in our spiritual worth, in our cultural dignity. This is where study of the scriptures, regular and continuous, and sadhana, constant and sincere, come to serve us. The study clearly points out the goal and the way – the sadhana yields to us the energy and vitality to walk the path and explode into the goal. These we must.

14. Harmony and Peace: Values for Tolerance

In the world today, we are living through an age of confusions and tensions, both within and without us. The external challenges persecute us and render our lives unhappy and sorrow ridden. The intelligent philosophy of the Rishis advises man 'to live in harmony' with the situations in life and steadily work on to meet them with discretion and constant application. When we live thus for a period of time, a subjective poise develops, giving us inward peace and tranquility, which, thereafter, remains unaffected by external threats and onslaughts.

Revered Shri Vethatheri, Maharishi says 'has beautifully

written that Harmony is a precious treasure of human life'. Real success, satisfaction, and happiness are the different facets of harmony. If one is to enjoy the benefits of life to the fullest, it is necessary to develop and maintain harmony; and for this understanding the philosophy of nature is required.

Harmony should be maintained in all spheres of life, and these are:

- Between body and life;
- Between wisdom and habits;
- Between self and society;
- Between the purpose of life and the method of living.; and
- Between will and nature.

The more one understands life, the more one will achieve harmony; and success will be proportionate to that. No doubt harmonizing life is a difficult task, but it is worth all the striving, for it is the only way to equip oneself to enjoy life to the fullest extent and to reach the goal of life, which is the perfection of consciousness. By the development of knowledge man comes to understand the cause and effect system which is the law of nature.

15. Values of Devotion and Dedication

Of the innumerable techniques prescribed by the rishis for self-development, the most popular ones are the path of selfless dedicated service (karmayoga), the path of discriminative knowledge (jnanayoga), and the mystic path of self-development through disciplined contemplation (raja-yoga).

According to Sage Narada, true devotion for the Lord is superior and nobler to all these, because devotion is the final outcome of all other methods of self-development.

This supreme devotion is indeed, as a technique, even superior to the path of action, the path of knowledge, and the path of disciplined contemplation. (Narada Bhakti Sutra II:I:25)

All the other paths are the means that take the seekers to the final goal of spiritual experience, but in devotion there is very little difference in essence between the means and the end, between the way and the goal. Love alone is love's own end and fulfilment. Devotion is both the means and the end. As long as residual vasanas (inherent tendencies) are still lingering in the devotee's personality, so long is devotion only the path. But when, as a result of his love for the Lord, his vasanas disappear totally, a stage comes when his supreme love itself becomes the Lord of love Supreme.

Than all other paths, devotion is the one most readily available and most easily attainable. (Narada Bhakti Sutra VI:1:58). Having dedicated all activities unto Him, the devotee should turn all desire, anger, pride, and so forth toward Him alone (Narada Bhakti Sutra VI:2:65). Having gained this supreme devotion, the devotee attains perfection and immortality and becomes extremely satisfied. (Narada Bhakti Sutra I:1:4)

Acharya Vinoba Bhave says: Knowledge, love, and constant effort are the three legs on which life stands. If one of the legs of a tripod is broken, it cannot stand, since all three legs are needed. This is also the condition of life. Even if we logically distinguish between devotion (bhakti), knowledge (jnana), and action (karma), we cannot divide them in experience. The three together make up one great entity.

G. Chandralekka Rao in an Article; value education for college students "rightly feels that realizing this need our curriculum needs to insist on educating the young students in the art of living with values. If learning remains detached from value judgements, scholarship runs the risk of degenerating into indifference. Value judgements actually enhance the accuracy of learning, teachers, therefore, should be aware of the important role they are called upon to play as professionals and citizens, as agents of development and change. They must make an effort to light a candle instead of cursing the darkness and sow the seeds of value education with a fond hope that they would diffuse their own fragrance towards the creation of a just and new society as they sprout and blossom. Can we be good role models if we are not ethical ourselves?

University education which is worthwhile should lead

to the development of integrated personality and inculcate values like patriotism, spirit of national unity and a healthy appreciation of the rich variety of cultural expressions and promote a humanistic outlook. It is only in the highest education stage that the students can be enabled to acquire Intellectual, democratic and aesthetic values and a deeply felt concern for the environment.

The content of value oriented post-graduate education should include: (a) a yearning for knowledge and capacity to utilize it for the good of the society, (b) Democratic education, (c) Aesthetic education, (d) a course in ethics, (e) spiritual education, and (f) provision for activities involving values.[37]

Case Study

Education with Value Focus

Sri Sathya Sai Institute of Higher Learning Prasanthi Nilayam (AP).

Sri Sathya Sai Institute of Higher Learning Prasanthi Nilayam (Andhra Pradesh) set-up on November 22, 1981, by Bhagavan Sri Sathya Sai Baba which grew out of the Colleges founded earlier by Bhagavan Sri Sathya Sai Baba at Anantapur, Andhra Pradesh, Whitefield (near Bangalore, Karnataka) and Prasanthinilayam, Andhra Pradesh.

Bhagavan, in His Divine Message to the students, announced that the main purpose of establishing the Institute of Higher Learning was to help them cultivate self–knowledge and self-confidence, so that each one of them can learn self-sacrifice and earn self-realization. He defined the goal as spiritual upliftment, self-discovery and social service through love and detachment.

The consistent endeavour of the university since its inception has been to develop core courses bringing out value-orientation in an appropriate manner, blending of science and spirituality, providing interaction between head and heart through self-reliance programmes and co-curricular activities, designing Awareness and Foundation courses and incorporating these as part of the curriculum with credits.

The philosophy of education of the Institute is based on the appreciation of the need to provide full scope for the development of body, mind and heart. Discipline, duty and adherence to basic human values are deeply appreciated as the best qualities of students in the Institute. These are being observed in various situations in the hostel, on the playground and in the Campuses and during the celebration of various festival and organization of festivals and other important functions. It is precisely because of the importance of these activities for the overall development of personality, that the Institute attaches great importance to integral items of education like Yogasanas, games and sports, attendance in morning prayers and meditation, attendance in universal prayers and participation in morning assembly talks, attendance in classes and social work/self-reliance programmes. These are incorporated in the total system of our education offered in the Institute.

A society without values will cease to be human. The more human values are cherished, the better will be the growth of society, the nation and the world. We cannot rest content with an educational system which is confined to academic achievement. It has to promote human virtues simultaneously. The main problem of our education today is how to adapt the spiritual and cultural traditions we have inherited from the past to our present day life.

The Institute believes that teaching of values cannot be confined only to specific programmes such as Awareness Programme under Undergraduate and Postgraduate Courses and foundational courses in Professional Studies. Values will have to be presented as a part and parcel of teaching of the subject. In the process of teaching of various subjects, whether it is physical sciences, biological sciences, social sciences or Commerce and Management, the values are appropriately incorporated in the subjects in order that the students would appreciate and imbibe the practical applications of values in their day-to-day living.

Even research is value-based. For years, the Chemistry department has been focusing on the Chemistry of Natural Products, and in particular on the possible use of various native plants for producing drugs. Many of the Dissertations of the students of M.Tech. [Computer Science] address the needs of the Sri Sathya Sai Institute of Higher Medical

Sciences [popularly known as the Super-Specialty Hospital]; and so on.

On the sports field, the stress is less on competition and more on collective enjoyment. Indeed, the events presented on the Institute's Annual Sports -and Cultural festival held every year on January 11th are carefully planned to promote such a spirit.

"We do not need today a new faith or creed, nor a new system of education. Nor need we create a new society. All we need are men and women who have pure and loving hearts. Their hearts must be filled with sacred feeling. The transformation has to be effected in the minds of the people."

"Our educational institution (University) is making an endeavour so that in a few years from now we shall have thousands of these students who will scatter themselves to all parts of the world. The uppermost thing for the students is that they should futher this moral aspect of ours." Most of the research studies carried out in the field of value education revealed the following:

1. Educational system at present is not congenial to value promotion.
2. Teachers, themselves lack knowledge and rationale of values. They do not follow values.
3. Literature on value education is limited. Whatever is available is not of good quality.
4. Students are enamoured by modern fashion.
5. Families are also forgetting their role as the first school of citizenship.
6. Materialism has left no place for ethical and moral values.
7. Leaders have no values.
8. The aim of students is to pass the examination and not personality development.
9. Negative values like drinking, smoking, gambling are common among teachers and students.

Conclusion

The worst days of a serious threat to Indian society are over. Under foreign domination and western influence we had developed the foolish notion of degrading everything, morals, ethics and spirituality and were easily swept-off our feet by the glamour and glitter of the exotic. The wonderful phenomenon that is taking place now is that we are returning to these things which have lent stability and strength to our culture over the centuries. Because the various educational programmes launched by the NCERT, UGC and other organizations (such as Sri Sathya Sai Organization) ranging all the way from nursery to post-graduate level, are bringing into proper focus the valuable ingredients of our culture. By far the most important aspect of these programmes is that besides giving a theoretical and conceptual base in the curriculum they also seek to transform the quality of life through inculcation of human values of peace, love, truth, spirituality, right conduct, ahimsa and, above all, national character which, in effect, represent the highest and the noblest in our culture system.[38]

About ethical or approved conduct Apastamba-Dharma-Sutra (22.14) enjoins:

Absence of anger, elation, indignation, avarice, delusion, vanity and enmity; speaking truth; moderation in eating; refraining from exposing others' weak points; freedom from jealousy; sharing one's good things with others; sacrifice; straightforwardness; gentleness; quietude; self-control; friendliness with other beings; absence of cruelty; contentment —these form the approved conduct for men of all stations of life. By observing them duly one becomes universally benevolent.

Suresh Prasad Singh in his Article "Emerging values in modern Education" suggests an integrated vision to promote value education. To quote him: The power of modern education can be better realized by achieving a happy integration of utility and value, integration of body and mind, emotions and ideas, individual and society, and the world. The vision of progress must not be devoid of human element, the aspect of vision which makes the progress meaningful and purposeful. The progress that is aimed at the desired, is an assertion of the powers of human imagination, and soothe fruits of this progress must be realized with the ends of humanity in mind. The tools of change are powerful but their application must be human and they must be employed for pious purposes.

In the wake of the phenomenal developments on the educational front, re-orientation of values. In the post-modernist education assumes special significance. Here are certain concrete recommendations for tempering utilitarian pursuit of together education with desirable ideals and visions of human happiness:

(a) Education must promote rational outlook on life and scientific approach to issues confronting the real life situations;
(b) An imaginatively framed course in fundamental freedom and human rights must constitute curriculum of our degree and post-graduate levels curriculum;
(c) Power that education generates must be employed for constructive human purposes;
(d) Education must develop sensitivity to environment and must foster human ethos for the enjoyment of the fruits of progress;
(e) Humanism should be the central concern of education in all circumstances, and it must promote quality concern for corporate behaviour and corporate life; and
(f) Education must be able to develop a working mechanism to fight the evil of consumerism and acquisitive culture so that environment may be protected and development may remain sustainable.

In New Delhi Conference on "Quest for New Perspectives", held on July 9-10, 2003 feels that:

As we reflect today on the theme of dialogue of civilizations, it seems imperative that education should be so developed that a new mentality is created which spontaneously turns to dialogue rather than to conflict, which spontaneously responds to the call of interchange, and which is spontaneously eager to see problems from various points of view and which is capable of synthesizing different points of view without sacrificing uniqueness of various truths that are synthesized. We have to develop particularly a new curriculum that aims at explaining the basic theme of human progress as a mighty expression of an adventure of continuous self-exceeding. This curriculum should inspire students to work for unity even while rejecting uniformity; this curriculum should also encourage students to respect cultural diversity. Finally this curriculum should develop a new science and art of living together which necessitates adhence to the law of mutuality rather than conflict and the law of variety of expressions rather than any uniform monotone. It may also be urged that since science and technology characterize a large part of modern civilization, we should develop a new curriculum where by a fresh impetus is given to scientific studies that are in harmony with the study of values. There is, today, an increasing awareness that unless science and value are blended together, humanity will have to face a great peril, the peril of inner human suffering even in the midst of increase of knowledge and increase of material comforts. It is in the hands of educationists today to develop a new dimension in education so that education can not only build the defences of peace in the minds and hearts of people but also build bridges between the past and the future, and serve the great ends of the dialogue among civilizations.

What is now needed is a concerted action at the development of a curriculum that can bring home to the students three important lessons, namely, (i) that the entire humanity shares one basic impulse towards progress and by sharing this impulse humanity can be seen as one vast surge of adventure which aims at continuous self-exceeding; (ii) that humanity, in its mature developments, tends to reject uniformity and adopts the law of unity that permits and respects cultural diversities; and (iii) that the future progress of humankind is bound up with the development of a new science and art of living together which necessitates adherence to the law of mutuality rather than conflict and the law of varied expressions rather than any uniform monotone. Education should aim at strengthening democratic and universal human values and respect for human rights.

Education is the most powerful instrument for preparing a mind which can promote the culture of dialogue. (See Chart 1.2).

Notes and References

1. R.P. Dhokalia, External Human Values and World Religions, New Delhi, NCERT, pp. 109-10.
2. *Ibid.*, p. 10.
3. Kulwant Pathania, Fostering Values in Education: Some Suggestions, *University News*, June 26-July 02, 2006, p. 6.
4. Sidhdheshwar Sharma, Professional Ethics and Value Education in Teacher Education, in *University News*, April 3-09, 2006, p. 10.
5. *Ibid.*, p. 11.
6. V.S. Malimath, Role of Universities in imparting True Education in *University News*, May 7-13, 2007, p. 22.
7. His Excellency Lord Swraj Paul, Hard Work and Integrity have no Equal, in *University News*, Feb. 19-25, 2007, p. 19.
8. V.S. Malimath, "Role of Universities in Imparting True Education", *University News*, May 7-13, No. 45, p. 19.
9. *University News*, April 23-29, 2007, p. 1.
10. Quoted in Anitha Shetty, *et. al.*, Value Education: Need of the present generation in *University News*, Oct. 13, 1997, p. 12.
11. Quoted in N.P. Sinha, Towards inculcating values in Education, in *University News*, Oct. 22-28, 2001, pp. 1-2.
12. Swami Gautamananda, Values in our Education, in *Values: The Key to a Meaningful Life*, Ramakrishna Math, Madras, India, pp. 83-85.
13. *University News*, Dec. 9, 1996, p. 22.
14. R. Satya Rajiv, Human Values in University Management, in *University News*, Value Education in India, New Delhi, 2001, pp. 86-87.
15. R. Natarajan, *University News*, July 21-22, 2003, p. 16.
16. Sri Aurobindo, The Synthesis of Yoga, 1976, Sixth Edition, Sri Aurobindo Ashram, Pondicherry, p. 2.
17. Prashant Bhushan, Stemming the Tide of Corruption in *IJPA*, July-Sept., 1995, p. 472.
18. S.R. Maheshwari, Ethics for Civil Service in India, in *IJPA*, July-Sept., 1995, pp. 505.
19. O.P. Dwevedi, Administrative Theology, *IJPA*, July-Sept., 1990, pp. 418-19.
20. N.R. Naganhathan, A Charter of Ethics, Reading Material for Trainees (Some abstracts).
21. *The Tribune*, dated 11.9.2000.
22. Jaideep Singh, The Enlightened Organization, in *IJPA*, April-June, 1979, p. 44.

23. Swami Jagadatmananda, Learn to Live, Vol. 2, Ramakrishna Math, Chennai; India, 2000, pp. 154-57.
24. H.H. The Dalal Lama, Education for Peace, in *Journal of Value Education*, Vol. 2, No. 1, January 2002, p. 1.
25. Swami Purnananda, Making Life Valuable by Imbiding values, in *Journal of Value Education*, Vol. 2, No. 1, January 2002, pp. 30-31, (NCERT).
26. *Ibid.*, p. 15.
27. K. Muralicharn, Value in Education: A Changing Concept, in *University News*, January 7-13, 2002, p. 2.
28. Hemanta K. Khandai, Value Oriented Approach from Primary to University Education, *University News*, March 31 to April 6, 2003, pp. 9-10.
29. Swami Sachidananda, Vision and Values for National Regeneration, *Journal of Value Education*, Vol. 2, No. 1, January 2002 (NCERT), pp. 70-71.
30. H.H. Jagadguru's Madras Discourse Acharya Call, Part III, Peetam Kanchipuram, 1998, pp. 66-67.
31. *Ibid.*, p. 192.
32. *Ibid*
33. Nageshwar Rao and R.P. Das, Bringing values back: The Role of Teachers in Higher Education in *Journal of Value Education*, Vol. 2, No. 1, January 2002, p. 89.
34. J.S. Rajput, Symphony of Human Values in Education, NCERT, December 2001, New Delhi.
35. Learn to Live, Vol. I, *op. cit.*, pp. 139-41.
36. R.D. Dhokalia, External Human Values and World Religions, NCERT, New Delhi, 2001, pp. 10, 13, 24.
37. H. Venkataiah, Value Education, Curriculum for Graduates and Post-Graduates in *University News*, June 22, 1998.
38. Girijesh Kunal, How to inculcate value education through teacher education, *Journal of Value Education, op. cit.* pp. 118-19.

2

Family and Values

The need of value education has been emphasized in previous chapter. However, it is very difficult to impart value education in the context of present environment. It has been rightly said that it is easy to destroy the mountains than to change the minds of the people.

Value-education is virtually going to emerge as a new science for inspiring human values in our highly scientific and technologically advanced society. This is the challenge in front of today's techno-globalism—the creation of value-based human beings. Einstein's brain should be combined with Buddha's heart to stop the devastation of Nagasaki and Hiroshima. Napoleon's dynamism should be combined with Vivekananda's prophetic passion for helping human beings to manifest their divinity and Ramakrishna's universal love, respect and acceptance of all religions should be combined with the spirit of intense religious revival which is emerging all over the world today.[1]

Rockfeller wrote at the end of his life: "There is more to life than the accumulation of money. . . . The best way to prepare for the end is to live for others. That is what I am trying to do."[2]

In his memorable speech after the first atomic explosion Oppenheimer declared the need for human values in science:

CHART 2.1

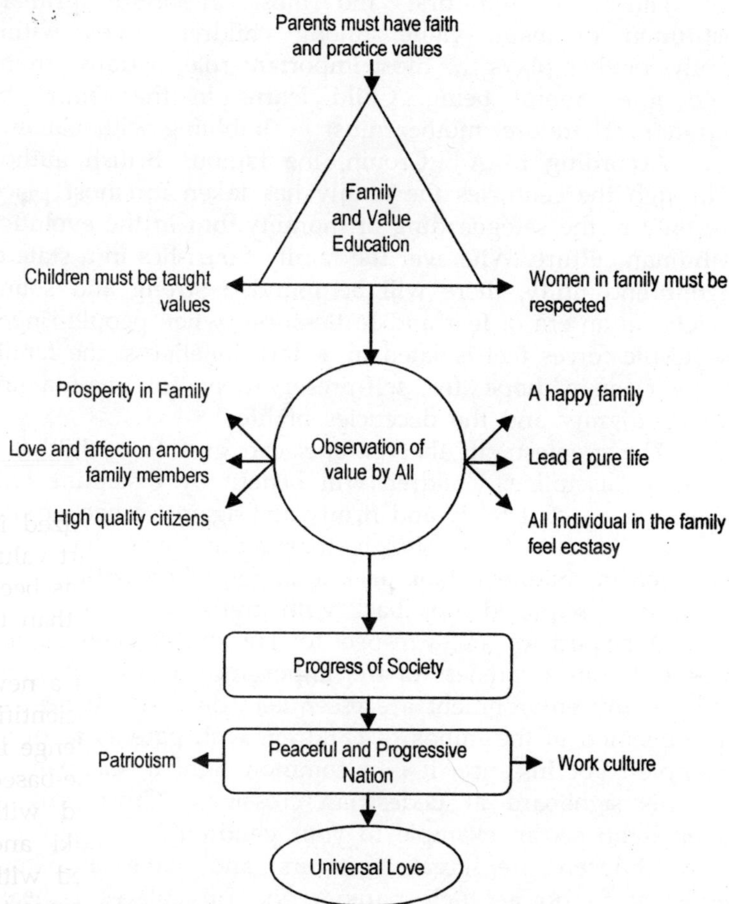

"We are men too. We cannot forget our fellow men. I mean also our deep moral dependence in that the value of science must lie in the world of men, that all roots lie there."[3]

Methods

It is not easy to inculcate value education by one agency. We require multi-agency concept to promote value education. Positive efforts from all directions can create positive value among people. Let us discuss some of them.

I. Family

Family is the first and most important primary institution to instill value among children. Even within family, mother plays the most important role in transforming child to a moral being. Child learns in the family by imitation. Therefore, mother must be bubbling with values.

According to A.J. Cronin, the famous British author, "Through the centuries the family has taken foremost place, not only in the safeguarding of morality, but in the evolution of human culture. Wherever the family flourishes in a state of vigour and unity, there will be found a strong and sound society. In an era of fear and restlessness, when people ringed by hostile forces feel isolated in a dark loneliness, the family is their main hope for self-preservation, for maintaining human dignity and the decencies of life."

The greatest gift that parents can give to a child is a sense of discipline. Children will benefit by discipline only when it is exacted fairly and firmly and against a background of love. Studies have shown that adults who had been punished in childhood look back in anger, whereas those who had been disciplined look back with gratitude.

A respect for life, a respect for law, traffic rules, public-prosperity, an awareness of the importance of a clean, green and healthy environment are essential values which need to be implanted in the minds of children, with parents as prime examples. For instance, it is a common sight in Germany to see this signboard at pedestrian crossings: 'Cross only by green light: set an example to your children'.[4]

Children are great imitators and have a natural tendency to do as their parents do. This places a heavy responsibility on parents to lead their lives in such a way that they are talking, walking examples of a set of values which they wish to impart to their children. Many are the times when children are told not to tell lies, but the very next moment they are confused to find their parents asking them to tell a caller that they are not at home. Isn't it a common experience to hear a child say, 'My father told me to tell you that he is not at home'?

There is only one real magic in this life that can move mountains and turn dreams into reality. That magic is

"Believing in yourself." Only those who believe in themselves and in their capacity to meet challenges are able to face life with courage. Almost anyone can achieve anything if only he believes in himself.[5]

All of us—whether we know it or not and whether we like it or not—are shaped by the cultural heritage from which we evolve. A very large part of whatever success I have had in life has been largely lodged in the traditions of this part of the country. The energy and constructive dynamism that is so much part of his ethos is an invaluable asset anywhere in the world. The appreciation of family values that we, and indeed most Indians, cherish provides an emotional security and sense of responsibility rare in today's society. We must preserve these attributes because they are the bedrock of character and without character any success is superficial.[6]

The greatest illusion of our people is their infantile belief in the legal solubility of all problems. In the wise words of Lord Hailsham, the former Lord Chancellor of the UK, 'We might do well to remember that in the whole realm of human relations there is no field more vulnerable to corruption, dishonesty, chicanery, and sheer quackery and charlatanism that contested litigation, criminal and civil, commercial, matrimonial, testamentary, or resulting from personal injury, real, imagined, or invented. We might also do well to consider that few of the safeguards we have achieved against these evils have been achieved by government interference or by parliamentary legislation. They have been brought about by the steady application of self-regulatory procedures and disciplines. . .[7]

If one maintains his upright character in all situations (whether dealing with friends or foes or strangers), such a conduct alone deserves the name of justice. Just as the beam of a balance stands level when it rightly weighs things, so also a noble man must maintain his level of character unbiased and such an impartiality is an ornament to him.

Strive with ceaseless effort to work your way along the path of righteousness as far as you can in all aspects of conduct.

Sister Christine, another great disciple of Vivekananda wrote:

"Some of us believe that if Swami Vivekananda's ideas regarding the education of woman are carried out in true spirit, a being will be evolved who will be unique in the history of the world. As the women of ancient Greece were almost perfect physically, this one will be her complement intellectually and spiritually—a woman, gracious, loving, tender, long–suffering, great in heart and intellect, but greatest of all in spirituality."[8]

Role of Family in Educating the Children and other Family Members to Imbibe Values

Family has been regarded as the cornerstone of society. It forms the basic unit of Social organization and it is difficult to imagine how human society could function without it. In general, the family has been seen as a universal social institution, as an inevitable part of the human society. It has been regarded as good institution both for individual and society. Mukul Sharma in his article, "Goodness may involve a lot of brains" in *Economic Times* (26.6.2007), feels that we must learn from insects to promote good family values. To quote him: "Social insects such as wasps and termites are known to help each other with no mutual tradeoffs or benefits to themselves. Among bees, for example, there are whole classes of sterile members that exist solely for the care and protection of others—often at the cost of their own lives. This phenomenon that had baffled even Darwin who wrote about it in the Origin of Species as "one special difficulty, which at first appeared to me insuperable, and actually fatal to my theory." Today, we know that such behaviour is for the greater good of the whole colony which is regarded as a "superorganism." It's something like our body's cells which continuously die so that we can go on living. Our family members must learn from these social insects to make it an inspiring institution

MacIvor and Page hold that the family is a definite and long-term group defined by sexual relationships that reproduce and bring up children. It may include other blood relations also but it is mainly formed by living together of man, woman and their children. The unit formed by their living together is called family. According to Davis, Family is "a group of persons whose relations to one another are based upon consanguinity and who are therefore kin to another." According to Burgess and Locke, "A family is a group of persons united by the ties of marriage, blood or adoption, constituting a single household, inter-acting and inter-communicating. With each other in their respective social role of husband and wife, mother and daughter, brother and sister, creating and maintaining a common culture."

Family is the first home of citizenship. All the values essential to enjoy life are learnt in families where roles are differentiated. Mother is first and most important teacher of the child from whom he/she would learn values of life like truthfulness, honesty, love, respect to elders and selfless service, etc. However, because of the disintegration of joint family system and degradation of women, the families became problems. The families were engulfed by domestic violence, child abuse, subjugation of women, maltreatment of older people, etc. Thus a family which was heaven for all its members became a hell with all sort of problems—drinking, gambling, disobeying, beating, etc.

In the 21st Century, domestic violence would increase more due to the changed life style, i.e. increasing use of alcohol, luxuries of life beyond capacity, lust for more money, etc. This is going to be a world-wide phenomenon. Domestic violence is a slow poison which is swallowing the ingredients of family life. Such a situation is causing problems of health to the members of the family and is a source of constant tension.[9]

The menace of domestic violence is beyond description as it is like an iceberg and whatever we see outside in public, it is negligible. If we take up the definition of Domestic Violence in a broader sense then hardly any house is saved from its clutches. However, here we may take a narrow definition when domestic violence takes physical from and results in torture, beating, causing physical and mental tensions to women and children so that they get tired of their life. The women are denied food and good place to sleep, etc. It is not restricted to a particular area or types of people. Its tentacles are spreading in every area. However, the gravitation of violence against women in rural areas are more prevalent as compared to cities. The interesting feature of this is that it is found even among educated religious-minded people as well. Such a horrible situation causes havoc and make life of women and children miserable. What are the causes of it? Why is it on the increase? Why can we not make it a sweet home where peace prevails? Lets us analyse the causes of domestic violence—

1. Joint families disintegrated into nuclear families. Joint family system has disintegrated resulting into lack of guidance, control, and affection to newly married. Joint family system was a shock absorber.
2. Husband dominates wife causing irritations. The husband dominates wife which is not acceptable to her. It becomes more serious when wife is also employed. There is no body to help them to sort out differences.
3. Husband and wife start doubting about extra-marital relations causing quarrels, fights and even suicides. It is very difficult to amicably settle such issues.
4. Interference of the parents of the girl in the husband's family—Frequent visit of parents and other family members of girl's side cause tension and interference. This makes the husband and his family angry resulting into quarrels and disputes.
5. Husband if in business or service is starved of funds, he asks the wife to make arrangements from her parents causing domestic violence. This is not one time activity but a long–term problem. This results into all sorts of domestic violence.

Drinking habits of the husband make the life of the wife a hell. The drinking is becoming a common phenomenon. This results into wastage of money, poor health and bad habits like beating wife, children causing Domestic Violence.

Before we discuss about inculcating values in family, let us discuss about the need of good relationship between husband and wife as from their harmonious relationship, children can imbibe good values.

Mahatma Gandhi nicely said that "To call women the weaker sex is a libel; it is man's injustice to woman. If by strength is meant brute strength, then, indeed woman is less brute that man. If by strength is meant moral power, then woman is immeasurably man's superior, has she not greater intuition, is she not more self-sacrificing, had she not greater powers of endurance, has she not greater courage? Without her man could not be. If non-violence is the law of our being, the future is with woman. Who can make a more effective appeal to the heart than woman"?

Dr. Brenda Gael MsSweeney observes, "We must ask ourselves—when the female half of the world is living with the daily threat of physical violence or mental violence, are we truly free"?

Mata Amritanandamayi Devi in her article, "Women Power: Break free to gain Spiritual Wisdom" in *Hindustan Times,* dated May 16, 2000, rightly mentions that in ancient India, the Sanskrit word a husband used to address his wife was patni (the one who leads the husband through life); dharmapatni (the one who guides her husband on the path of dharma or righteousness and responsibility); and sahadharmacharini (the one who moves together with her husband on the path of dharma). All these terms imply that traditionally women were meant to enjoy the same status as men in society, or perhaps even a higher one.

In reality all men are a part of women. Every child first lies in the mother's womb as a part of the woman's very being. Women are essentially mothers, the creators of life. Is God a man or a woman? The answer to that question is that God is neither male nor female. God is "That." But if you insist on God having a gender, then God is more female than male because the masculine is always contained within the feminine. Masculine energy is static. A man's mind easily becomes obsessed with his thoughts and actions. The mind and intellect of a man usually get struck in the work that he does, and because of this, the most men cannot separate their professional life from the family life. Feminine energy, on the other hand, is fluid like a river. That's why each woman has a dharma towards the world and to herself. Along with men, she should shoulder equal responsibility in the growth and development of society.

Our ancient scriptures say, "where women are respected, there dwell the Gods." But this maxim, instead of gaining world-wide momentum has lost its value even in India where it originated. When one reads the newspapers in the morning, the news is related to violence especially on women. Physical assault, rape, dowry deaths, murders, the list is endless. Moreover, most of the violence on women goes unreported, so the crimes, that do get reported are just the tip of the iceberg.

Mahatma Gandhi himself wrote, on women's role in *Harijan*, (February 14, 1940), "My opinion is that, just as fundamentally man and woman are one, their problem must be one in essence. The soul in both is the same. The two live the same life, have the same feelings. Each is a complement of the other. The one cannot live without the other's active help. But somehow or other man has dominated woman from ages past, and so woman has developed an inferiority complex. She has believed in the truth of man's interested teaching that she is inferior to him. But the peers among men have recognized her equal status."

We are sure that new millennium would usher an era where women can enjoy the life in full and in all fields to ensure socio-economic justice. To awaken people, it is the women who must be awakened. Once she is one the move, the family moves, the villages moves, the nation moves.

J.S. Mill and Hariet Taylor Mill ". . . the principle which regulates the existing social relations between the two sexes—the legal subordination of one sex to the other—is wrong in itself, and now one of the chief hindrances to human improvement . . . it ought to be replaced by a principle of perfect equality, admitting no power or privilege on the one side, nor disability on the other."

Empowerment of Women being one of the primary objectives of the Ninth Plan, efforts were made to create an enabling environment where women can freely exercise their rights both within and outside home, as equal partners alongwith men. This was realized through early finalization and adoption of the 'National Policy for Empowerment of Women' which laid down definite goals, targets and policy prescriptions along with a well defined Gender.

Development Index to monitor the impact of its implementation in raising the status of women from time to time

In the words of Justice Krishna Iyer:

"The poignancy of the Indian women's condition is that she is a slave, bonded labour, bought, sold, raped and murdered, eve-teased and dowry burnt, employment-wise exclude *de-facto* and even by rules profession-wise banished into the background and in industry and agriculture and science and technology silently barred from entry or promotion."

It is the urgency and basic requirement of new millennium to provide women freedom, justice and equal status to empower them by equipping with rights to find their place in modern India. Women empowerment is not a piece meal approach but a holistic one wherein the legislature, executive, judiciary and the people of India bring about the revolution for the cause of women.

The following values may be kept in mind while dealing with women in the family and society.

- Enhance self-esteem and self-confidence in women.
- Build a positive image of women by recognizing their contribution to the society, polity and economy.
- Develop in them an ability to think critically.
- Foster decision-making and action through collective process.
- Enable women to make informed choices in areas, like education, employment and health especially reproductive health.
- Ensure equal participation in the developmental process.
- Provide information, knowledge and skill for economic independence.
- Enhance access to legal literacy and information related to their rights and entitlements in the society with a view to enhance their participation on an equal footing in all areas.

God created human race—male and female. He made neither of them superior to the other; on the other hand, he created them for a harmonious existence together. Therefore, the challenges that lie ahead of us cannot be met unless they are approached with a sense of humility and with a sense of togetherness with men. While some of them can be met exclusively by women, they can achieve more by pooling the resources of all. Thikurral mentions the following values for the welfare of the family—

- There is nothing nobler than the resolution of a person who says: I will not remove my hand from the work that I have begun for promoting the welfare of my family.—1021
- When persistently guided by manly effort and full knowledge, that will surely be the means of raising the status of the family.—1022
- If a man resolves: "It is my duty to raise the status of my family" and begins to exert himself with that purpose, then destiny itself may support and hurry to meet him on the way with the offer of success.—1023
- If a person has the unwavering determination to increase the status of his family and accordingly exerts himself without slackering, then success of its own accord will approach him straight.—1024
- If a person when he is tempted to promote the welfare of his family adopts faultless means then the whole world will circle round him as kith and kin.—1025
- If a person has the ability to raise his family to a higher status he will be considered a great hero and a courageous leader, by people at large.—1026
- On the field of battle in the midst of numerous soldiers it is the courageous hero who must face the front of the struggle. Similarly, in the midst of the several members of the family the burden of promoting the welfare of the family falls on the shoulders of the able member.—1027

- In an attempt to promote the welfare of the family you cannot wait for a proper season. Nor can you stand idle because of false pride.—1028
- He who is destined to remove every difficulty from his family, he is certainly going to improve it.—1029
- When adversity saps the foundation of the family, if there is no bold and able member to support it then such a family will fall in ruins.—1030

Methods to Promote Values in Family

1. Love

Love is the elixir of life. It has been found to have power even to cure physical and mental disorders. One who has hatred in his mind not only loses his mind, but also undermines his health and life. On the other hand, love, sympathy, and friendship not only contribute towards building one's peace of mind, but also create a balanced outlook. A man who develops these qualities will acquire serenity, joy and peace in spite of all external circumstances.

2. Enthusiasm

To make life worthwhile and fruitful, we must generate enthusiasm within ourselves. Generation of enthusiasm will take place when we discover for ourselves a goal and attach ourselves to the Altar with a spirit of dedication, reverence and love. Once we have surrendered ourselves to it, the ideal itself will provide us with the inspiration and strength. Then nothing can hinder the progress of our march towards that Goal and the ideal. The love for the ideal will overcome and vanquish all the hurdles from the ideal, and if it comes to that, life itself will be cast-off with a smile in dedication at that Altar. That was how Bhagat Singh could walk to the gallows with a smile on his face. What is important is that one should choose the right ideal . . . an ideal worthwhile even if it comes to sacrificing one's own life in the endeavour. The ideal should be inspiring, it should arouse the spring of activity in us. Thus, the discovering of the ideal is the secret of generating in ourselves Dynamism and

Vitality in its fullness.[10] Bhagat Singh could do it because of the teachings of his parents.

3. Promoting Basic Values

Time is now calling to come together to promote and exemplify values such as tolerance, non-violence, sympathy and compassion for the well-being of others and to create a viable and sustainable family for the future. We must come together to dialogue, to build trust and mutual understanding to eliminate suspicion, fear, tension, insecurity and greed. This can be achieved only with the quality of self-restraint and the spirit of goodwill. Domination, coercion and the threat of force must stop. We must cultivate peace and harmony in our family. None of these can be legislated, but are possible through education in values and spirituality. Education should be given to families to provide respect to women which in turn would be reflected in children rooted in basic values as well as respect to elder members of the family if living with the joint family. Children would consciously and unconsciously imbibe the values being in practice in the family.

It is a good thing to begin to learn at an early age that to lead an efficient life and obtain from one's body the maximum it is able to give, reason must be the master of the house. And it is not a question of yoga or higher realization, it is something which should be taught everywhere in every school, every family, every home, man was made to be a mental being, and merely to be a man—we are not speaking of anything else, we are speaking only of being a man—life must be dominated by reason and not by vital impulses. This should be taught to all children from their infancy. . . The first thing which should be taught to every human being as soon as he is able to think, is that he should obey reasons which is a super-instinct of the species. Reason is the master of the nature of mankind. One must obey reason and absolutely refuse to be the slave of instincts. And here I am not talking to you about yoga. I am not talking about spiritual life, not at all; it has nothing to do with that. It is the basic wisdom of human life, purely human life; every human being who obeys anything other than reason is a kind of brute lower than the animal. That's all. And this should be taught everywhere; it is the basic education which should be given to children.

Usually all education, all culture, all refinement to the sense and the being is one of the best ways of curing instinct, desires, and passions. To eliminate these things does not cure them; to cultivate, intellectualise refine them, this is the surest means of curing. To give the greatest possible development for progress and growth; to acquire a certain sense of harmony and exactness of perception this is a part of the culture of the being of the education of the being. Education is certainly one of the best means of preparing the consciousness for a higher development.[11]

4. Harmony in Family

Harmony among all members of family is basic for promoting good values among family members. All members must understood their role and carry out their duties sincerely. This would be a supporting family where values would be ingrained in all the members.

'Harmony is a precious treasure of human life'. Real success, satisfaction and happiness are the different facets of harmony. If one is to enjoy the benefits of life to the fullest, it is necessary to develop and maintain harmony; and for this understanding the philosophy of nature is required. Harmony should be maintained in all spheres of life especially in family and these are:

- Between body and life;
- Between wisdom and habits;
- Between Individual and Family;
- Between self and family;
- Between the purpose of life and the method of living; and between will and nature.

The more one understands family, the more one will achieve harmony; and success will be proportionate to that. No doubt, harmonizing family is a difficult task, but it is worth striving, for it is the only way to equip oneself to enjoy life to the fullest extent and to reach the goal of life, which is the perfection of consciousness. By the development of knowledge family members come to understand the Cause and Effect system, which is the Law of Nature. Harmony would be beneficial to all members of the family and would promote good values in theory and practice. Harmony in family can promote harmony in the cosmos.

To quote Swami Chinmayananda: The life of harmony can be lived by rising above our limited egocentric view of things and happenings, and expanding our mind to accommodate a constant awareness of the totality of the world, the entirety of mankind and the vastness and wholeness of the universal problems. When this total and consummate perception is developed and maintained, man's individual problems sink into insignificance and absurdity. Our life of harmony with the ampler scheme of the cosmos brings in our heart an inward peace and poise. When poise is maintained within us problems and challenges vanish like mist before the rising sun.[12] Harmony is basic for all the members of family.

5. Peace

Peace is a basic value for promoting good will in the family. A family in peace can achieve perfection and its individuals will be a source of strength to family and society.

The essence of vedic scriptures emphasize God realization and attainments of everlasting peace, as the main aim of human life. The training for this must start from family. All religions aim at the following:

- People must live in harmony without harming others;
- Help people who are suffering;
- Love other living beings as they love themselves;
- Share whatever they get with others; and
- Show love and compassion towards fellow beings.

Humanitarianism will blossom only when all people realize the fact though place, appearance and name separate us, however, we are basically one and united with the same soul and source. Let us meditate, analyse, realize and be in

Peace and Happiness. For all these family education and family peace are basic requirements as society is made up of families.

6. Holistic Education

We should not teach industrial values but must follow holistic values which can make a family a heaven for its members. In this computer age, we should not be left helpless to suffer in life. There is no scarcity of providence of Nature. All the problems and pains are the results of human beings aggressive nature and wrong doings. The imprints of animalistic behaviour, snatching the prosperities of others and enjoying sensory pleasures at the cost of fellow-beings should be changed or neutralised completely by a world-wide plan. This is impossible to implement through political force or economic reforms, here and there, bit by bit. The spiritual path is the only right and sure way to change the behaviour of the mankind by long-term plan. The beginning for this must be made in the family. Families should be educated in basic values which can warn them against all evils.

7. Positive Attitude

All the members must have positive attitude which can enhance the reputation and prestige of the family.

Education today is a peculiar thing because it is not bringing about any valued transformation in anyone. This should not be so. We expect a transformation, but it does not come, for a transformation can happen only with knowledge, with the discovery of truth. Knowledge of the truth transforms a person, but education does not. This is the tragedy of our lives, that in spite of so much education, our lives have not changed. We are still the same.

In a very precise statement, Adi Sankaracarya has given the purpose of knowledge. He says that the result of knowledge is the elimination of falsehood. This implies that if I understand something as false, I withdraw myself from it; and when my wrong concept has gone, then my wrong conduct or vulgarity also comes to an end. Until now, however, we have based our lives upon certain concepts, many of which are false; consequently, the activity arising from them is also false.

When real knowledge takes place, humility comes, for after a person discovers the truth, he realizes how foolish he has been and no one is proud of his foolishness. When we wake up to true knowledge, all of our sufferings come to an end, and we become totally different persons. Yet, at present, we are living under a spell of ignorance and wrong understanding. Our education, rather than removing these false concepts is strengthening them. Since we are people of learning, we should become free from all of our wrong concepts; we should wake up from this dream.

When a person works with inspiration, he never gets tired or exhausted. When man works only for himself, there is perspiration; but when he works for a noble goal there is inspiration. In cases where a man cannot dedicate his actions to the lord, even if he works for some ideal or goal he will derive tremendous strength from his chosen altar of dedication. The nobler the goal, the greater will be the strength he gains. This is the beauty of love and dedication which brings efficiency in life.

In Sanskrit there is a beautiful verse which says, "He really lives in whose living countless people live." What is there to say about a man when even his death becomes an inspiration? He laughs at death. Death cannot destroy him. One who has fulfiled his life and has blessed and inspired many others alone can be called a successful person. He alone is proficient and he alone can be called efficient. Such is the success from which we get great happiness and the strength to face whatever situations confront us. This is where sorrow ends. Such a life is an inspiration to others.[13]

8. Constructive Actions

Family members must engage themselves in constructive activities and not waste their time in useless pursuits. Dalai Lama says: "I believe that life is meant to bring us happiness. Negative actions always bring pain and sorrow, but constructive actions bring us pleasure and joy. The most important thing is transforming our minds. In our daily lives compassion is most effective. We all want to be happy and one of the most important foundations for happiness is mental peace. From my own limited experience

I have found that the greatest inner tranquility comes from the development of love and compassion. The more we care for the happiness of others, the greater our own sense of well-being. Cultivating a close, warm-hearted feeling for others automatically puts the mind at ease. This helps remove whatever fears or insecurities we may have and gives us the strength to cope with any obstacles we may encounter. It is the ultimate source of success in life."

9. A chapter on family life may be included in the school curriculum indicating the broad parameters of family life. What should be the contents of school curriculum about family? These can be:

- (a) Need of family
- (b) Co-operation among family members
- (c) Cleanliness and good environment of home
- (d) Respect for elder members of the family
- (e) Sharing of goods happily
- (f) Eating food together
- (g) Soft speaking
- (h) Love and affection
- (i) Prayers to one's God
- (j) Enjoying and participating in family functions.

If the members of family follow some principles families and home can be heavens on earth.

10. Religious places may be encouraged to lecture on family life quoting ideal examples of Ramayana. Ethical values may be ingrained in the minds of children. Religious places like temples, Gurdwaras, Churches must tell the people who come for different functions the importance of family life. Religious preachers can tell them the benefits of happy family. They can hammer to the people that the first God is to serve their parents and do their family duties honestly. In this way, there can be good relationships between the families and religious places. Religious place can arrange camps for children, parents and elder members of the family and preach them their duties.

Values of Dharma in the Family

Nivedita R. Bhide in her article, "Values in Family" rightly states: In the Indian social system the unit of society is not an individual but a family. Traditionally, every person's life is divided into four stages. In the second stage, called Grihasthashrama, a person takes to family life and is expected to serve society. Our forefathers, the rishis, had conscientiously set the family on firm foundations so as to ensure the stability of society. It is this admirable family system which led many historians to comment that the law and order, culture, and personal virtues did not suffer in India even under foreign rule or in times of war.

The principle which predominantly ruled in the family was Dharma, a word which defies definition in English. 'Family' does not mean a group of people related to each other by law or blood and living together. It is a social unit with a definite purpose—namely, man-making and nurturing of society.

Family is an institution. An institution can function effectively only if it follows the rule of continuity and change. The entry of a newly-wed bride into the house of her husband is an important landmark in any family. She is the child of the present and represents 'change' whereas the in-laws act as the link connecting the past to the present. They ensure continuity in a family. Both the bride and the in-laws have to understand and love each other to allow an uninterrupted progress in the family. The holding together or the breaking apart of a family generally gets decided at this point, namely, the entry of a daughter-in-law. In our tradition, the wife is called a Saha-dharmacharini, meaning, one who practices Dharma along with her husband. This dharma includes the traditions of her new family. How she treats her parents-in-law is usually a good indication of how her children will treat her when she gets old. For the parents-in-law, the bride is Lakshmi incarnate of the house. If they want their family to prosper—if they want peace, happiness, and wealth for the family—they have to keep her happy. If she is unhappy, the whole household gets disturbed. It is through mutual understanding and loving care that the highest good in any family is attained.

11. Holistic View

Hedi and Nik Boesten in their article, "Three Points of View" rightly suggests:[16] If a man and woman marry for love, they are in perfect harmony in thought and emotion right from the start. Instead, they want to accept one another just as they are, with different developments, and if possible complement one another. From then on, they should bear all responsibilities, perform duties and take decisions together and each can rely on the other. This helps enormously in coping with difficulties at work and in everyday life.

At the same time a process of mutual maturing begins: giving in, showing consideration, accepting the common fate, and giving up selfish desires. This takes place all the more quickly, the earlier the desire for children arises. Then selfless service is required. It culminates in the recognition of the fact that during the children's stay of about twenty years with the family, they are merely given into the care of their parents and that parents must learn to release them unconditionally when the time comes. In this way humility, contentment and kindness can grow and in old-age, wisdom, which we in our childhood so appreciated in the older generation.

Today the problem for parents in the West is that children are increasingly questioning the traditional family values. They no longer just want to take them over by way of obedience, but accept them only when they have understood their relevance and value after a period of time. and a maturing process. Often the only help is if the parents have patiently and constantly set an example and are open to questions, even to have themselves called into question. From the point of view of the parents, the special value of the family today lies in helping the growing generation to develop and expand healthy and stable self-confidence, teaching them to be responsible and self-critical, and setting an example in the religious conviction that everything is meaningful. From the latter arises an avoidance of too pessimistic thoughts about the future and an inner tranquility, perhaps even a cheerful prevailing mood.

There is a tendency among some women today to downplay the role of a traditional mother in favour of a career. We should be aware, however, that there are many women who enjoy being a wife and mother, not because they are incompetent to pursue a career, but because they derive greater satisfaction from these. According to C.E. Barker, an analytical psychotherapist, 'One of the tragedies of this modern science soaked society with its obsession for technology, is that mothers now tend to think their contribution to the world is of little account. It assumes that motherhood is a temporary affliction imposed on woman which severely interferes with her fight to show herself as good as man. Alas, such woman have no idea that the job of being a mother and offering a tiny human being her identity, warmth, protective love and tenderness, determines the health, well-being, security, stability and sanity of the coming generation."

Barker continues, 'A generation of good "mothering" would make an unbelievable contribution toward producing a civilization that would work for stability and peace.' Swami Vivekananda sums up the greatness of motherhood in simple words: 'The Position of the mother is the highest in the world, for it is the one place in which to learn and exercise the greatest unselfishness.' The media can be educative and not merely informative; sensitive.

It is high time that in the new millennium, we must revive the institution of family with old values, traditions, love, affection, enthusiasm, truthfulness, honesty, etc. From families, individuals would promote these qualities in the society and the cosmos and usher new era of harmony and peace.

Truthfulness and honesty are the two pillars to sustain human existence and happiness. These imply that the persons following these values have no contradictions in thoughts and actions. An honest and fruitful person earns confidence and trust from all. He stands like a rock. Honesty is not to be proved or shown from inside rather it is a conviction from within and is as pure as God. All the religions of the world advocate the practice of Truth. Love is the religion of the universe which can keep all people united. All these can be learnt in a family.

The emphasis should be more on performance rather than paper planning. Khalil Gibran has rightly said that

"Believing is a fine thing, but placing those beliefs into execution is a test of strength. Many are those who talk like the roar of the sea, but their lives are shallow and stagnant, like the rotting marshes. Many are those who lift their heads above the mountain tops, but their spirit remain dormant to the obscurity of the caverns."

Let us have a great ideal, an ideal that will startle us with its greatness. That is the only kind of an ideal to hold before our minds eye and to work for. Little by little our imperfections and difficulties will vanish and instead of regarding life as a drudgery, instead of shrinking from it, we shall bless this life which offers so many opportunities. We shall find joy even in the little daily tasks and wherever we are placed we shall know happiness. This must begin in the family.

Conclusion

The great occupation of women should be beautify life; to cultivate, for her own, sake and that of those who surround her, all her faculties of mind, soul, and body; all her powers of enjoyment, and powers of giving enjoyment; and to diffuse beauty, elegance, and grace, everywhere. If in addition to this the activity of her nature demands more energetic and definite employment, there is never any lack of it in the world; if she loves, her natural impulse will be to associate her existence with him she loves, and to share his occupations; in which, if he loves her (with that affection of equality which along deserves to be called love). She will naturally take as strong an interest, and be as thoroughly conversant, as the most perfect confidence on his side can make her.[14]

Between the hum-drum of the daily academic activities, the inculcation of civic and social duties was never forgotten. Education was not imported merely for the sake of culture or for the purpose of developing mental and intellectual powers and faculties. Its primary aim, among others, was also to promote social efficiency and happiness. The graduates, who were not to lead an isolated or self-centered life, had to perform their duties as a son, a husband and a father conscientiously. They were taught that their wealth was not solely their own or of their family's but a part of its should be spent on chaitable works. They had certain social duties which were emphatically reflected in the convocation address given to these students on the eve of their graduation from the University. The art graduates were told:

"Speak the truth, Do your duty. Neglect not the daily study. . . . Do not swerve from the truth. Do not swerve from duty. Do not neglect what is useful. Do not miss opportunities to be great. Do not neglect the daily duties of learning and teaching. . . . Do not neglect the rituals due to the Gods and fathers."

"Let your mother be to you like unto a god. Let your father be to you like unto a god. Let your teacher be to you like unto a god. Let your guest be to you like unto a god."

"Whatever actions are blameless, those should be followed, not other. Whatever good works have been performed by us, those should be emulated by you, not others. And there are some Brahmanas better than we. They should be comforted by you by giving them a seat."

". . . Thus conduct yourself. This is the rule. This is the teaching. . . . This is the command. Thus should you observe. Thus should be observed."[15]

Let us end quoting the values for householders Dharma in Thikkural:

> He who is esteemed as a householder is one who standing firm in the path of virtue serves to support the other 3 orders. ...41
>
> A householder lives true to his virtue when the supports the ascetics, the indigents, and the destitute ones who take refuge in his house in their last moments. . . .42
>
> Elders on death-bed, God, Guests, Relatives, and Oneself, to cherish these five is the main duty of the householder. . . .43
>
> If a householder shares his meal with others, what he obtained by just means, his family line will continue long without a break. ...44

If home life is based on love and virtue, then that life will have its perfect grace and reward. ...45

If one wants to live as a householder, let him live according to the path of righteousness prescribed for him. What benefit would be achieve by adopting any other path? ...46

If a householder lives his life without swerving from the path of righteousness ordained for him, he will occupy the foremost place among all those that strive for spiritual realization. ...47

One who lives the faultless home life according to the path of righteousness and shows to others how to walk the correct path, will have his domestic life nobler than that of the ascetics who practice stern austeristics. ...48

Domestic life par excellence is that which is based upon virtue. The other course of the ascetics if faultless is also praiseworthy. 49

He who enjoys on earth a faultless domestic life may claim the citizenship of heaven with the Gods. ...50

Notes and References

1. Swami Jitatmananda, Value Education, *op. cit.*, p. 4.
2. M.L. Burke: "Swami Vivekananda in the West: Vol. 1, 487-88, Advaita Ashrama, Calcutta.
3. R. Oppendeimer, Letters and Recollections: Cambridge Harvard University, Press 1980, p. 292.
4. Values, The Key to a Meaningful Life, A Vedanta Kesari Presentation, Sri Ramakrishnan Math, Madras, 600 004.
5. Ashoo Reddy, Home, Sweet Home, in Values, *op. cit.*, pp. 75, 76 and 81.
6. His Exellency, Lord Swaraj Paul, Hard Work and Integrity have no equal, in *University News*, Feb. 19-25, 2007, p. 19.
7. Nani A. Palkhivala, Time for National Introspection, in Values, p. 114.
8. Reminiscences of Swami Vivekananda; Advanita Ashrama, pp. 2-7.

9. UNIFEM and Support Service to Counter-Violence against Women in Haryana.
10. Swami Chinmayananda, A Manual of Self Unfoldment, *op. cit.*, p. 42.
11. The Sunlit Path, Passages from conventions and writings of The Mother, Sri Aurobindo Ashram, Pondicherry, India, 1984, p. 7.
12. Swami Chinmayananda, Kindle Life, pp. 40-41.
13. Swami Tejomayananda, Right Thinking, CCMT, Mumbai, pp. 5, 29 30.
14. John Stuart Mill and H.T. Mill, Early Essays on Marriage and Divorce, Alice and Rossi (ed.) Essays on Sexual Equality, p. 225.
15. Chandni Saxena, "Role of Ancient Indian Universities in Value Orientation to the Contemporary Indian Society", *University News*, 44, January 30, 2005. p. 30.

3

Society and Values

Lord, make me an instrument of your peace,
Where there is hatred, let me sow love, where there is injury, pardon;
Where there is doubt, faith; where there is despair, hope,
Where there is darkness, light, where there is sadness, joy
O Divine Master, grant that I may not so much seek to be consoled as to console,
To be understood as to understand; to be loved as to love.
For it is in giving that we receive, it is in pardoning that we are pardoned; and it is in dying that we are born to eternal life.

—*Prayer of Saint Francis of Assisi*

Man/woman is social by nature. Man's nature is such that he/she cannot afford to live alone. No human being is known to have normally developed in isolation. Necessity also compels man to live in society. Many of his needs will remain unsatisfied if he or she does not have the cooperation of his fellow beings. Every individual is the offspring of a social relationship established between man and woman. Man

CHART 3.1

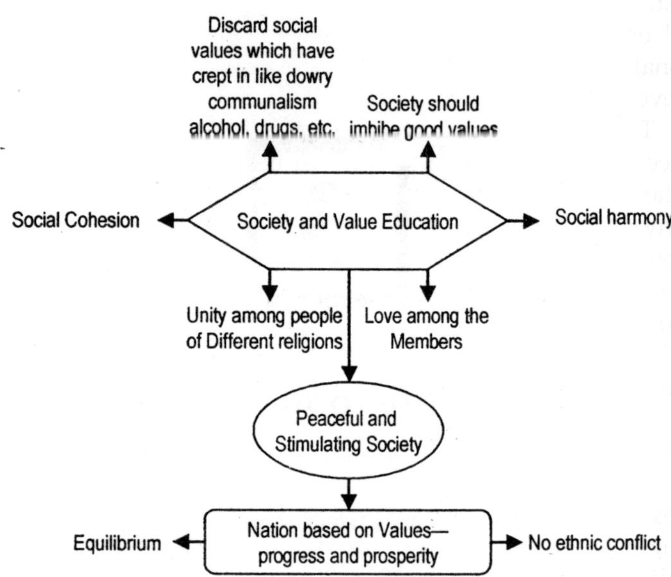

lives in society for his mental and intellectual development society preserves our culture and transmits it to succeeding generations. It both liberates and limits our potentialities as individuals and shapes our attitudes, beliefs, morals and ideals. The mind of a man/woman without society, as feral cases show, remains the mind of an infant at the age of adulthood. The cultural heritage directs our personality. Thus, society fulfils not only physical needs but also determines our mental conditions.

We seem to be passing through a crisis of values in our social and political life which gives special urgency to the question of values in education. It is commonly deplored that crime, violence, cruelty, indifference to human values, greed and spite have spread to all aspects of our life including the education sector. Altruism, selfless service to fellow human beings and idealism are things of the past. Sensitivity to the beauty in art, literature, nature and life in general are very much on the decline. Lack of social cohesion, national disintegration has become patently manifest and our democratic social order is under severe stress. Social tensions, unrest, prejudices and complexes transmitted through the social environment vitiate the quality of life. Narrow castiest regional, linguistic and communal platforms divide the people as never before." (Reddy and Sarma, 2003).[1]

The Oxford English Dictionary defines ethics as the science of morals or moral principles. Values, norms, standards, morality like expressions are also considered synonyms to this expression and recently "social responsibility" has also been used. It has, but to me, something to do with the sense of right or wrong—what is permissible and what is done.[2]

Before founding BHU, Malviya had said: "To revitalize India as a Nation, it is necessary to feed her youth with old spiritual and moral values and religion must be made a part of education based on Indian ideals.[3]

To achieve real happiness you have to imbibe ideals, values and principles, acquire the right qualities and adopt the right attitude. Primacy must be accorded to character and morality. Aim high in life and regard failures as pillars of success. Be optimistic and ever smiling. Your constant endeavour in life should be to become a good person. This can be achieved by thinking good, speaking good and doing good. Goodness implies quality of caring, compassion, kindness, benevolence, sacrifice, love of truth, humanism, tolerance, harmony, non-violence and morality. Virtue always follows goodness; cultivate good habit and make goodness a habit; for man without goodness is not better than a beast. The truly great are not those who have more money or brains or higher status or position. What really matters is whether you have been kind and helpful to others. This can be achieved when you expand your capacity to love and not to hate others. Love begins when we care for others and take trouble to bring comfort to those in pain and suffering. This is the best way to be happy and this is the best way to be great.[4]

The importance of educated human power for the social and material progress of the country is, without doubt a necessity and needs no over emphasis. But the human progress encompassing economic and social aspects is being hampered because of the low level of value-consciousness amongst the different sections of the society. Character formation is even more important for the well-being of the individual and of the community than mere cultivation of intellect. Development of moral, ethical, and social concepts is essential to a satisfying personal philosophy, to a career consistent with the public welfare, and to a sound professional attitude for the development of every phase of personality.[5]

B.H. Briz Kishore, Chairman, National Council of Rural Institute and former Member, University Grants Commission, Ministry of Home Resource Development, Government of India, Shakar Bhavan, Fateh Maidan Road, Hyderabad delivered the Bajaj Endowment Lecture at Gujarat Vidyapeeth, Ahmedabad on Sept. 19, 2003. He said, "The objective of the ethical education programmes is to involve students in an exploration of different value-dimensions of life, which go into making a good man, a good life and good society. An integrated personality is visualized as one, which reflects a harmonious balance of all these varied values. It includes discussions on spiritual, ethical, aesthetic, cultural, societal and human values. This is the way to be truly and fully humane for understanding and cultivating their value-standards that can relate to them through their own life experiences."—(Excerpts)[6]

According to Cooley, "society and individual do not denote separate phenomena but are simply collective and distributive aspects of the same thing. Without society the individuals cannot survive. The close dependence of the individual upon his social milieu makes it possible to account for some aspects of human behaviour without reference to psychological characteristics. But the individual is not a passive instrument of society. He is to be seen as an active being who not only does action but also innovates and modify the behaviour and actions. The individual also resists restrictions imposed by the society which may disturb the social equilibrium.

Individual and society are inter-dependent. The relationship between them is not one sided, both are essential for the comprehension of society. Society consists of a number of individuals who live in it and create and recreate it. This creation and recreation of society by men/women is a continuous process which has been going on since the human species came into being. But when one fine morning some people sat down and decided to form a society. In fact, society and individual are two inseparable dimensions of same reality. There cannot be a society without individuals and we cannot think of survival of an individual apart from society.

Simplicity and high thinking leads to happiness and truthful life. The great prophets, scholars and saints believed in and practiced simple living and high thinking. The simple living and high thinking go together. Simple living while on the one hand blesses the doer, on the other hand, it helps others to ensure sustainable development. Acharay's call Part 2 (H.H. Jagadguru's in his Madras Doscourses) has beautifully explained the need and rationale of simple living.

"High thinking is inconsistent with complicated material life based on high speed imposed on us by material workship. All the graces of life are possible only when we learn the art of living nobly."

Simplicity and high thinking promotes the following qualities in human beings:

1. Simple living protects the people practicing simplicity from evil habits like smoking, drinking, etc.
2. Simple living and high thinking help in the development of mental perfection and firmness.
3. Simple living makes the person practicing it beautiful externally and internally.
4. Simple living promotes the quality of selfless service.
5. Simple living promotes disciplined life.
6. Simple living leads to creativity and betterment of society.

A society thrives best when it is composed of men and women who are intelligent, hard working, honest, and dutiful. A good society means a society where the average men and women are good. One or two great men do not determine its character. A great man or woman may be born in society and under any conditions, but that is no indication of an ideal society. An ideal society is one which gives opportunity to every individual to grow—grow physically, intellectually, and morally. IT places an ideal before the individual and urges him to grow according to that ideal. Not only that, it also creates conditions conducive to such growth.

Real beauty eventually lies in simplicity. The simpler the life the easier it is to live with.

Life is meant to bring us happiness. Negative actions always bring pain and sorrow, but constructive actions bring us pleasure and joy. The most important thing is transforming our minds. In our daily lives compassion is most effective. We all want to be happy and one of the most important foundations for happiness is mental peace. From my own limited experience we have found that the greatest inner tranquility comes from the development of love and compassion. The more we care for the happiness of others, the greater our own sense of well-being. Cultivating a close, warm-hearted feeling for others automatically puts the mind at ease. This helps remove whatever fears or insecurities we may have and gives us the strength to cope with any obstacle we may encounter. It is the ultimate source of success in life.

As individuals what is particularly important is that we develop a kind heart, a sense of love, compassion and respect for others. We believe it is important that issues like working for peace in the world do not merely remain the business of politicians and diplomats; we should all be involved. The shape of the future is of great interest to all of us. I am convinced that even if only a few individuals try to create mental peace of happiness within themselves and act responsibility and kind heartedly towards others, they will have a positive influence in their community.[7]

The twentieth century was marred by conflict and war. Therefore, it is especially important that we take steps to ensure that this new century will be characterized instead of by non-violence and dialogue, the preconditions of peaceful co-existence. Contentment does not depend upon externals; it changes with our mental attitude. John Milton wrote:

The mind in its own place, and in itself.
Can make a heaven of Hell, a hell of Heaven.

Vedanta says: We cannot change the world, we can only change ourselves. The world is like a dog's curly tail. No matter how hard we try to straighten it, it will always curl up again and again. We matter how hard we try to streaigthen it, it will always curl up again. We can only straighten ourselves. Whatever after due consideration and analysis you find to be conductive to the good to the benefit and to the welfare of all beings, that doctrine, believe in, cling to, and take as your guide.[8]

Whatever result a person intends to achieve he may succeed in realising it according to his idea provided he pursues his end with a steadfastness of will.

If India is to attain economic prosperity, social well-being, intellectual advancement, national integration, and the rejuvenation of her ancient spiritual culture and values drastic changes in the ethos of the people must be brought about.[9]

A society is the summation of individuals. The values of a society are determined by its individuals, and the force of inequality in society strengthened by selfish considerations, has to be kept under control.

The force that can hold society together is moral force, Dharma, the consideration for the other person. This deep value in mankind, which enhanced becomes altruism, is possible only in an atmosphere of "toned-down materialism" and assertion of the Spirit. If the individuals value sense gratification and money, the society will be materialistic; if the individuals value intellectual pursuits, the society will be advanced in science and technology; if the individuals value the arts, the society will be cultured. Only if the individuals place the highest value on spiritual awakening, will the society be a peaceful one.[10]

Every society big or small, simple or complex has a boundary. It has a time and space dimension. Individuals living in a particular society feel that they belong to each other. As compared to other societies they are similar in terms of language, dress, food, habits and the type of houses they build for themselves. Those who speak different languages, eat different types of food, put on different style of dresses and build their houses in different ways are considered as outsiders.

Society in 21st century has become materialistic, exploitative, prone to criminal activities that is why society has become polluted. Criminal elements in a society are the leaders of society. How can we expect the assimilation of individuals in such a society? What is needed is a social change by pure and God fearing individuals to purge society of its bad elements or make them change by adopting good values, thereby leading to transformation of society. Such individuals rather than being engulfed by wrong values, must promote positive values.

Independence is the very essence of manhood and he who has disengaged himself from this slavish dependence upon the world of objects for gaining his flashes of joys, is truly independent. Other are only beings, who, like feathers in the summer breeze, are tossed about hither and thither by the problems and challenges of the world.

A man may be tossed about by uncertain storms of life but the solution to it lies in his own efforts in finding an ideal in life and then raising his personality from the level of petty emotions to the loftier heights of the chosen ideal. The secret of success in life thus lies in keeping the head above the storms of the heart. A successful man never allows his faculty of discrimination and judgement to be disturbed by the rising tides of his emotions.

For a harmonious and a better quality of life in the twenty-first century, what is required is a new national as well as global socio-political agenda for the establishment of a new social order with a sound foundation of physical culture, mental culture and soul culture, all working hand-in-hand to produce the enlightened, educated and complete man of genuine culture. This enjoins integration of physical sciences with the science of spirit or spiritualism. If materialism is a quest for a better quality of outer life, spiritualism is the quest that begins with the ascent of man and society towards humanism and pursuit of eternal human values that will guarantee the advancement of contemporary civilization and the glory of man and society. The integration of the two is imperative for the betterment of mankind by putting an end to the prevailing disequilibrium, disharmony and disorder in the human life at all levels from home to the global village. It would elevate man to his higher spiritual status as he would be fully aware of the divinity in himself as well as in all creatures—of the fatherhood of God, the fellowship of humanity and the brotherhood of man. Whenever and wherever spiritual qualities are lacking in man, there is nothing to prevent the society from falling into decay.

Lawrence A. Kimpton observes that: "A great university is a community of men and women who wish to know about man, society, the world of nature, and the things of the spirit. It is a place where the codes of nature are broken, the secretes of the universe are exposed."

Amongst all the living-beings, man is the most evolved creation in the universe. Unlike other creatures a man's life has to possess some meaning beyond mere self-preservation or existence. He is the only living being who is relatively free to make his own destiny. And if he has to make his destiny, it has to be guided by certain values which could become the illuminating forces of his life process. According to Dr. P.N. Mathur (1986), these values for man, which provide the prime motivating force behind his thought, emotion and action, have to be moral and spiritual if his socio-cultural and spiritual life has to be such as brings peace, progress and welfare for both the individual and society. This was precisely the reason why the ancient Indian Universities which mirrored the great ideals of a great nation called India and its society, worked to create an understanding of the spirit of its civilization. These universities imbued the rising generations with the traditions of a great society who, for centuries sustained on such human values which nurtured free minds of men and urged them on to full and fair enquiry which brought wisdom into human affairs.[11]

Let us be dedicated to an accepted and well-tested ideal and let us develop the courage to live our convictions fully, entirely and wholly. This intellectual honesty to live true to our conviction in full dedication to the ideal adds a serene cadence to our individual life. The success and beauty of the individual life help to build the glory and effectiveness of the society/nation.

Our firm belief today is that the joys we experience through our senses lie in the objects of the world. Consistent with this belief, we are constantly engaged in acquiring, possessing and aggrandizing more and more wealth. But a little reflection reveals to us that the acquisition and possession of wealth is no measure of the quantum of one's happiness. We are but too familiar with the striking contradictions in life between a millionaire sitting and mourning in his palatial apartments and ill-clad peasant roaring in ecstatic joy amidst his poor circumstances. Happiness, therefore, is measured by the tranquillity of one's mind.[12] It does not mean that all the members of society are exactly similar in taste and habits but by and large members of society are alike and they belong to a particular geographical area.

In this age of science and rapid technological development, our life has become complicated and stress has become our companion. We are trapped in the mire of political controversies. In order to earn our living and for our own survival we have to face intense competition everywhere. Conflicts and violent confrontations between different religious groups, castes and classes, whether hidden or open, have disturbed our balance. In these circumstances unless one knows how to maintain his inner peace and mental iquipoise, anxiety, worry and stress will undoubtedly overwhelm him. Mental disturbances affect the physical health of the person adversely. Neurophysiologists have proved this all over the world. It is better to nip worry, stress and fear in the bud, instead of allowing them to accumulate slowly and eventually produce a fatal illness. When such a disease progresses relentlessly, we rush helplessly to a physician. We can avoid such serious consequences of worry and stress if we learn to mould our lives on certain values and principles.

We are passing through critical times when the environment all around is unethical. K.R. Narayanan, former President of India, while delivering his address, on the eve of

Independence Day, on 14th August, 2000, was critical of the nexus between politicians and criminals, who are, in the process polluting the environment of the country. The malpractices in every sphere have become cancerous and are engulfing the entire system geared to provide good standard of living to people. It is creating stress both among the people as well as the people in power. T.N. Chaturvedi in his Editorial on the Special Number on Ethics in Public life remarked.[13]

The potential damage and threat to the political fabric of a system is not dependent on the character of government, i.e. whether it is an activist or limited in scope. History shows that neither a capitalist nor a socialist nor a welfare state is immune to the corrosive evil of corruption. The standards of conduct and behaviour of people in political authority have their malignant influence in other walks of life in society. The ethical dimensions of how influential and powerful people conduct themselves in private life and the public domain set a precedent for the lesser human beings and groups in society to follow or to seek justification for their own self-seeking or even scandalous conduct. The perniciousness ripple-effect encompasses all segments of society. It is not only the public systems that are under attack. The people harbour grievances against trade, industry, business, academia, medical and other professional groups and organizations. The evil within and outside the government circle, is thus, not limited to any narrow confines. Similarly, the influence of ethical conduct in positive terms is also not contained or concerned with only some specific sections and select groups but is relevant to the entirety of society and its wider network of relationships. As is often said, the moral basis for the unity and stability of society demands that ethical restraints must operate not only in respect of individuals but also organized groups—be they industrial, business and trade associations, labour unions, political parties, military and civil services, judiciary, non-governmental organizations, academic or professional associations, agriculturists organisations, etc. apart from government itself. The all-pervading and inter-locking nature of ethics in public life is to be comprehended in all its manifestations and dimensions. This is borne out by history in different times and ages and also by the prowess of civilization today.

The scandals and cases of corruption, kickbacks, bribery, extortions, lying and deception by government all over the world, in both developed and developing countries at different times, are too many and too well-known to need any enumeration. In the wake of many cases of nepotism, influence peddling, corporate bribery, corruption, illicit operations, business malpractices, and unhealthy nexus between politics, administration and business coming of public notice at the time of the World War II, the US Senate set-up a sub-committee under Senator Paul Doughlas, which submitted its report, commonly known as the Report on Ethical Standards in Government. This attracted attention allover the world and the various nuances of ethics in governance were discussed, researched and commented upon in various forums.

Vohra Committee has been quite vocal in portraying the decaying environment engulfing the basic framework of the Indian constitution and social life of the people.

To quote from the Vohra Committee:[14] The big smuggling Syndicates, having international linkages, have spread into and infected the various economic and financial activities, including havala transactions, circulation of black money and operations of a vicious parallel economy causing serious damage to the economic fibre of the country. The Syndicates have acquired substantial financial and muscle power and social respectability and have successfully corrupted the Government machinery at all levels and wielded enough influence to make the task of Investigating and Prosecuting agencies extremely difficult; even the members of the Judicial system have not escaped the embrace of the Mafia.

Justice V.R. Krishna Iyer has even blamed the elite clan for joining the criminals and make the nation stink by their frivolous activities. To quote him:[15]

Lawyers, Doctors, Company Secretaries, Chartered Accountants, Engineers and Scientists, not to speak of the talented bureaucrats, are all slowly selling their souls for a mess of pottage. Even the leaders in the professions have let us down. People when they are maltreated by officials get stressed and suffocated causing anxieties, fears, suffer tensions, stress. That is why, stress among people is on the increase.

Norm is a standard for judging the behaviour of any societal form or function. Every society has such norms which regulate the behaviour of its members. Norms are shared by the members and they feel sentimental about them. Norms are part of the cultural heritage. For example, paying respect to the elders, parents, taking care of the children, avoid trespassing on some one's private property or not to pay a courtesy call on your friend at odd hours lest he feels disturbed. Purpose of the norms is to regulate the behaviour of individuals in society. People behave according to these norms and also expect others to do the same. In brief, norms are products of social interaction, transmitted through social heritage, shared in common which regulate the behaviour.

If there are large number of people who cherish the well-tested norms built for common good, the society is bound to be a source of bliss from which would radiate fragrance of good values to make life of individuals idealistic.

A nation is built by the individuals comprising it. When each individual in the society or nation puts forth his effort in the direction indicated in the scriptures and reconstitutes his personality, then that society or nation grows dynamically, permeating peace and glory to one and all. Let us therefore, awake, arise and rebuild our nation and ourselves.[16]

Values

Like norms values are essential for the maintenance of order and control in the society. Values are standard of judgement by which things and actions are considered as good or bad, moral or immoral, beautiful and ugly. Through values choices can be made among alternatives and specific courses of action can be judged as appropriate or inappropriate. Values deal not so much with what is but with what ought to be. In a way they express moral imperatives and facilitate organized activity to control the behaviour of individuals in society.

The term cultural pluralism means the co-existence of several sub-cultures within a given society on equal terms. The advocates of pluralism hold that cultural differences within a society should be retained in so far as these differences do not conflict with the major value and norms of the dominant culture. They believe that culturally diverse groups can live in harmony and that mutual understanding rather than assimilation should be the goal. Therefore, cultural pluralism implies the cultural heterogeneity with ethnic and other minority groups maintaining their identity within the society.

The Indian nation today, contrary to the expectation of the father of the Nation, Mahatma Gandhi, is not a peaceful country and despite the tremendous improvements it registered in the various human development aspects, violence seems to be spreading like cancer. Violence of different sorts dominate the general scenario sending shock waves all around. Mass killings, rioting and destruction of other's property at the slightest provocation seems to have become the order of the day. No part of India can claim to be free from this scourge.

The odds before humanity appear to be imponderable. From religious violence, physical violence, economics of violence, etc., humanity has now moved over to a period of 'terrorist violence and counter-terrorist violence which is more deadly. It is hoped that the power and glory of non-violence would continue to influence thinkers, social activists, policy-makers, administrators, writers as well as the common man, as is evident from the various campaigns and determined movements, led non-violently in different parts of the world now. The declaration by UNESCO of 2000 AD as the 'Year of Non-violence' is yet another mile stone in humanity's striving towards building a non-violent world 'Vasudhaiva Kutumbakam' as espoused by Indian sages several centuries ago.[17]

In addition, there are reports in newspapers, T.V., Radio, about murders, rape, extortion, abductions, snatching of ornaments, thefts, etc. which result in the total collapse of society. Corruption is spreading like cancer. Today the society and country is polluted. Drinking, sex, gambling, night clubs have become a daily feature. Society is not keeping its members under accepted values. Under such a situation individuals should engage themselves to purge the society of its bad values and bring in the accepted values to make the life of the people happy.

How dear is the thought that a time will come when there will be no more hunger on earth, no more exploitation, no more social injustice; also there will be freedom for all, peace and amity between man and man, and life will be easy and comfortable for everybody! This has been man's dream ever since he has learnt to think, formulate his wishes and plans, decide his priorities, and much later, also recognize that his fate is interlinked with his fellow-beings, even his environment. But how is it that this dream has not yet come true?

This indeed is a riddle. Man has grown much over the centuries in every direction. He has proved his supremacy over Nature and can now do things that once seemed impossible. On the physical plane he is much better off than ever before. Yet the overall outlook of the world remains as grim as ever. Take the case of food. Given the present scale of food production, hunger need no longer be a problem; yet many people starve for various reasons, chief of them being trade manipulations by clever people. As regards exploitation, if one knew in how many covert and overt ways it goes on! Despite all the protestations of goodwill by people in power, the weak continue to be exploited. So also social injustice. Its crude forms may have changed but it continues as ruthlessly as ever. Love and amity are words much talked about as they always have been but the world is nowhere near seeing any semblance of them in practice. The common man helplessly looks on while evil forces go on playing havoc among themselves.

Why is the situation like this? One cynical view is that this is how the world is constituted and there is nothing one can do about it. As they say, it is like a dog's tail which will always remain curly and you can never make it straight. No doubt you can help improve the situation in some areas, but may be in doing so you will create problems elsewhere. The argument seems to be that good and evil go together and you cannot have one without the other. You can never have a world in which there is no wrongdoing, no injustice, no cruelty, no hardship. These will continue though their forms may change from time to time. Not only will these evil things continue but also their counterpart, the good things, will continue. Philosophically, this may be true, but man has no right to stop fighting evil. It is his duty as well as privilege to carry on his fight against evil. He alone can dare dream that some day he will be able to .convert the earth to a paradise. The story of civilization is the story of the struggle he is making in this direction. He may or may not succeed but he keeps on struggling though he perhaps does not know and does not even want to know.[18]

A population living in a geographical area would not by itself constitute a nation. It is just a mere number, a multitude of human beings. But, when the members live together with an integrated programme and strive with diligence and devotion for the achievement of a common goal, one sees the formation and glorious achievements of a nation.

As long as human beings live disintegrated; each one self-centered and seeking his private ends, regardless of others, with no allegiance whatsoever to a common cause, they can never make a nation. The scientific, economic and political philosophies have, time and again, given out revolutionary schemes, which present an artificial look of integration during the initial enthusiasm, but, by themselves, none of these schemes can ever succeed in creating or building up a true nation.

A united country, wherein each citizen is inspired to give out his very best in a spirit of selfless dedication, demanding nothing for himself except the privilege of serving the country, develops into a mighty nation asserting itself with power, prestige and strength.[19]

The dynamics of togetherness is, therefore, to be discovered immediately—more so in context of the present world. The answer to this great challenge of the times assures us of a continued future as a happy, united and progressive nation serving as a beacon for the restless world to follow and gain a more rewarding peace and a more meaningful progress.

Human mind today is completely out of control, flowing in all directions. It is like a river in spate. Our primary attempt should be to prevent the flow spreading in all directions by controlling, harnessing and regulating it. This is achieved by reinforcing the banks. In the river of thoughts, the intellect represents the banks, which decide the direction of flow. Hence, the intellect has to be chastened and chiseled with the help of the scriptures. [20]

A change in thoughts can be effected by three methods, namely, by reducing the quantity of thoughts, by improving the quality of thoughts and by giving a different direction to the thoughts.[21]

In order to live and to bring out the maximum happiness from ourselves, to work out the best for ourselves, everyone of us must have a goal in life, a mission, an inspiring ideal; looking up to that ideal and hitching our eyes to it, we must work on in the world outside. Thereby, the work becomes chastened; the work itself become its own reward for the individual and a great joy wells up in his mind, not in terms of what he gets on the first of the month, but what he gives to the society as best as he can, from the place where he is.

The great Acaryas have said that having discovered a great goal, surrender yourself to that goal and act towards it drawing your inspiration from that goal, and thereby discover a new column of energy. Do not allow this energy to be dissipated in the futile memories of the past, regrets or failures, or in the imagined sorrows of the future, or in the excitement of the present. Thus, bring that entire energy focused into activity. That is the highest creative action in the world outside. Thereby the individual who is till now considered most inefficient finds his way to the highest achievement and success.[22]

Let us discuss some values which need be followed by individuals in a society as well as society should uphold them. This is not an easy task. Associations, communities, social groups must work in preserving the values which can make a society richer and healthy.

Selfishness

Selfishness is the root of all trouble in the world. Individuals, communities and countries fall out because they are selfish. If there are wars, it is because some nations are too selfish. Some amount of selfishness is natural but it can be excessive and when excessive, it becomes dangerous. It is at this point that some sort of check is called for. Even within a family or community, if there is too much selfishness, it has to be curbed. The necessity for a State to frame laws and devise a machinery to enforce those laws arises because of this selfishness. The laws evolve through centuries of experience and most of them remain unwritten. Within certain limits, selfishness is legitimate, even welcome, but where it exceeds those limits, the offending member or members may have to face expulsion. This happens even in the animal world. In man's case, the check is more rigid; the criterion of his progress is how selfless he is.

This is what is regarded as liberation, liberation from the bondage which narrow selfishness imposes on a man, the kind of selfishness which flows from the feeling that you, as an individual, have a separate identity from others. When this selfishness is gone, you have the feeling that you are one with others, as if your own self is extinct, 'killed'.[23]

The Dalai Lama, while speaking on the occasion of the Theosophical Society of India's centenary celebration, put his finger on the real problem when he said that at the root of the troubles which afflicted man today lay on his own pride and selfishness. He said that there could be no peace on earth so long as man continued to neglect moral values. Progress in science and technology was good, but this, he pointed out, needed to be matched by advancement in moral qualities if chances of conflicts were to be minimized. Leadership rooted in character and welfare of humanity to reform society through good values is essential.

It is clear that it is not enough for a world leader to be politically astute. It may be an additional qualification, but the essential requisite is for him to have a character that will command respect from all including those who disagree with him. People aspiring for world leadership have to have something of the moral stature that characterized Buddha and

Christ. They must have the same compassion and wisdom so that the weaker nations may feel that their interests are safe in their hands. As world leaders, they must accept the responsibility of helping the weaker nations grow stronger. If there is any injustice done to them, they must see it redressed quickly. Now that technology has unified the world, they must help this unity grow stronger and more meaningful by promoting the spirit of co-operation and friendship among the nations. The world's problems are not merely political and economic. They are also moral. Life's purpose is not accumulation of wealth and pursuit of sense—pleasure, but higher development—morally and spiritually. World leaders should never tire of repeating this. But they themselves should set an example in this respect. [24]

Viewed against this, the way some gurus are operating in India and abroad is bound to cause concern. They perform weird tricks to convince the world of their powers, but is religion magic? True religion raises a man's moral stature. It makes him a better man, better in every respect. A guru's credentials are to be judged in terms of these qualities. If a guru does not possess these qualities himself, how can he confer them on other? Can an unlighted lamp light other lamps?

Buddha had found peace and joy himself and was anxious that his fellow men share them with him. He noticed much of man's misery was of his own making. The seat of the trouble is within man himself. It is a mistake to look outside for its cause and remedy. The solution Buddha offers is simple, practical, and without any philosophical claptrap. He places the onus on man himself and not on any god or goddess, or that unknown factor called Fate. What man needs is self-restraint. The word 'samyak' which he uses while spelling out how man should conduct himself is very significant. It means restrained, according to the prevailing norms. The right thought, the right speech, the right action—the emphasis always is on the word 'right' in whatever man does. The entire eight-fold path which Buddha chalks out for man to attain nirvana is nothing but a cautious tight-rope walk between that which is pleasant (preyas) and that which is really good (shreyas). There are people who first act and then think. Buddha wants that they should first think and then act. His advice is: Ask yourself if what you are going to do is right by the accepted moral standards. If not, avoid it.[25]

Morality and Ethics

Man is basically human because he has a kind heart. Else, he is inhuman. He has intelligence, so he is rational. Else, he is sub-human. This rational human being draws ethics for the welfare of humanity all over the globe. There are human rights, human responsibilities meant for observance by all. Webster's dictionary suggests different shades of meaning to the synonyms: moral, ethical, virtuous, righteous and nobel. They all basically mean 'conforming to a standard of what is right and good'. "Moral implies conformity to established and sanctioned codes of accepted notions of right and wrong. ETHICAL may suggest the involvement or more difficult or subtle questions of rightness, fairness or equity. VIRTUOUS implies the possession or manifestation of moral excellence in character. RIGHTEOUS stresses guiltlessness or blamelessness and often suggests sanctimonious; NOBLE implies moral eminence and freedom from anything petty, mean or dubious in conduct and character."

Having been born as human beings, let us not be unethical. Every profession has certain ethics. Under no circumstances should we violate the professional ethics. A teacher is unethical if he does not teach with affection when a student approaches him or her to learn. A doctor is unethical if he or she does not treat the patient on account of insufficient money or fees. A lawyer is unethical if he uses his brain power to defend crime and presents his arguments to get acquittal for a criminal. So are the various professional ethics. Above all, is the human ethics. To be unconcerned to the society's needs, if a person enjoys luxury, he is the most unethical. So does Swami Vivekananda rightly say: "Him I call a traitor who having been educated at the cost of the millions of poor and innocent people enjoys the luxurious life without paying any attention to improve their lot." Let every man shine as an ethically excellent one.[26]

In his memorable speech after the first atomic explosion

Oppenheimer declared the need for human values in science: "We are men too. We cannot forget our fellow men. I mean also our deep moral dependence in that the value of science must lie in the world of men, that all roots lie there."[27]

Rockfeller wrote at the end of his life: "There is more to life than the accumulation of money. . . . The best way to prepare for the end is to live for others. That is what I am trying to do."[28]

Sister Christine, another great disciple of Vivekananda wrote:

"Some of us believe that if Swami Vivekananda's ideas regarding the education of woman are carried out in true spirit, a being will be evolved who will be unique in the history of the world. As the women of ancient Greece was almost perfect physically, this one will be her complement intellectually and spiritually—a woman, gracious, loving, tender, long-suffering, great in heart and intellect, but greatest of all in spirituality."[29]

Guru Nanak said: "Duryodhana was ruined in dishonour. He forgot God the creator. He who persecutes God's saints must come to grief."[30]

In his Karma Yoga Vivekananda explained the wonderful power of words.

Look at the power of the word! There is a woman weeping and miserable; another woman comes along and speaks to her a few gentle words. The doubled up frame of the weeping woman becomes straightened at once, her sorrow is gone and she already begins to smile. Think of the power of words! They are a great force in higher philosophy as well as in common life. Day and night we manipulate this force without thought and without inquiry. To know the nature of this force and to use it well is also a part of Karma Yoga.[31]

Avoid Social differences based on caste

In trying to remove the evils of social differences, Swami Vivekananda was against all strife, for that will weaken the nation. So he said:

"Therefore, it is no use fighting among the castes. What good will it do? It will divide us all the more, weaken us all the more, degrade us all the more. The solution is not by bringing down the higher, but by raising the lower up to the level of the higher. And that is the line of work that is found in all our books, inspite of what you may hear from some people whose knowledge of their own scriptures and whose capacity to understand the mighty plans of the ancients are only zero. What is the plan? The ideal at one end is the Brahmana and the ideal at the other end is the Candala, and the whole work is to raise the Candala up to the Brahmana. Slowly and slowly you find more and more privileges granted to them.[32]

Tolerance and harmony

Dr. S. Radhakrishnan defines the Indian concept of toleration in a beautiful sentence in his remarkable book (Eastern Religions and Western Thought, p. 317): 'Toleration is the homage that the finite mind pays to the inexhaustibility of the infinite'.

The only way to worship an infinite God is not to take a copyright on Him after your experience of Him through your religion, but to accept and respect the spiritual experiences of other religion also, in the knowledge that the infinite is inexhaustible. That attitude alone can make you not only tolerate other religions but also to accept them with reverence. This is mature Indian wisdom which alone can help to transform religions from mutually weakening colliding units into mutually co-operating dynamic forces working for human betterment and world peace.

What must be the high level of character—excellence of the person in whom you have this all—enveloping universal attitude, sympathy and understanding! Sri Ramakrishna himself was one such embodiment of this universality. To him went not only believing men and women of all sects, but also persons with agnostic and scientific attitudes. Sri Ramakrishna welcomes all of them with love and respect. In his life one may see one of the highest types of human excellence.

The last note that Vivekananda struck in the inspiring music of his Parliament of Religions speeches from 11th to 27th September, 1893, was the world-wide proclamation of this very age-old Indian wisdom (The Complete Works, Vol. I, p. 24).

If the Parliament of Religions has shown anything to the world, it is this: It has proved to the world that holiness, purity and charity are not the exclusive possession of any church in the world, and that every system has produced men and women of the most exalted character. In the face of this evidence, if anybody dreams of the exclusive survival of his own religion and the destruction of the others, I pity him from the bottom of my heart, and point out to him that upon the banner of every religion will soon be written, in spite of resistance: 'help and not fight', 'Assimilation and not destruction', 'Harmony and Peace and not Dissension'.

The Ethics of National Integration

The capacity and fitness of the higher brain to undertake and fulfil this high function is directly proportional to its freedom from slavery to man's sensory apparatus and its appetites, to the pressures and pulls of lower nature. The higher brain, with its powers of reason and imagination, may stultify itself by functioning as the tail-end of the sensory apparatus. It may, on the other hand, redeem itself and also man by becoming true to itself, by becoming truly higher. It is ethical discipline, what Vedanta calls sama and dama—discipline of the mind and the senses—that helps the higher brain to thus redeem itself and become the agent also of man's redemption. This is the reason in its true form, what Vedants calls buddhi. Referring to the evolutionary significance of this development of the higher brain, neurologist, Grey Walter, in his book, 'The Living Brain', exclaims (p. 18):

For all mammals, homeostasis meant survival; but for man, emancipation.

This, the spiritual growth of man, is thus a fact; the more we know the science and technique of this growth, the better for us and for our nation. Physical and intellectual growth we know and recognize, the second less palpably than the first. A baby is born with about seven pounds of body weight. Every day it increases in weight. It drinks its mother's milk to be followed by other types of food and drink and it grows steadily until it becomes a full-grown healthy man or woman of 150 or 200 pounds. This is the palpable physical growth of man; and we ensure it by appropriate means of physical nourishment. Equally important, though less obvious, is his mental growth. A village boy is timid and without confidence. He is sent to school. Within a few weeks, he gains in knowledge, in alertness, in self-confidence. He develops a sense of his individuality; and this continues until he becomes, may be, an intellectual giant, or a giant of will; this is the mental growth of man, which we ensure through appropriate mental nourishment, through education, institutional and non-institutional. These two types of growth are necessary, but not sufficient. There is a third growth, most vital and significant, but least recognized, without which the other two will prove his undoing; without which his search for fulfilment will result in unfulfilment and defeat. This is his spiritual growth, which finds expression in ethical awareness and social feeling to begin with, and finds its consummation in the experience by him of the infinite, universal and divine dimension of his personality, the Atman.[33]

I do hope that, as remarked by me earlier, the self-criticism which is evident in our nation today, and which is a sure sign of the basic health of our society, will slowly generate the necessary moral forces to cure the nation of its present ailments. The ailment is a moral ailment and the remedy has to be a moral remedy. We all desire that our nation should be healthy, physically as well as mentally. We have achieved some notable successes in tackling our physical diseases. We have practically conquered malaria which was such a scourge even two decades ago. We are on the way to conquer the scourge of tuberculosis, with leprosy next to the list. As a result of these measures, we have considerably raised the nation's life expectancy from about 29 to about 60 years since our independence, besides improving the general health of the nation. But the greatest challenge to the nation today is the malady that afflicts its mind and heart. Cynicism, self-centredness, and utter unconcern for others are more deadly than the most deadly physical diseases and the viruses that cause them; for they corrode the nation's resolve to stay free, to be united, and to march onward to progress. We cannot be blind to the fact that this disease has already invaded our body-politic, including our youths. We have to take energetic measures to arrest the further progress of this disease and to eliminate it from the body-politic. And the nation has to be alert thereafter to see that these deadly mental viruses do not invade our society again. This is the responsibility of every patriotic citizen. We have no king or emperor ruling over us today as in the medieval and other periods. We live under a democratic set-up which derives its strength from its free, disciplined, responsible and responsive citizens to whom service of the nation is politics and religion is one, and in whom the nation has its guarantee of unity, strength and continued progress.[34]

Discipline: Individual and Collective

Discipline is much talked about these days but very little practiced. At home in educational Institutions, in offices, on playing-field, in society—there is hardly any discipline anywhere, though, in these places as elsewhere, those who wield authority never tire of stressing the importance of discipline. Those for whom discipline is recommended, however, have the feeling that people who talk so much about discipline are the very people who need it most. Often enough, the critics, say, people wax eloquent about discipline only because they want to silence their guilty conscience which constantly rebukes them for not following the rules they are laying down for others. Whatever that may be, the picture seems to be grim. At home today parents' control over children is nil. If 'control' is suggestive of a kind of relationship which modern psychology totally opposes, there is not even that much-needed and innocent-looking association which can help guide children through the different years of their adolescence. Similarly, in educational institutions. Gone are the days when teachers were dictators in the classroom. Now they try to be 'equals', yet not with much success. On the playing-field the situation is worse. The players want to win by any means, fair or foul, more often foul. As regards spectators, the less said the better. It has now become a common feature that whenever there is a competitive match going on, police have to be on hand to prevent rioting among the spectators.

Why is there so much indiscipline today? One reason is that man has suddenly become conscious of his power. There was a time when people depended upon each other for their very survival. The weak depended upon the strong, the young upon the aged. Now, the State takes care of them. The need for an individual to depend upon another is now much less than ever before. Also, there is no feeling of others. Men and women have become ego-centric, they live for themselves only. They want to be free and by freedom they mean a condition in which they can do whatever they please.

But how can family or society survive or an individual develop if there is no discipline? Freedom certainly is necessary, but discipline is more necessary. Only a highly disciplined person is free. Such a person needs no outside agency to control him, he controls himself. Till an individual reaches that stage, he certainly needs discipline. He should welcome guidance, even control, till he is really free, that is, fully disciplined. The purpose of discipline is to grow till discipline is no more needed.

The need for collective discipline is just as great. No nation can be great unless it is a disciplined nation. Collective discipline reflects collective will. Unity in thought and action is the essence of collective discipline. How can this unity be obtained? One way is by coercion. It may be political or moral coercion, but discipline voluntarily accepted for a common purpose which is dear to all.

Discipline, individual or collective, is the outcome of a long process of self-negation, sacrificing one's own interests for the sake of others. When the self dominates, there is no discipline, individual or collective.

A society thrives best when it is composed of men and women who are intelligent, hard-working, honest, and dutiful. A good society means a society where the average men and women are good. One or two great men do not determine its character. A great man or woman may be born in any society and under any conditions, but that is no indication that that is an ideal society. An ideal society is one which gives opportunity to every individual to grow—grow physically, intellectually, and morally. It places an ideal before the individual and urges him to grow according to that ideal. Not only that, it also creates condition conducive to such growth. If society has to progress, even if it has to survive, the individual must give precedence to the collective well-being as against his own.[35]

No one knows what exactly an ideal society is like, for it does not exist. All one knows is that it is a society which allows the maximum freedom to the individual, while giving him every possible opportunity to grow. It protects the weak and defenceless, also ensures justice and equality. It expects every individual to grow, not only materially but also morally, in his human qualities. An ideal society creates an environment where an ideal individual can grow. An ideal individual need not be told what his duties and obligations are. He knows and fulfils them, without being asked. He is his own guide, own mentor, he is Law unto himself. His social conscience abhors the idea of selfishness. He lives for others. The highest good for him is the good of all. His concern is for all, specially the weak, the helpless. He stakes everything for them. Buddha was one such individual. So also Christ. So also Ramakrishna. And there have been others. Society can justify itself only if it produces such individuals.[36]

Bata K. Dey, has sounded an alarming bell to save the nation from the onslaughts of unethical values dominating all walks of life and spoiling the entire fabric of the society. To quote him: "Public life is in a desperate state today, with vice-regal regalia dominating it with its fierce ferocity and crushing criminality, sounding the death-knell of ethicality, morality and value-system. There is dire need to save it. Public men—at whatever station of life they function—must be 'men' for the public; leaders must 'lead' and, most importantly, politicians must stop 'politicking'. Public opinion—which is often branded as meaning neither public nor opinion—must be built up against acceptance and tolerance of unethical behaviour and action by anybody, howsoever high and mighty he may be. Crisis of confidence—which admittedly is a function of culture—must be restored in public life; otherwise, the ancient civilization that we boast of will be no more; there will remain no public, no life, worth living, without ethics.[37]

The vacuum created because of traditional and 'old-fashioned' values drawn from religious sources and based on common sense being discarded in favour of materialism and self-individualism, clearly points to the need for a code of ethics. As a matter of fact, no specific standards were left sacred against which the conduct of public officials (as well as business people) could be measured. And as clergy and religious leaders were told to keep out of the onslaught of corruption, dishonesty, sleaziness, deception and selfish individualism. That protective layer in the body politic is needed back. For no nation or a society, irrespective of its political and religious orientation, can live in a moral vacuum. There have to be some articles of faith (drawn from the societal culture, traditions, and religions) governing our lives, which must be resurrected and strengthened. We already know that one cannot legislate honesty and good behaviour; these have to come from within. For that, one has to look to our religions where such attributes are considered sacred. But, one does not acquire such attributes by thinking alone; these have to be drilled in the thinking process of the officials. But that could be possible if their moral consciousness is raised so that they are able to fight against the forces of corruption, favoritism, and malpractice. Otherwise, they will continue to be adrift in the sea of amoralism, of which the prevailing administrative culture has come to symbolize. It is to prevent further decay that they ought to think in terms of drawing on their priceless spiritual and cultural heritage. Thus, there is a need within the secular domain of the administrative culture to seek the spiritual guidance. Only by demonstrating high standards of personal integrity, fairness, justice and by regarding their work as Dharma, public officials may be able to arrest those insidious forces which have penetrated the foundation as well as the structure of India's administration. Such is the requisite of a moral government.

Moral values, in simple terms, are the values that tell us what is the right, proper and acceptable way of behaving. Moral values are indispensable for good governance. An efficient and technologically sound administrative machinery, unless it stands on high moral pedestal, does not serve the public, but it services a self-perpetuating and exploitative system.[38]

All human beings are born free and equal in dignity and rights. The inherent dignity of all members of the human family is the foundation of freedom and justice and peace in the world as given in the Universal declaration of human rights in its preamble. Human rights are the moral claims, which are inalienable and inherent in all human individuals by virtue of their humanity alone. These are the rights of all human beings, because they are born in human family. The concept of human rights and the human rights movement is getting more and more impetus in today's social and political background because it is now universally accepted need that human rights are essential in human lives and hence they must be protected.[39]

Human rights and duties are beautifully Ingrained in the ancient Sanskrit Literature which is quite evident from the concept of Vasudhaiba Kutumbakam (the whole universe is a family) and Nara Narayana Universal prayers in vedic Benediction also supports the same view.

> "Let all be happy
> Let all be free from diseases
> Let all see the auspicious things
> Let no-body suffer from grief."
>
> "(Sarve Bhavantu Sukhinah,
> Sarve Shantu Niramayah
> Sarve Bhadrani Pashyantu
> Maa kaschiddukhabhagebhavat."

Similarly a prayer in Shiksha Vali of the Taittiriya Upanishad also stresses the same

> "May He (God) protect us both together
> May He nourish us both together
> May we work jointly with great energy
> May our study be vigorous and effective
> May we not hate anyone
> Let there be peace, Peace and Peace."

Ancient Sanskrit Literature allows individuals to enjoy wealth and happiness but are guided by Dharma so that they may not come into conflict with Dharma (righteous path).

Right to equality is perhaps the most fundamental right without which happiness is impossible. Unjust discrimination always results in misery and unhappiness to those discriminated against. The Vedas, which constituted the primordial source of Dharma declared a charter of equality in the Vedas. It is worth-quoting:

> "No one is superior (ajyestasa) or inferior (akanishtasa) All are brothers (ete bharataraha). All should strive for the interests of all and should progress collectively.
>
> Let the strength to live with mutual co-operation be firm in you all.
>
> —(Rigveda, Mandala 10, Sukta 191, Mantra 4)

Today humanity binds us together because the global society has created oneness of mankind. Human rights and their co-relative human duties are founded on eternal and universal human values and ideals transcending all man-made boundaries—civilization, cultural or geographic. In our times of social, political and economic globalization, additional values are being questioned and challenged and so education as a social institution is confronted with new challenges in respect to the view of man, one's perception of knowledge and the educational aims and the vision of good life and values and its substantive features. The goal of elevation of man's awareness and consciousness, and of enlightenment of his soul with a view of making a new harmonious multi-cultural world order and a more humane civilization requires a synthesis of varieties of cultural and religious diversities of materialism with spiritualism and of the values, ideals and the spirit of all major religions of the world. This further underlines harnessing of every branch of knowledge and the union of moral and secular values with constitutional and legal norms. Revival of the duty-oriented society, a spiritual basis and balancing of human rights and duties as co-relatives and spiritual regeneration of the entire human life through education in a wider sense, can pave the way for a harmonious, just and peaceful global order. Moral and spiritual source of rights and duties enjoins tenacious pursuit of worthy ideals and human values.[40]

The modern world is marked by a widespread explosion of knowledge and tremendous achievements in Science and Technology, coupled with a general decline and reversal of human values as well as an alarming deterioration of moral and mental health both of individuals and societies. The recent spate of crimes, violence, terrorism, and drug abuse makes us aware of the significance of human values, without which human life loses all meaning. It is also evident that a mere economic prosperity and material wealth cannot result in a lasting well-being of mankind. The inner strength of mankind springs from within, which seems ill-nourished now.[41]

Conclusion

Today, the world as a whole is passing through a supreme crisis in all its history. The old world with its thoughts, opinions, and institutions is in a state of rapid dissolution; none can yet see clearly the shape of things to come. Deeply imbedded in the modern consciousness is a desire of the creation of a stable civilization. Thinkers in the East and the West give expression to this urge when they speak of the future world order. If the future is to witness the emergence of a world civilization, the collective wisdom of mankind has to be utilized for its realization. The greatest contribution shall come not from sects and creeds or parties and leaders, but from the spiritual benefactors of humanity, like Krsna, Buddha, Jesus and Mohammed. The present world—context, with its gushing passions and high aspirations, somewhat resembles the conditions that obtained in India in the age of the Mahabharata war when the message of the Gita was delivered. In these days of conflict, struggle, and confusion, we can have not better guide to show us the path to freedom and peace than the message of the rational, universal, and comprehensive spirituality which Krsna taught in the Gita over 3,000 years ago. It is God's message to man—eternal, ancient and ageless. Momentous problems are there before us which stagger the wisdom of the earth's bravest and best. Let us hope and pray that the new interest that is evident in many quarters in the 'Song Celestial', as Edwin Arnold called the Gita, may be productive of real and lasting benefit to humanity at large.[42]

In an article appeared in the *Economic Times*, July 5, 2007, "Stop Chasing Your Thoughts", by Parmhansa Sri Nithyananda observes: Society, in the form of political or religious institutions, controls you through fear and greed. These institutions believe that unless you are prodded by fear and greed, you cannot be effective, productive and valuable. But productive, effective and valuable to whom? It is certainly not for any advantage to your own self, but perhaps to the benefit of these institutions. . . . When you stop seeking meaning you will fall into inaction, tamas, for a brief period, till you start seeking the source of your thoughts and move into satva. You will feel the effect of inner healing, and you will understand that the universe does take care of you. Shanti Path teaches us:

Let there be balance in the space!
Let there be balance in the sky!
Let there be peace on the earth!
Let there be calmness in waters!
Let there be growth in plants!
Let there be growth in the trees!
Let there be grace in all Gods!
Let there be bliss in the Brahman!
Let there be balance in everything!
Let there be peace and peace!
Let such peace be with everyone of us!

—Shukal Yajurveda 36-17.

The Rain may pour on all parts of the world timely and sufficiently.

Good grains may grow abundantly to the satisfaction of all living beings.

The leaders of all nations may progress in spiritual knowledge and do good services to humanity.

If the mind of the people of all nations to pure and is

CHART 3.2

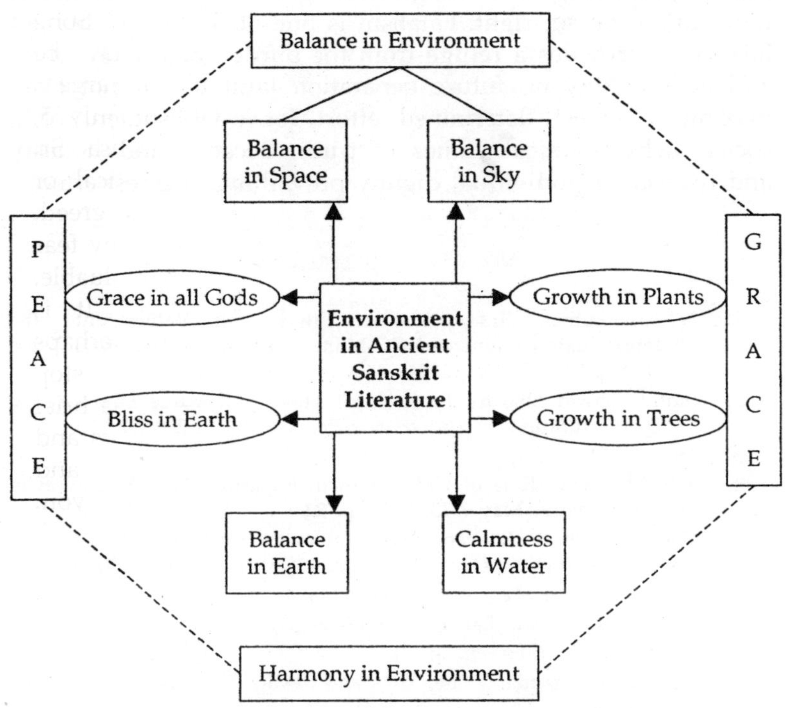

eager to serve others, there will be peace and bliss at individual level as well as global level.

"The whole world may enjoy prosperity, happiness and peace."

Man's capability to transform his surroundings can bring to one and all the benefits of development and also an opportunity to enhance the quality of life. Wrongly or heedlessly applied, the same power can do incalculable harm to human beings and to human environment.

Let us be realistic that the goal of regeneration of values cannot be achieved overnight. There is no instant remedy like instant coffee. It will be a long process which will require unflagging determination and sincerity. The task of regeneration of ethical values is stupendous. But so are the stakes, the preservation of the ethical fabric of our nation.

Therefore, let us not despair and indulge in the luxury of fatalism, thinking that things have gone so far wrong that they cannot be set right. Fatalism is one of the great alibis of history. It provides a refuge from the burden of responsibility and action. May no future generation fault us for not even making a honest determined effort for establishment of a society where ethical values of truth, decency and honesty and respect for individual dignity prevail and are respected.[43]

Notes and References

1. N. Sivakumar, 'Integration of Ethics and Values into the Undergraduate Commerce UGC Model Curriculum, *University News*, 42(39) Sept. 27-29, Oct. 2004.
2. Sidhdheshwar Sharma, Professional Ethics and Value Education in Teacher Education, in *University News*, April 3-9, 2006, p. 10.
3. *Ibid.*, p. 11.
4. V.S. Malimath, Role of Universities in imparting True Education in *University News*, May 7-13, 2007, p. 22.
5. B.H. Brizkishore, Education with Ethics for reading a scientific and non-violent society, *University News*, 42(06), Feb. 9-15, 2004, p. 14.
6. *University News*, Feb. 9-15, 2004, p. 14.
7. His Holiness, Dala Lama, ALIYAR, 2002.
8. Living Wisdom, *op. cit.*, p. 219.
9. Swami Bhajananda, Value, Yoga and Reality, in *Values: The Key to a Meaningful Life*, A Vedanta Kesari Presentation, Shri Ramakrishna Math, Madras, 1996.
10. Swami Swabhananda, Peace in Living Wisdom, Sri Ramakrishna Math, Madras, 1995, p. 88.
11. Chandni Saxena, Role of Ancient Indian Universities in Value-orientation to the Contemporary Indian Society, *University News*, Jan. 30-Feb. 6, p. 26.
12. Swami Chinmayananda, Kindle Life, CMMT, Mumbai, 2002, pp. 7, 8-11.
13. T.N. Chaturvedi, Editorial, *IJPA*, July-Sept., 1995, pp. ix-x.
14. India, Report of Vohra Committee, (Chairman, N.N. Vohra), para 6.2.
15. Justice V.P. Krishna Iyer, Ethical Entropy in Public Life, in *IJPA*, July to Sept. 1995, p. 350.
16. Swami Chinmayananda, Kindle Life, Central Chinmaya Trust, Mumbai, 2002, p. 25.
17. N. Radhakrishnan, Violence Free Society Campaign, in *Journal of Peace and Gandhian Studies*, Vol. 5, No. 1, January 2004, pp. 92-107.
18. Swami Lokesh Warananda, Practical Spirituality the Ramakrishna Mission Institute of Culture, Calcutta, 1995, pp. 245-46.

19. Swami Chinmayananda, Kindle Life, pp. 48-50.
20. Swami Chinmayannanda, Kindle Life, *op. cit.*, pp. 64.
21. *Ibid.*
22. Swami Chinmayananda, Kindle Life, Central Chinmaya Mission Trust, Mumbai.
23. Swami Lokeshwarananda, Practical Spirituality, *op. cit.*, pp. 15-16.
24. Swami Lokeshwarananda, Practical Spirituality, *op. cit.*, p. 34.
25. Swami Lokeshwarananda, Practical Spirituality, *op. cit.*, pp. 40, 55-56.
26. K. Subrahmanyam, Value Education, Vivekananda Prakashan Trust, Pondicherry, 2006, pp. 51-53, 63.
27. R. Oppenheimer, Letters and Recollections, Cambridge Harward University Press, 1980, p. 292.
28. Challenge of Education, New Delhi, GOI, 1985, p. 15-25.
29. Remembrance of Swami Vivekananda, Advaitya Ashram, p. 27.
30. Sikhism, Panjabi University, Patiala, 1969, p. 108.
31. Swami Jitatmananda, Value Education, *op. cit.*, pp. 77-78.
32. Swami Vivekananda of India and her Problems, *op. cit.*, p. 84.
33. Swami Ranganathananda, Philosophy of Service, Advaita Ashrama, Kolkata, 2003, pp. 18-19.
34. *Ibid.*, pp. 60-61.
35. Swami Lokeswarananda, Practical Spirituality, *op. cit.*, pp. 121-22.
36. *Ibid.*, pp. 86, 132.
37. Bata K. Dey, Ethics, Maladies and Remedies in *IJPA*, July-Sept., 1995, p. 461.
38. N.R. Ranganathan, A Charter of Ethics, Reading Material for Trainees (Some abstracts).
39. Mrs. Snehal Fadnovas, Impact of Women's Rights Movement on the Development of Human Rights in South Asian Countries, in *Journal of Human Rights*, Vol. II, No. 1, Nagpur.
40. R.P. Dhokalia, External Human Values and World Religions, New Delhi, NCERT, 2001, p. 10.
41. R.P. Dhokalia, External Human Values and World Religions, New Delhi, NCERT, pp. 109-10.
42. Swami Ranganathananda, Eternal Values and A Changing Society, Vol. I, (Philosophy and Spirituality), Bharti Vidya Bhavan, 1994, p. 113.
43. S.J. Soraligee, Regeneration of Ethical Values, *University News*, July 16-22, 2007.

4

Education System and Values

Educational system is the right place to impart value education both as an independent subject and part of other subjects.

Sri Sathya Sai Baba says, "The educational system of a country is like a bank on which the nation draws a cheque whenever it requires strong, reliable, skilled workers. If it goes bankrupt, as ours is nearly gone today, it is a national disaster. If the system is overhauled and lubricated, the next generation is assured of good leaders, and what is equally essential, good followers." (Ramamurthy, 2005)

Value-education is virtually going to emerge as a new science for inspiring human values in our highly scientific and technologically advanced society. This is the challenge in front of today's techno-globalism—the creation of value-based human beings. Einstein's brain should be combined with Buddha's heart to stop the devastation of Nagasaki and Hiroshima. Napoleon's dynamism should be combined with Vivekananda's prophetic passion for helping human beings to manifest their divinity and Ramakrishna's universal love, respect and acceptance of all religions should be combined with the spirit of intense religious revival which is emerging all over the world today.[1]

To quote Swami Vivekananda: "we want that education

CHART 4.1

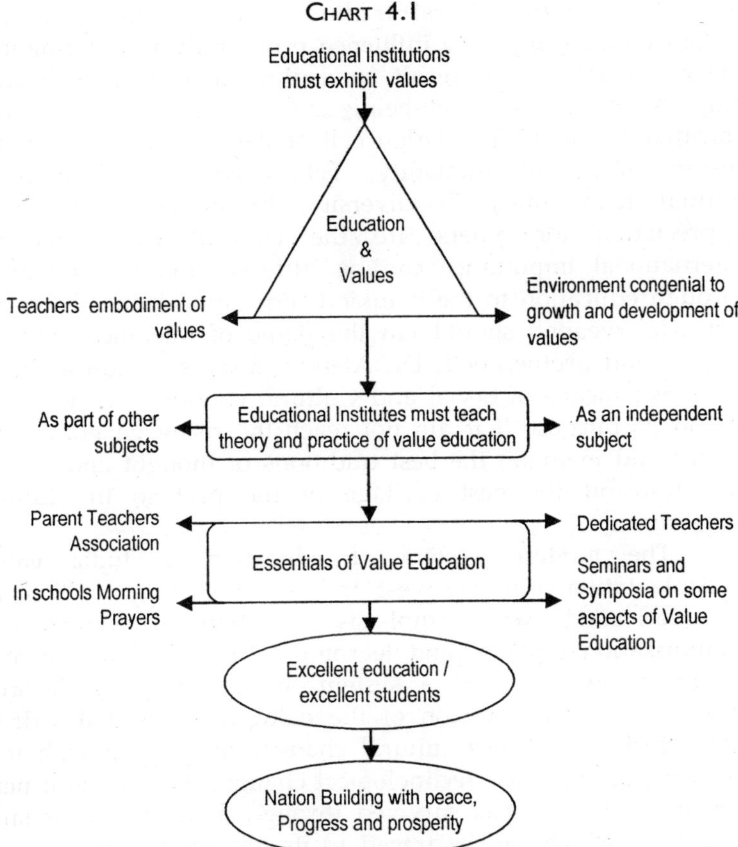

by which character is formed, strength of mind is increased, the intellect is expanded, and by which one can stand on one's own feet. . . . Education is not the amount of information that is put into your brain and runs riot there, undigested, all your life. We must have life-building, man-making, character making, assimilation of ideas. If you have assimilated five ideas and made them your life and character, you have more education than any man who has got by heart a whole library. . . . Infinite strength is religion. Strength is Goodness, weakness is sin. All sins and all evil can be summed up in that one word: weakness. . . It is weakness that is the source of all selfishness. It is weakness that makes men injure others."[2]

The Indian cultural traditions based upon idealism, morality and spirituality influence profoundly in determining the curriculum. As a result curriculum in our country lays emphasis on material well-being and cultivation of moral and spiritual pursuits. The clarion call of the current period is to restore unity of humanity. Fellow-feeling, co operation, mutual help, unity in diversity, brotherhood love and appreciation for others are the cultural values having international importance can be diffused and disseminated through education to the mankind. Education being the most powerful weapon should fan the flame of tolerance, mutual respect and brotherhood. Dr. Aletkar observes: "Education is the Chief means of Social and Cultural continuity and it will fail in its purpose if it did not reach the rising generation to accept and maintain the best traditions of thought and action and transmit the best heritage of the past to the future generations."

The modern system of education in India is a transplantation from the west and requires reorganization. It is overloaded with emphasis on bookish knowledge, memorization of facts, and learning tested by examinations. Hence, today we need a system of education which lays stress on the transmission of the cultural ideals and values and which also brings cultural changes in keeping with the modern scientific and technological changes. We are sure that the Indian culture has survived through the ages and is still in a form which can be traced to its ancient origin.[3]

Atharvaveda says "Truth, right attitude, concentration, aptitude for leaning and complete dedication these human values sustain the earth." The cultivation of these values among children is the immediate function of the education even though it is becoming difficult in present condition of the society. Material, physical and spiritual values together can help to process the cycle of Dharma, Artha, Kama and Moksha. This concept has a great implication to present system of life where the meaning of Dharma is totally misunderstood. Education needs to instill devotion in the people towards their motherland and faith in Sanathana Dharma.[4]

Qualitative change in the contemporary values of our

youth must be brought about. Educational institutions and particularly universities have an important role and a heavy responsibility to discharge in this connection. The aim and function of any university cannot be simply to teach its students the techniques of bread winning. It should also foster an individual's spiritual growth by transmission and inculcation of ethical values. The pride of any university would legitimately be that its students are not merely brilliant economists and scientists, students who are excellent in their respective fields of endeavour, but they are also good citizens whose actions are guided by sound ethical principles, persons who are tolerant and respect human rights of fellow citizens, and serve humanity in their own way. In other words persons with moral character.[5]

Value orientation to higher education is no longer a luxury; it is necessary. The techniques outlined above are by no means exhaustive. The purpose of this is not so much to talk of the 'why' of value education but to emphasise the 'how' of it. It is said that if the 19th century belonged to Europe and the 20th century to America, the 21st century verily belongs to Asia. As the country prepares itself to take its rightful place amongst the comity of nations, higher educational institutions have a yeoman role to play in the task of nation-building. The edifice of a strong and happy nation can be sustained only if it is built on the bedrock of a vibrant value system in tune with our national ethos.

M. Karpaga Vinayagam, Hon'ble Chief Justice, Jharkhand High Court, Jharkhand, delivered the Convocation Address on 22nd Convocation of Bharathiar University, Coimbatore on 22 January, 2007. He said, "The meaningful education should stimulate all aspects of human intellectual potentials. You should not simply emphasize on needs of responsibility and the authority of knowledge, science, technology and management, but you should also uphold the values supported by the time honoured and potentially valuable disciplines of the humanity. It is true that there is explosion of knowledge, but we should not forget that there is an erosion of values. There is no replacement for essence of values. It is essential that the students acquire knowledge and understanding of the facts with a sense of respect to the values. You must be morally good, otherwise you with your specialized knowledge will resemble as a well trained dog than a harmoniously developed man." Excerpts[6]

It is evident that the importance of ethics and values in education systems are re-emerging. Especially for sustenance and growth in this LPG period, they are very essential. To prepare future citizen of multi-dimensional capabilities, rather than a one-dimensional personalities and also to provide wisdom with knowledge, the importance of ethics and values is re-established. This is also essential for the Role of Universities for spreading value system in the society.[7]

The Indian ethos from the extreme north to the extreme south has been shaped by our own religious, economic and cultural factors. The western culture, which we are now trying to ape, on the other hand, is built around comfort and enjoyment of the body. Indian ethos talks of rhythm, natural harmony, and being in tune with this rhythm by a value-oriented life. When we are in tune, we are in a state of dynamic equilibrium, a state of bliss, 'Ananda'. Education is the means to know and to experience this bliss and to give us the life skills for it, not just job skills.[8]

Malvinder Ahuja in his article, "Preferences of teachers on Social Values according to their experience and Subject Area" feels that the observation of Education Commission (1964-66) that the destiny of India is now being shaped in her class room, may be extended a step further to say that it is the teacher in the classroom who is shaping the destiny as he has a powerful influence on his pupils. So there is an urgent need of improving the knowledge and teaching competence of a teacher to inculcate in him healthy professional attitudes and desirable qualities and values.

Swami Vivekananda feels that job of education system is to create an environment in which students consciously and unconsciously learn the essential values. To quote him:

Values dictate human behaviour—it is a dynamic term involving ideal modes of conduct, that shape one's vision of life, Ethical values include one's capacity to be one's own self, to harmonise the contradictions within and to be of service to others. Higher education can enhance qualitatively by giving depth to each curriculum and emphasizing those values of life which are beyond the phenomenal subject and add eternity to education.

Seminars, conference, workshops in ideas and problems related to ethical values serve the twin purpose of maximizing one's potential and also illuminating the mind through the experience of many. Indeed, lessons in ethics may not be effectively preached from the platform, but they need to be practiced by every member who plays a role in the system. Those who regard education only in cognitive terms, are sceptical about the teaching ability of values. Ethical values can be cultivated fortuitously by examples from lives of religious and spiritual leaders, along with extracts from scriptures of the world that are of a universalistic nature. The detached atmosphere of an academic institution, can be used to study the deepest ideologies with an open mind.[9]

Ramamurti Committee enumerated some of these values in the following manner: "Democracy, secularism, socialism, scientific temper, equality of sexes, honesty, integrity, courage and justice (fairness), respect for all life forms, different cultures and languages (including tribal), etc. constitute the mosaic of values which is vital to the unity and integrity of the country. The content and process of education should be all pervasively informed by these basic values." (Ramamurti 1990: 276)

No one was ever taught by another. The teacher spoils everything by thinking that he is teaching. Within man is all knowledge, and it requires only an awakening, and that much is the work of the teacher . . . You cannot teach a child any more than you can grow a plant. The plant develops its own nature. . . All that mass of energy was there confined. The gigantic intellect, we know, lies coiled up in the protoplasmic cell.[10]

According to international communication on Education, "the aim of education is to transform a person into a complete man. It results in a perfect integration of physical, emotional, intellectual and spiritual capabilities of a person. We have to realize and put into action the true meaning of education. Right education leads to refinement of conduct. Good intellect alone can lead to happiness in the family, prosperity in the nation and peace in the world."

Prof. S. Sampath, Vice-Chancellor, Sri Sathya Sai Institute of Higher Learning, in his Tenth Convocation Address said: "The Sri Sathya Sai system of education has a goal that transcends the concept of building up a fabric of knowledge and skills . . . . Its grand aim is to produce a combination of action in the material world with deep yearning for spiritual enquiry, by creating a base to facilitate the transformation of secular values to "absolute values." The learner would then be enabled to play when the time comes, a meaningful role in society as a person in whom there is a symbiosis of worldly concerns and spiritual ideas."

National Education Policy (1986) expressed the same view: "In our culturally plural society, education should foster universal and eternal values oriented towards the unity and integrity of our people. Such value orientation should help eliminate obscurantism, religious fanaticism, violence, superstitution and fatalism."

Role of Education

No ideal, ideology, institution or religion is self-operative. It is through human agency alone that ideals and institutions established for their realization are made operational. History bears witness to perversions, distortions and abuse or misuse of ideals and institutions for the reason that human being is essentially imperfect though he seeks perfection. It is true that perfection is not attainable by imperfect beings, however, it is always worthwhile attempting and this depends largely upon a meaningful education of man with a view to fertilizing the soil within so that the vessel may bear rich, juicy and truthful fruits. Sustenance of human values, ethics and morals in human society and spiritual enlightenment of man seem to be decidedly more effective and meaningful goals of educational philosophy to follow. It is principally inadequate appreciation of the essentially spiritual nature of man and prevailing disrespectful attitude towards the role of true religion of spiritualism in protecting and promoting the spiritual core of human beings which accounts for the crisis of our times.[11]

The Mother Education: Part I

Education to be complete must have five principal aspects corresponding to the five principal activities of the human being: the physical, the vital, the mental, the psychic and the spiritual. Usually, these phases of education follow chronologically the growth of the individual; this, however, does not mean that one of them should replace another, but that all must continue, completing one another until the end of his life.[12]

With very few exceptions, parents are not aware of the disastrous influence that their own defects, impulses, weaknesses and lack of self-control have on their children. If you wish to be respected by a child, have respect for yourself and be worthy of respect at every moment. Never be authoritarian, despotic, impatient or ill-tempered. When your child asks you a question, do not give him a stupid or silly answer under the pretext that he cannot understand you. You can always make yourself understood if you take enough trouble; and in spite of the popular saying that it is not always good to tell the truth, I affirm that it is always good to tell the truth, but that the art consists in telling it in such a way as to make it accessible to the mind of the hearer. In early life, until he is twelve or fourteen, the child's mind is hardly open to abstract notions and general ideas. And yet you can train it to understand these things by using concrete images, symbols or parables. Up to quite an advanced age and for some who mentally always remain children, a narrative, a story, a tale well told teach much more than any number of theoretical explanations.[13]

A true mental education, which will prepare man for a higher life, has five principal phases. Normally these phases follow one after another, but in exceptional individuals they may alternate or even proceed simultaneously. These five phases, in brief, are:

(1) Development of the power of concentration, the capacity of attention.
(2) Development of the capacities of expansion, widening, complexity and richness.
(3) Organisation of one's ideas around a central idea,

a higher ideal or a supremely luminous idea that will serve as a guide in life.

(4) Thought-control, rejection of undesirable thoughts, to become able to think only what one wants and when one wants.

(5) Development of mental silence, perfect calm and a more and more total receptivity to inspirations coming from the higher regions of the being.[14]

Education is knowledge imbibed with values and wisdom. Else the knowledge may prove to be dangerous and sow in the mind the seeds of destruction to the serious detriment of humanity. We need that education, which is knowledge with ethics, so as to condition the students' behaviour and character by which they not only successfully pass the journey through life but also spread the fragrance of their presence in the society, conscious of their responsibility and discharging the trust that the society places in them.[15]

National Integration

The nation today is going through a critical stage in its evolutionary growth. Divisive and destructive forces are on the increase. There is an urgent need for all peace-loving responsible citizens of India to unite in a nation-building endeavor. Ours is the largest functioning democracy and the oldest living civilization on earth. Since our Independence in 1947 we have made great progress in science and technology, communication, transportation, agriculture, industry and a number of other fields. There is much we can be proud of. At the same time, there are also serious crises facing the nation today. Though India had won its political freedom and had become a sovereign democratic republic way back in 1947, we Indians are yet to develop a 'citizenship' consciousness. We still continue with our 'subjective' mentality, expecting the Government and political leaders to do everything for us. We are angry when the Governments do not deliver results as to our expectations. We destroy public property and disrupt public life to express our anger and disagreement.

India is counted among the poorest and most corrupt countries of the world in spite of her abundant human and material resources. More than 300 million of Indians are still illiterate. They also continue to live in abject poverty even after 60 years of political freedom. Communal and political violence are on the increase all over the country. The disparity between the rich and the poor are ever widening. India urgently needs a 'Second Freedom Struggle' which has to be much more powerful than the first. All responsible and patriotic citizens of India must unite in this historic task. Nation-building initiatives and efforts must come from enlightened citizens of character and courage. When such citizens and initiatives are lacking in a country, that nation is sure to fall into corruption and moral decay. This is what is happening to India today. Responsible citizenship and duty consciousness alone can redeem India.

The responsibility for building a great new India lies with the citizens of India. The government and government servants as well as political parties and political leaders can only help the citizens in fulfiling their duties. Responsible citizenship is the basic principle and prerequisite of true democracy. Mahatma Gandhi in a letter dated 27th Jan. 1948 had said, "The Congress has won political freedom, but it is yet to win economic freedom, social and moral freedom. These freedoms are harder than the political, if only, because they are constructive, less exciting and not spectacular."[16]

Two reports on education (1985, 1986) released by the Government of India admits: "There is too much emphasis on Western ideas, and teachers under training do not get exposed adequately to Indian philosophical and psychological concepts of education." "Progressive erosion of values . . . amongst teachers as well as students . . . is seen as a highly dangerous development. 1985 report asserts the need of 'democratic', 'moral', 'spiritual values', and an 'operationally viable value system' which will be at the same time, 'scientific'. Fortunately India has awakened in a big way to answer this long felt need.[17]

UNESCO Report 1982 says that, "The physical, the intellectual, emotional and ethical integration of the individual into a complete man is a broad definition of the fundamental aim of education."[18]

An American writer writes:

"In our educational system, as in many other areas of our national life, we are carried away with toys of our technology and profiteering and marketing that goes with them. Their widespread use is leaving the inner child untouched, undeveloped, often unmotivated and dissatisfied and increasingly violent as his undirected and unfocussed energies look for some kind of expression. He becomes our juvenile delinquent when in reality our greatest national problem, from our unnecessary slums to our highest seats of power, is "adult delinquency."[19]

The Parliamentary Standing Committee on Human Resource Development in its Eighty-first Report on Value-based Education (1999) has highlighted that Truth (Satya), Righteous Conduct (Dharma), Peace (Shanti), Love (Prema) and Non-Violence (Ahimsa) as the Core universal values, which need to be identified as the foundation stone on which the value-based education programmes can be built-up. All the religions of the world have also emphasized that non-violence, tolerance and peace are the fundamental components of humanity. Great philosophers and social thinkers of East as well as West have seen education as a process leading ultimately to spiritual development. UNESCO in the context of peace, refers education not only to general education acquiring cognitive capital but ability to live together.

Prof. R.T. Deopurkar rightly observed that values in the educational systems of modern India need to be revised in the light of the values in the educational systems in ancient India and their critical evaluation, because the educational systems in free India can best be developed on the sound foundation of the values of our own history, traditions, conventions and heritage. We may take the best elements of the east and the west, both ancient and modern, and try to develop our own national values in modern Indian education. Any blind imitation of a foreign scheme is bound to fail to flourish on the native soil if it does not take into consideration our own past history, traditions, conventions and heritage of values in life and education.

The present crisis in the system of education starting from primary to University Education is the crisis of values which are being frequently violated by students and teachers. The indiscipline, crisis of character and infighting are the result of business approach in education.

Most of the research studies carried out in the field of value education revealed the following:

(a) Educational system at present is not congenial to value promotion.
(b) Teachers, themselves lack knowledge and rationale of values. They do not follow values.
(c) Literature on value education is limited. Whatever is available is not of good quality.
(d) Students are enamoured by modern fashion.
(e) Families are also forgetting their role as the first school of citizenship.
(f) Materialisation has left no place for values.
(g) Leaders have no values.
(h) The aim of students is to pass the examination and not personality development.
(i) Negative values like drinking, smoking, gambling are common among teachers and students.

Preamble of UNESCO Constitution observes: "As wars begin in the minds of men, it is in the minds of men that defenses for peace must be constructed."

Education is the basis of social transformation and national reconstruction. As mentioned in the Report of Kothari Commission on Education way back in 1966, the destiny of the nation is being moulded in the classrooms of India. If we are to succeed in building a great new India of peace and values, we need to make Peace and Value Education part of our educational system. We also need to promote Peace and Value Education among the people of India. In response to this challenge of the era, Peace and Value Education as mentioned in Chapter A-3 was made the core component of National Regeneration Movement (NRM) from 2001. It was found that promoting Peace and Value Education among the people of India needs an organization of dedicated volunteers. In response to this felt need, Swami Sachidananda Bharathi founded 'Dharma Bharathi Mission' on 30th Jan. 2003. NRM had to concentrate its efforts on developing DBM and promoting Peace and Value Education ever since then.

With 'Desh Vandana—2007' National Regeneration Movement, (NRM) is being synergised and expanded to make it a 'Second Freedom Struggle' for the economic, social and moral freedoms of India as envisaged by Mahatma Gandhi. Peace and Value Education and Gandhian Liberative Campaigns will be the two important components of NRM hereafter. Dharma Bharathi Mission (DBM) will be responsible to promote and coordinate the Peace and Value Education component of NRM. Dharma Rajya Vedi will be responsible to promote and coordinate the Gandhian Liberative Campaigns.

Role of Education in Promoting Ethical Values

1. Education Helps in Speedy Acquisition of Accumulated Knowledge

Education can pass on distilled knowledge of ethical values to students at a very fast rate. Ethical education must be based on sacred documents written by enlightened souls. In addition, the teachers teaching these ethical issues must be scholars and embodiments of these ethical values.[20]

2. Education Promotes Refinements of Senses

Usually all education, all culture, all refinement of the senses and the being is one of the best ways of curing instincts, desires, passions. To eliminate these things does not cure them; to cultivate, intellectualize, refine them, this is the surest means of curing. To give the greatest possible development for progress and growth, to acquire a certain sense of harmony and exactness of perception, this is a part of the culture of the being, of the education of the being. Education is certainly one of the best means of preparing the consciousness for a higher development. Education of right type can sublimate the energies of students to achieve higher spiritual, goals of life.[21]

Physical as well as mental purity is absolutely necessary. Sometimes we make the mistake of only physical purity because it is so much more difficult to achieve true mental purity. There are many who satisfy themselves by taking baths, but who do not trouble themselves to have a pure mind. It is, however, impossible to concentrate a dirty mind on higher things.

3. Unfolding Mental Potentialities

The potentialities of mind are unlimited. These can produce excellent results through training of mind in a regular and systematic way. Mind has more potentialities than mega computers. There is no parallel of it. "You have a mental instrument with many possibilities, faculties, but they are latent and need a special education, a special training so that they can express the Light. It is certain that in ordinary life the brain is the seat of the outer expression of the mental consciousness; well, if this brain is not developed, if it is crude, there are innumerable things which cannot be expressed, because they do not have the instrument required to express themselves. It would be like a musical instrument with most of its notes missing, and that produces a rough approximation but not something precise. Mental culture and Intellectual education change the constitution of our brain, enlarges it considerably, and as a result, the expression becomes more complete and more precise.[22]

4. Promotes Crystallising of Thought

Every average person has the capacity to practise concentration although it is usually directed towards persons or objects of gain and enjoyment presented to him by the world. In order to follow the spiritual life, no new faculties need be created all of a sudden. The old capacities and tendencies are to be given a Godward turn without diminishing their intensity, and then the worldly man is transformed into a spiritual man.

The usefulness of work is nothing else but [this]: to crystallise this mental power. For, what you learn (unless you put it in practice by some work or deeper studies), half of what you learn, at least, will vanish, disappear with time. But it will leave behind one thing: the capacity of crystallising your thought, making something clear out of it, something precise, exact and organized. And that is the true usefulness of work: to organize your cerebral capacity.[23]

वितार्का हिंसादय: कृतकारितानुमोदिता लोभक्रोधमोहपूर्वका ।
मृदुमध्यास्मित्रा दु:खज्ञानानन्तफला इति प्रतिपक्षभावनम् ॥

—Raj Yoga Sutras

Negative thoughts and emotions, such as violence, whether committed, abetted, or caused through greed, anger or delusion, and whether present in mild, medium or great intensity, result in endless pain and ignorance. Thus, there is the necessity for pondering over the opposites.

5. Achievement of True Freedom

It is almost impossible to pass from the mental being-even the most perfect and most remarkable—to the true spiritual life without having realized this ideal of moral perfection for a certain period of time, however brief it may be. Many people try to take a short-cut and want to assert their inner freedom before having overcome all the weaknesses of the outer nature; they are in great danger of deluding themselves. The true spiritual life, complete freedom, is something much higher than the highest moral realizations, but one must take care that this so-called freedom is not an indulgence and a contempt for all rules. One must go higher, always higher, higher; nothing less than what the highest of humanity has achieved.[24]

6. Guard Against Despair

Despair is never a necessity for progress, it is always a sign of weakness and tarmas; it often indicates the presence, of an adverse force, that is to say, a force that is purposely acting against sadhana.

In all circumstances of life one must always be, very careful to guard against despair. Besides, this habit of being somber, morose, of despairing, does not truly depend on events, but on a lack of faith in the nature. One who has faith, even if only in himself, can face all difficulties, all circumstances, even the most adverse, without discouragement or despair. He fights like a man to the end. Natures that lack faith also lack endurance and courage.[25]

7. Perfect Development of Reasoning

It is a good thing to learn at an early age that to lead an efficient life and obtain from one's body the maximum it is able to give, reason must be, the master of the house. And it is not a question of yoga or higher realization, it is something which should be taught everywhere, in every school, every family, every home: man was made to be a mental being, and merely to be a man—we are not speaking of anything else, we are speaking only of being a man—life must be dominated by reason and not by vital impulses. This should be taught to all children from their infancy. . . . The first thing which should be taught to every human being as soon as he is able to think, is that he should obey reason which is a super-instinct of the species. Reason is the master of the nature of mankind. One must obey reason and absolutely refuse to be the slave of instincts. And here I am not talking to you about yoga, I am not talking about spiritual life, not at all it has nothing to do with that. It is the basic wisdom of human life, purely human life: every human being who obeys anything other than reason is a kind of brute lower than the animal. That's all. And this should be taught everywhere; it is the basic education which should be given to children.[26]

8. Control Impulses

From the time you are quite young the work of your educators is to teach you to control your impulses and obey only those which are in conformity with the laws under which you live or with the ideal you wish to follow or the customs of the environment in which you are. But whether it is good or bad, mediocre or excellent, it is always the result of a mental control over the impulses. Where your parents tell you, "You should not do this", or when they say, "You have to do that", this is a beginning of education for the mind's control over the impulses.[27]

Swami Yatishwarananda says that attachment in any form may be enough to muddle the brain and bring about spiritual ruin in the mind of the aspirant, but when attachment and anger combine, the whole mind becomes chaotic, and all progress is stopped. All struggle for the higher life comes to an end when passion has its sway over a person. We should not give an opportunity for passion to sway us. It is the nature of the mind to think, and if we do not give good and pure thoughts to the mind by avoiding all old impure associations, it is bound to think of bad and impure ones. So be up and doing. Always be on your guard and follow the path intelligently and assiduously.

9. Perfection of Goal

When we reach perfection which is our goal, we shall perceive that the truth we seek is made up of four major aspects: Love, Knowledge, Power and Beauty. These four attributes of the Truth will express themselves spontaneously in our being. The psychic will be the vehicle of true and pure love, the mind will be the vehicle of infallible knowledge, the vital will manifest an invincible power and strength and the body will be the expression of a perfect beauty and harmony.[28]

K.C. Pant feels that there are a few more things which education must have inculcated in us—the ability to live one's truth, the ability to live one's truth is what is currently known as walking the talk and talking the walk, i.e. one should know what he says, and only says that he can do. If there is a huge gap between thought and action, word and deed, style will replace substance. This may seem attractive in the short-term, but it cannot be sustained. [29]

10. Promoting Value of Rights to Equality

Right to quality is perhaps the most fundamental right without which happiness is impossible. Unjust discrimination always results in misery and unhappiness to those discriminated against. The Vedas, which constituted the primordial source of Dharma declared a charter of equality in the Vedas. It is worth-quoting:

> "No one is superior (ajyestasa) or inferior (akanishtasa) All are brothers (ete bharataraha). All should strive for The interests of all and should progress collectively.
> Let the strength to live with mutual co-operation be firm in you all.
>
> —(Rigveda, Mandala 10, Sukta 191, Mantra 4)
> Atharvanaveda—Samajnana Sukta.

11. Promoting Values to Guarantee Human Rights

The tradition of democracy in India is founded on the values of equality and equity, the tolerance and respect for freedom and human dignity and these find expression in the constitution of India. In order to obtain the full realization of these values, there is an imperative need of spreading education and awareness amongst the citizens about these rights as protected by the State with the aim that progress comes within the framework of a respect for human rights and social justice.

The traditions of democracy in India is founded on the values of equality and equity, of tolerance and respect for freedom and human dignity and these find expression in the Constitution of India. In order to obtain the full realization of these values, there is an imperative need to spread education and awareness amongst the citizens about these rights as protected by the State with the aim that progress comes within the framework of a respect for human rights and social justice.

12. Promoting Values of Human Excellence

Dr. M. Lakshmi Kumari in her forward to Yoga in Education, Vol. I by Dr. H.R. Nagendra and Sri T. Mohan Swami Vivekananda Yoga Prakashan states that the aim of all education, undoubtedly, is the attainment of human excellence and perfection, not just in any field of knowledge or activity but life in totality. Education should be the means to fashion excellent characters out of the very ordinary human raw material. This means culturing of the qualities of head and heart in a way congenial to the growth and development of oneself and other around him. In practical life, this has to be translated as qualities of truthfulness, righteous living, purity in personal life, self-confidence, integration of body, mind and intellect, love and compassion towards all living beings and surrender to Almighty. These are steps leading to the unfoldment of perfection already in man. Such a truly education and cultured man alone can meet the challenges, internal and external, in a positive way, converting them into opportunities, helping in his ultimate evolution. Pursued further, one's entire thought, behaviour and life itself would come to express the spiritual oneness of the creation and this would be the manifestation also of the divinity inherent in man. A truly educated man, like a true scientist, satisfied with nothing but the one truth, has to be necessarily spiritual as well.

Swami Vivekanand stressed on man-making, character-building education. To quote him, "Education is not the amount of information that is put into your brain and runs riot there undigested all your life. We must have life-building, man-making, character-making assimilation of ideals. We want education by which character is formed, strength of mind is increased, the intellect is expanded, by which one can stand on one's feet. What we want is Western science coupled with Vedanta, Brahmacharya as the guiding motto and also Shraddha and faith in one's own life." Education is the panacea for all the ills affecting us individually, socially and nationally.

A man of excellence does not believe in his own welfare and development. He is keen to promote the welfare of all as in their welfare lies his own welfare. In Mahabharata, the Victory of Pandvas was because, the persons on their side were highly skilled, spiritual and desireless while on the other side, that is Kauravs were desirous of usurping the territory of legal heirs. Ram Rajya in Ramayana was based on the Character of Ram and his brothers.

Contents of the Value Education

When we reach perfection which is our goal, we shall perceive that the truth we seek is made up of four major aspects: Love, Knowledge, Power and Beauty. These four attributes of the Truth will express themselves spontaneously in our being. The psychic will be the vehicle of true and pure love, the mind will be the vehicle of infallible knowledge, and vital will manifest an invincible power and strength and the body will be the expression of a perfect beauty and harmony.[30]

Education to be complete must have the five principal aspects corresponding to the five principal activities of the human being; the physical, the vital, the mental, the psychic and the spiritual. Usually, these phases of education follow chronologically the growth of the individual; this, however, does not mean that one of them should replace another, but that all must continue, completing one another until the end of his life.

(a) Physical Education has Three Principal Aspects

(1) Control and discipline of the functioning of the body, (2) An integral, methodical and harmonious development of all the parts and movements of the body, and (3) Correction of any defects and deformities. "Lastly, we must, by means of a rational and clear-seeing physical education, make our body strong and supple so that it may become in the material world a fit instrument for the truth-force which wills to manifest through us."

"In this sound and balanced life a new harmony will manifest in the body, reflecting the harmony of the higher regions, which will give it the perfect proportions and the ideal beauty of form.[31]

(b) Vital Education

Of all education, vital education is perhaps the most important, the most indispensable. Yet it is rarely taken up and pursued with discernment and right method. There are several reasons for this: first, the human mind is in a state of great confusion about this particular subject, secondly, the undertaking is very difficult and to be successful in it one must have endless endurance and persistence and a will that no failure can weaken.

Generally, all disciplines dealing with the vital being, its purification and its control, proceed by coërcion, suppression, abstinence and asceticism. This procedure is certainly easier and quicker, although less deeply enduring and effective, than a rigorous and detailed education. Besides, it eliminates all possibility of the intervention, help and collaboration of the vital. And yet this help is of the utmost importance if one wants the individual's growth and action to be complete.[32]

One must gain a full knowledge of one's character and then acquire control over one's movements in order to achieve perfect mastery and the transformation of all the elements that have to be transformed. "The vital being in us is the seat of impulses and desires, of enthusiasm and violence, of dynamic energy and desperate depression, of passions and revolt. It can set in motion everything, build-up and realize, it can also destroy and mar everything. It seems to be, in the human being, the most difficult part to train. It is a long labour requiring great patience, and it demands a perfect sincerity, for without sincerity one will deceive oneself from the very first step, and all endeavour for progress will go in vain."[33]

(c) Mental Education

A true mental education, which will prepare man for a higher life, has five principal phases. Normally these phases follow one after another, but in exceptional individuals they may alternate or even proceed simultaneously. These five phases, in brief, are:

(1) Development of the power of concentration, the capacity of attention.
(2) Development of the capacities of expansion, widening, complexity and richness.
(3) Organisation of one's ideas around a central idea, a higher ideal or a supremely luminous idea that will serve as a guide in life.
(4) Thought-control, rejection of undesirable thoughts, to become able to think only what one wants and when one wants.
(5) Development of mental silence, perfect calm and a more and more total receptivity to inspirations coming from the higher regions of the being.

"To complete this movement of inner discovery, it is good not to neglect the mental development. For a mental instrument can be equally a great helper a great hindrance. In its natural state the human mind is always limited in its vision, narrow in its understanding, rigid in its conceptions, and a certain effort is needed to enlarge it, make it supple and deep."[34]

(d) Psychic and Spiritual

Every human being carries hidden within him the possibility of a greater consciousness which goes beyond the bounds of his present life and enables him to share in a higher and a vaster life. Indeed, in all exceptional beings it is always this consciousness that governs their lives and organizes both the circumstances of their existence and their individual reaction to these circumstances. What the human mental consciousness does not know and cannot do, this consciousness knows and does. It is like a light that shines at the centre of the being, radiating through the thick coverings of the external consciousness.

The path to that realization is long and difficult, strewn with snares and problems to be solved, which demand an unfailing determination. It is like the explorer's trek through virgin forest in quest of an unknown land, of some great discovery. The psychic being is also a great discovery which requires at least as much fortitude and endurance as the discovery of new continents.[35]

The destruction of impurities through austerities brings about powers to the body and senses. When austerities, self-imposed disciplines, are practiced, great will is developed, and the abilities of the physical body and senses are extended beyond what is considered normal.

(e) Love and Affection

Love is the elixir of life. It has been found to have power even to cure physical and mental disorders. One who has hatred in his mind not only loses his mind, but also undermines his health and life. On the other hand, love, sympathy, and friendship not only contribute towards building one's peace of mind, but also create a balanced outlook. A man who develops these qualities will acquire serenity, joy and peace in spite of all external circumstances.[36]

Swami Vivekananda said, "The whole world is eager to receive pure love. We should distribute it without expecting anything in return. Give it, with no desire for a reciprocation."

A Guide Book on Living Values, a publication of the Braham Kumaris World Spiritual University beautifully observes that in a better world, the natural law is love, and in a better person, the natural nature is loving. Love is the principle which creates and sustains human relations with dignity and depth. Spiritual love takes one into silence, and that silence has the power to unite, guide and free people. Love is the bedrock for the belief in equality of spirit and personhood. When love is combined with faith, that creates a strong foundation for initiative and action. Love is the catalyst for change, development, and achievement.

"Love knows no defeat. Love is sure to win, if not today, tomorrow, if not tomorrow, after centuries. Love is sure to bring victory in its wake. What is important is whether you love your brothers. I don't take note of what the newspapers say. Have faith in the omnipotence of love. If you are capable of unselfish love, you are all-powerful."

What instills a feeling of unity in us is truth. Love is truth; hatred is untruth. Hatred divides us and causes enmity between us. It separates men from men. Hence, it is faulty and false. Hatred is a destructive force. Love is a unifying force. It binds people together, mother, child, family, cities, the whole world, the animals-get united. The driving force behind harmony of life is love.

(f) Avoidance of Materialism

Materialism and all its miseries cannot be conquered by materialism. . . . The whole of western world is sitting on a volcano, which may burst tomorrow, go to pieces tomorrow. . . . It is spiritual culture and ethical culture alone that can change wrong racial tendencies for better", warned Swami Vivekanada in the late 19th century.[37]

(g) Encourage Positive Thoughts

Gautama Buddha says that what we are now is the result of our thoughts. Thoughts shape and determine our life. If our thoughts are good, happiness follows us like a shadow. If our thoughts are wicked, grief is sure to pursue us. Jesus Christ, "Whatsoever a man soweth, that shall he reap."

Karma is a psychological law and acts primarily in the psychological realm, the physical circumstances being merely the means whereby the psychological purpose is fulfiled.

What the entity is today is the result of what it has been in days and experiences ages past. For life is continuous, and whether it is manifested in materiality or in other realms of consciousness, it is necessary for its unfoldment.[38]

(h) Encourage Strength, Discourage Fearlessness

Strength, strength is what the Upanishads speak from every page. This is the one great thing to remember; it has been the one great lesson. That need be taught, strength it says, strength, O man, be not weak. Are there no human weaknesses?—says man. There are, say the Upanishads, but will more weakness heal them; would you try to wash dirt with dirt? Will sin cure sin, weakness cure weakness? Strength, 0 man, strength, say the Upanisads; stands up and be strong. Vivekanand says:

"Strength, Strength is goodness; weakness is sin. If there is one word that you find coming out life a bomb from the Upanishads, bursting like a bomb-shell upon masses of ignorance, it is the word fearlessness. And the only religion that ought to be taught is the religion of fearlessness. It is fear that brings misery, fear that brings death, fear that breeds evil. And what causes fear? Ignorance of our own nature", "this is a great fact: strength is life; weakness is death. Strength is felicity, life eternal, immortal, weakness is constant strain and misery."

It is weakness, says the Vedanta, which is the cause of all misery in this world, weakness is the cause of suffering. We become miserable, because we are weak. We lie, steal, kill and commit other crimes, because we are weak. We die because we are weak. Where there is nothing to weaken us, there is no death nor sorrow. We are miserable through delusion. Give up the delusion and the whole thing vanishes. "All the strength and succour you want is within yourselves. Therefore, make your own future. . . . The infinite future is before you; and you must always remember that each word, thought, and deed lays up a store for you, and that as the bad thoughts and works are ready to spring upon you like tigers, so also there is the inspiring hope that the good thoughts and good deeds are ready with the power of a hundred thousand angles to defend you always and for ever."

(i) Detachment

The object of the Gita is to discover a golden mean between the two ideals of action and of contemplation, preserving the merits of both. Karma-yoga is that golden mean in which the merits of both the ideals are happily integrated. It advocates a life of activity with detachment as the guiding spirit and one's spiritual unfoldment as the goal of one's activities. Thus, it discards neither ideal but integrating the spirit of renunciation of the one and the activitism of the other, it purifies and elevates man. This fusion of the two ideals in Karma-yoga gives due regard to social welfare on the one hand and on the other leads an individual to the fulfilment of his spiritual aspirations. Thus, the Gita ignores neither the society nor the individual. It does not advocate a life of inaction but instead recommends a life of intense action in which self is effaced in all its aspects.

कर्मणैव हि संसिद्धिमास्थिता जनकादय: ।
लोकसंग्रहमेवापि सम्पश्यन् कर्तुमर्हसि ।।

—3/20 Bhagavad Gita

It is though action (without attachment) alone that Janaka and other wise men reached perfection. Having an eye to maintenance of the world order too you should take to action.

सक्ता: कर्मण्यविद्वांसो यथा कुर्वन्ति भारत ।
कुर्याद्विद्वांस्तथासक्त्तचिकीणुलोकसंग्रहम् ।।

Arjuna, as the unwise act with attachment, so should the wise man, seeking maintenance of the world order, act without attachment. The devotion, zeal and earnestness with which a mother nurses her child. On account of her natural affection and attachment for the child as well as the prospect of receiving some return for her services in her old age, cannot be found elsewhere; even so he who possesses natural attachment for actions and the enjoyments that are obtained through them, and faith in the scriptures which prescribe them, duly performs all actions enjoyed by the scriptures, with all their attendant limbs, with sincere faith, reverence and earnestness.

(i) Spiritual Happiness

Pursuing material and spiritual happiness and the welfare of mankind can lead any organization confidently into the future. The essence of all this is "management from the heart" and it is much closer to our way of life than anybody else.

A publication of the Brahma Kumari's world's spiritual University "Living Values" beautifully puts people speak of peace of mind. Happiness of mind is a state of peace or bliss in which there is no upheaval or violence. Peace within the self creates faith in the intellect. The flute of happiness plays softly and constantly in the minds of those who have such faith. No matter how adverse or challenging a situation may be, there is fearlessness, for the power of faith gives the guarantee of ultimate victory. As the intellect becomes enlightened by spiritual wisdom, there are less mood swings and doubts in the hearts. An individual becomes better able to payoff debts of pain and sorrow while maintaining a healthy account of happiness. In a world where all relationships have accounts of happiness and sorrow, the greatest lesson to be learned about being happy is: "Give happiness and take happiness, don't give sorrow and take sorrow."

Happiness is prosperity which comes from self-sovereignty. Self-sovereignty means being master over the mind, intellect, personality traits, and physical senses of the body, being complete with all powers and virtues; and attaining a perfect balance between masculine and feminine characteristics. There is that state of perfection within each human soul. On the spiritual quest in search of such perfection, the intellect goes through a process of discovering its divine nature.

(j) Environment Value in Educational Institutions

Cleanliness and beautification of environment is the most important value which directly affect the mind and spirit of the students whether it may be primary, secondary or higher education institutions.

The students spend large time of the day in school/college/university. However, most students consider education as a drudgery to be avoided and postponed on one pretext or the other and this makes their life dull, insensitive and non-creative. In contrast, if the students take pleasure in getting education, they can remain active, healthy and efficient. Life would thus remain always joyful. The quality of education content and the situational context are equally important for gaining intellectual satisfaction. While much has been written about the working of educational institutions, enough attention has not been paid to the ambience/environmental factors which are so critical for ensuring the desired outputs.

It is commonly seen and felt that the teachers do not seem to be bothered about the place they are working, its surroundings and the general atmosphere. A visit to most educational institutions would reveal the following:

(i) The outlay of the educational institutions is dull, shabby and disorderly. Various pieces of furniture do not match, and are so positioned that it appears to be lying scattered and uncared for.

(ii) The bath rooms are stinking, making it unbearable unusable. Besides, drinking water of good quality is not available, which leads to many diseases among students.

(iii) Disorderly parking of vehicles outside the educational institutions premises causes inconvenience to visitors and the whole place looks like an unorganized market area.

(iv) The teachers and administrative staff come to the educational institutions at their own time, disregarding all norms of punctuality, depicting an attitude of apathy and indifference causing poor impact on students.

(v) Building maintenance is poor and it appears that teachers have no concern with the surroundings. Most of the walls and floors have been spoilt by spitting, throwing refuse, painting and pasting posters/slogans, etc.

(vi) We find many useless articles, equipments, papers, etc. scattered all over, causing repulsion for any visitor. There is no display of aesthetic sense in decorating the building and its exteriors with plants, flowers, etc.

(vii) We find that most teachers start quarreling with the parents on one pretext or the other, assuming themselves to be the owners of the educational institution rather than being public servants/ facilitators.

(viii) There are no occasions for intellectual discussions, lectures, symposia, etc. wherein the teachers and students can open up and suggest ways of improving the educational institutions outlook, work culture and administrative practices.

(ix) Holidays are observed on important days without having even adequate knowledge about them and the necessity felt for celebrating them. In this way teachers fail to convey the good values to students.

The question is how to manage all these inputs? How to make the quality services available? Although above issues are considered to be peripheral and incidental yet these are actually the pre-requisites for building an efficient institution. These are considered to be unimportant but otherwise, these are the pre-requisites on which to build efficient educational organization. For example, a good educational layout helps in the following:

1. Proper utilization of space.
2. Effective work flow.
3. Speedy communication.
4. Better use of class equipments.
5. Proper supervision.
6. Necessary comfort and reduced fatigue.
7. High morale of the students and faculty.
8. Improved overall efficiency of the educational institution.

Building Management

Buildings should be well maintained to keep the minds of students happy as well as to create good image in the minds of the visitors. Most of the educational institutions buildings are in dilapidated conditions. PWD, an organization created at the union and state levels to maintain and upkeep these buildings has failed to discharge its duties because of corrupt practices as well as shortage of staff and finances. What can be done to maintain buildings?

(i) Each building should be placed under the control of a caretaker, who must examine the building at regular intervals and note all the problems being faced.

(ii) A committee should be constituted and empowered to effect the required changes.

(iii) White washing and painting of walls and doors respectively should be done as and when required instead of fixed intervals. Maintenance contracts may be awarded accordingly.

(iv) Safety of the buildings should be regularly examined and those found unfit for occupation should either be demolished or reclaimed in order to prevent danger to the life and property.

(v) Adequate lighting and fan arrangements may be made as per the need of each room/seating patterns rather than sticking to uniform standards of space.

(vi) Leakages in buildings may be checked in time so as to avoid permanent damages.

(vii) Modifications/alterations may be made only under the advice of architects having innovative ideas for efficient and effective use of space.

Management of Furniture and Equipment

Furniture is essential to provide comforts and working atmosphere to students. Furniture costs money and hence must be used carefully and maintained properly. We can take the following steps to make the furniture serve our purpose.

(i) Proper assessment of the needs of all class–rooms and offices may be done before ordering new equipment, It has been seen that because of lack of coordination furniture at one place is lying surplus while at another place it is in demand causing artificial scarcity. Sometimes the stores are full of old furniture which can be made of good quality with minor repairs and polishing while the orders are placed for buying fresh furniture.

(ii) Peons employed for the upkeep of furniture need be trained in the upkeep of furniture through regular dusting, spraying to avoid rusting and keeping them in good conditions.

(iii) Furniture should be neatly arranged to provide aesthetic and presentable outlook.

(iv) Every year/every single article of furniture should be physically counted and examined for repairs, polish or condemnation, etc.

(v) Furniture, which is unserviceable and beyond repairs, needs to be condemned rather than piling them up in stores and wasting precious space.

(vi) The students and teachers should be convinced about the importance of cleaning, inspecting and keeping equipment in god order; of reporting defects immediately and of returning equipment to its correct place after use.

(vii) There is no easy way to convince the staff and students of the need to clean equipment and to keep it in good condition. The best way is for the teachers to set a good example by ensuring that equipments are cared for and kept in a good condition (dirty or damp equipment deteriorates more rapidly than when it is kept clean and dry).

(viii) An inspection check–list and inspection schedule should be drawn up and duties decentralized among responsible students and teachers who should help in detecting discrepancies and taking remedial action.

Thus, good management can take care of the management of equipments by:

- Instructing and motivating students to feel responsible for the equipment they use,
- Ordering supplies when needed,
- Storing them safely, and
- Controlling their use.

The salient advantages of such a system would be:

(a) Reduction in the idle time and continuous availability of equipment.
(b) Increased life of the equipment.
(c) Continued service
(d) Less operational costs.
(e) Satisfactory quality of services.
(f) Safety of operation

Management of Redundant Articles

Educational institutions are full of redundant articles and no one takes pains to write them off. These articles on one hand present an ugly look and on the other hand block the space, especially in large educational institutions, where the value of space is quite prohibitive. Thus articles/papers/equipments which have become useless need to be discarded as early as possible. How can we go about it? We suggest a few measures as follows:

(i) There should be stock taking in every class-room and offices once a quarter to identify of what is relevant and what is not. This exercise would help in disposing of unwanted articles.
(ii) The auctioning of discarded items should be decentralized to teachers. The depreciated value rather than book value should be criteria for evaluating the auction bids.
(iii) Removal of redundant articles should thus be a continuous process.
(iv) There may be many articles like fans, tube lights, heaters, boilers, etc. which have become outdated or inefficient. These need to be discarded on regular intervals and substituted by efficient models.

Maintenance of Public Conveniences

Bathrooms and toilets in educational institutions premises are the most essential infrastructural component for students, and teachers as well as visitors. They should be kept clean, as cleanliness is next to godliness. Many of the diseases are the product of insanitary conditions besides causing physical discomfort and inconvenience to the users. We suggest here the following actions to keep them clean:

- (i) Sweepers engaged for cleaning bath rooms may be given training by pinpointing the importance of cleanliness in the upkeep of bath rooms.
- (ii) Necessary materials like phenyl, cleansing agents, etc. may be supplied regularly.
- (iii) Some students may be appointed to supervise the upkeep of bathrooms regularly and maintaining a record of the action taken.
- (iv) Bathrooms may be constructed away from classrooms so that the stink does not adversely affect the students and teachers.
- (v) Students, teachers and visitors may be requested to keep the bathrooms clean.
- (vi) Sufficient water arrangements may be made.
- (vii) Privatisation of cleanliness of bath rooms can be tried.

Supply of Potable Water

Water is the basic requirement of every human being. Most of the students get health problems and infections because of poor quality of water. They cannot afford bottled water available at a high cost. The organization should attend to management of supply of good water for all students, teachers and visitors. The following can be done in this direction:

- (i) Water storage should be done in clean tanks. Besides tanks should be washed on Saturdays/ Sundays when schools are closed. Besides insecticides like potassium per magnate may be used once a month to keep the water infection free. Tanks which have become too dirty should be discarded.

(ii) Students and visitors should be requested not to waste the precious resource, i.e. water. Taps may not be kept open.
(iii) Plastic jugs and glasses used for taking water are mostly dirty. They need be regularly cleaned and well maintained.
(iv) Contract for mineral water at cheap rates may be tried if feasible.
(v) Water testing may be got done through laboratories once in six months to assess its quality.

Management of Vehicles

This is an age of vehicles as most of the students, teachers and visitors use cars/scooters to come to educational institutions especially in higher education institutions. Parking of these vehicles has become a big challenge and even nuisance. We suggest the following to mange vehicles:

(i) Parking zones may be earmarked separately for cycles, scooters and cars so that there may be clear cut demarcation.
(ii) Vehicles of the staff who are to park for the whole day should be done separately from visitors as their movement would be limited. Parking rules may be framed and in case of violation, huge fines may be imposed as a deterrent.
(iii) Persons may be engaged to guide the vehicle owners. His salary can be paid from the collections made from vehicle owners.

Punctuality

The value of Punctuality which was cherished by all has become a casualty causing great problems. It is good for better time management. There is a lot of indiscipline among teachers who remain absent without leave. Besides they come late and go early, thus making themselves available only for a short period. How to ensure punctuality? We suggest some techniques to ensure punctuality:

(1) Head of educational institutes should show seriousness about this issue by calling for all teachers to be punctual as a preventive and educational measure.
(2) Induction training may be given to all teachers to be punctual as preventive and educational measure.
(3) Late arrivals should lead to deduction of half day casual leave and 3 consecutive defaults invite censure and adverse entry in ACR.
(4) Punching of cards to mark attendance can be introduced.
(5) Habitually non-punctual teaching and administrative staff may be served warning/censures/stoppage of increment and even suspension including termination.
(6) Extra-benefits in the form of deputation of training, other assignments, etc. may be refused to those who are not punctual.
(7) Strict monitoring may be done to prohibit late coming.

The Administration Reforms Commission (ARC) has rightly stated that the healthy functioning of the administration depends not only on the competence of its personnel, but also on the maintenance of a high standard of personal conduct and the observance of discipline. It is, therefore, essential that there should be a clearly enumerated code to correct official behaviour and a provision for the punishment of those who deviate therefrom. There would, of course, also be provision for punishing slackness and inefficiency.

Punctuality enforcement is not a difficult task provided the culture of non–punctuality is discouraged. Teachers are being paid for devoting time and time is money. How can we pay them if they are not producing. The Indian educational institutions are suffering a lot on this count. Government of India and state Governments must give top priority to this issue as we find that because of non-punctuality of doctors, teachers, administrative staff, people suffer a great agony in waiting for them. The government must be harsh and no leniency should be exhibited to persons who are not punctual. This is the first and foremost requirement of any administrative and academic excellence and responsive administration.

Behaviour Management

Most of the problems today are the result of rude behaviour of majority of teachers towards students. Their behaviour has alienated the students from the good functioning. How to go about it. We may suggest the following remedies:

(i) Training may be imparted in the art and science of communication.
(ii) Teachers using filthy language should be dealt with strictly by imposition of fines or recording the demeanour in the confidential reports.
(iii) A column about behaviour should be incorporated in ACR.
(iv) Teachers should be encouraged to be polite, nice and courteous. Superiors should set a personal example by observing same standards while dealing with their bosses as well as subordinates or members of public.
(v) Supervision should be done strictly and if required dialogues of students and teachers depicting different situations—very negative, negative positive, very positive, be recorded for training purposes. To quote Aristotle, "Anyone can become angry—that is easy. But to be angry with the right person, to the right degree, at the right time, for the right purpose and the right way is not easy."
(vi) A new concept called Equilibrium thinking has been tried out with police trainees both with veterans having thirty years experience and freshly recruited officer trainees. Several of the trainees reported remarkable breakthroughs in managing anger and other emotions. Equilibrium

is produced when positive values or vices are balanced. The positive values need to be affirmed or reinforced and the negative values need to be denied, weakened and uprooted. The same may be used in educational institutions.

Current success literature talks only of the power of positive thinking but mere positive thinking does not generate sufficient power to overcome the challenge to ingrained negative attitudes, habits forces and values. Mere positive thinking does not produce an equilibrium that comes from a habit of self–realization. The method is quite simple. Continuously hold the words Beat it to Beat it in one's mind. In order to overcome anger, continually issue the following commands to self:

1. Be calm	Beat anger
2. Be gentle	Beat stress
3. Be peaceful	Beat tension
4. Be patient	Beat impatience
5. Be poised	Beat imbalance
6. Be tactful	Beat tactlessness
7. Be cheerful	Beat depression

It takes only about 10 seconds to run the series of commands through one's mind. So even if one repeats the exercise, ten times a day it will take only 100 seconds.

The repetitive reinforcement on a daily and continuous basis will help in internalizing values and overcoming flows and weaknesses. Equilibrium thinking lends itself to the all round development of the human personality and character. Prabhat Kumar, the then Cabinet Secretary of India in his article, "A Responsive and Effective Government" rightly stresses the need for making the administration sensitive to the citizen's needs. To quote him:

We are now on the threshold of the twenty-first century. In the new millennium, above all, the government would need to re-invent itself to become citizen-friendly. It would need to limit its role to core functions such as security, law and order, social services, creation of infrastructure and macro-economic management. Greater delegation and decentralization of authority and responsibilities would need to be introduced at all levels. A combination of citizens' Charters and the Right to Information would ensure greater accountability in the administrative systems. The process of consultation with the participation of citizens in decision-making would gradually become more pronounced in order to ensure accountability. At the same time, good citizenry would also need to be emphasized for all round development of the society. Besides enjoying their rights, the citizens would need to behave responsibly and perform their duties to the state. Clearly defined ethical standards would also need to be adopted by the civil servants as well as politicians. In order to achieve all this, innovative use of information technology would be critical.

Do's	*Don'ts*
1. Make haste slowly.	Don't merely make haste.
2. List areas of interface.	Don't be unrealistic.
3. Phase out areas for introduction of small steps.	Don't take on more than you can commit.
4. Involve students and staff in formulating and implementing it.	Don't involve only senior teachers in the formulation and implementation.
5. Prepare a master plan for formulation and implementation over five years and budget for it.	Don't rush into an overall package for the whole educational organisation.
6. Win students' confidence with small highly visible measures.	Don't promise more than you can deliver.
7. Remember, students charter is a process, constantly evolving.	Don't look upon it as a one-time exercise with a final outcome.

8. Inform the students of the proposed commitments	Don't inform the students unless you are sure of delivering the service.
9. Use simple language	Don't use difficult language or jargon.
10. Train your staff.	Don't leave yourself out.
11. Delegate power.	Don't centralize.
12. Set-up system for feedback and independent scrutiny.	Don't continue blindly without regular, periodic reassessment of performance.

Celebration of Festivals and Important Events

In order to promote patriotism, national integration and enlightened citizenship, it is essential that the educational institutions should celebrate festivals and important events for small duration wherein, the following activities can be undertaken:

1. A brief lecture about the purpose of festival/ event.
2. Cultural programme.
3. Discussions.
4. Simple tea and snacks.

Such acts would promote the bond of friendship among the students and teachers in the educational organization and help in building a good team. This would also take care of regionalism, caste and narrow loyalties.

We have to register Indian culture in the minds of students and teachers which is the source of most of values.

Beautification of Environment

Internal and external physical environment should be soothing and stimulating to generate enthusiasm, activity and high spirits among students. A visit to most of the educational institutions reveal that no attention is paid by administration to this aspect.

Suggestions to improve environment in educational institutions:

(i) Plants in pots may be kept at various locations. These may be changed according to the season. The weeds should also be regularly removed through contract arrangements. Students may be involved in this process.

(ii) Proper spraying may also done to ensure infection-free atmosphere. Some sprays with fragrance may also be used. Spread of rodents, flies, mosquitoes should be checked.

(iii) Proper play cards may be displayed for the guidance of visitors.

(iv) Dustbins and waste paper baskets may be provided to avoid littering and proper disposal of waste material.

(v) Preparation of tea/coffee or any other article may be banned in the individual rooms. Tea/coffee, etc. can be had only in the canteen. Canteen should be equipped with proper exhaust fans to avoid pungent smells.

(vi) Good ideas may be written on the board specially provided for the purpose at the entrance of the building to infuse good thoughts.

(vii) If there is space surrounding the educational institutions, it should be well maintained. There should be regular removing of the congress grass and weeds and planting of flowering plants depending upon the season.

The dynamics of educational institutions management can thus be summarized in graphical form as on next page.

Dynamics of Managing Aesthetic Values

The task before the educational institutions/administration today is to manage the appropriate inputs in such a way that the educational organization strive towards excellence.

	EDUCATIONAL INSTITUTION	
Beautification of internal and external environment		Feeling of pride and belongingness.
Students' welfare through essential facilities		Sense of well–being and satisfaction among students
Inculcation of values of punctuality and good behaviour among teachers and students		Responsive, accountable and student centric administration
Efficient conduct of teaching in classrooms		Proper use of time and money
Joint celebration of festival events to inculcate values		Team spirit
Input		Output (Good values ingrained among students)

We can thus conclude that the dynamism in the educational institutions cannot be declared by fiat, nor can it be generated artificially imposing systems, procedures and job demands. The enthusiasm and the aesthetic sense of students about their educational institutions is a priceless corollary of effective management. Without it, the whole management effort can easily become a kind of drudgery, never moving beyond a mechanical process with little sense of personal involvement. The students have a great potential which need be optimized through the development of their attitudes and philosophy through aesthetic development.

Role of Teachers in Value Education

In order to impart value education we need teachers at all levels of education system who can be effective in molding the minds of the students for understanding and practice of values.

In order to intensify the establishment of an integrated educational system on the issues of peace, human rights and democracy, training of teachers in value education becomes essential. Teachers must 'glow in' their profession. They should never 'glow out' and become 'burn outs'. Teachers are to awaken the lives of others and work as supermen' for the creation of a sense of human values.

The Revised Programme of Action, 1992, mostly

reiterated the NPE, 1986 and the provisions made in the POA, 1986. It has aptly described of "Teacher performance is the most crucial input in the field of education. Whatever policies may be laid down, in the ultimate analysis, these have to be interpreted and implemented by teachers, as much through their personal example as through teaching-learning process."

In addition, the personality of the teacher must be embodiment of values. The teacher must possess qualities of head and heart and these qualities in the domain of value education require intimate relationship between teacher and taught. We are today passing through crisis of character among teachers as large number of cases are being reported in newspapers, TV, police stations, etc. where teachers indulge in unethical activities like harassing female students, having sexual relations with them and torturing them to undertake tuitions. Therefore, it is imperative to select right quality of teachers who really can impart education in their discipline as well as value education.

Thus, there is a great need to infuse civic consciousness, patriotism and discipline among the students through education, adult education and functional literacy. Former President Sanjiva Reddy while inaugurating the Silver Jubilee Celebration of Kurukshetra University on January 11, 1980 has rightly said that India is in need of a new educational system which will look upon the child as a bud that opens up petal by petal and which needs the sunlight of the ideals of truth, beauty and goodness. Only such citizens would be able to contribute to national prosperity in whatever field they may be engaged as it has been rightly said that not gold but only men can make a nation great and strong.

Let us mention in the context of higher education the present callousness of teachers. Faculty members are the life and blood of the University. The University authorities through material and non-material incentives, need to keep them motivated so that they can achieve excellence so that an excellent academic environment exists in the University. S.K. Mukerji in his lecture "Challenge in the Management of Higher Education in India", (Zaheer Science Foundation

Lecture, 1978), rightly stresses the role of teachers. To quote him:

"He is the central figure in whom the University sees its past glory and around him it builds its future dignity. A teacher must be constantly searching, researching, criticizing and learning and making himself fit for his calling. A failure on his part can mar all other grandiose structure of the university. If he fails to understand this and its importance, nothing can save a University from stagnation and degeneration."

S.P. Srivastava in his article, "University Education in India: Current Problems and Future Challenges" observes that next to the problem of unmanageable numbers, the problem of indifferent teaching and research is no less serious. The crowded-classrooms, the inadequate infrastructure for teaching and research, the market-like atmosphere in many colleges and residential universities, the growing incidents of students indiscipline, and frequent closures of colleges and universities have combined to contribute to teaching and research being relegated to a low priority, next only to admission and examination. Teachers blame the students for many ills of the university system, and the students, in return, accuse teachers to be negligent in the performance of their primary duties. Accusations and counter-accusations notwithstanding, the fact remains that in large number of colleges and universities teaching is a casualty and chaos is the norm.

Notwithstanding the long list of problems which teachers find troublesome and terrible, nobody could, however, deny that teachers, for reasons good, bad and indifferent, have not showed up a collective will of the teaching community to improve the academic atmosphere of the colleges and universities. On the contrary, as the opinion goes, they too have contributed to the mess our higher education is in. One big reason is that most of our universities and colleges no longer have many brilliant and committed teachers.[39]

K. Abdul Gafoor in his article, "Teachers as Professionals" observes that on the basis of the discussion, becoming a member of the teaching profession means that you make the following commitment. That teachers have—

(i) to reach an acceptable level of competence and skill in teaching; enabling to become an effective teacher; and to understand the body of knowledge about how people learn and how teachers can teach;

(ii) to continuously develop professional knowledge and professional judgement through experience, further learning, reflection and research;

(iii) to be publicly accountable to our work, to the head, parents, inspectors; and

(iv) to set personal standards and conform to external standards for monitoring and improving our work.[40]

Let us mention the quality of teachers in educational systems which can promote value education.

"Some say knowledge is power
Other say, the above is not true
Character is power and wealth"

—*Satya Sai Baba*

"Our Young minds have to be ignited
This ignition is more powerful
Compared to any source on earth
Under the Earth, above the Earth"

—*Dr. A.P.J. Abdul Kalam*, Former President of India

Need of creating an urge for acquiring knowledge, values, character building among students by teachers, students have immense potentialities: What is needed is harnessing of this energy by teachers through various techniques.

In Indian thought the teacher is the source of inspiration and also a model for the development of moral and human values—not only among his pupils, but also in the society. The teacher's task is not merely to impart knowledge. He has also to mould the character of his pupils and through them the character of the entire society. Character building includes the development of moral as well as human values.

Dr. Rajammal P. Devadas, Chancellor, Avinashilingam Institute for Home Science and Higher Education for Women, Coimbatore delivered the Convocation Address at the Annual Convocation of the Government College of Education for Women, Coimbatore. She said, "the essence of teaching lies in creating an insatiable love for knowledge in the learners, a love that will not die when they leave the educational institution, but will continue to influence them till the end of their lives. The real success of a teacher lies in helping children to grow into worthy human beings with courage to face the problems in life, with an inner strength that is the result of good character and community living."

The main aim of education is to shape the character of youth and make them persons of high morality and worthy citizens of the nation. Values have to be inculcated by providing activities and experiences inside and outside the educational institution that promote values. Values are related to both cognitive and affective domains and hence in addition to giving a knowledge of values, integration of value system into the personality of the youth leading to character formation is essential. This can be done by creating an institutional climate wherein the student-teacher relationship is friendly and based on faith. To achieve this the teachers should strive to have a clean image among the students by being honest, sincere and punctual. By following professional ethics and by devoting more time for discussion with students, teachers should present themselves as ideals.

Need of providing learning atmosphere by teachers of higher education institutes

The primary function of the teachers in universities and colleges is to provide learning atmosphere to students so that he may be able to cultivate his mind, skills and character in order to lead a purposeful life and contribute to the well-being and growth of the society around him. It is helpful, even without going into many details, to visualize a number of competencies befitting specific objectives which may be desirable to cultivate through the educational process, competencies such as:

(i) On the cognitive side—knowledge of facts, phenomena and theories, understanding and application of this knowledge to new and unknown situations; ability to gather knowledge through first hand study of books as well as situations; to analyse and creatively synthesise thoughts and ideas;

(ii) On the side of skill—ability to observe, explore and experiment, competence to present and discuss ideas, to give and obtain cooperation in a team, to organize work and people for carrying out tasks undertaken; and

(iii) On the effective side—resourcefulness, self-reliance, capacity for disciplined, hard work, sense of responsibility and inclination towards justice, fairplay and helpfulness towards others, lack of prejudice or pre-judgement in all spheres, initiative and openness to change and experience.[41]

Rapport with the Students

Students' development depend to a large extent upon the teachers who are competent professionally and understand the art and science of developing rapport with the students.

Education is a process of human enlightenment and empowerment of the achievement of a better and higher quality of life. A sound and effective system of education results in the unfolding of learners' potentialities, enlargement of their competencies and transformation of their interests, attitudes and values. A remarkable feature of higher education system of the present day is the phenomenal growth in its size and spread. Despite this quantitative expansion, quality is deteriorating continuously giving rise to the cause for serious concern. To improve quality of higher education several schemes like Faculty Development Programme, University Leadership Programme, National

Eligibility Test, Academic Staff College, Autonomous College and National Assessment and Accreditation Council have been launched by UGC. These schemes have been in operation for quite some time now, but the success is not remarkable. This is because of their half-hearted and ritualistic implementation.

A teacher should have:

- Commitment to the learner which can be seen in his love for the learner, readiness to help them and concern for their all round development.
- Commitment to society: Awareness and concern about the impact of teacher's work on the degree of advancement of families, communities and nation.
- Commitment to the profession, i.e. internal acceptance of the role and responsibility of the teacher's profession, no matter under what circumstances one entered it.
- Commitment to achieve excellence, care and concern for doing everything in the classroom, in the college and the community in the best possible manner.
- Commitment to basic human values-genuine practice of professional values as impartiality, objectivity, intellectual honesty, national loyalty, etc., with consistency.[42]

K. Walia in an Article, "Thoughts of Radhakrishnan on Value Education" in *Journal of Value Education*, Vol. I, No. 2, July 2001 states that Dr. Radhakrishnan felt that the students were not trained to approach life problems with the fortitude, self-control and sense of balance which our new conditions demand, thus, students become a danger to themselves and to the society. He hoped that universities would pay greater attention to this side of education. He further observes that the Student Unrest and Indiscipline—all these things are mainly traceable to the lack of proper nutrient to the human spirit. Few are able to sustain them properly, to give them food for the spirit, music for the soul, gymanastic for the body and the religion for the whole mind, the whole totality of the human being, we will be able to develop a better nation. The distinguished educationist found a widespread sense of dissatisfaction and frustration among the youth in the country. He remarks that "If these things are to be removed and if the young men and women are to be persuaded to enlist themselves in the work of internal consolidation and development, it is essential to emphasize national unity, rapid economic development and a pure, clean and honest administration. We must put-down the forces that impair our national unity, retard our economic progress and endeavour to raise students by efficiency and honesty in our administration."

Dr. Radhakrishnan always appealed and pleaded to the young men and women: "Mother India expects of you that your lives should be clean, noble and dedicated to selfless work."

Dr. Radhakrishnan observes that "we do not wish to train mere specialists and technicians but civilized human being."

NIEPA in its report Best Practices in Education, New Delhi, 2001 observes that human values are the need of the hour, not only in educational institutions but in every walk of life and throughout the world. Human value cannot be promoted merely by repeating the words Sathya, Dharma, Shanti, Prema and Ahimsa. The heart cannot be transformed by lessons in a classroom. What is needed are the persons who will provide the stimulus and the encouragement to bring them out. The world cannot be changed by mere preaching. It is only through action and practical examples, in all educational institutions, can the impulse for change be intensified. When teachers and elders practice disciplined and regulated life and when human values are fully imbibed by them, the students will automatically follow. The ideal being "End of education is character."

N.K. Ambasht and Ajit Singh in their article, "Education of Learners in Life Coping Skills and Emerging Need" in *Journal of Value Education*, Vol. 1, No. 2, July 2001, CONCERT observe that the present scenario in the country demands immediate significant interventions to help students to withstand/overcome stresses, strains and frustration, depression, etc. One of the significant interventions is to train the students to acquire life coping skills and develop desirable attitudes. This has to be a deliberate and planned effort. Graded curricular inputs have to be made from early years of education to the higher and professional level of education.

About education, Tagore said, "I do not put my faith in any new institution, but in the individuals all over the world, who think clearly, feel nobly and act rightly, thus becoming channels of moral truth—Education must include the development of man's spiritual powers and help to build a harmonious, self-confident personality, "the whole man" the liberated man with vision of "Yatra Vishwam Vabati ek Needam"—The "(Vasudhaiv Kutumbkam)."

Dr. M. Lakshmi Kumari, President, V.K. Yogas, Kanyakumari, says that, The aim of all education, undoubtedly, is the attainment of human excellence and perfection, not just in any field of knowledge or activity but life in totality. Education should be the means to fashion excellent characters out of the very ordinary human raw material. This means culturing of the qualities of head and heart in a way congenial to the growth and development of oneself and others around him. In practical life, this has to be translated as qualities of truthfulness, righteous living, purity in personal life, self-confidence, integration of body, mind and intellect, love and compassion towards all living beings and surrender to Almighty. These are steps leading to the unfoldment of perfection already in man. Such a truly educated and cultured man alone can meet the challenges, internal and external, in a positive way, converting them into opportunities, helping in his ultimate evolution. Pursued further, one's entire thought, behaviour and life itself would come to express the spiritual oneness of the creation and this would be the manifestation also of the divinity inherent in man. A truly educated man, like a true scientist, satisfied with nothing but the one truth, has to be necessarily spiritual as well.

To build a truly great character is the most glorious of human achievements. Such a man-making education, in which India has all the technical know-how, handed down from time immemorial, should form the basis of our national efforts in the field. In most exquisite words have our ancient Masters sung the glory of such a true education:

> Asato maa sadgamaya,
> Tamaso maa jyotir gamaya,
> Mrutyor maa amrutam gamaya,
> Om Shanti, Shanti, Shanti.
> Lead Me From the Unreal to the Real,
> Lead Me From Darkness to Light,
> Lead Me From Death to Immortality,
> Om Peace, Peace, Peace.

Vivekananda wanted teachers to stand out as Rishis—the symbol of purity and integrity. Vivekananda explains: "Be pure first and you will have power. The chaste brain has tremendous energy and gigantic will power. Continence gives wonderful control over mankind. The spiritual leaders of men have been very continent and that is what gave them power."[43]

"There is no allegiance possible where there is no character in the leader and perfect purity ensures the most lasting allegiance and confidence."[44]

"When you are a Rishi you will find others obey you instinctively. Something mysterious emanates from you which makes them follow you, makes them hear you, makes them unconsciously even against their will carry out your plan. That is Rishihood."[45]

Narayan Prem Sai in his article, "Dive into the Ocean of Tranquility and Peace" in *Times of India*, dated June 29, 2007 observes that Prayer is not a time-bound process. Let it be a perpetual state. Let your life blossom with the divinity within. So let your every deed be guided by His thoughts. Think that you are just the means, the Lord is the doer. Do not act in haste. Ensure that you carry out your work with a calm and selfless attitude. Work done with patience and quiescence proves to be more efficient.

In the beginning, you will tend to forget. We are so used to leading a restless life that peace continues to evade us. To retain peace within try the above methods again and again. As they become habitual, you will feel Supreme benediction in the form of peace. You will feel one with God. All mental agitation, perplexity and ficklessness will steadily wane. You will lead a peaceful and happy life. When clouds form in the skies, we know that rain will follow, but we must not want for it. Nothing will be achieved by attempting to interfere with the future before the time is ripe. Patience is needed.

Father Edward Joseph Flenagan (1886-1948) of America was a priest trained in the Catholic tradition. He took up the mission of reforming juvenile delinquents who got into the bad company of criminal gangs and committed various crimes like murder, robbery, violence and cruelty. In the Boys' Town founded by him there were orphans of all races and faiths. The efforts that he made and the patience that he showed in transforming delinquent children into citizens of good conduct and behaviour are without a parallel.

Flenagan firmly believed that children could be won over by a person of ideal conduct whom they would imitate, and not by-admonition, rebuke and punishment. Here is an incident narrated in 'Father Flenagan of Boys' Town', which points at the secret of how Flenagan succeeded in converting a boy who was murderously cruel and violent.[46]

Dr. Sarvapalli Radhakrishnan "help the students to think rightly, make them feel nobly, let them do rightly, above all let them posses the spirit of compassion (Karuna), universal love and brotherhood so that we can live together in a global village as "brothers and sisters." In this context Rigvedic wisdom says, 'Let us burn our inner wisdom to remove the darkness of society. Let the noble thoughts come from all corners'. If the students are prepared on these ideals, they will not be only civilized citizen to serve the nation but also they will have the potential to save the disintegrating society. They will be able to face and overcome the challenges of terrorism, hatred, communalism and attempt to twist religion for political purpose.

Education must be based on certain basic values, which we have inherited through ages as part of our heritage. Of course, those values are to be interpreted in the context of changing situation and environment. The purpose of education would be to generate queries in the mind of the learner to find out the rationality or otherwise of each and every act.[47]

Education is just not gathering mere information and putting them in the brain so that they cause riot in the mind, if it is not properly assimilated. The objective of the education is to enlighten oneself to be rational, compassionate and responsible to the society. All of us are the social products and everyone has the responsibility to the society. We are the output of investment the society has made in us, and therefore society can claim a dividend upon us. We are obliged to pay such dividend. This we call our Social obligation.[48]

The quality education is nothing but preparing for quality life. The elements of quality education, i.e. excellence in operations; conformity to accepted way of doing things, value for money; purpose-oriented approach and ability to transform are also the essential requirements of quality life. The quality elements which you have practiced in your learning, research and outreach activities need to be extended to your future career and social life activities making a difference to the quality of life in the society. Quality, essentially is an attitude of mind. The close link between the quality education and quality of life should be understood and practiced. This gives content and meaning to the transformative role of education.[49]

Co-ordial Relations between the Teacher and Students: Values of Respect, Love and Affection

Swami Lokeshwarananda observes that according to the Indian tradition, a teacher is like a lighted lamp from which other lamps may be lighted. This underlines the fact that a teacher must himself be a highly educated man, otherwise he is not entitled to teach. Can a blind man lead another blind man.

But it will be a mistake to think that academic qualification is the only criterion of a teacher. He may have encyclopaedic knowledge, but to this must be added moral excellence of the highest order. He need not teach high moral principles, he has to live them. A teacher should be an example of what is best in man. He can inspire by what he is and not by what he knows. 'To know is to be'—runs a popular dictum in India. Knowledge is useless if it does not make a man perfect—perfect not merely in skills and abilities, but also in character.

The teacher's task is to impart knowledge but to do this, he must first enkindle in the pupil a thirst for knowledge. He must also train his pupil's body and mind, train his faculties, so that the pupil can use them to his best advantage. Mind is man's most powerful organ. A healthy mind under control is man's best friend and guide. Given such a mind and a desire to learn, a student can learn by his own efforts, with the assistance of the teacher or even without. In fact, one learns best when one learns by one's own efforts, for how much knowledge can a teacher pass on to his pupil also, the knowledge that the teacher imparts may turn out to be outdated, if not also wrong. The most a teacher can do is to give his pupil a sense of direction, that is, tell him what to learn and how to learn it and also how to apply that knowledge for his own good and the good of his community.

The relationship between the teacher and the taught is exactly like the relationship of the gardener and the flowers on the bush. The gardener does not create the flowers from the soil and the manure; the flowers must themselves come from the bush. The gardener can only tend its roots, water it, protect it, see that it has the correct amount of sunlight and shade—all these externals he can provide. But no more gardener can guarantee the blossom; it can come only from the bush itself.

Similarly, the teacher's job is to nurture the student with right thoughts. The student must be given a conductive and protective environment where he or she need not overstrain to live. But the blossoming—the real fragrance and beauty of the personality—must come from within.[50]

What is now needed is a concerted action at the development of a curriculum that can bring home to the students' three important lessons, namely, (i) that the entire humanity shares one basic impulse towards progress and by sharing this impulse humanity can be seen as one vast surge of adventure which aims at continuous self-exceeding; (ii) that humanity, in its mature developments, tends to reject uniformity and adopts the law of unity that permits and respects cultural diversities; and (iii) that the future progress of humankind is bound up with the development of a new science and art of living together which necessitates adherence to the law of mutuality rather than conflict and the law of varied expressions rather than any uniform monotone. Education should aim at strengthening democratic and universal human values and respect for human rights. Education is the most powerful instrument for preparing a mind which can promote the culture of dialogue.

Children and School Environment

Children are the parents of the future and what they learn is likely to be applied for the rest of their lives. Moreover, children have important roles within the households—taking care of younger brothers and sisters, fetching and storing drinking water and so on. If brought into the developmental process by increasing their knowledge about health and disease prevention, they can function as change agents within their families.

The school teacher is held in high esteem not only by the children but also by their parents and the community at large. The students can develop hygiene habits by emulating the teacher. Also, the school teacher can influence the parents and community members on issues related to sanitation.

The school can also serve as a demonstration centre for the sanitation package—the garbage pit, soakage pit and sanitary latrine for adoption by household and the community.

The School Sanitation aims at inculcating hygienic habits in the school children through health and hygiene education and improving the living conditions of the parents and the communities to which they belong. It is, therefore, important to ensure that the influential members of the communities, including Panchayat members and the parents are involved in the implementation of the day-to-day activities of the school and also contribute voluntarily towards the construction, repair and maintenance of the water and sanitary facilities. The main features of the strategy are—

(a) Awareness creation in school children about the concept and components of sanitation.
(b) Inculcation of hygiene practices in school children.
(c) Involvement of parents and the community.
(d) Improving access to water and sanitation facilities within schools.
(e) Cost sharing for better ownership of the sanitation facilities provided.
(f) Development of communication materials.
(g) Involvement of students and teachers in the operation and maintenance of the sanitation facilities.

Let us take the example of Primary Education:

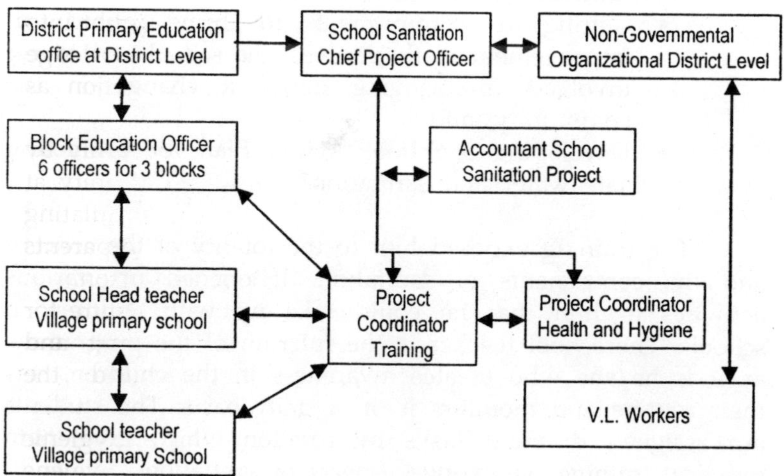

To ensure effective implementation of the project, it is imperative that the functionaries from the various line departments and non-governmental organizations are suitably oriented. In order to sensitize those involved in the project, a series of orientation workshops have been conducted for functionaries from the district, block and village levels. Functionaries at the district and block level include—the DPEO, District Health Officer, CDPO, BEOs and so on and at the village level—Anganwadi workers, Panchayat members, PTA members, etc.

Training of teachers is a key element for the effective implementation of the school sanitation project.

- Giving a working knowledge of relation between water, sanitation, hygiene behaviour and health; the seven components of sanitation;
- Creating an awareness about their importance as role models, resulting adoption of proper hygienic practice themselves;
- Suggesting activities for inculcation of hygienic habits among children;
- Imparting information and skills in operation and maintenance of the safe water and sanitary facilities by involving children;
- Getting a commitment to bring about an improvement in themselves, the school and to get involved in bringing about a change in the community; and
- Developing a School Action Plan for promoting safe water and sanitation?

The training exposed him to the totality of the concept and the components of sanitation. It opened up various activities to him that he could take up with children in schools. The school teacher is the fulcrum of the programme as it is he/she who creates awareness in the children, sets their routine and monitors it on a daily basis. The students are assigned different tasks by rotation which give them practical training on various aspects of sanitation.

Daily Routine of the Teachers and Students

- Morning assembly with a thought for the day.
- Presenting a write up and speech on the theme for the day.

- Children monitor the personal hygiene habits of other children—check for clipped nails, clean teeth, clean appearance and footwear.
- The children committees ensure proper storage and handling of drinking water, use the garbage pits and cleanliness around water sources.
- Children plant and water trees in the school compound.

- **Disposal of garbage**—look after collection of garbage into the bins in the school, undertake emptying of bins into the garbage pit and covering the pit with mud.
- **Storage of drinking water**—are responsible for cleaning the pot/jug in which drinking water is stored, filling the water storage pitcher with drinking water and keeping the storage pot covered. Ensuring proper handling of drinking water is the responsibility of the teacher, along with the committee members.
- **Cleanliness of the toilets**—look after the cleanliness of the toilet. These children clean the toilet in the morning by throwing water in the toilet and sweeping it. They also clean it once before they leave for the day.
- **Personal hygine**—checking of personal cleanliness of the students, checking if they have bathed, combed their hair, trimmed their hair and clipped the nails. At first the teachers used to send the children who had not bathed back home. Now, the children from these committees have the authority, in case the need for sending a child back arises. These instances are now very rare.
- **Environmental sanitation**—ensuring proper drainage of waste water by clearing drains from water source, watering plants and planting trees in the school.

Cleaning and maintenance of the water and sanitation facilities is as important as their installation.

The challenge is to make best use of the interrelationship between the school and the community for improved sanitation and hygiene—

(a) The involved community offers support to the school Sanitation project, or at least does not work against it. Community members contribute financially, in kind, or provide labour to improve facilities in the schools.
(b) Effectiveness of the project in terms of health benefits of children increases community sanitation and hygiene practices also change.
(c) Community involvement facilitates a broader impact of the project.

Discussing the school sanitation project in the PTA meetings has helped the parents to come forward and participate in whatever way they could. The process of creating awareness on hygiene issues can begin with the children's involvement in a mapping exercise.[51]

Prayers

In schools, generally the school starts with the prayer in the morning where all students assemble at one place. Different schools use different songs in the praise of God or nation. Whatever the nature of song, it must contain many values inherent in it. The teachers can use this opportunity to impart value education after the prayer. Students can be encouraged to speak. Value education is easy for students to understand but difficult to follow. Therefore, we must impart value instruction in such a way as to be understood and followed by students. It must be a continuous affair as value education is the most important than other subjects, values can help the students to improve the quality of life.

Alexis Carrel, who received Nobel Prize in medicine, in 1912 wrote: "Prayer is not only worship; it is also an emanation of man's worshipping spirit—the most powerful form of energy that one can generate. . . the only power in the world that seems to overcome the laws of nature."

Educational institutions must teach the students about

the use of words, sentences and language—we must know that the proper use of words can solve difficult problems easily. If a person is ailing and if we use the polite and soothing words, his grief can be lessened. Words are not words but they have the force of values behind them. Teachers must teach values through his subject teaching.

In *The Tribune* dated May 22, 2007 a feature appeared by Kanwalpreet, "Inculcating Values" by stating that Values and Ethics were reflected at the beginning of each day in the assembly in the school. Our chests puffed up with pride as we sang the school anthem· followed by the national anthem. With the education system getting revamped in the past few years, what changes have occurred in the assembly?

Ms. Komal Anand, Principal of the junior wing of Yadvindra Public School, Mohali, says: "I believed the assembly is the best way to start the day. We have assemblies for different classes where the children get to show their talent. We start with a small prayer to thank God and ask Him to bless our friends and families. There are times when a child says an impromptu prayer if a near and dear one is in distress. The child goes home with a lighter heart. "Show and Tell" encourages the children to show to their friends whatever drawing, model is special to them. Each section puts up a small act to clarify concepts. The classes IV and V read out news while for the tiny tots, the assembly means a place where they perform as a group."

Dr. Harish Dhillon, Principal, Yadvindra Public School, says, "we teach courtesy beside spiritual enlightenment to our students through this platform. We reward students for little acts of honesty and motivate them to achieve higher goals. We develop their public speaking skills and reinforce values." Prayer is a pillar of strength for us. We offer ourselves to God and get power to go through the day without hurting anyone. There are girls who come up with different problems and the prayer bring succour to them."

The school assembly has evolved into an institution by itself. The students don't have to wait for the annual function to showcase their talent. The assembly gives a chance to each and every child, around the year to blossom.

Story Telling and Drama

Story-telling and Drama are the best means for value-education through words. One drama of Harishchandra revolutionized the life of Mohandas K. Gandhi who made sacrifice and truth as the foundation of his life. One drama of Shri Chaitanya Lila by Girish Ghosh brought a wave of pure devotion to God in a totally Westernized Calcutta. Even Sri Ramakrishna went to ecstasy by seeing the drama. In pre-Shakespeare days Morality plays used to educate the masses on the need of moral life. In thousands of Indian villages the age-old stories of Rama-Sita, Hanuman, Krisna and Gopis – are being staged regularly in order to bring elevation of the masses. The annual Ramleela drama in Delhi, and the Rasleela dance and music of Vrindavan are outstanding examples of value-education even in 21st century.[52]

Lessons for Value-based Administration

The present day educational institutions have several lessons to learn from the Indian heritage. These include:

- To promote ethical behaviour, the institution must have a basic goal or philosophy of promoting social and national welfare. Unfortunately we find that educational institutions today have become centers of business and therefore have lost their original focus. This leads to deterioration in ethical behaviour, which must be urgently rectified.
- Teachers and administrators who are the leaders of educational institutions must first set an example to others by their conduct. This is clearly evident from educational institutions of ancient India. However, this is missing in today's educational system. Teachers have lost their authority as models of character. This needs to be changed to improve the system.
- It is necessary to modify admission procedures to clearly emphasise on character of students. But current day educational institutions focus more on competence of the students at the time of admissions. The entrance examinations to several

prestigious institutions emphasise mastery of subject knowledge. In this process, an even more important facet namely character of the students gets ignored. The level of unrest and indiscipline in the campuses bear testimony to this.

- According to the Indian heritage, the most important criteria for promotions was the character of the teachers. In several educational institutions today, promotions of teachers and administrators are based on experience and patronage. The Indian education system can reach lofty heights, when it pays attention to this important facet of rewarding teachers and administrators based on their character.
- Teachers must treat their students lovingly as their own children. They must work for the betterment of students. This close bondage was reflected in the ancient Gurukulas. However, today this relationship has been desecrated into a commercial relationship, with no scope for love, reverence and concern. Teachers must change their attitudes towards students to create this sacred bond.
- Students were inculcated into socially responsible behaviour in ancient India. They were taught that 'Service to Society is Service to God'. However, it is unfortunate to note that no emphasis is placed on social responsibility today. This leads to highly individualistic behaviour with no concern for the society.
- The undercurrent of education as per the Indian heritage was spiritual transformation. Today the emphasis has shifted to secular education with spirituality playing no role in education. This needs to be rectified to inculcate value-based administration in educational institutions.

Let us . . . with utmost speed, pioneer and propagate a holistic educational philosophy for the twenty-first century based upon the following premises:

- That the planet we inhabit and of which we are all citizens—Planet Earth-is a single living, pulsating entity; that the human race in the final analysis is an interlocking family—Vasusdhaiva Kutumbakam as the Veda has it; and that differences of race and religion, nationality and ideology, sex and sexual preference, economical and social status—though significant in themselves—must be viewed in the broader context of global unity;
- That the ecology of planet earth has to be preserved from mindless destruction and ruthless exploitation and enriched for the welfare of generations yet unborn; and that there should be a more equitable consumption pattern based on limits to growth not unbridled consumerism;
- That hatred and bigotry, fundamentalism and fanaticism, and greed and jealousy whether among individuals, groups of nations, are corrosive emotions which must be overcome as we move into the next century; and that love and compassion caring and charity, and friendship and co-operation are the elements that have to be encouraged as we transit into our new global awareness;
- That the world's great religions must no longer war against each other for supremacy but co-operate for the welfare of the human race, and that through a continuing and creative interfaith dialogue, the golden thread of spiritual aspiration that binds them together must be strengthened instead of the dogma and exclusivism that divides them;
- That holistic education must acknowledge the multiple dimensions of the human personality—physical, intellectual, aesthetic, emotional and spiritual—thus moving towards the perennial dream of an integrated individual living on a harmonious planet. (Singh, 1996: pp. 226-27)

Conclusion

In Sanskrit there is a beautiful verse which says, "He really lives in whose living countless people live." What is there to say about a man when even his death becomes an inspiration? He laughs at death. Death cannot destroy him. One who has fulfiled his life and has blessed and inspired many others alone can be called a successful person. He alone is proficient and he alone can be called efficient. Such is the success from which we get great happiness and the strength to face whatever situations confront us. This is where sorrow ends. Such a life is an inspiration to others.

We read in the Taitiriya Upanisad that after the completion of education, the teacher advises the outgoing students. Thus, Speak the truth, practise Dharma, never deviate from study, help the teacher through wealth in his mission of diffusion of knowledge, and become a householder and beget good progeny. Also give, give and give (sraddhaya deyam, etc.). Truthfulness means straight forwardness in thought, word and deed. It means to think noble, relevant thoughts only, to express them when necessary in a precise language, and act in harmony with one's thoughts. Thus the speech of the truthful has the strength of his whole personality behind it. Therefore, it cannot fail, says the yoga-sutra. In fact, in realizing the highest knowledge, truthfulness occupies the highest place, he that speaks truth always is sitting on the lap of God, as it were, says Sri Ramakrishna. The speech of a truthful person unfailingly produces its effect, i.e., it impresses its purport on the heart of the hearer, brings fearlessness to the speaker himself ! More truths are revealed spontaneously to such a truthful man. Thus, truthfulness is a great value in education.

From truthfulness come honesty, punctuality, cleanliness, orderliness, simplicity, etc. Truthfulness is the guard against tall duplicity, cunningness and hypocrisy. It saves the student from many a false step. It makes him work hard to get sound knowledge rather than putting up an appearance of it ! It gives him an inner urge to confess his failures to the teacher and thus, get corrected. A true student will be humble to accept and apologize when he is in the wrong. This great quality attracts the love and solicitation from the teacher.[53]

The education as is obtained today is not at all aimed at character-building with the result that we find even highly educated men who have so much of power and service machinery at their command fail miserably when tackling problems in the right way, in the human way, in the interests of our nation. Highly talented individuals are there in every field, second to none, but devoid of patriotic fervour and personal integrity, the impact they produce is minimal. Today, we are urgently in need of men and women of character, integrity and dedication and of tremendous capacities happily blending dignity of man with dignity of labour.

Concentration of mind, its purity and chastity alone can bring out the amazing qualities and capacities that lie hidden in the human mind. Lack of these has created a student community who are debilitated, inhuman, selfish and indifferent to human values Swami Vivekananda stresses the value of shraddha, faith, as one of the most potent factors capable of elevating human life. He wanted this "Life-saving, great, ennobling, grand doctrine" to be taught to our children from their very birth. Where the different streams of consciousness in man, namely, concentration of mind, purity of life, faith in oneself, strength of body and fearlessness of mind are combined together in a single personality, the force of that character becomes invincible. Men of such stature alone can rebuild a shattered society. It is such men that our educational system should create to safely carry over our country to the 21st century.

D.S. Kothari observed in this regard: The fundamental values of life, integrity, pursuit of truth and idealism cannot be sustained by embalming these in monuments and memorials or by inscribing them in textbooks. High ideals and great national goals are meaningless, unless we strive for them passionately and ceaselessly. And each generation has to recreate, revitalize and renovate these through hard work and sacrifice, otherwise ideals and values wither and decay and goals fade away.

A teacher who practices virtues attains spiritual merit. Thus the Manusmriti (2.160), declares that a teacher whose speech and thoughts are pure and perfectly guarded gains the full rewards of a spiritual life. Further a person who passes all his life with his teacher and serves him reaches the highest goal of life (i.e.) spiritual beatitude. (2.249)

Mukul Sharma in his article in *Economic Times* dated 21-8-2007 quoting Einstein and Lord Buddha observes: "Our task must be to free ourselves from the prison by widening our circle of compassion and the whole of nature in its beauty." As usual, Einstein was not given to merely posing problems or querrying nature with conundrums. Instead, he believed in answers. His solution here is to startle that the same thing had struck the Buddha too some 2500 years ago, namely, enlarge the capacity of consciousness by showing and showering compassion for and on all living creatures.

The true value of a human being is determined by the measure and the sense in which they have obtained liberation from the self. Here we see the crux of the problem—the ego which stands between us and the goal of deliverance. Einstein believed we would require a substantially new manner of thinking about ourselves if humanity was to survive—and that any religion of the future would have to be a cosmic one, transcending the personal self and any personal God we might adhere to. And, more importantly, that it should be based on a religious sense arising from the experience of all things natural and spiritual as a meaningful unity.

Notes and References

1. Swami Sitatmananda, Value Education, Sri Ramakrishna Ashrama, Rajkot, 2003, p. 4.
2. *Ibid.*
3. Tarulata Devi, "The Cultural Impact of Vedic Education in Ancient India, *University News*, Jan. 30-Feb. 05, 2006, pp. 44-45.
4. Quoted in H.C. Hemamalini, "Values of Sustainability in the Traditions of Indigenous Indian Knowledge and their Implications, *University News*, Jan. 30 –Feb. 5, 2006, p. 6.
5. Soli J. Sorabjee, Regeneration of Ethical Value, *University News*, 45(29), July 16-22, 2007.
6. M. Karapaga Vinayagam, The Prime Goal of Education, *University News*, May 28-June 3, 2007, p. 19.
7. P. Sivaswaroop, Resilence of Ethics and Values in Higher Education,

Pre-requisite for Providing Value Orientation, *University News*, Jan. 10-15, 2005, p. 16.

8. Ranjana Bhatia, Value Education in Teacher Education: Issue of Concern, *University News*, Dec. 18-24, 2006, p. 11.
9. Neelanjana Pathak, 'Good Means for Good Ends: Towards Value-Centred Higher Education', *University News*, 44(34), Aug. 21-27, 2006.
10. Complete Works of Swami Vivekananda, Advaita Asharama, Calcutta, Vol. 5: 336, 410, 2-239-40.
11. R.P. Dhokalia, *op. cit.*, p. 13.
12. The Mother Education, Sri Aurobindo Ashram, Pondicherry, 1997, p. 9.
13. *Ibid.*, pp. 10-11.
14. *Ibid.*, pp. 24-25.
15. R.C. Lohati, Intellectual, Moral and Physical Aspects of Education, in *University News*, May 16-22, 2005, p. 18.
16. Acharya Guru, National Regeneration Movement Navasrushti International Trust, 2007, pp. 1-2.
17. Challenge of Education: New Delhi, Govt. of India, 1985, pp. 15-25, 69.
18. Learning to Be, UNESO, 1972, pp. 154-57.
19. Swami Vivekananda by Eleanor Stark, Portsmouth, Peter E. Randall, Publisher, USA, p. 171.
20. Sri Aurobindo Ashram, Pondicherry, India, The Sunlit Path, Passages from Conversations and Writing of the Mother, 2001, Shri Aurobindo Trust, p. 5.
21. *Ibid.*, p. 7.
22. *Ibid.*, p. 119.
23. *Ibid.*, p. 119.
24. Sri Aurobindo Ashram, Pondicherry, India, The Sunlit Path, Passages From Conversations and Writing of the Mother, 2001, Shri Aurobindo Trust, p. 5.
25. *Ibid.* p. 119.
26. *Ibid.*, p. 6.
27. *Ibid.*, pp. 5-6.
28. Sri Aurobindo Ashram, Pondicherry, "The Mother Education, Part One, Essays on Education with Commentaries", 1997, Shri Aurobindo Trust, 1989, p. 8.
29. *University News*, 20-26, Oct. 2003, p. 15.
30. Shri Aurobindo Ashram, Pondicherry, The Mother Education, Part One, Essays on Education with Commentaries, 1997, Shri Aurobindo Asrham Trust.
31. *Ibid.* p. 87.
32. *Ibid.*, p. 22.
33. *Ibid.*, pp. 23, 83.
34. *Ibid.*, pp. 24-25, 77.
35. *Ibid.*, pp. 30, 33.

36. Swami Jagadatmananda, Learn to Live, Vol. 2, Sri Ramakrishna Math, Chennai, 2000, pp. 173-74.
37. *Ibid.*, p. 3.
38. *Ibid.*, pp. 323-24.
39. S.P. Srivastava, University Education in India, *University News*, 37/18, May 3, 1999.
40. K. Abdul Gafoor, Teachers as Professionals, *University News*, 38/27, July 3, 2000.
41. R.N. Prasad, University and Political Development in Independent India, in *University News*, Oct. 4, 1999, p. 4.
42. Vandan Mohd. and Veena A Mohd., Crisis in Higher Education, Causes and Remedies, in *University News*, 41/2, May 26 to June 1, 2003, pp. 7-9.
43. Swami Vivekananda, Raj Yoga, Advaita Ashram, 1992, p. 209.
44. Complete works of Swami Vivekananda, Advaita Ashram, Calcutta, Vol. 8, p. 135.
45. *Ibid.*, Vol. 3, p. 396.
46. Swami Jagadatmananda, Learn to Live, Vol. I, pp. 36-37, Sri Ramakrishna Math, Chennai, 2000.
47. Pranab Mukherjee, Unity of Manmind, *University News*, July 26-Aug. 2, p. 15.
48. *Ibid.*, p. 13.
49. V.S. Prasad, Education for Social Transformation, in *University News*, March 8-14, 2004, pp. 15-16.
50. Swami Purnananda, Making Life Valueable by imbibing values in *Journal of Value Education*, Vol. 2, No. 1, January 2000, (NCERT).
51. UNICEF, A better World for Children, School Sanitation in Ambala, India, Delhi.
52. Swami Jitatmananda, Value Education, Sri Ramkrishna Ashram, Rajkot, 2003, pp. 77-78.
53. Swami Gautamananda, Values in our education, in *Values: The Key to a Meaningful Life*, Sri Ramakrishna Math, Madras, 1996, pp. 88-90.

Yoga and Values

योगश्चित्तवृत्तिनिरोधः ॥ 2 ॥

Yoga is the control of thought—waves in the mind

—Patanjli Yogsutra

Water flows continually into the ocean
But the ocean is never disturbed;
Desire flows into the mind of the seer
But he is never disturbed.
The seer knows peace. . ....
He knows peace who has forgotten desire
He lives without craving;
Free from ego, free from pride.

—Bhagavad Gita

Remain in bliss in this world,
Fearless, pure in heart,
Wake up in bliss every morning,
Carry out all your duties in bliss,
Remain in bliss in weal and woe,
In criticism and insult,
Remain in bliss unaffected,
Remain in bliss pardoning everybody.

—Rabindranath Tagore

CHART 5.1

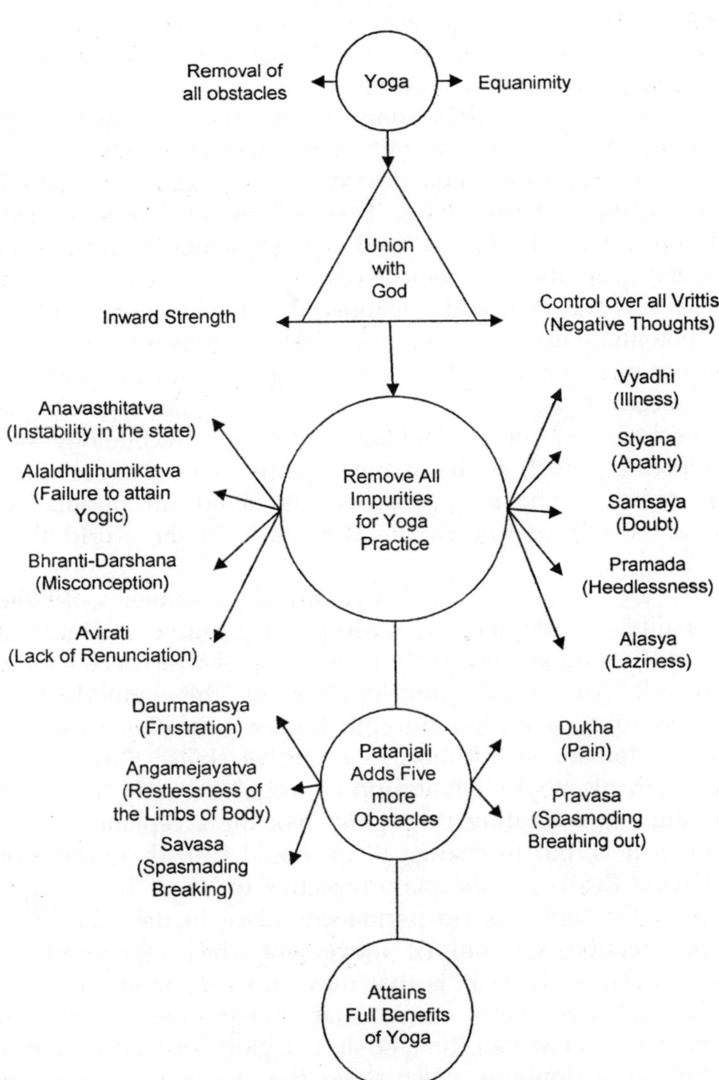

Yoga encompasses all values and includes all values which sharpen the human beings in achieving their material, intellectual and spiritual goals. Yoga can promote theory and practice of all values essential for personality development. The theory and practice of yoga enrich the quality of life through the values inherent in Yoga. Yoga if followed earnestly can create happy family life, social life and peace and prosperity in the Universe.

Prof. T.R. Anandharaman, in his article, "Yoga for the Incoming Millennium" clarifies that Yoga constitutes without any doubt one of the India's many priceless gifts of perennial value to the human value. Despite being a very ancient tradition, it has all along proved ever so modern and relevant to every generation to seekers of human perfection. As the Science of Total man and Technology of Conscious Evolution, its potentialities has always been immense and its contributions manifold as well as in tune with the needs of the concerned age, whether it was the bygone age of the "Upanishads" or the present age of Science, Technology and Engineering. Infact, as this planet awaits the next millennium, Yoga seems to have approached its zenith in popularity, fascination and usefulness in more parts of the world than ever before.

Yoga helps in the overall development of the personality of people. The concept of positive health and lifelong learning are relatively new concepts which need to be promoted. An overall development of the individual is intended to be achieved through higher education using an affective domain in addition to cognitive skills.[1] Shri Kumar Swamiji in his book "Dimension of Yoga" strongly feels that Yoga aims at recreating the world. Not the acceptance of the world as it is, but to change it, to mould it in the pattern of the Divine Reality, is the main objective of Yoga. To say this, is to say that evil has no permanent place in the scheme of things. Creation is a complex movement which represents the various notes and rhythms that make up the grand harmony of the spheres. This music that moves the cosmos is magnificent and wonderful and is the glory of God manifest therein. But a doubting voice raises the question, is there not some chaos in this cosmos? Is there not a confusion in this concord? Is there not a walpurgis night in this winning light? Yes, there is. In the order of creation, first there is the consciousness and division of trenchant separation of good and evil. This is the outlook of individualized consciousness. Next, as the consciousness grows and encompasses the whole existence, good and evil are both embraced and are found to form a secret harmony. This is the outlook of the cosmic consciousness. There is still a higher status, the status of transcendence in which evil is not simply embraced but dissolved and even transformed into supreme reality of which it is an aberration, a projection or a lower formulation. In Yoga the total eradication of evil from the world and human nature, with a remoulding of terrestrial life in the pattern of the divine Reality, is viewed not as a mere concept but as a concrete fact.

Yoga deals with the problems of human nature and human psychology through a vast repertory of practical methods which aim towards purification, regulation and awakening of human potential. At present, yoga is passing through a momentous period of growth consolidation and expansion with its rapid integration into modern society. Many institutions dealing with the theory of Yoga and its practice have come up. At many levels we can see changes and new developments as yoga is being applied in different facets of life in a variety of new ways, such as a form of therapy, a technique of health and stress management.

Modern man is all set for a revolution after nearly four centuries of continuous growth. From the era of blind faith and superstitutions he has progressed an era of rational thinking, experimentation, matter-based approach and its fascinating applications to comfort his living. The strides of this growth encompasses all facets of life including education (science and technology-orientated) and the very direction of growth of an individual (economy-based) and a country (measured with the yardstick of GNP). Tremendous growth has been made in understanding the structure of this physical universe and the laws governing them.

The two major challenges of this era of science and technology—viz. stress and pollution have become the true triggers for the new revolution. If pollution is working at the material front to direct man towards better ecological and appropriate technology, the challenge of stress is shaking the very foundations of the matter-based objective approach of science. As we glide through the decades of transition, our understanding is bound to encompass a greater spectrum of the universe—life, mind, psyche, etc.

India, known for its wisdom has given us the Upanisads, the quintessence of the VEDAS, and a saga of knowledge. From these books of knowledge—Vedas, Upanisads, Yoga texts—are emerging new rays of hopes which are essential to face the new revolution.[2]

Scientific and technological progress all over the globe has made man highly sensitive, critical and also creative. Sharp to the core, his intellect has gained tremendous power of analysis. The left side of his brain is highly developed, helping him to unravel the subtle mysteries of nature and understand clearly the general law of nature. Technology has helped man reap the benefits of its use. Autonomation and computers have brought great speed and sophistication in all our interactions. In search of happiness we are propelled by a desire to increase our living standards by acquiring more and more comfort giving objects and experiencing sensual pleasures. To satisfy this desire we are always on the lookout to earn more and more. In the process, we have become very active and have overcome our lethargy.

Associated with this growth is the emergence of two basic challenges: pollution and stress. The challenge of pollution is being tackled effectively but not met totally. Strict pollution control measures in the industrial sectors and extensive research leading towards the use of ecologically friendly technologies, have certainly yielded dividends. But on the second front, in spite of extensive research all over the globe, a decreasing quality of life, increasing health hazards, social unrest, student unrest, etc. traits which are all different expressions of stress, have shown no trend of decrease. On the contrary, over the last two decades, it is rather on the path of ascent.

The current mechanistic world-view, the matter-based approach the increased dependence on science and technology and the associated lifestyle have to undergo basic changes towards embracing a more holistic world-view and a healthier and more harmonious lifestyle. Emotion trainings and harnessing of the will-power—the growth of the right side of the brain in general—are then the associated adjuncts for such a holistic understanding and also for a healthier and harmonious living. And that is what Yoga offers.

Today, man is subjected to a large number of stressful situations in the modern fast way of life and his balance is frequently disturbed. The system is constantly kept under sympathetic stimulation without enough time for the parasympathetic to do its job. This repeated sympathetic stimulations lead to intermittent upsurges of heart rate, blood pressure, poor digestion, elevated blood glucose, etc. When this happens over a number of years it become a habit for the heart and the blood vessels to remain in stimulated state and they lose the capacity to come back to the resting levels. This is the main cause for the increasing incidence of high blood pressure and diabetes among people today.[3]

Youth in the system of higher education represents a tremendous potential for society, provided it is channeled in the right direction, the enthusiasm, initiative and idealism of young people can help others, including the elderly, the handicapped, the poor, and in so doing can create a happier and more balanced society.

Unprecedented challenges face the youth of today, said Dr. Hiroshi Nakajima, Director-General of WHO, in a message to the world assembly of Youth. And he added that young people may be given opportunities "to demonstrate their creativity, energy and commitment to solving their own problems and helping to build a healthy future for the entire community in which they live."

Unwise life-styles pose the biggest threats to students' health. Innovative judgments, a tendency to show off, or the desire to keep up with their fellows—all these incline them towards risk-taking behaviour. This may include experimenting with dangerous substances like alcohol or drugs, driving too fast on the highway, or simply defying adult society.

In many cases, the cigarette is the very first contact young people have with the life-styles of adulthood. This first encounter often occurs at a very early age: by the time they reach their teens, they may already be unable to break the smoking habit. It is vital that they should be aware of the short-term and long-term risks that smoking represents to their health.

The risk destroying their most important assets; the health and physical fitness through laziness and lack of exercise, rash driving and traffic accidents, suicide or attempts to suicide, slow suicide through the use of alcohol, smoking, dung abuse, excessive intake of tea and coffee, unprotected sexual encounters, sexual misadventures like rape, sexually transmitted diseases, teenager pregnancies and abortions or unwed child births. The ill-effects on their health can extend far into later life. Accidents are estimated to disable permanently three times as many as they kill, smoking and alcohol can store epidemics of respiratory diseases, liver damage and cancer. Teenager pregnancy can kill mother or child or else leave them physically and mentally handicapped. Needless to conclude that in some countries youth is the only age-group in which mortality and morbidity rate is rising, due to these ills of modern society. Alcohol and unemployment is behind alarmingly large number of deaths through accidents and suicide (Jerome, 1980).

Before a dam was constructed on Satluj River, at Bhakra, the water resource was not only wasted but it resulted in floods, leading to loss of life and property. The same is true for youth resource. The idle youth is not only a waste, but also the tide of this unutilized energy can result in negative development wasted in the field of health and economy. The youth can be our best resource if they are healthy and if their joyous energy is channelised for building a better society. The potential energy of youth has to be converted into kinetic energy with understanding, support and technological knowledge and its use should be made to build modern India. Much needs to be done both for and by young people. It is not sufficient merely to have activities directed towards youth. If the aims and objectives of International Youth Year, 1985, and the WHO Global Strategy for Health for All by the year 2000 are to be achieved. Serious efforts of collaborative action by everyone—young and old are needed. The youngsters of today, with their capabilities, energy and commitment, represent a vital resource; they must be partners in the quest for a just future.

Life of students in higher education is becoming more and more artificial and they are travelling more and more away from natural living. In order to return to natural life, they should practice Yoga and learn to live more in consonance with nature and cosmic consciousness.

We see the disinterest and inevitable suffering among many students. It has been realized that every individual contains hidden potential, which when developed allows him to attain pertinent bliss, inner peace and the ultimate goal of our existence.

A brief discussion with students revealed the following problems of students in the system of higher education:

(a) Lack of interest in studies
(b) Lack of vitality, enthusiasm and eagerness
(c) Enamored by affluent environment leading to alcoholism, smoking, gambling, etc.
(d) Irregular in food habits
(e) Not interested in exercises and games
(f) Drudgery in life
(g) No aim in life
(h) Lack of reading habits
(i) Not following any regular course of life
(j) Full of tensions, worries and agitations
(k) Lack of peace-restlessness
(l) Lack of concentration
(m) Problematic both at home and in a college
(n) Bad company
(o) Aimless life.

How can we overcome the problems inflicting the personality of students in higher education system? How can we channelise their potential energy into kinetic energy to make them enjoy the bliss of life? How can we stimulate students towards holistic approach? How can we make them develop their personality in totality? How can we check students from indulging in bad habits—alcoholism, smoking, gambling, etc.? How can we educate them to put them on right track? The only answer is the need of imparting yoga education which can solve all the problems simultaneously. It requires understanding and practice of science and practice of yoga. First let us understand the meaning of yoga.

Meaning of Yoga

Patanjali defines yoga as complete suppression of all mental modes or processes (cittavrttinirodha).[4] Vyasa defines it as absorptive concentration (samadhi). It is a universal attribute of the mind.[5] All persons can attain yoga by repeated practice (abhyasa) and detachment (vairagya).[6]

Swami Satyananda Sanswati in his book, "Asana Pranayama Mudra Bandha," (Bihar School of Yoga, Munger, Bihar, Indium, 1999) comments that, "Yoga is not an ancient myth buried in oblivion. It is the most valuable inheritance of the present. It is the essential need of today and the culture of tomorrow." The Yogic culture of tomorrow is something towards which we have to strive, we have to try to attain. Yoga has been the culture to strive, we have to try to attain. Yoga has been the culture of ancient India and the ancient civilization of the world, and it is going to be the culture of tomorrow. It is the science of today which we have to learn, which we have to accept, and which we have to understand. It is a science which deals with the developments of the human personality and which leads to the awakening of untapped energy sources within the brain and mind. The practice of yoga is not new. Ancient rishis, saints and sages have been talking about it for the last fifty thousand years. They spoke about it, not as a religion or philosophy, but as a way of life which could lead to the development and awakening of our consciousness and energy.

Yoga bestows inner strength, sharpens our intellect, teaches us to control our emotions and brings a rare concentration and efficiency into our action and work, marking one do the right thing in the right way at the right time and that is why. Yoga is defined as a skill in action.

From finite to infinite it is the journey of everything in this Universe. Yoga can speed up this journey by giving a spiritual content and dimension to all human efforts. Every institution working in the field of human upliftment—religious or secular—should understand the newly emerging—but for us, as old as our spiritual heritage—vision of Reality and adjust and adopt measures to ensure this new dimension in their growth. Scientific research, experimental verification, application in day-to-day life, etc. must strengthen the hands of Yoga practitioners so that they can take up the challenges posed by the modern age. This is Vivekananda Kendra's approach.

The mother in her Diary for all times: The Great Adventure says, "Yoga means union with the Divine, and the union is effected through offering—it is founded on the offering of yourself to the Divine."

For most people, however, yoga is simply a means of maintaining health and well-being in an increasingly stressful society. Asanas remove the physical discomfort accumulated during a day at the office sitting in a chair, hunched over a desk. Relaxation techniques help maximize the effectiveness of ever-diminishing time off. In an age of mobile phones, beepers and twenty-four hour shopping, yogic practices make great personal and even business sense.

The word yoga is derived from the Sanskrit root 'yuj' meaning 'to unite', 'to combine', and 'to integrate', which means total integration of the physical, mental, intellectual and spiritual aspects of the human personality.[7] Yoga is a way of life, propounded by Patanjali in a systematic form.

Yoga is an exact science. It aims at the harmonious development of the body, the mind and the soul. Yoga is the turning away of the senses from the objective universe and the concentrations of the mind within. Yoga is the turning away of the senses from the objective universe and the concentration of mind are eternal life in the soul of spirit. Yoga aims at controlling the mind and its modifications. The path of Yoga is an inner path whose gateway is your heart. Yoga is harmony between the individual and the cosmos, between thought and action, between soul and God, between Organism and respiration.

Yoga is the discipline of a mind, senses and physical body. Yoga helps in the co-ordination and control of the subtle forces within the body. Yoga brings in perfection, peace and everlasting happiness; one can even have increased energy, vigor, vitality, longevity, resistance, calmness, and good sleep at times by the practice of Yoga. The practice of

Yoga will help people to control the emotions and passions and resistance power increases and removes the disturbing elements from mind. It will enable them to keep a balanced mind and remove fatigue and get concentration, self-sufficiency, impertinence, pride, luxury, name, fame, self-assertive nature, abstinence, idea of superiority, evil company, laziness, over eating, meat eating, over work, attachments, too much talking, smoking, drinking are some of the obstacles in the path of Yoga.[8]

Swami Parmahansa Niranjanananda in his book 'Yoga Darshan: Vision of Yoga Upanishads' (1993) Bihar observes that the aim of yoga is to take one from the impure aspect of the mind towards the pure aspect, from a state of scattered desire to a state of balanced desire, where the desire becomes positive, constructive, and self elevating, where the desire does not limit us to the external environment only, but also encompasses the inner dimensions. By transcending the impure mind and obtaining purity of mind and by awakening the faculties of the pure mind, one attains transcendence or mukti. One must go from the impure to the pure, and awaken the faculties of the pure mind in order to attain transcendence.

Aspects of Yoga Values (See Chart 5.2)

The science of Yoga has its roots in Upanishads, Veadas, Bhagavad-Gita, Yogavashishta of Vashishta, Hathayoga Pradipika, and the Yoga Sutras of Patanjali. However a detailed classical work could be found in the Yoga Sutras of Patanjali, which dates back roughly to 300 B.C. The Yoga Sutras serve as the basic text for an in-depth study on this great science. Pathanjali called it Ashtanga Yoga, i.e., science having eight limbs or constituents, viz.,

1. Yama
2. Niyama
3. Aasana
4. Praanaayaama
5. Prathyaahaara
6. Dhaarana

7. Dhyaana
8. Samaadhi

यम – नियामासन – प्राणायाम – प्रत्याहार, धारणा – ध्यान – समाध्योष्टावङ्गगनि ।

—Pantajli Yogasutra 2.2.9

(I) Yama

The first discipline of restraint (yama consists in non-injury (ahimsa), truthfulness in thought and speech (satya), non-stealing (asteya), sexual restraint (brahmacarya), and non-acceptance of unnecessary gifts.[9] These are negative virtues. Non-injury (ahimsa) consists in the absence of cruelty to all creatures in all possible ways and at all times. It is tenderness, good will, and kindness for all living beings.[10]

A truthful person must have valid thoughts in his mind, speak them out correctly, excite similar thoughts in the hearer's mind, and his words must be conducive to the welfare of all creatures.

Yama is based on the principle that above all religions, human religion is the best. (Abstinences) viz., Ahimsa (Non-injury), Sathya (Non-falsehood), Astheya (Non-stealing), Aparigraha (Non-acceptance or non-hoarding of things beyond our bear necessities of life) and Brahmacharva (Non-deviation from one's on personal laws of nature).

Steady intellect is a natural and spontaneous state for a man of realization. Since he knows the truth, nothing in this world can disturb him. Even ordinary people and spiritual aspirants can derive immense benefit by cultivating a steady intellect. Intellectual, conviction about Reality may help us to develop a steady intellect to a certain extent.

He is a man of steady intellect whose mind is not disturbed by the pair of opposites, namely, happiness and misery, victory and defeat, gain and loss, praise and blame, attachment and hatred, honour and dishonour, heat and cold.[11] Sri Krishna has given a beautiful illustration in the Bhagavad Gita (2.70), of a steady intellect.

आपूर्यमाणमचलप्रतिष्ठं समुद्रमापः प्रविशन्ति यद्वत ।

CHART 5.2

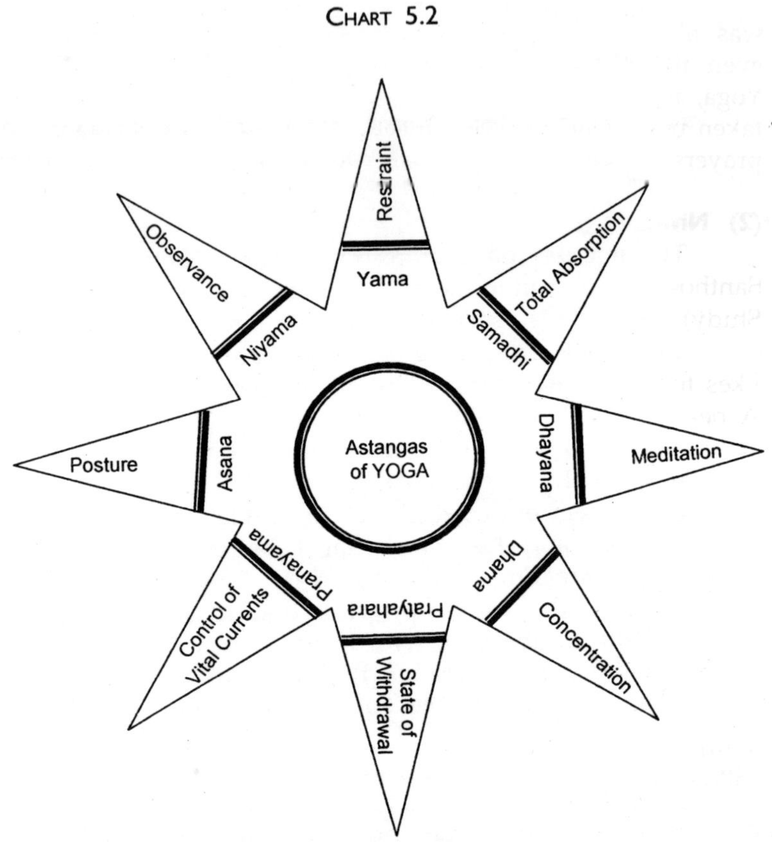

'Water enters into the sea from all directions but the sea remains full and unchanged.'

Prof. T.R. Anantharaman observes that a little reflection on the five Yamas, or restraints, will bring out, however, their enormous importance in the maintenance of what one would today refer to as external or social ecology. It is though their sustained practice that one can hope to establish a peaceful, harmonious and happy social environment, which is a sine qua non for real progress of any type in case of individuals or groups, who form part of a community or nation. No wonder, Patanjali calls them Saarvabhauma, supreme or universal obligatory for all and under all circumstances. It was also not a chance coincidence that Mahatma Gandhi, even though he was not a full-fledged votary of classical Yoga, included all the five Yamas in the eleven vows to be taken up seriously for practice and repeated every day in the prayers by the inmates of his Ashram.

(2) Niyama

These are the observances viz., Shoucha (Purity), Santhosha (Contentment), Tapas (Austerity), Swadyaaya (Self Study), Eswara Pranidhaana (Total surrender to the Supreme).

Thirst for knowledge is inherent in man and no one likes to be ignorant. Knowledge alone can remove ignorance. A beautiful verse in Chanakya Niti (XVII-17) says:

ज्ञानं नराणामधिको विशेषः ।
ज्ञानेन हीनाः पशुभिः समानाः ॥

'What distinguishes a man from an animal is his capacity to acquire knowledge. Without knowledge men are equal to animals.'

Spiritual knowledge comes through direct experience of Truth, but very few can reach that state. Others have to follow the path of discrimination, using their intellect.

There is a popular saying:

स्वदेशे पूज्यते राजा विद्वान् सर्वत्र पूज्यते ।

"The king is honoured only in his kingdom whereas a learned person is honoured everywhere.[12]

This is a great psychological truth discovered by the Yoga system long ago. It is a commonplace of modern Ethics. Mackenizie says, "It is generally better to escape from our defects, not by thinking about them and trying to elude them, but by fixing our attention on the opposite excellences. It certainly seems a more effectual method as a rule to expel our evil propensities by developing good ones rather than by seeking directly to crush the evil ones.[13]

(3) Aasana

Asana means a state of being in which one can remain physically and mentally steady, calm, quiet and comfortable. In the Yoga Sutras of Patanjali there is a concise definition of yogasana: "Sthiramsukhamaasanam", meaning that position which is comfortable and steady. So, we can see that yogasanas in this context are practiced to develop the practitioners' ability to sit comfortably in one position for an extended length of time, as is necessary during meditation.

In raja yoga, asana refers to the sitting position, but in hatha yoga it means something more. Asana are specific body position which open the energy channels and psychic centres. They are tools to higher awareness and provide the stable foundation for our exploration of the body, breath, mind and beyond. The hatha yogis also found that by developing control of the body through asana, the mind is also controlled. Therefore, the practice of asana is foremost in hatha yoga.

This Involves practice of physical Postures for correcting any deformities or physical ailments. Hatha Yoga Texts claim that there are as many as 84000000 postures.

The third discipline is bodily posture (asana). It is a steady and pleasant posture of the body. It should not move. It should not be painful. It should not distract the mind. There are many kinds of postures, padmasana, virasana, bhadrasana, svastika, and the like. The various postures of the body are the means of controlling it and keeping it healthy and fit. They tone up the nervous system. They can be learnt from experts. The control of the body is the basis of the yoga discipline.

They are controlled by means of practice and non-attachment. Patanjli Yogasutras-12.

Practice is the repeated effort to follow the disciplines which give permanent control of the thought-waves of the mind. Yogasutra-13 Practice becomes firmly grounded when it has been cultivated for a long time, uninterruptedly, with earnest devotion. Yogasutra.[14]

The practice of yoga prevents psychosomatic disorders/diseases and improves individual's resistance and ability to endure stressful situations. As a primary prevention, yogic exercises should be advised to drive the benefits of prevention of diseases, promotion of health and for therapeutic purposes.

(4) Praanaayaama

This limb deals with practice of breathing exercises involving rechaka, puraka, antara kumbaka and bahya kumbhaka (inhalation, exhalation, internal retention and external retention) thus exercising our lungs—the ventilators of our body.

The fourth discipline is breath control (pranayama). It consists in controlling natural breathing and subjecting it to a definite law. It consists in slow and deep inspiration (puraka), retention of breath (Kumbhaka), and slow expiration (recaka).[15] These three functions should be performed for definite periods. The time of inspiration, the time of retention of breath, and the time of expiration should be in the proportion: 1, 4 and 2.

Breath Control is conducive to concentration of mind. It removes the crust of affliction from illumination of the sattava of the mind. It removes the demerit which observes discriminative knowledge. Breath control is the supreme austerity. It purges the mind of impurities and generates illumination of knowledge.[16]

The term pranayama is derived from the Sanskrit term 'prana' which means the 'vital principal'. The vital principle permeates the brain and the nervous system of an individual. It is the source of volition, enthusiasm, spontaneity and happiness in an individual. He spreads the same in the environment which also becomes pure.[17]

Pranayama is the method of rhythmic regulation of breath. It produces stability in the body, and equanimity in the mind of an individual. The subtle physiology of an individual gets purified through regular practice of pranayama. The body of an individual becomes free from leanness, obesity, crookedness, etc. through regular practise of pranayama. Swami Vishnu Devananda states:

Pracchardana-vidharanabhayam va pranasya

It is also achieved by the expulsion and retention of the breath.

This is a reference to the practice of pranayama as a method of purification. Regulation of the breath gives control over the thought waves, for control of breath is directly related to control of mind. There are many pranayama exercises, each of which has a special effect on the autonomic nervous system and the psyche.[18]

We do not pay any serious attention to breathing, the most important of all our bodily functions. It has never occurred to us that a great deal of our physical and mental troubles are due to the fact that we do not breathe correctly. Life and breath are synonymous. We live as long as we breathe. We start our life with the first breath and end it with the last breath. We never stop breathing whether we are awake or asleep. We can exist without food for weeks and without water for a few days but without air we cannot exist even for a few minutes. Air is the most important nourishment for our blood. All the activities of body from digestion to creative thinking depend upon the oxygen supply through breathing; yet we treat breathing with utter indifference. If there is a deficiency in the supply of oxygen, the process of ionization will be incomplete and the food is partially assimilated. Nearly 50 percent of delinquency in minors is due to oxygen starvation which is the result of shallow breathing and lack of fresh air.

The habit of shallow breathing is one of many unnatural habits that modern civilization has forced upon us. It has been proved that in the civilized world only babies can breathe in a natural way. Shallow breathing is directly or indirectly responsible for a number of physical and mental diseases ranging from nervous disorders to common colds. To function properly the brain requires three times more oxygen than the rest of the body. If it does not get its due allotment, it exacts it from the body supply. That is why brain workers often possess a poor physic and a bad health. Deep breathing not only nourishes the whole system but also cleanses it.

Prana is not mere breath but it is cosmic energy. It is a life giving principle which pervades the whole atmosphere. It is manifested in every form of existence—organic and inorganic. By breathing exercises it is possible to raise the degree of circulation of Prana in the body. The surplus of Prana is stored in the solar plexus which is the battery of human body.

(5) Prathyaahara

If the mind is withdrawn from external sensible objects, the external senses are automatically withdrawn from them. They do not follow their objects, but they follow the mind. They are fixed on those objects only on which the mind is fixed. The restraint of the external senses depends upon the restraint of the mind. It can be acquired by repeated practice, resolute will, and sense control.[19]

The five disciplines of restraint (yama), observance (niyama), bodily posture (asana), breath-control (pranayama), and sense-control (pratyahara) are the external aids to yoga (bahirangasadhana). The last three disciplines, fixation of mind (dharana), meditation (Dhyana) and absorptive concentration or ecstasy (samadhi) are the internal aids of yoga (antarangasadhana) They directly lead to conscious ecstasy (samprajnatasamadhi).[20]

(6) Dhaarana

This involves concentration of mind, it is true that the main stumbling block in increasing our knowledge is lack of concentration. The ever-increasing aberrations in the mind with the advent of age would really worsen the situation unless the mind is cultured through yogic techniques. Everything is possible to those who can concentrate, and so we are encouraged to preserve, to break through the barriers of ordinary sense perception and to press forward fearlessly in our search for inner knowledge. The physical strength gained in a gymnasium can be used later for practical purposes. The mental strength gained through these exercises in concentration can be used for the most practical purpose of all; to unite ourselves with the Atman.

विशेका वा ज्योतिष्टमति ।। 36 ।।

(7) Dhyaana

Dyaana involves relaxed dwelling of the mind for a longer duration on the object of meditation. Fixation of attention on an object to the exclusion of other objects leads to meditation, if the cognition produced by it continues unbroken for a long time. There is a continuous stream of similar cognitions of the contemplated object undisturbed by dissimilar cognitions.[21]

(8) Samaadhi

The meditation involves the continuous flowing of mind energy and steady focusing on the object of meditation effortlessly for a longer and longer time. The very essence of yoga is merger of individual soul with that of universal soul, a state of super consciousness. This essence is achieved through Samaadhi only. Fixation (dharana), meditation (dhyana) and absorptive concenration (samadhi), on the same object together are called samyama. They are the internal aids (antarangasadhana) to conscious ecstasy, while restraint, observance, bodily posture, breath control, and withdrawal of the senses from their objects are the external aids (bahirangasadhana) to it. But they are the external aids to super conscious ecstasy.[22]

Swami Sivananda in his article "Religious Education and Practice of Yoga" mentions the causes of stresses and strains and suggest meditation as has been laid down in all our ancient Sanskrit scriptures.

"Watch your mind very carefully. Be vigilant. Be on the alert. Do not allow the waves of irritability, jealousy, hatred and lust to disturb you. These dark waves are enemies of peaceful living, meditation and wisdom. To some it is very difficult to keep the mind unruffled and pure, the causes being deep-rooted worldly Samskaras, unfavourable surroundings, and the predominance of extrovert tendencies. To some, of course, evil thoughts are not a problem at all. They appear occasionally as a passing phase without doing much havoc. The very fact that evil thoughts give you mental suffering is a sign of spiritual progress; for many do not have that much of sensitiveness."

In nutshell Meditation is the process where the mind of a person is attracted towards God without interruption and is always keen to set in prayer from the core of heart. Prayer and Japa always help in supplementing and complementing meditation.

A massive qualitative change takes place within Man along with the awakening of Prajnaa and gradually leads him on to the status of a Sthita-Prajnaa (Man of Steadfast Illumination or Wisdom), whose hallmarks are described in many old Sanskrit texts, particularly in those dozen beautiful verses towards the end of the second chapter of the Bhagvad Gita, the immortal and inspiring dialogue between Arjuna and Lord Krishna. At this stage of Man's evolution into expanded states of consciousness, words and exhortations are of only limited use. Only regular reflection and meditation under the direction of one's own pure intellect or a qualified teacher can contribute to progress in this realm, which has been differently referred to as transcendental, mystical, religious, spiritual, super-conscious, supramental, supernatural, etc. by its explorers in different parts of the world and in different ages. Whatever the name, this higher realm of consciousness is filled with Light and Joy unbounded.

Classification of Yoga

There are four yogas—Bhakti Yoga, Karma Yoga, Jnana Yoga and Raja Yoga—to realize the Divine, where is the need to practise Buddhi Yoga? The answer is that even to practice the four yogas one has to take the help of Buddhi.

Shri Krishnan says in the Bhagavad Gita (18:57):

चेतना सर्वकर्माणि मयि सन्यस्य मत्परः ।

बुद्धियोगमुपाश्रित्य मच्चितः सततं भव ॥

"Resigning mentally all actions to Me, regarding Me as the supreme goal and resorting to Budhhi Yoga, ever fix your mind on Me.

Bhakti Yoga

Devotion mixed with discrimination is an ideal path.

Without discrimination devotion ends in mere sentimentalism or emotionalism. Therefore, the place of Buddhi in Bhakti yoga is very significant. When the Lord is pleased with His devotees, he bestows His grace in the form of pure intellect. Sri Krishna himself promises in the Bhagwad Gita (10.10):

तेन सततयुक्तानां भजतां प्रीतिपूर्वकम् ।
ददामि बुद्धियोगं तं येन मापुयान्ति ते ॥

"To those who are ceaselessly devoted to Me and who worship Me with immense love, I grant Buddhi yoga by which they come to Me." A concentrated mind alone is a fit instrument for prolonged and deep meditation on the Divine. Intellect alone can do this since it is superior to the mind and the senses.

Dhayana Yoga

The mind is superior to the senses and the intellect is superior to the mind. Through the constant practice of meditation, we gain control over our senses and mind, which helps us to develop the power of concentration.

Karma Yoga

No one can renounce work but if we learn the skill of performing work, the same work will release us from the bondage of Karma.

Sri Krishna clearly says that even to perform work in the right spirit one must exercise his intellectual faculty. Even a little work, done with the spirit of self-sacrifice and dedication, gives a sense of fulfilment. Therefore, intelligent people always choose the path of selfless work using their discriminative faculty. To work and yet to be free from the effects of work requires subtle understanding of the secret of work and such understanding comes from Buddhi. Sri Krishna says in the Bhagvad Gita (2.39)

नराणामधिको विशेष: ।
ज्ञानेन हीना: पशुभि: समाना ॥

"Being endowed with such intellect you will get rid of the bondage of actions, O Pratha."

Jnana Yoga

Discrimination between the real and the unreal is called Viveka. Buddhi alone has the capacity to determine the real nature of an object. In the path of knowledge, the aspirant has to realize the Truth by constant reasoning and through Buddhi alone this can be done. Sankaracharya emphasizes this view in the Vivekachudamani (versa: 16):

मेधावी पुरुषे विद्वानूहपोहविचक्षण: ।
अधिकार्यात्मविद्यायामुक्तलक्षणलक्षित: ।।

> "An intelligent and learned man skilled in arguing in favour of the Scriptures. . . . is the recipient of the knowledge of the Atman."[23]

Ordinarily we speak of four Yogas, the royal roads to Reality, viz. Jnana, Bhakti, Raja and Karma Yogas. Strangely enough, the Bhagvata does not recognize Rajayoga as an independent path. It speaks of only three. Sri Krishna says to Uddava: "I have propounded three Yogas for the welfare of mankind. They are Jnana, Karma and Bhakti and there is none other anywhere. Jnana Yoga for those who are disillusioned with the world and have given up Karma; Karmayoga for those who hanker after worldly pleasures and are attached to Karma; and Bhaktiyoga for those who happen to hear about Me and My sports and are attracted by them, yet are not totally free from worldly pursuits nor are very much attached to them." (Bh. II.10, 6.7, 8.)[24]

Though the Bhagvata does not accord an independent status to Patanjali's Yoga, it recommends and incorporates all its limbs in the practice of meditation. Yama, Niyama, Asana, Pranayama and the whole host are there, may be in a slightly modified form. (Vide Bhag. 11.14; 32-35; and 11.19.33.35).[25]

According to Aurobindo's Yoga is to want to transform oneself integrally, it is to have a single aim in life, such that nothing else exists any longer, that alone exists. And so one feels it clearly in oneself whether one wants it or not; but if one doesn't one can still have a life of goodwill, a life of service, of understanding; one can labour for the work to be accomplished more easily—all that—one can do many things. But between this and doing yoga there is a great difference. And to do Yoga, you must want it consciously.

Impact of Yoga on Life of People

The ancient literature is full of philosophy, science and techniques of channelising the potential energies of people and their life long journey. But How?

The answer is compulsory education of Yoga from school to university level in graded manner. Let us mention some of the facts which can be developed by Yoga Education to improve the personality of students.

(a) Holistic Development of Personality

Holistic Development of Personality, i.e. physical, mental and spiritual. This coincides with the definition adopted by World Health Organization. Health is a state of physical, mental and social well-being and not merely the absence of infirmily. Yoga offers us a holistic lifestyle of bliss, peace, creativeness, emotional balance and physical well-being.

The concept of 'mental equanimity' is more satisfactory than the concept of mental health because the former alone can produce spiritual development in an individual. When consciousness of subject and object disappears and only the meaning remains, it is called samadhi. Samadhi is a merging of the mind into the essence of the object of meditation. Nothing exists but that pure awareness.[26]

Mind is the most powerful part of the human system. It is a Super Computer. Teachers in the systems of Education don't realize its potential or devise ways and means to harness this most important source. Education system can achieve excellence, provided they know the secret of tapping students mind. We generally notice that most of the students do not mentally position as one or the other problems concerning their education continuously bogs them down. Many of them become mental wrecks and a liability on the education system. The higher education systems instead of solving their problems, cause further deterioration. 25 percent of students in every higher education system are a liability and the other 75 percent are not contributing as per their potential. Teachers should try to create positive mental attitudes among the students. Positive mental attitude is a state of mind that reflects the strength of students' belief in what they do. It generates inner and voluntary emotions which enhances motivation, resulting in positive thoughts. Positive thinking is the key to development and is result-oriented.

The ancient Indian philosophers laid stress on mental equanimity for the general well-being of individuals. The mind of an ordinary person is usually very restless. Myraids of desire produce upheavals in the mind of an individual. Over and above this, the mind of an ordinary person is afflicted by several tensions.

The ancient Indian Philosophers maintained that if the mind of an individual usually remains in a disturbed state, he is very likely to develop pathological symptoms. An individual with pathological mental symptoms quite often develop certain pathological organic symptoms because there is very close relationship between the body and the mind of an individual. The mind of an individual becomes free from anxiety and miseries, if there is peace in his mind."

The mind is a reservoir for numerous powers. By utilizing the resources which are hidden within it, one can attain any height of success in the world. If the mind is trained, made one-pointed and inward, it also has power to penetrate into the deeper levels of our being. It is the finest instrument that a human being can ever have.

Holistic approach to health represents a revisioning of the human endeavour to restore order in the organismic functioning, that has occurred in the past several centuries with the medical profession. The holistic health movement is the reflection of the growing dissatisfaction among the professional as well as lay people about the capacity of modern medicine in delivering the health care. A shortcoming of modern medicine is its failure to recognize the interactive nature of the different aspects of human existence viz. physical, psychological social and spiritual in the etiology of illnesses and in the maintenance of health and well-being.

Since modern medicine is itself a development within the framework of science, many have argued that the change needs to be brought about in the very framework. Thus, holistic movement is viewed as a by-product and manifestation of the contemporary thrust on the revision of the scientific framework. One can find this trend in the works of behavioural, natural and social scientists which are contributing for major change in the worldview. It involves a fundamental shift in cognition leading to radical alterations in the belief and assumptions about the nature of the universe, about the human nature, about organism environment interaction, and about the nature of consciousness. The newly emerging worldview is described as holistic paradigm.

In the final analysis, the physical, social, mental and spiritual balance is the most desirable for holistic health. Unless a person is physically fit and active; he cannot perform at his best level. On the other hand, it is the mind, which accounts for 80 percent of physical and social problems. These are called psychosomatic diseases. Lastly, it is the spirit which ultimately directs the mind and through it to the body. The teachers should devise ways and means to ensure synergy of the physical, social, mental and spiritual capabilities, which would release the infinite potential powers of the students and generate efficiency and happiness in the society.

(b) Control of negative thought waves in the mind

When Patanjali speaks of "control of thought waves", he does not refer to a momentary or superficial control. Many people believe that the practice of yoga is concerned with "making your mind a blank"—a condition which could, if it were really desirable, be much more easily achieved by asking a friend to hit you over the head with a hammer. No spiritual advantage is ever gained by self-violence. We are not trying to check the thought-waves by smashing the organs which record them. We have to do something much more difficult—to unlearn the false identification of the thought waves with the ego-sense. This process of unlearning involves a complete transformation of character, "renewal of the mind", as St. Paul puts it.

(c) Creation of positive Attitude

To attain success in life and to reach the desired goal one must have a positive attitude. Faith in oneself and in God, courage, strength and fearlessness are the characteristics of a positive intellect. For a man of intense faith nothing is impossible in this world. That person alone who is ready to undergo any amount of suffering and face any difficulty can reach the goal. One should never harbour negative thoughts, like 'I am only a householder', 'I am a sinner', 'I am good for nothing', 'I am weak'. Such negative thinking can do tremendous harm to our personality.[27] Swami Vivekananda stressed this idea again and again. He was very particular that our younger generation must cultivate positive ideas. He says, "He is an atheist who does not believe in himself. The old religion said that he was an atheist who did not believe in God. The new religion says that he is an atheist who does not believe in himself."

(d) Vast Intellect

Visala Buddhi is that characteristic of the intellect, which transcends all narrow and selfish ideas and embraces the whole world. When a person lets go his individuality and identifies himself with the whole existence, he is called a man of vast intellect. We bow down to the great sage Vyasa because he possessed this vast intelligence.

नमोस्तु ते व्यास विशालबुद्धे: ।

(Gita Dhyana Sloka, 2)

Swami Vivekananda wanted our people to develop such an intellect. In one of his lectures delivered in Madras he said, 'We want that education, by which character is formed, strength of mind is increased, the intellect is expanded and by which one can stand on one's own feet.' Further he said, 'Expansion is life, contraction is death.'

A person who is only interested in himself is like a prisoner. He remains confined within the four walls of his house, without any concern for the outside world. He is quite happy with himself and is not aware of his spiritual dimension. There is no expansion of heart. A little spiritual growth will help us to expand our intellect. The same Divine dwells in the heart of everybody and we are one spiritually. Therefore, we must change our attitude towards others.

Sri Krishna shows us how to develop this vast intellect (6.32):

> ज्ञानं आत्मौगाग्येन सर्पत्र समं मण्यति योऽर्जन ।
> सुखं वा यदि वा दुःखे स योगी परमो मतः ॥

> 'He who judges pleasure and pain everywhere bothersome standard as the one he applies to himself, that yogi is thought to be the highest.

The idea is, the man of vast intellect (Visala Buddhi) empathizes with the joys and sorrows of all beings as his own. He understands the sufferings and shares the happiness and miseries of others. Through this teaching Sri Krishna exhorts us, to love others as we love ourselves. Be full of kindness and compassion, identify yourself with others and partake of their joys and sorrows. Why? Because unity underlies this apparent diversity.

The man of vast intellect breaking all barriers embraces the whole world. A selfish man on the other hand feels miserable when others are happy and feels happy when others are suffering. This is called Bheda Buddhi. He always wants to preserve his separate identity. Such a man does not hesitate to harm others for selfish purposes. Because of his deluded intellect, he divides people into different categories, depending on their caste, creed, religion, sex, social status, just to exploit them for his selfish motives. What happens to such a man?[28]

All the great religions of the world have come out of one Truth. If we follow religion without practicing the Truth, it is like the blind leading the blind. Those who belong to God love all. Love is the religion of the universe. A compassionate one transcends the boundaries of religion and realizes the undivided, absolute Reality.[29]

(e) Decisions based on deep thinking

Our decisions, motives, actions should always be

guided by serious and deep thinking and not by mere impulse or emotion. A calm and study mind alone is fit to discriminate between right and wrong. We find a beautiful verse in the Katha Upanishad which can guide our intellect to make the right choices (1.2.2):

श्रेयच्श्र प्रेयच्श्र मनुष्यमेतः तौ सम्परीत्य विविनक्ति धीरः ।
श्रेयो हि धीरोऽभिप्रेयसो वृणीते प्रेयो मन्दो योगक्षेमाद्वृणीते ।।

'Both the good and the pleasant present themselves to a man. The calm soul examines them well and discriminates. He prefers the good to the pleasant; but the fool chooses the pleasant out of greed and avarice.'[30]

(f) Strengthen spiritual power

Spiritual strength is the highest strength, the next being intellectual and the last, physical. Those who have made considerable progress in spiritual life alone can experience spiritual strength; till then we have to depend upon intellectual strength. Intellectual conviction is possible only through right understanding. Regular study of the scriptures, teachings of great luminaries and discussions on spiritual matters help us to develop right understanding.

The Taittiriya Upanishad says (1.19):

स्वाध्याय प्रवचनाभ्यां न प्रमदितव्यम् ।

'Do not be careless, about learning and teaching'.

Since it is difficult to keep the mind always on the spiritual plane, it is better to engage it in intellectual pursuit, lest it should go down to the physical and sensual level.

Thirst for knowledge is inherent in man and no one likes to be ignorant. Knowledge alone can remove ignorance. A beautiful verse in Chanakya Niti (XVII-17) says:

ज्ञांन नराणामधिको विशेषः ।
ज्ञानेन हीनाः पशुभिः समानाः ।।

What distinguishes a man from an animal is his capacity to acquire knowledge. Without knowledge men are equal to animals.

Spiritual knowledge comes through direct experience of Truth, but very few can reach that state. Others have to follow the path of discrimination, using their intellect.

There is a popular saying:

स्वदेशे पूज्यते राजा विद्वान् सर्वत्र पूज्यते ।

The king is honoured only in his kingdom whereas a learned person is honoured everywhere.[31]

(g) Helps in sorting out psychological problems born out of tensions, conflicts, etc.[32]

What most psychologists ask their patients to do is to yield to the demands of the unconscious. In some cases this may release the inner tensions. But this may not be permanent and may even be more harmful. The super conscious is at present unknown to us, but that does not mean that it is the same as the unconscious mind of the psychologists. It can be attained through spiritual disciplines. It is the source of supreme peace and bliss. More than all, it gives man the feeling of wholeness, the feeling of supreme fulfilment.

(h) Strengthen Will Power

Development of will power is a problem that is often faced by everyone of us. If we can exercise our body and buildup its strength gradually, there is no reason why the same cannot be done with our mind! By denying ourselves small pleasures and temptations to begin with, we can gradually but surely build up our will power. The example given by the Holy Mother of the farmer who could lift a bull because he used to carry it daily since the time it was a small helpless calf, can give us much-needed encouragement here also.[33]

Fear is the greatest of all foes. It is a devil residing with. Fearlessness is the first rung on the ladder of freedom.

To cultivate the quality of humility is one step toward

enlightenment. By being humble we gain much and lose nothing. Prayer and contemplation strengthen our will power in cultivating this inner quality.

(i) Understanding the Purpose of Life

Swami Rama feels that "If a human being remains constantly aware of the purpose of his life and directs all his actions toward the fulfilment of that purpose, there remains nothing impossible for him. Those who are not aware of the purpose of life are easily caught by the whirlpool of miseries."

A human being is fully equipped with all necessary healing powers, but does not know their usage. The moment he comes in touch with the healing potentials within, he can heal himself. All the powers belong to only one God. A human being is only an instrument.

(j) Nutrition for Yogic Persons

Swami Vishnu Devananda in his book 'Meditation and Mantras' has rightly said that, What is consumed by the human body correlates directly to the efficiency with which the brain functions. Recent studies show that certain red food colouring creates hyperactivity in children, and that refined sugar can cause emotional instability. These are just two examples of substances that are often heedlessly consumed without understanding their effect on the body and mind.

Several years ago vegetarianism was, in a sense, an underground-practice. A person who refrained from eating meat was viewed with a certain amount of curiosity, if not suspicion. Today it is quite a different story. Health food stores and vegetarian restaurants are prevalent. There is a growing awareness that our health is directly affected by what we eat. Many diseases can be cured by a change in diet or a short period of fasting, with no medications at all. This is true not only of physical disorders, but of many mental difficulties as well. It is particularly important that pregnant mothers have this awareness; too often they do not realize the effect of their diet on the developing fetus.

There is no doubt that, "You are what you eat", a subtle part of what is consumed becomes the consciousness.

Those who have changed from a meat to vegetarian diet notice a corresponding change in consciousness. There is a certain grossness that disappears, and the awareness becomes finely tuned.

In the Bhagavad-Gita three types of food have been mentioned which produce three different types of dispositions in individuals.

A person becomes healthy, moral, religious, intelligent and creative by regularly taking, sattvika food.

Sattvika spreads sattvika and the Cumulative effect is purity of environment.

आयु: सत्वबलारोग्यसुखप्रीतिविवर्धना: ।
रम्या: स्निग्धा: स्थिरा हृद्या आहारा: सात्त्विकप्रिया: ।।

xvii/8 Bhagavad Gita.

Foods which promote longevity, intelligence, vigour, health, happiness and cheerfulness, and which are sweet, bland, substantial and naturally agreeable, are dear to the Sattvika type of men."

कट्वम्ललवणात्युष्णतीदणरुक्षविदाहिन: ।
आहारा राजसस्येष्टा दु:खशोकामयप्रदा: ।।

xvii/9 Bhagavad Gita.

Foods which are bitter, acid, salty, overhot, pungent, dry and burning, and which cause suffering, grief and sickness, are dear to the Rajasika type of men.

यातायामं गतरसं पूति पयुषितं च यत् ।
उच्छिष्टमपि चामेध्यं भोजनं तामसप्रियम् ।।

xvii/10 Bhagavad Gita.

Food which is half-cooked or half-ripe, insipid, putrid, stale and polluted, and which is impure too, is dear to men of a Tamasika disposition.

Research Studies about Impact of Yoga on Lives of People

P.K. Hassanagas *et al.* in their article, Yoga in the

Culture of Labour based on research have come out with the following conclusions:[34]

1. Practising yoga helps in improving the general health of the volunteers.
2. The psycho condition is reinforced and the mental capabilities are increased. The concentration and the memory are developed. Self-confidence, self-discipline and working capability are increased.
3. The capability for removing the psychophysical fatigue is increased.
4. The influence of the harmful factors from the working conditions to health is decreased because the immunity and the resistance of the body is reinforced and the participants learn how to protect themselves.
5. The number of the injuries is decreased as a result of increase of the self-consciousness, self-control of the body and the brain.
6. The number of absences due to illness is decreased.
7. The efficiency and the productivity increases leading to profits.

Nedungade V. Haridas in the article, "Physiological and Philosophical Aspects of Yoga" states that:[35]

Yoga science is a well proven treasure and it is up to us to tap the yoga power to relax and rejuvenate our mind, increase our physical strength, expand our spiritual awareness, improve our concentration, help our body use oxygen and nutrients more effectively and to prevent illness and retard old age.

In conclusion, a quotation is taken from His Holiness Swamy vishnudevananda "Health is wealth—peace of mind is happiness—yoga shows the way."

Pavlos K. Hassanages *et al.* in their article, "Yoga and Cardio Vascular Diseases" state:[36]

Our results show remarkable influence of yoga on eliminating and alleviating of chronic psycho stresses, increasing of self-control, self-confidence and self-discipline which help to eliminate other risk factors and to undertake responsibility for improving one's own health and the quality of living which in turn helps in preventing coronary disease.

Dr. (Mrs.) Hemalatha Murthy in his article, "Management of Respiratory Diseases by Yoga,"[37] states that yoga gives us solace, confidence, redeems all our miseries, obsession, conflicts. It is suitable to all and all times. It helps the persons to change their attitude and bring a tremendous change in way of life which is simple and which is very necessary, unless, there is no true solutions to all the problems and illnesses. Right knowledge of yoga burns out the likes and dislikes, ego and ignorance and there is establishment of Pure Bliss, which is natural state of a being.

For the management of stress in order to combat the so called stress-induced disorders all the above discussed areas should be tapped. Yoga way is more holistic, which offers the lifestyle of bliss, efficiency, emotional equipoise, mental clarity, intellectual sharpness and physical well-being.

Swami Harshananda in his article, "Attainment of Yoga" mentions that knowingly or unknowingly, all of us are struggling to get peace. As long as our mind is in pieces and the pieces are in ceaseless mutual conflict, peace eludes us. It is only when we learn to put these pieces together so as to make the mind whole and integrated that we gain the peace of Kaivalya. This is easier said than done. However, with competent guides like Patanjali who are ever eager to help out of infinite compassion, this task should not be that difficult.

Patanjali, the great master of the Yoga system, calls these pieces of the mind as vrttis, modifications, which are ever arising and never subsiding. Yoga or union of the individual self with the Supreme Self will result through Yoga or Samadhi, when these Vrttis are controlled, suppressed and eliminated, by the right kind of discipline and training. This discipline and training is also Yoga.[38]

Dr. S.C. Manchanda,[39] Professor and Head; Department of Cardiology, All India Institute of Medical Sciences, New Delhi has depicted the role of Yoga lifestyle in Coronary Artery diseases in his "Research Study of Reversal of Coronary Heart Disease through Preksha Meditation with

Reference to Coronary Atherosclerotic Reversal Potential of Yoga Lifestyle Intervention." According to the study, forty-two male patients (mean age 51.0 + 9.5 range 32-72 years) with angiographically proven CAD were included. Patients in the control group (n=21) were managed on conventional medical therapy (with control of risk factors, AHA step 1 diet, moderate aerobic exertion), while those in the yoga group (n=21) were advised strict lifestyle modifications and yogic exercises as detailed below. The yogic lifestyle intervention programme consisted of:

(a) Yogic Lifestyle Methods—
   (i) Health rejuvenating exercises: a set of movements for improving the general tone of the body and to improve coordination.
   (ii) Relaxation exercise (Kayotsarg): a method of complete relaxation to prepare the body and mind for mediation.
   (iii) Breathing exercises (Pranȃyama).
   (iv) Yogic postres for stretch relaxation (Asanas).
   (v) Preksha meditation (preksha means seeing deeply within).
   (vi) Reflection on moral values (Anuvrat and Anupreksha.)

(b) Stress Management (relaxation, breathing exercises and Preksha meditation).

(c) Dietary control.

(d) Moderate aerobic exercises.

The change in the lesion severity was classified into regression (10% absolute reduction in diameter stenosis), no significant change <10% change in diameter stenosis) or progression (>10% absolute increase in diameter stenosis). In the Yoga group, 3 (5%) lesions showed progression, 46 (75%) lesions showed no change while 12 (20%) lesions showed regression. In the control group 22 (37%) lesions showed progression, 36 (61%) showed no change while 1 (2%) showed regression.

Yoga lifestyle intervention is beneficial in improving the symptoms and exercise capacity, lowering weight and serum lipid levels. It also retards the progression of coronary atherosclerosis in patients with severe coronary artery diseases and reduces revasularisation procedures.

In ancient India the early Yogis were a group of mystics and scientists to whom the relationship between the mortal man and an immortal spirit was of great interest. They set about to find ways and means of uniting these two during the earthly life of man. They spent not decades but centuries in making their experiments with different methods of concentration, meditation and relaxation; with various breathing processes, postures and foods. When they finally succeeded in their experiments, they systematized the result of their findings and called it the science of Yoga. The aim of Yoga is to achieve reintegration of the individual consciousness with the cosmic consciousness.[40]

The aim of Yoga is to completely alter one's personality and outlook so that he is able to face all problems of life with equanimity, while pursuing to achieve the ideals which he cherishes. It is a complete break with normal waking consciousness. It is neither a condition of vain pursuits and frustrations of waking life, nor a condition of mere dreaming, nor even condition of absence of quality as in deep sleep, but a condition of calmness and tranquility of mind in daily pursuits. As Gita describes with an analogy, he is one into whom all desires enter as waters into these and is ever motionless though constantly being filled (11.70). He enjoys and suffers like all human beings; he has passions, fears and rages like all human beings; but unlike the ordinary human beings, he is able to maintain tranquility through them all.

Swami Lokeshwarananda feels that, "The world-wide interest which yoga has aroused is encouraging, but is not without its dangers. Already yoga centres have cropped up in many places in India and abroad, where yoga is being taught by people least qualified to do so. If yoga were only a physical exercise, no serious objection could be raised against this; but yoga is an integrated science whose sole purpose is to help to improve his spiritual life. At the moment, yoga's popularity rests on the proven physical benefit it brings. It keeps the body slim, strengthens the digestive organs, keeps off common diseases like colds, helps one preserve one's youth and beauty, and so on. The claim is also made that it can cure more serious diseases, but the claim has yet to be tested. As man's chief worry is about his body, no wonder yoga is becoming increasingly popular. More and more people are crowding round these yoga centres, hoping to push back their advancing age or retain their fast-fading beauty. That yoga has a higher purpose is hardly realized. So much fuss is made over its physical advantages that many have now come to think it is nothing but another form of physical exercise. This suits the self-styled teachers because they know little or nothing about its other advantages."

Swami Aseshananda observes that Yoga has been erroneously interpreted as crystal gazing, fortune telling, fire eating, and other types of miracle-mongering. Yoga has nothing to do with any kind of miracles or occult practices. Yoga is a rational method of self-discipline and purification of the heart. "Blessed are the pure in heart, for they shall see God", says Christ.

Conclusion

Systematic and regular practice of Yogic techniques viz. Postures, Pranayama, Mudras, Bandas, Shat-Kriyas, Concentration, Meditation and diet regulations under experts guidance and certainly not from books alone, will go for to build up the lost muscle tone of various organs, glands, nerves, etc. mental clarity, positive attitude towards life, and in removing physical and mental restlessness and physiochemical process as the stress creates nerves disorders due to modern hectic, pressurized, frustrated living.

It has been reported in the ancient literature that Yogic practice brings change in various hormonal and physiochemical process in the human body by operating at the higher levels in the nervous system.[41]

> "Yoga helps in maintaining good health and gives
> resistance, stamina, vitality and vigour to the body.
> Yoga is the best curative and preventive medicine
> Yoga leads to chittanasa which is moksha
> Yoga practitioners should not become Bhogi
> If no Yoga—no health, no peace, no life."

Notes and References

1. Xth Plan of University Grants Commission, New Delhi, 2002, p. 51.
2. Dr. H.R. Nagendra and Dr. R. Nagarathna, News Perspectives on Stress Management, Swami Vivekananda Yoga Prakashana, Bangalore, 2003, Preface.
3. *Ibid.*, pp. 2 3.27.
4. YB ii (2).
5. YS I (2).
6. YS (i) 12.
7. R.H. Singh, "Yoga and Health, Science and Philosophy of Indian Medicine, Baidyanath Bhawan, Nagpur, 1978.
8. Dr. C.H. Sudarshan, Yoga for Better Health, in Nisargopcar Varta, National Institute of Naturopathy, Pune, May 2001.
9. Y.S. H. 30.
10. Y.B. R.M. ii 30.
11. Swami Srikantanada, The Intelligent Way to Yoga, Sri Rama Krishna Math, Chennai, 2001, pp. 30-31.
12. Swami Srikantananda, *op. cit.*, p. 66.
13. Manual of Ethics, 1935, p. 341.
14. Y.S. R.M. YB (i) 46.
15. Y.S. ii 49, 50.
16. Y.S. ii 53, UB RM ii 52.
17. Swami Sivananada, Practice of Yoga Quoted in Swami Devananda, *op. cit.*, p. 60.
18. Swami Vishnu Devananda, *op. cit.*, p. 161.
19. YS YB MP ii 54.
20. YB iii, YS, YB iii 7.
21. RM iii 2.
22. YS YB iii, 4, 7, 8.
23. Swami Siddhinathananda, Yoga in Srimad Bhagavata, Yoga and Its various Aspects, Sri Ramakrishna Math, Madras, pp. 160-61.
24. Swami Srikantananda, *op. cit.*, pp. 7-11.
25. Swami Siddhinathananda, Yoga in Srimad Bhagavata, Yoga and Its various aspects, Sri Rama Krishna Math, Madras, pp. 160-61.
26. Swami Vishnu Devananda, *op. cit.*, p. 177.
27. Bata K. Day, Ethics: Maladies and Remedies, in *IJPA*, July-Sept. 1995, p. 46.
28. Swami Srikantananda, *op. cit.*, pp. 56-57.
29. *Ibid.*, pp. 40-41.
30. *Ibid.*, p. 17.
31. *Ibid.*, 65-66.
32. Swami Yatishwarananda, Meditation and Spiritual Life, Ramakrishna Ashram, Bangalore, 1983, pp. 17-18.
33. *Ibid.*

34. P.K. Hassanagas, "Yoga in the Culture of Labour based on Research", Arya Vidya Sala Kottakhal and University of Calicut, Holistic Life and Medicine, Sixth World Congress on Holistic Life and Medicine held at Calicut, Kerala, 5-7 July 1996, pp. 127-28.
35. Nedungade, V. Hardias, Physiological and Philosophical Aspects of Yoga.
36. *Ibid.*, p. 150.
37. Dr. (Mrs.) Hemlatha Murly, "Management of Respiratory Disease by Yoga." National Institute of Naturopathy, Pune, *op. cit.*, p. 12.
38. Swami Harshanand, "Attainment of Yoga Maladies and Remedies", in *Yoga: Its various aspects*, Sri Ramakrishana Math, Madras, pp. 203-04.
39. Manchanda, S.C. *et al.*, "Research Study of Reversal of Coronary Heart Disease through Preksha Meditation with reference to coronary atherosclerotic reversal potential of yoga lifestyle intervention." A Research Study conducted by AIIMS, Deptt. of Cardiology, New Delhi, pp. 1-8.
40. Swami Prabuddhananda, Yoga in Daily Life, In *Yoga: Its various Aspects*, Shri Ramakrishna Math, Madras, pp. 70-71, 121-22.
41. Dr. C.H. Sudarshan, *op. cit.*, p. 20.

APPENDIX 5.1

The UGC Scheme for Promotion of Yoga Education and Practice and Positive Health in Universities

1. Introduction

Yoga promotes physical and mental health. It disciplines the mind and improves the power of concentration. Therefore, it is ideally suited for those who are involved in intellectual pursuits. The concepts of positive health and lifelong learning are relatively new and need to be strengthened. Yoga is a discipline, based on meticulous practice and requires very modest infrastructure and money. The Commission has formulated a scheme for promotion of yoga education and practice in the Xth Plan and a new component of positive health is being added to this scheme.

2. Objective

To impart special education in various areas like yoga, positive health, career, personality development, etc. for the overall development of students, teachers and non-teaching staff of universities.

3. Eligibility/Target Groups

All eligible universities which are included under Section 2(f) and have been declared fit to receive central assistance under Section 12(b) of the UGC Act of 1956, are covered under the scheme. The target group is students, teachers and non-teaching staff of universities.

4. Nature of Assistance

The UGC will provide grants to the selected universities upto the end of Xth Plan period only, i.e. 31st March, 2007. Thereafter the scheme is required to be taken over by the concerned universities under its maintenance budget. The UGC will provide financial assistance as under:

The Universities may charge Rs. 50 p.m. per head as a token fee from the students/teachers non-teaching staff interested to participate in its yoga center activities for meeting the recurring expenditure.

Yoga

Sl. No.	*Items*	*Financial Assistance under the scheme*
1.	Equipment/Furnishing	Rs. 1,00,000 (one time grant)
2.	Honorarium to instructors – maximum two (2)	Rs. 1,80,000/- p.a. @ Rs. 7500/- p.m. (Rs. 7500 x 12 x 2 = 1,80,000

The minimum qualifications for yoga instructors shall be as under:

1. Post-graduate degree (full time course) in Yoga/ Yogic Science/Yoga Therapy/Yoga Studies, etc. from a recognized university.

Or

2. Post-graduate diploma (full time of at least one year course) in Yoga/Yogic Science/Yoga Therapy/Yoga Studies, etc. from a recognized university or an eminent institution with a well established reputation in the field of yoga, with a minimum experience of two years in yoga teaching and practice.

Positive Health

Assistance will be provided for organizing 3-5 days awareness programme by inviting guest speakers/experts, etc. These programmes could be from amongst the following:

1. General counseling
2. AIDS
3. Drug Abuse
4. Sex education and reproductive health
5. Art of healthy living
6. Stress management
7. Sound Body and mental health

Any other programme on similar subject/nature can also be covered.

S. No.	Activity	Financial Assistance
1.	For organizing 3-5 days awareness programme	Rs. 25,000 per programme

6

Ancient Scriptures and Values

Paramahamsa Sri Nithananda in its Economic Times article, "Truth is stronger than fact" in *The Economic Times* observed that West has always focused on facts, while the East has focused on truth. As a consequence the west moved forward in science while the east moved forward in spirituality.

When the great sages of the east looked inwards and realized the truth of their existence, they expressed these in the form of scriptures, the sruti and sastra. In order that the common man could understand these spiritual truths, some of these masters wrote the purana, the epics.

These epics created role models who exemplified these truths that they had experienced in a form that anyone could understand. The Puruana had characters like Rama and Krishna who the ordinary person could identify with and follow. These characters were based on truth not on fact. When Valmiki talks about the monkeys that occupied Kishkinda, the numbers he uses are so large that Kishkinda could not have physically held so many monkeys. What he is referring to is the impact of those monkeys upon Rama and his mission. When Krishna as a child killed monsters and when Hanuman lifted a mountain, the incidents were meant to convey the truth and impact of the incident upon human consciousness.

CHART 6.1

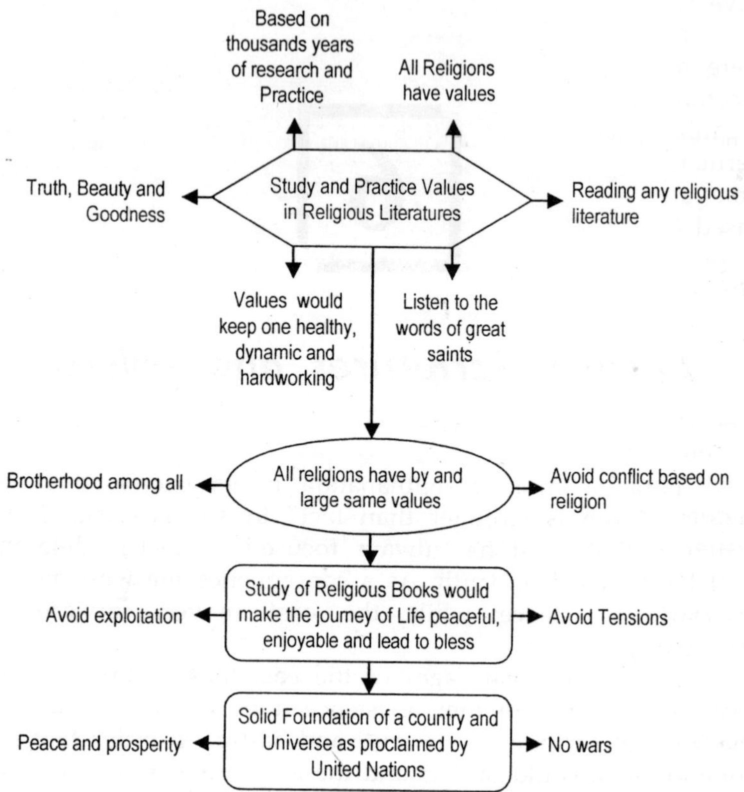

Incidents as recorded in the purana are metaphysical, not physical. They are not factual history but truthful experiences. Our sages recorded not day-to-day history, but only those incidents that impacted upon the collective consciousness.

When a scientist conducts an experiment to prove his theory, he does so in three dimensions. These are the easily understood dimensions of length, breadth and depth. A master goes beyond these in his inner experiments to discover truth. He travels in space and time as well. He experiences, expresses and records what is permanent in different space and time dimensions. It may be difficult for you to grasp and accept this, but this is the truth. This is why our scriptures have withstood the test of time and cultures.

Expressions of the experiences of our great masters were recorded as sruti. The rules and regulations that they recommended based on these experiences for societal organization were the smruti. Sruti was the truth and permanent. Smruti were facts that needed to change over time and space. Spirituality is based on sruti. Religion is based on smruti. Both need to be used for every day life, as theory and practice. However, one needs to understand the difference between truth and facts. Truth transcends facts; spirituality transcends religions.

Paramahamsa Sri Nithyananda in his article, "Idol worship is not an idle ritual" in *Economic Times* dated 28th June 2007 observes that there are two problems. One is that all our sacred scriptures need understanding at different levels of energy, actually seen. Very few are able to understand beyond the gross physical energy level. It is not a matter of learning Sanskrit words. Anyone can look up a dictionary and translate; it is a matter of rising in energy to the required level of understanding.

The second is the loss of connection between our sacred scriptures and the rituals that followed from them; between the sruit and smruti. Without this connection, rituals seem meaningless and are performed without meaning. It is the duty of spiritual masters to reestablish this connection.

Temples have been created not for idle worship. Most of our great temples are built upon or created by enlightened Masters who imbued them with their own energy. When you pray in an energy field like that, your prayers do come true. It is like a projector that magnifies a slide on to a screen. The same way your prayers are projected into reality through the energy of the temples and the energized idols. The energy enables your body, mind and spirit to be focused on what you sincerely wish for resulting in fulfilment.

The Taittiriya Upanishad which advocates the study and teaching of the scriptures, particularly stresses the inculcation of moral and human values. The moral values, rita, satya, dama and sama have to be imbibed. The human values viz., serving the atithi and manusha (guests and other human beings) have to be developed. Education is not mere swadhyaya pravachana but the concurrent practice of rita, satya, dama, sama, etc., along with study and learning.[1]

The guidelines and the programmes for the implementation of the moral and human values in Indian thought will give an idea of the earnest effort of our forefathers to foster these values in all walks of life. They bestowed sufficient thought on the basic nature of man, took into account his noble and ignoble tendencies, the effort he has to make to adjust himself to nature and to his fellow beings. They identified Rita, i.e., the principle of harmony and progress as the basic principle of moral and human values. Man's conduct has to be based on this principle of harmony. To achieve this harmony he has to avoid the conflict between man and man, man and nature, and within himself he has to avoid the conflict between his emotions and rational faculties. All the moral and human values formulated in Indian thought are based on this principle of harmony and aimed of achieving this harmony that makes life meaningful and worth living.[2]

The social and cultural traditions of India have evolved in the course of thousands of years through the mixing up of the social institutions, customs, values and beliefs of different races and communities. Some traditional values of Indian culture are very well enshrined in well known prayers, phrases or statements, like, 'Satyam, Shivam Sundaram', (truth, goodness and beauty), Sa vidhya, ya Vimuktaye (Knowledge is that which leads one to salvation), 'Sakal Bhumi Gopal Ki' (All the lands belong to the Lord). Our scriptures, religious books, commentaries on niti (policy) and folklore are mines of our cultural traditions.[3]

In the words of Dr. Radhakrishnan: Though faith in the Supreme is the basic principle of the Indian tradition, the Indian state will not identify itself with or be controlled by any particular religion. This view of religious impartiality, of comprehension and forbearance, has a prophetic role to play within the national and the international life. The religious impartiality of the Indian state is not to be confused with secularism or atheism. Secularism as here defined is in accordance with the ancient religious tradition of India. It tries to build-up a fellowship of believers, not by subordinating individual qualities to the group mind but by bringing them into harmony with each other. This dynamic fellowship is based on the principle of diversity in unity which alone has the quality of creativeness.[4]

Ecthoing this conviction in the concluding portion of his Autobiography, astro-physicist R.A. Millikan says:

It seems to me that the two great pillars upon which all human well-being and human progress rest are, first, the spirit of religion, and, second the spirit of science—or knowledge. Neither can attain its largest effectiveness without support from the other. To promote the latter, we have universities and research institutions. But the supreme opportunity for everyone with no exception lies in the first.

Concluding his treatment of India in *Our Oriental Heritage* (written in 1935), the first volume of this series on *The Story of Civilization,* the American philosopher and historian, Will Durant, says (p. 633):

'One cannot conclude the history of India as one can conclude the history of Egypt, or Babylonia, or Assyria; for that history is still being made, that civilization is still creating. . . .

'It is true that even across the Himalayan barrier India has sent to us such questionable gifts as grammar and logic, philosophy, and fables, hypnotism and chess, and above all, our numerals and our decimal system. But these are not the essence of her spirit; they are trifles compared to what we may learn from her in the future. As invention, industry, and trade bind the continents together, or as they fling us into conflict with Asia, we shall study its civilizations more closely, and shall absorb, even in enmity, some of its ways and thoughts. Perhaps, in return for conquest, arrogance, and spoliation, India will teach us the tolerance and gentleness of the mature mind, the quiet content of the unacquisitive soul, the calm of the understanding spirit, and a unifying, pacifying love for all living things.'

Unfortunately, most modern men and women do not know anything beyond the sense-life. Pleasures and material comforts have mesmerized us, as it were. If this trend continues, the whole civilization will collapse, as did the

Roman civilization. Swami Vivekananda therefore warned the West that unless it makes spirituality its aim in life, its civilization would not last. Science and technology cannot give us values. Values cannot come from the body either. This body is composed of the genes, which are by nature selfish; they cannot think of other people. Therefore, we have to overcome this attachment to the body, to the senses, and attain something higher and abiding. We have to seek an answer to the question, what lies above the sensory level? India got the answer from the Upanisads long, long ago. There is one passage in the Katha Upanisad that says that our body has muscular energy, but it is very ordinary, very gross. Inside the nervous system, there is a little more subtle energy. Still deeper is the psyche. That is more subtle, and has more energy. Thus, we find that human resources are organized on an ascending scale of subtlety, immensity, and inwardness. And the highest is the Atman.[5]

Says Swami Vivekananda in his address to the Chicago Parliament of Religion: This period, this capacity to discover spiritual truths, is not a national Indian monopoly; Indian thought holds that it is a universal phenomenon. In fact, Vedanta, or Sanatana Dharma holds that it is this very effort and its culmination that constitutes religion; religion is anubhava, realization and not a matter of mere belief or conformity, creed or dogma.

In the words of Dr. Radhakrishnan (Recovery of Faith, 202):

"Though faith in the Supreme is the basic principle of the Indian tradition, the Indian state will not identify itself with or be controlled by any particular religion. . . . This view of religious impartiality, of comprehension and forbearance, has a prophetic role to play within the national and the international life. The religious impartiality of the India state is not to be confused with secularism or atheism. Secularism as here defined is in accordance with the ancient religious tradition of India. It tries to build up a fellowship of believers, not by subordinating individual qualities to the group mind but by bringing them into harmony with each other. This dynamic fellowship is based on the principle of diversity in unity which alone has the quality of creativeness.

Echoing this conviction in the concluding portion of his Autobiography, astro-physicist R.A. Millikan says:

"It seems to me that the two great pillars upon which all human well-being and human progress rest are, first, the spirit of religion, and, second, the spirit of science—or knowledge. Neither can attain its largest effectiveness without support form the other. To promote the latter, we have universities and research institutions. But the supreme opportunity for everyone with no exception lies in the first.

F. Max Muller observes that if I were to look over the whole world to find out the country most richly endowed with all the wealth, power, and beauty that nature can bestow - in some a parts a very paradise on earth—I should point to India. If I were asked under what sky the human mind has most fully developed some of its choices gifts, has most deeply pondered on the greatest—problems of life, and has found solutions of some of them which well deserve the attention even of those who have studied Plato and Kant—I should point to India. And if I were to ask myself from what literature, we, here in Europe, we who have been nurtured almost exclusively on the thoughts of Greeks and Romans, may draw the corrective which is most wanted in order to make our inner life more perfect, more comprehensive, more universal, in fact more truly human, a life, not for this life only, but a transfigured and eternal life—again I should point to India.

That very hope will give light to our minds, strength our hearts, and steadiness to our feet. That hope cannot find a better expression, and this talk cannot find a more fitting conclusion, than in the following exhortation of Swami Vivekananda made in the course of his lecture on 'The Mission of the Vedanta' delivered in Kumbakonam in 1897 (Complete Works of Swami Vivekananda, Vol. III, p. 193).

Teach yourselves, teach everyone his real nature; call upon the sleeping soul and see how it awakes. Power will come, glory will come, goodness will come, purity will come, and everything that is excellent will come, when this sleeping could (of man) is roused to self-conscious activity.

Swami Ranganathananda in his book, "Man the known and Man the Unknown" observes that the Chhandogya

Upanishad formula said: Tattwamasi, tattwamasi. When I consider myself as a machine, as a body, the Upanisads gently reminds me of the truth: "Don't equate yourself with things or the body-mind-complex. This is not your true dimension. There is something higher—'there is man the unknown beyond man the known'. What a beautiful conception it is! I only wish to say that the German philosopher Kant, was the first to distinguish between two rivers of knowledge—phenomenon and the noumenon. Whatever is revealed through senses is called phenomenon and its plural is 'phenomena'. Behind the phenomena is this 'noumena', the thing in itself, as he put it in German. But that thing in itself is unknown and unknowable. Vedanta said long before that it is unknown but not unknowable. Why? It is your own Self; it is not a thing to be known. 'You are the knower, you are the infinite one', that is the language of Vedanta. "Don't make yourself as an object. You are the Eternal Subject, ever free'.

Vedas

Says Swami Vivekananda in his address to the Chicago Parliament of Religions: "By the Vedas no books are meant. They mean the accumulated treasury of spiritual laws discovered by different persons at different times. Just as the law of gravitation existed before its discovery and would exist if all humanity forgot it, so it is with the laws that govern the spiritual world. The moral, ethical, and spiritual relations between soul and soul and between individual spirits and the Father of all spirits, were there before their discovery, and would remain even if we forget them."

The discoverers of these laws are called Tsis (sages), and we honour them as perfected beings. I am glad to tell this audience that some of the very greatest of them were women.

This rsihood, this capacity to discover spiritual truths, is not a national Indian monopoly; Indian thought holds that it is a universal phenomenon. In fact, Vedanta or Sanatana Dharma holds that it is this very effort and its culmination that constitutes religion; religion is anubhava, realization, and not a matter of mere belief or conformity, creed or dogma.

All animals have awareness of the outer world, but only man has awareness of the inner world. This has exposed a wonderful dimension in the heart of nature which it is the duty of science to explore. The scientific need for this exploration is backed by the entire development of biology during the last hundred years. In man, nature has disclosed a 'within' view of itself by itself. This recognition was lacking in science till now; and its recognition now is bound to put modern science on the track of that deepest mystery of all existence—the true Self of man. Man appears as a miniature edition of nature; and in man, with his mysterious properties of thought, ego, self-awareness, and moral awareness, the scientific mind has got scent of the deep mystery of nature thus revealed.

And this was what Vedanta succeeded in discovering ages ago in India—the 'within' of the universe, the pratyak rupa, or inner form, of the universe, through the pratyak rupa of man. This is what the great sages of ancient India did, and a few descriptions of their experiments, very simple condensed, descriptions, occur in the Upanisads. There is one in the Katha Upanisad (IV:I). A certain bold spirit said to himself: 'Let me try to understand what is inside'. The mind and the senses have the natural tendency to turn outwards. It is a mighty task to turn them inwards. But this man was a dhira—a hero, courageous and intelligent. He found the pratyat-atman, the inner self, which is also the self of the universe, by the tremendous technology of turning the mind and senses within. By training the mind, and turning its energy inwards, step by step, in a scientific detached manner —it is a stern discipline, like walking on the razor's edge (Katha Upanisad II, 14)—we find a new world opening up, a new dimension of the human personality, the birthless and deathless Atman, the Self, of the nature of pure awareness. That was the work that the Upanisads did, that was the work that Vedanta did, and that is the work that India has continued to do even to our time; and the latest of such explores of the inner world were Sri Ramakrishna and Swami Vivekananda.

Upanisads

The principal Upanisads are accepted to be those which Sankaracharya chose to comment upon; they are ten in number and enumerated in the Indian tradition as follows: Isa, Kena, Katha, Prasna, Mundaka, Mandukya, Taittiryia, Aitareya, Chandogya and Brhadaranyaka.

In his lecture on "Vedanta and Its Application to Indian Life", the Swami says: (Complete Works, Vol. III, Eighth Edition, pp. 237-38):

'Strength, strength is what the Upanisads speak to me from every page. This is one great thing to remember, it has been the one great lesson I have been taught in my life. Strength, it says, strength, O man, be not weak, are there no human weaknesses?—says man. There are, say the Upanisads, but will more weakness heal them, would you try to wash dirt with dirt? Will sin cure sin, weakness cure weakness Ay, it is the only literature in the world where you find the word *abhih,* 'fearless', used again and again; in no other scripture in the world is this adjective applied either to God or to man . . . And the Upanisads are the great mine of strength. Therein lies strength enough to invigorate the whole world. The whole world can be vivified, made strong, energized through them. They will call with trumpet voice upon the weak, the miserable, and the down-trodden of all races, all creeds, all sects, to stand on their feet and be free. Freedom—physical freedom, mental freedom, and spiritual freedom—are the watchwords of the Upanisads.[6]

What the Upanisads Contain?

In the Upanisads, we get an intelligible body of verified and verifiable spiritual insights mixed with a mass of myths and legends and cosmological speculations relating to the nature and origin of the universe. While the former has universal validity, and has a claim on human intelligence in all ages, the latter forswears all such claim. All positivistic knowledge contained in any literature, including religious literature, is limited and conditioned by the level of contemporary scientific knowledge. Modification, and even scrapping, of much of this knowledge due to subsequent advances has affected the truth-validity of much of man's literary heritage, including his religious and philosophical ones.

The spiritual insights of the Upanisads, however, are an exception to the tyranny of time. Subsequent scientific advances have not only not affected their truth-value but have, on the contrary, only helped to reveal the rational basis of their insights and enhance their spiritual appeal. This is no wonder, because these insights are the products of an equally scientific investigation into a different field of experience, namely, the world of man's inner life.[7]

According to some scholars, Sankara also commented on an eleventh Upanisads the Svetasvatara. In his commentary on the Brahma-Sutra, he refers to four more, namely, Kausitaki, Jabala, Mahanarayana and Paingala.

Gita

Bhagvadgita which is called the Gospel of Humanity deals with metaphysics, religious outlook and ethical codes recommends a strenuous life but does not give any room for selfish impulses. Gita is the philosophy of karma (action) based on jnana (knowledge) and supported by Bhakti (devotion). Gita implies that the self-effort is the keynote for success. It gives advice to be self-reliant, be bold, be manly and cheerful, do one's duty with a sense of devotion, develop a balanced mind, humility, purity, self-control and service to others. It gives the message that, to fight against the evil is the duty of man, Nishkama Karma or selfless devotion to duty is the advocated value for everyone in the present time. Dharma is the universal guiding force to attain self-perfection and social harmony. Ancient Indian Education was mostly value-based and aimed at the cultivation of such virtues like truth, goodness, beauty, non-violence, sincerity, honesty, respect, altruism, compassion, love and duty. Certain virtues or ethical modes sustain the glory of the earth.[8]

Today, the world as a whole is passing through a supreme crisis in all its history. The old world with its thoughts, opinions, and institutions is in a state of rapid dissolution; none can yet see clearly the shape of things to come. Deeply imbedded in the modern consciousness is a desire for the creation of a stable civilization. Thinkers is the

East and the West give expression to this urge when they speak of the future world order. If the future is to witness the emergence of world civilization, the collective wisdom of mankind has to be utilized for its realization. The greatest contribution shall come not from sects and creeds or parties and leaders, but from the spiritual benefactors of humanity, like Krsna, Buddha, Jesus, and Mohammad. The present world context, with its gushing passions and high aspirations, somewhat resembles the conditions that obtained in India in the age of the Mahabharata war when the message of the Gita was delivered. In these days of conflict, struggle, and confusion, we can have no better guide to show us the path to freedom and peace than the message of the rational, universal, and comprehensive spirituality which Krsna taught in the Gita over 3000 years ago. It is God's message to man—eternal, ancient, and ageless. Momentous problems are there before us which stagger the wisdom of the earth's bravest and best. Let us hope and pray that the new interest that is evident in many quarters in the 'song cesteial', as Edwin Arnold called the Gita may be productive of real and lasting benefit to humanity at large.[9]

Among the leaders of thought and action who have appeared on the Indian horizon, none stands so unique for nobility of thought and versataility of character as Bhagavan Sri Krsna, the great teacher of the Bhagavad Gita. With the increasing popularity of the Gita in modern times, a growing appreciation of the personality of Sri Krsna is becoming evident. In the West, Carlyle, Walt Whitman, and Emerson were the first to respond to the spiritual beauty and philosophic depth of the Gita. Did not Burnouf, the French translator of the Gita, write that 'no greater book has ever come from the hands of man'?[10]

The Gita is not an original work in the sense in which we usually understand the term, though it is supremely original statement of what Aldous Huxley calls 'The Perennial Philosophy'. It is a continuation of the ancient philosophy that you find in the Upanisads. The Gita summarizes the essential teachings of Vedanta and presents them in a popular manner. That is why it has become the scripture of the vast masses in this country. When we study the Gita, we are not merely studying the Upanisadic philosophy, but also the ethical implications of that philosophy. We want ethical guidance, and the Gita provides it. A metaphysics which speaks of the highest Reality without reference to everyday life will not be of us much use to us. Therefore, the sublime ethical implications of the Vedanta are elaborated in the Gita.

From all these considerations the Gita has assumed an importance in our life, and that importance is increasing day-by-day. In his preface to the English edition of the Gita by Charles Wilkins, Warren Hastings, the first British Governor-General of India, declared the 'the writers of the Indian philosophies will survive, when the British dominion and shall have long ceased to exist and the sources which it yielded of wealth and power are lost to remembrance'. Since these lines were written, the Gita has been establishing an ever-widening empire in the hearts of men and women both in the East and the West. Its appeal to the thinking minds of India in the past, is in sharp contrast to the indifference and often hostility displayed by the modern mind to the scriptures and prophets of the world. The source of this power lies in the two importance features of its message— its rationality and its universality.[11]

Duty: The First Stage of Ethical Discipline

To this end, the Gita gives a two-fold advice. Firstly, all work, whether pleasant or unpleasant, should be performed in the sense of duty. What does this imply? That work by itself is neither high nor low, but the preferences of the ego evaluate all work according to its whims. It is at this stage that man seeks for a comfortable life and a comfortable religion. The sense of duty teaches us to disregard the false values which the ego has attached to life and work. This negation of the ego and its values is also the transcendence of the ego itself. This helps us to realize the second characteristics of the saksin, namely, freedom from limited vision or, what amounts to the same thing, getting universality of outlook. Secondly, by not caring for the fruits of our actions or by being unattached to them, we are asked to realize the first characteristics of the saksin, we are asked to realize the first characteristic of the saksin, namely, detachment. The only condemnation of the Gita makes of those who work with various selfish motives is that they are men of small understanding: krpanah phalahetavah, and defines karma-yoga as dexterity in action: yogah karmasu kausalam. It extols this attitude in these words. (Gita, 51) The Wise, possessed of this evenness of minds abandoning the fruits of their actions, freed for ever from the fetters of life, attain that state which is beyond all evil.

In its comprehensive vision of the drama of human life on earth, the Gita ever seeks to impart to man a sense of purpose and direction, which is spiritual freedom and perfection; prevents him from getting stuck up in a static sect or system, by exhorting him to move on and grow and develop; and inspires him with a spirit of active tolerance and fellowship, by gently pointing out to him that the goal is one, through the paths are many. The modern world, with its prevailing confusion of values and ends, has need to capture this vision of the Gita and turn its course, in the beautiful language of the Vedic hymn (Brhadaranyaka Upanisad, I, 3.28); from the unreal to the real, from darkness to light, and from death to immortality:

Asato ma sat gaṃaya;
Tamaso majyotir gamaya;
Mrtyor ma amrtam gamaya

From the unreal lead me to the real, from darkness lead me to light, from death lead me to light, from death lead me to immortality.

The Upanisadic vibrations of truth and beauty, goodness and love, became caught in a later stage in a mighty condenser of personality, who shook up India spirituality and politically during his earthly career round about 1400 B.C. and whose voice continues to shake up even today. Sri Krsna, the author of the Gita, has affected Indian thought and life in such a profound way that has no parallel in India or elsewhere; his influence is both intensive and extensive.

If we abstract the Krsna element from the Indian heritage, it will be reduced to almost elementary proportions.

He has entered into our religion and philosophy, mysticism and poetry, painting and sculpture; music and dancing, into all that pertains to the varied life of a people advanced in culture and civilization. His personality has a charm for all varieties and levels of people. He has been and continues to be the perennial 'pied piper' of the Indian heart and intellect, drawing all to him, our girls and our boys, our saints and our sages, our intellectuals and our artists, our stateman and our diplomats. The Bhagavata Purana of a later age, gave expression to the wonder of generations when it stated that Sri Krsna is God Himself, unlike other avataras who were merely aspects and parts of Him (1.3.28). Where shall we seek for this mesmerism of Sri Krsna, for this focusing of affections and loyalties of a whole people, except in the character of that person and the character of his people?

The great epic, The Mahabharata, illumines the India of a heroic and creative age. The galaxy of its heroes belongs to a wide range of the lovable and the hateful, the righteous and the wicked, the gentle and the ferocious, the admirable and the detestable. The one character that dominates this galaxy, alike by its force and charm as by its loftiness and brilliance, is Sri Krsna. Respected by the sages and loved by the people, feared by the wicked and sought after by the good, full of tender solicitude for the welfare of women and the masses, and honouring those to whom honour is due, the Mahabharata depicts Sri Krsna as a rare hero, at once human and divine, engaged in shaping the mind and face of the India of his time, through a long life characterized by ceaseless activity on the one hand and calm detachment on the other. The Mahabharata describes the tumultuous scenes of national welcome which the citizens of Indraprastha and Hastinapura used to accord to Sri Krsna, their leader, during his rare visits to India's capital.[12]

Values in Srimad Bhagavad Gita

Selected Slokas

Given below are the five verses from Bhagavad Gita (Chapter XIII, from 7th to 11th enumerating the important values. The original Sanskrit test is followed by the transliteration in and the meaning:

अमानित्वमदम्भित्वमहिंसा क्षान्तिरार्जवम् ।
आचार्योपासनं शौचं स्थैर्यमात्मविनिग्रहः ।।

13/7 (Srimad Bhagavad Gita)

Amanitvamadambhitvamahimsa ksantirarjavan
Acaryopasanam saucam sthairyamatmavinigrahah.

Absence of pride, freedom from hypocricy, non-violence, forbearance, straightness of body, speech and mind, devout service of the preceptor, internal and external purity, steadfastness of mind and control of body, mind and the senses.

इन्द्रियार्थेषु वैराग्यमनहंकार एव च ।
जन्ममृत्युजराव्याधिदुःखदोषानुदर्शनम् ।।

13/8 (Srimad Bhagavad Gita)

Indriyarthesu vairagyamanahankara eva ca,
Janmamrtyujaravyadhidukhadosanudarsanam

Dispassion towards the objects of enjoyment of this world and the next, and also absence of egotism, pondering again and again on the pain and evils inherent in birth, death, old age and disease.

असक्तिरनभिष्वङगः पुत्रदारगृहादिषु ।
नित्य च समचित्ततवमिष्टानिष्टोपापात्तिषु ।।

13/9 (Srimad Bhagavad Gita)

Asaktiranabhisvangah putradaragrhadisu
Nityam ca samacittatvamistanistopapattisu

Absence of attachment and the feeling of mineness in respect of son, wife, home, etc. and constant equipoise of mind both in favourable and unfavourable circumstances.

Dharma was then the chief factor that shaped men's lives. As the artistic sense colours the entire outlook of the artist and gives a touch of individuality and beauty not merely to his painting or music but also to his writings and discourses, nay, even his walking, eating, and sitting, so also dharma was meant to give a holy, blissful, loving, and heroic turn to the outlook of its votary and introduce its distinctive fragrance and sweetness into all the activities of his daily life. Through his thoughts and manifold contacts each individual was to evolve steadily and dedicate his virtues to the service of society.

Valmiki has wisely upheld the ideal of dharma which has a comprehensive sweep and which enables its votaries, irrespective of their vocation or status in society, to enjoy inner perfection and freedom while dedicating their virtues to the welfare of others. If this ideal, exemplified by the sage in the motives and activities of his numerous characters, is grasped and put into practice, all the creeds may survive the present crisis, work side by side without the feeling of hostility, and make people intelligent, efficient and self-sacrificing enough to solve the problems of the family, country, or even of the world as a whole.

Ramayana

Rama is presented in every context as the ideal man. There were occasions on which the great rsis, or the celestials, stood before him with joined palms and urged him to remember that he was the supreme Being Himself. But he seldom moved from the position that he was a mere man, Rama, son of Dasaratha. No doubt he is described as the possessor of all the virtues a man can inherit or acquire, but there is not the least suggestion that he obtained them just because he was divine and not because he underwent the necessary discipline laid down for ordinary men. If he developed subtle intelligence, or philosophic wisdom, and could excel in military feats, or in answering controversialists, or even in singing, it was only because he diligently engaged himself in the study of the respective subjects and in serving his seniors and preceptors of the respective subjects and in serving his seniors and presceptors.

The Ramayana, along with the Mahabharata and the Puranas, constitute the epic literature of India, comprising the Iṭihasa and the Puranas, the study of which has been rightly stressed as necessary for the correct interpretation of the Vedas. For over two thousand years, the Ramayana, like Mahabharata, has been influencing deeply the religious and moral thought as well as the literary production of India. In fact the Ramayana and the Mahabharata are, declared Swami Vivekananda, 'the two encyclopedias of the ancient Aryan life and wisdom portraying an ideal civilization, which humanity has yet to aspire after. According to Macdowell, Probably no work of world literature, secular in its origin, has ever produced so profound an influence on the life and thought of a people as the Ramayana.

The Ramayana gives a many-sided picture of perfect life. We are accustomed to regard such a life as one led far away from the turmoils of the work a day world in some forest retreat and characterized by an unbroken cause of introspection or meditation leading up to a state of mental equipoise or illumination. The Ramayana, however, does not stop with this partial view. For along with the ascetics who embarked upon such severe discipline, we are always shown the figure of Rama himself, towering above them all the honoured by these very ascetics as the special manifestation of the Lord for the protection of dharma. We are thought face to face with a series of difficult, baffling, and tragic situations, and shown how Rama and the other principal characters react to them and ultimately tide over them without swerving in the least from the highest principles of spiritual life laid down in the scriptures. Inner perfection issues out in virtuous action which overcomes evil and transforms the evil-doer is thus Valmiki's main theme.

Ramayan is an ideal scripture which suggests as to how family, social and national values can create an ideal state popularly known as Ram Rajya. In such a state there is no scope of any problem—law and order poverty, social conflicts and justice. We shall discuss briefly some values enshrined in Ramayana which can be a source of solace to the present day world engulfed in crisis of all types. Ramayana's approach to all problems were based on ethical and moral values which are a product of remuneration. When Lord Rama was asked to go to priests for fourteen years, his brothers, mothers got annoyed and wanted him to disobey the king and get control of the whole kingdom. On keeping the views of his family members Lord Rama remembered:

If this kingdom and all that we experience, including our bodies, were true in the ultimate sense, then it would have been proper for your to make an effort on the lines proposed by you.

- Enjoyments are momentary like streaks of lightning appearing in the clouds. So also is life—it is like a small drop of water sprinkled on a red hot piece of iron.
- For men in the grip of the serpent of Time, To long for these extremely temporary enjoyments is like what it is for a frog to cry for food when it is already in the mouth of a serpent.
- Man struggles day and night in various kinds of work for securing objects of enjoyment for his body. But, the truth is that the body is different from the true Self.
- For all creatures, extremely temporary is the association with their kith and kin like father, mother, sons, brother, wife and others. It is only like the association that the traveller has in a way side inn or even like pieces of wood floating down a river.
- Fortune is unstable like a shadow. So is youth, like a wave in a water receptacle. Sexual enjoyments are dream-like and unsubstantial. Life, after all, is of very short duration, yet, strangely enough all living beings run after these values as the be-all and end-all of life.
- This transmigratory life resembles a dream. It is full of suffering arising from diseases. It is as evanescent as a castle in the air, but yet foolish man goes after it.
- Sunset and sunrise mark the ebbing away of life. We see all around others succumbing to old age

and death. But still man does not realise that this is his fate also.

- Without realising that every day and every night that he is now enjoying, mark the termination of those that have gone before, the foolish and unreflective man blindly runs after enjoyments. He does not realise the rapidity with which time rolls on.
- The contents of our life-span are like water kept in an unbaked pot. It leaks out and is exhausted every moment. Like enemies, many kinds of diseases are ever ready to attack and destroy the body.
- Old age and disease are ever assailing the body, and in their wake death too is watching for the opportune moment to pounce upon man like a tigress.
- In this world you find that man thinks of his own body as 'I'—of this body which is only a synonym for worms, dirt and ashes. With reference to such a despicable thing like this body, he feels that he is a world-renowned king.
- How can this body be the spirit (Atman)—this body which is nothing but a combination of skin, bones excreta, women, blood, etc.? It is extremely changeful also. How can such a body be identified with the Atman?
- Lakshmana! This body for the love of which you say you are going to destroy the world—this identification with the body is the cause of all evil.
- The conviction that 'I am the body' is what is called Avidya (ignorance). The conviction that 'I am not the body but the light of Consciousness, is called Vidya (knowledge)'.
- Avidya is the cause of transmigratory life, and the eradication of it is accomplished by Vidya. Therefore, all who aspire for liberation should every cultivate Vidya. In the cultivation of Vidya, the chief obstructing factors are passions like lust and anger.

- Of all these, anger is the greatest obstruction. For, overcome by anger, man murders even his father, brother, well-wishers and friends.
- From anger arises distress in mind. Anger keeps on tightly ties to the transmigratory life. Anger effaces a man's righteous tendencies. Therefore, anger is to be abandoned by all means.
- Anger is man's most terrible enemy. Desires and longings of the heart constitute the Vaitarani—the river of hell difficult to cross. Contentment is Nandanavana, the forest of Nandana—the garden of heaven. Peace at heart is verily Kamadhenu—the heavenly cow of plenty.

Control your Mind and be Calm

- Therefore practise calmness of mind. Thereby you can avoid having enemies. The Atman is distinct from the senses, mind, Prana, Buddhi and other categories. Pure and changeless, the Atman is the universal self-conscious intelligence shining without the help of any other entity (svayamjyoti). As long as one does not realise the distinctiveness of the Atman from the body, the senses and the Prana, so long will one be subject to the sufferings of transmigratory life, including death. Therefore, everything of the Atman as residing in the heart in complete separation from the body-mind complex. While knowing the Atman thus, follow the ways of the world at the same time. Do not feel distressed. Enjoyments and sufferings befall man according to his operative Karma (prarabdha).
- Though coursing along the flow of worldly life and appearing to be the agent of various actions, one who knows the real Self is never bound by the good and evil fruits of actions.
- Being pure and unaffected within, one is not affected by Karmas. Always remember these instructions.

- Thus you will never fall a victim to the sufferings of Samsara; and you, too, O mother, keep in your mind all these truths that I have spoken to Lakshmana.
- You wait for my return. Your sorrows will not last very long. Living beings who are subject to their Karma cannot always live in the same situation, as different environments are required for the experience of the fruits of their Karmas. So it is not given to them to live always with the same people in the same place. They have to part according to the quanta of Karma coming to fruition.
- Men subject to Karma are like boats caught in a current of water. They go in different directions according to the speed and direction of the water. And after all, fourteen years will pass away like a moment.
- Mother! Abandon grief and permit me to go. If you do so, I shall be able to live in the forest peace.

512: One who acquires wealth by fraudulent methods and gloats over his success is as silly as a person who stores up water in an unbaked clay pot.

514: Real strength of mind in action consists in this, that you must proceed with your work unostentatiously without much publicity till you finish the work successfully. Any other course will disclose your purpose and ruin your cause.

514: It is easy for everyone to declare a precept and say, this must be done in this way, but to act in life according to the precept is very difficult.

658: All blessings in life are born of wealth. Knowing this importance of wealth, if a person hoards it without enjoying it himself or giving to others, his life will become a misery experiencing poverty in the midst of enourmous wealth, and starvation in the midst of plenty.

661: The wealth acquired by a person utterly bereft of

love and sympathy for his friends and relations, who austerely denies himself the enjoyment there of and cannot even think of the virtuous path of helping the poor and needy, will ultimately fall into the hands of aliens who are destined to enjoy it.

661: The praiseworthy conduct of a benevolent wealthy man who bountifully gives to the deserving and needy may temporarily result in the exhaustion of his wealth, just as the benevolent rain which sustains the whole society may be temporarily absent owing to drought.[13]

Real strength of mind in action consists in this, that you must proceed with your work unostentatiously without much publicity till you finish the work successfully. Any other course will disclose your purpose and ruin your cause.

It is easy for everyone to declare a precept and say, this must be done in this way, but to act in life according to the precept is very difficult.

Whatever result a person intends to achieve he may succeed in realizing it according to his idea provided he pursues his end with a steadfastness of will.

In executing an action that is clearly discerned to be the right one, the adequate course must be pursued with the steadfast will without hesitation or procrastination.

A person who possesses all other powers but is wanting in the power of action will not be appreciated as a desirable person by the world at large.

Sikhism

Guru Nanak was born on 15th April, 1469 A.D. in village Rai Bhoi District Talwandi now known as Nankana Sahib, in Pakistan. After marriage, Guru Nanak moved to Sultanpur where his sister's husband, Jai Ram, was in the service of the Lodi administrator of that pargana.

At the age of thirty, Guru Nanak left sultanpur to spend nearly twenty years visiting numerous places in and outside the Indian sub-continent. He saw shops, cities, their markets and centres of pilgrimage. During his sojourns, the

Guru came in contact with the religious beliefs and practices of his times. Through discussions and debate he not only tested but also enriched his experience. The path which he discovered through long and deep searching was offered to all who came in contact with him.

His teachings, contained in Guru Nanak Bani were later collected and preserved in the Adi Granth, the sacred book of the Sikhs. His writings constitute the most authoritative portion of the Adi Granth and are considered to be the primal creed of the Sikh faith.

The Adi Granth was compiled and edited by the fifth Guru, Arjan Dev. It is lengthy volume of 1430 large size printed pages in Gurmukhi script, containing hymns, not only of the Sikh gurus but also of 36 other Hindu and Muslim saints and bards, who wrote between the 12th and 17th centuries. This work was completed in A.D. 1604. The original compilation is said to be preserved at Kartarpur (district Jalanadhar) but the oldest copy now in use is the one which is placed in the Golden Temple the prime Sikh shrine. It was prepared by Bhai Mani Singh under the supervision of Guru Gobind Singh.[14]

According to Guru Nanak (1469-1538) the founder of Sikhism, God is formless (Nirankar). He is the Doer of Good (Sat Kartar). Sikhism is monotheistic, as is taught by the mool mantra (basic chant) of the Japji (morning prayer). God is one, His name is Truth, He is the Creator. He is without fear. He is inimical to none. His existence is unlimited by time. He is unborn, self-existent and can be realized through the grace of the Guru.

It believes in the Sahaj (achievement of equipoise or mental equilibrium). The haumai (ego) has to be transcended. Opposed to the ego is Hukam (Supreme Will), Seva (service), Gyan (Religious and Philosophical knowledge), Sahaj (Equipoise), Nam (Meditation) and Nirlaip (Philosophical Detachment). The Sikh sacred text is the Adi Granth or Granth Sahib, completed by the fifth Guru, Arjun Dev, the final version being of the tenth Guru, Gobind Singh. There are 5756 Shabads or verses.

This holy scripture of the Sikh faith, called variously, Sri Adi Granth (Primal Scripture), Granth Sahib (the holy

Granth) and Guru Granth Sahib is not looked upon by the followers of the Sikh faith in the aspect only of a book or scripture, but as the embodiment in visible form of the essence of the Person of the T[illegible] holy Gurus. Being the repository of the Divine Word [illegible]d, Nam) it is offered worship and not m[illegible] [illegible]ratio[illegible] religious assemblies of the Sikhs, the holy Granth is the presiding Presence; all who e[illegible]r, bow before it and make offerings, which may range from the humblest token of a copper coin to large sums of money or commodities. These offerings are believed to be made to the holy Guru, and are intended to be utilized for the accomplishment of religious objectives and philanthropic purposes. Wherever, the holy Granth is kept in state, with an attendant waving the fly-whisk (chanwar) over it, and recitation and Kirtan (holy music) and other due ceremonial performed, that spot becomes for that occasion a Gurudwara (Guru's Portal, A Sikh Temple). In the Sikh Temples the Granth Sahib is kept, brought out in state, prayers offered in its presence and at night-time taken to a duly appointed place for 'retirement'. It is thus, treated as a sacred Person, the Guru, rather than as merely a book.

The Granth Sahib consists of hymns of devotion to God, inspired reflections on the Divinely ordained cosmic order, the vision of the higher life and exhortation to man towards lifting himself to the state of spiritual peace and the attainment of liberation (mukti, moksha). Its form is throughout verse, built on the principles of Indian neo-classical tradition of music prevalent in northern India. Its language is predominantly medieval Hindi of the Braji variety, with variation of Punjabi, and in general in verbal terms that are akin to the popular spoken forms. In the vocabulary used, a large variety of language—traditions of India are drawn upon, including a fair deal of Persian and Arabic, which in the time of the holy Gurus in the fifteenth, sixteenth and seventeenth centuries had become well-established in the cultural tradition, especially of northern India. These two languages, brought with them by the Muslim invaders and rulers from abroad, had passed into familiar popular idiom, and were employed by the holy Gurus to emphasize the universal character of their message, which was directed to the Muslims no less than the Hindus and others.

Guru Nanak Dev, from time to time in the course of his holy ministry pou[illegible]d forth his vision in the form of hymns which are de[illegible]onal, deeply reflective and morally inspiring. These co[illegible] by hi[illegible] or some disciples to be written down. When he quit this mo[illegible]al world (153[illegible]), he left to his successor in the holy office of Guruship, Gu[illegible]u Angad Dev, a Pothi of his inspired compositions as the most precious legacy, to be preserved and its teachings spread among mankind. Guru Angad Dev, whose period of apostleship lasted from 1539 to 1552 added some compositions of his own, though their volume is slender. He was mainly amplifying the deeper meaning and significance of the teachings of the Master. His successor, the aged Guru Amar Das (period of holy ministry, 1552-1574) with the fervour of inspired devotion, added a large volume of sacred poetry (bani) to what he inherited from Guru Nanak Dev and Guru Angad Dev, and gave expression to deep devotion, philosophy and the higher moral vision. In his life-time he collected the entire body of sacred verse of his own composition and of his predecessors, along with the compositions of some of the Bhaktas or saint-poets of India whose teachings accorded in principle with those of Sikhism. This entire body of sacred verse was recorded in two volumes or Pothis which are still extant with the descendants of the Guru. These became, when some years later the holy Granth Sahib came to be compiled, the matrix for the sacred Volume itself.[15]

Guru Nanak was a spiritual teacher with a difference because he believed that the world was worth living. Instead of denouncing the world as unworthy he advocated that it was possible to live pure among the impurities of world through 'a disciplined worldliness.'

> "As the lotus live the detached in water
> Or as the duck floateth carefree on the stream,
> So doth one cross the sea of life by attuning himself
> To the world and enshrining the Lord in the heart.'

Guru Nanak disapproved of the practice of those who unwilling to fight the battle of life under the pretence of cultivating spirituality and shied away from worldly responsibilities. In the words of Payne, 'Guru Nanak realised that religion if it is to be a living force must be a practical religion, one that teaches mankind not how to escape from world but how to live worthily in it, not how evil is to be avoided but how it is to be met or overcome.' After completing his five long Udasis, Guru Nanak himself settled down at Kartarpur. Here, he led a normal family life and discharged secular functions as householder, for his wife and his two sons lived with him. The combination of 'piety and practical activity' exemplified in the life of Guru Nanak and his disciples, the concept of righteous living is meaningless except in the context of society. There is constant reference in his Bani to being in the world but not worldly. The ideal is to achieve saintliness as a member of society, to have a spiritual existence with the necessary material requisites—'rajmen jog kamayo.' According to Guru Nanak, his disciples should have a longing to meet Him (God) and thus only can they abide 'pure amid the impurities of the world.' In this way, Guru Nanak enjoined upon his devotees that while living in the world, they should maintain an absolute purity —purity of thought, word and deed.

According to Guru Nanak, the individual should devote himself whole-heartedly to the all pervading, Omnipresent, Omnipotent and Omniscient Lord and should lead a family and social life. Emphasis was laid on the life of a householder, all the ascetic orders were decried Asceticism exhibits defeatist mentality and passivity. It may lead to several evils and vices. One must work hard to earn one's livelihood and not to depend upon the mercy of others. Guru Nanak said, 'Those who work hard for their livelihood and give something in charity to the deserving can alone recognise the path leading towards the Lord.' The individual has not only to perform duties for self but also for his family and society. The service of humanity leads us towards the lord. This is the social aspect of the spiritual culture of Guru Nanak Bani.

Guru Nanak preached universal brotherhood and amity

among communities and nations. He advocated abolition of all distinctions based on caste and creed for he said:

> 'Call every one as high none is low for God,
> The only potter had fashioned all alike
> And his light pervades all creation,
> Whom call high and whom low,
> When we see the same God within all.'

Guru Nanak strongly condemned caste system and proclaimed that all castes were equal. To give a practical shape to his teachings in this regard, at Kartarpur he introduced the system of langar (common kitchen) and pangal (persons sitting together in rows to eat, formed the pangat). Here he himself dined with people of all castes and classes high or low. In the langar all dines together sitting on the ground without any distinction of caste, creed, religion or social status. Every one, from a prince to a pauper, was given the same treatment and was served the same food, prepared in the same kitchen and distributed in the same manner. A spirit of sacrifice, service and brotherhood was developed and the langer became a symbol of equality, fraternity and brotherhood. This is both secularism and socialism in the true sense of the words.

He declared that his preaching applied equally to people of all castes. He declared that caste and their prerogatives are not there in the next world and one can gain merit not through his birth in a particular caste but by the goodness of one's deeds. For sometime, he lived and dined with the so-called low caste Bai Lalo. He, therefore, preached equally of men by saying:

'There is one father, we are all his children.' His ideal of equality found practical expression in the common meals (langar) as well as the corporate worship (sangat) of the community at Kartarpur. His dharmsal at Kartarpur was open to all men and women irrespective of their caste or creed.

Guru Nanak advocated equality for women. He raised his voice to get them an equal status with men in the domain of religion and society. The sons and daughters are all the creation of God, with the same light of God in them, says Guru Nanak. He enabled women folk to win recognition as independent social entity and laid the foundation for their educational and social development. At Kartarpur, doors of his Dharmsal were opened for all men and women. Women not only listened to the hymns of the Gurus but they could also sing the hymns and participated in the preparation of langar. For the first time in India, men and women of all faiths, castes and creeds could sit together and eat in the common kitchen of the Guru. Bhai Gurdas says: 'Lok Ved Gur Gyan Vichari Ardh Sariri Mokh Duari, i.e., "A woman is one half of the complete personality of man and is entitled to share his secular and spiritual knowledge equally with him. She is the gate-way to his spiritual liberation." Without her participation in social and religious activities man is incomplete and so is society.[16]

An important postulate of the teaching imparted by the Granth Sahib is the significance of the Guru, the spiritual guide, holy Preceptor. The Guru's guidance being essential for spiritual upliftment of the disciple, all reverence, complete Trust is enjoined upon the discipline to be given to him. The Guru is no ordinary mortal; he is a divinely-inspired being, so completely attuned to the Supreme Being, as to share in His essence, to be identical with Him in spirit. Pronouncements exalting the Guru thus are to be met within the Scripture in several places. This is not man-worship or idolatry of any kind. As in the case of the identification of the Shabda, the holy word with God, the Guru, not in his mortal body which is perishable, but in his God experience is Divine and to be reverenced. In Gurubani, in a member of contexts, Guru or Satiguru also is meant to imply the Supreme Being, whereby confusion of interpretation may occur. The holy Gurus, in order to emphasize their humanity, have often employed epithets to themselves indicating extreme humility. In Japu, Guru Nanak Dev has in several Pauris designated himself as neech (lowly). In another place he has defined himself as becharya (helpless, humble).

In Sri Raga 29, Guru Nanak Dev has delineated himself, in the consciousness of being human, characteristics of a great soul, as a Dhanak, a caste held very low and living on hunting unclean animals and plunder. In this hymns he calls himself a thug (robber) and otherwise denigrates the lower self that attaches to the higher self. Very often the phrase in the closing line of a hymns may be Jana Nanak—Nanak, servant of God. This tradition of humility has descended from Guru Nank Dev to his spiritual successors.[17]

A conversation of Guru Gobind Singh with Bhai Nand Lal is of utmost importance. It gives the gist of duties a true Sikh should perform. Said guru Gobind Singh: 'O friend, hear me, this is a way of life for a disciple of the Guru. Rise in the early hours of the morning, take bath, recite Japji and Jap Sahib and meditate on the name of God. In the evening, join the sangat (congregation) and hear the recitation of Rahiras (praises of God) and the edifying sermons. Those who follow such a routine, always endure. Nand Lal, listen carefully to what I say. In these categories I subsist: the category of the Attributes, the category of the word of the Guru. That which the Guru teaches, men should hear and preach. Men should hear the Word of the Guru with love in their hearts and faith in their minds. This, the form of the Guru, the men should behold, day in and day out. Men should serve each other without pride and selfishness. Those who serve humanity, their service do I acknowledge, as the service of my person Listen, O Nand Lal thus humanity shall be freed and attain everlasting bliss.'[18]

Jainism

Mahavira (Great Hero) is the title of Vardhamana (probably 599-527 BC) son of Sidhartha, a minor prince of Magadha (now Bihar), and of Trishala, a princess of the important Lichchavi tribe of north Magadha. At the age of thirty, he renounced the world, although he had a wife and a daughter. He performed severe austerities in the forests, and at the age of forty-two, obtained supreme knowledge (kaivalya) and became a Jina (conqueror of passions) and Nirgrantha or Niggantha (without bonds). The rest of his life was spent in preaching and in founding a new religion, known as Jainism. Mahavira died at Pavapuri, near Patna. His death was not seen by his followers as they had all fallen asleep. All the lights of the universe had then gone off.[19]

Jainism Thoughts

The special feature of Jainism , as signified by its very name, is to be found in its practical teaching; and the chief feature of the discipline it prescribes is its extreme severity. It is not merely the discipline for the ascetic that is characterized by such rigour; that for the householder also, comparatively speaking, is so. Jainism, like so many other doctrines, insists not on enlightenment alone or on conduct alone, but on both. To these it adds faiths, describing right faith, right knowledge and right conduct as the three gems or the three precious principles of life.[20]

Corresponding to the two modes of inrush of karmas (bhavasrava and dravyasrava) are two kinds of control opposing this inrush, by actual thought modification of a contrary nature and by the actual stoppage of the inrush of karma particles, and these are respectively called bhavasamvara and dravyasamvara. The bhavasamvaras are: (1) the vows of non-injury, truthfulness, abstinence from stealing, sex-control, and non-acceptance of objects of desire, (2) samitis consisting of the use of the trodden tracks in order to avoid injury to insects (irya), gentle and holy talk (bhasa), receiving proper alms (esana), etc., (3) guptis or restraints of body, speech and mind, (4) dharmas consisting of habits of forgiveness, humility, straightforwardness, truth, cleanliness, restraint, penance, abandonment, indifference to any kind of gain or loss, and supreme sex control, (5) anupreksa, consisting of meditation about the transient character of the world, about our helplessness without the truth, about the cycles of world-existence, about our own responsibilities for our good and bad actions, about the difference between the soul and the non-soul, about the uncleanliness of our body and all that is associated with it, about the influx of karma and its stoppage and the destruction of those karmas which have already entered the soul, about soul, matter and substance of the universe about the difficulties of attaining true knowledge, faith and conduct and about the essential principles of the world, (6) the parisahajaya consisting of the conquering of all kinds of physical troubles of heat, cold, etc. and the feelings of discomforts of various kinds of cariole.

Next to this we come to nirjara or the purging off of the karmas or rather their destruction. This nirjara also is of two kinds, bhavanirjara and dravyanirjara. Bhavanirjara means that change in the soul by virtue of which the karma particles are destroyed left. When all the karmas are destroyed moksa or liberation is affected.

It may not be out of place to mention here that though the karmas of man are constantly determining him in various ways yet there is in him infinite capacity or power for right action, so that karma can never subdue this freedom and infinite capacity, though this may be suppressed from time to time by the influence of karma. It is thus that by an exercise of this power man can overcome all karma and become finally liberated. If man had not this anantavirya in him he might have been eternally under the sway of the accumulated karma which secured his bondage. But since man is the repository of this indomitable power the karmas can only throw obstacles and produce sufferings, but can never prevent him from attaining his highest good.[21]

Buddhism

In B.C. 567, Siddhartha, son of king Suddhodhana of the Sakya clan, was born at Kapilavastu. This clan had migrated to Kosala, so we are told, from the peninsula of Sind. Siddhartha left the world and adopted the vow of asceticism in B.C. 532. In B.C. 522, he began to preach in Magatha during the reign of Bimbisara, and was known by the name of the 'Buddha'. To suppress all desire and thereby to reach nirvana was the tenet that he preached. But owing to the prevalence of the Shaiva and Vaishnaya systems of belief, Buddhism was never able to make much headway in India. On the other hand, its influence was deep and widely felt in Tibet, China, Ceylon, and the Sunda islands. Buddha died in B.C. 487.[22]

Buddha (probably 563-483 B.C.) was born of a princely, oligarchic family, the Shakyas. His father Suddhodana's capital, was at Kapilavastu on the Indo-Nepal border, to the north of Basti district of modern Uttar Pradesh, in north India. Like Vardhaman Mahavira, he was a Kshatriya, or of the warrior class. Before his birth, his mother Mahamaya, had a dream that a great white elephant with a lotus flower in his trunk had entered her side. He was born in the Lumbini Gardens in Kapilvastu, while his mother was on her way to her parents' home, for confinement. She died at childbirth. At birth he stood upright, took seven steps and said, "This is my last birth."

It has been said that "the total literature of Buddhism is so large that it is quite impossible for a single individual to master it in his lifetime." But his basic teachings are simple enough. These are the Four Noble Truths:

(i) Life is full of suffering.
(ii) Suffering is caused by desire.
(iii) Only the elimination of desire can lead to a cessation of suffering.
(iv) Desire can be eliminated through the Eightfold Path.

The Eightfold Path

1. Right view—knowledge of the Four Noble Truths.
2. Right Aim—non-resentment, harmlessness, renunciation.
3. Right Speech—no lying, abusing, backbiting, idle talk.
4. Right Action—non-violence, no taking what is not given, no wrongdoing in sexual matters.
5. Right Living—giving up wrong living, livelihood by right living (for instance), giving up sale of liquor and dealing in animals for butchery).
6. Right Effort—creation of good conditions,
7. Right Mindfulness—self-control, thoughtfulness for others, etc.
8. Right Contemplation—calm contemplation in solitude.

(Digha Nikaya 11.312).

Rules for Monks (from the Khuddaka Patha)

- Avoid the taking of life.
- Avoid taking what is not given.
- Avoid unchastity.
- Avoid falsehood.
- Avoid fermented liquor, distilled liquor and intoxicants, giving rise to sloth.
- Avoid highly spiced meals.
- Avoid dancing, singing, playing music and seeing shows.
- Avoid the use of flowers, scents and unguents and the wearing of ornaments and decorations.
- Avoid the use of raised beds and wide beds.
- Avoid the accepting of gold and silver.[23]

According to Buddhist teaching, correct insight or right understanding is the first in the series of Eight Noble Steps leading to complete emancipation of a human being. This is called the Middle Path of Noble Eightfold path. These eight are:

(i) Right Understandings

Attainment of the knowledge and skill to know and see things as they really are. That is to acquire correct views about the world and significance of life.

(ii) Right Thoughts

Right understanding leads to thoughts of renunciation, good-will and non-violence in a determination to foster noble aspiration and endeavour and to be free from malice and ill-will.

(iii) Right Speech

Abstention from every kind of falsehood, slander, rude machinations and abusive language, foolish talk, chatter and gossip.

(iv) Right Action

Peaceful, honourable and pure in action and abstinence from injury to any living being, stealing, sexual lust, falsehood and intoxicants.

(v) Right Livelihood

Abandonment of wrong occupations and earning one's livelihood only by right methods. Specially mentioned as non-conducive to self-realisation are selling weapons of war, butchery, prostitution, slave-traffic and purveying of poisons and intoxicating drugs.

(vi) Right Effort

Suppression of evil and cultivations of good through assiduous self-discipline.

(vii) Right Mindfulness of Awareness

Self-mastery over all one's actions through constant awareness

(viii) Right Concentration

Mental equipoise of the state where one's whole body and mind are permeated with a feeling of purity and peace.[24]

The Main Tenets of Islam

The founder of Islam was the Prophet Muhammad (570-632). His teaching is known as Islam, or submission to Allah or God. Those who so submit, are known as Muslims. We know about Muhammad and his teachings from the Al Quran or Koran (Reading, Recitation) and the Hadith or Hadis, sayings of the Prophet.

The principal bases on which the Islamic system is founded are: (i) An inner consciousness and belief in the unity of God. His majesty, His immateriality, His mercy and His supreme love and power; (ii) Charity and brotherhood of mankind; (iii) Subjugation and regulation of the passions and natural instincts and tendencies by the exercise of intuitive reason and judgement with a view to converting them into moral qualities; (iv) Expression of heartful gratitude to the Giver of all good and the sole Nourisher of the world (Rabbal-Alamin) not only in one's daily prayers but also in serving His creatures as the faithful servant of the Most Gracious (ibad-ur-rahman); (v) One's accountability for all human actions, whether manifest, hidden or contemplated, in another existence and belief in the coming day of Judgement, the final account and rewards and punishments, and (vi) One's obligation to safeguard and promote the welfare of one's own soul as well as the welfare of one's fellow-beings.[25]

Significantly, the Quran declares unequivocally that:

God has sent His messages to all peoples throughout history from time to time and has left none without guidance (35:24, 13:7); all messages have emanated from a single source, the "Mother of All Books" (13"39) or the Hidden Book (56:78); the import of all messages is universal which renders it incumbent on all peoples to believe in all prophets without "separating some from the others" and so none can claim sole proprietary claims upon God's guidance (62:6, 2:94-95)

Values have been laid in Chapter 17, verses 22-37 of Quran:

"Put not any other God with Allah
Be kind and respectful to parents, especially in their old age
Give what is due to kinsmen, the poor and travelers
Be not wasteful
Slay not your children for the fear of poverty
Go not near fornication
Slay not the soul, which Allah has forbidden you to do, except for a just cause,
Draw not near to the wealth of the orphan
Fulfil your contracts, Give just measure and weight, follow not that of which you have no knowledge,
Walk not on the earth proudly."

The main tenets of Islam are given below:

The Four Truths are:

There is no god but God or Allah, the Merciful and the Compassionate and Muhammad is his Prophet. In Arabic this is La Illaha Lil Allah la, Muhammad ur Rasul Allah, Bismillah il Rahim ur Rahman. This is known as the shahada or kalma.

Allah has sent Muhammad as his last prophet, with the truth, which is enshrined in the Koran.

Belief in resurrection and the Day of Judgement (Keyamat).

Belief in taqdeer or predestination by Allah, who in stern but also merciful and compassionate. The judgement is according to righteousness.

The Five Pillars of Islam are:

Belief in Allah and his Prophet Muhammad.

Prayers or namaaz or salat, five times a day.

Zakat, religious tithe, two and a half per cent of one's earnings, for the poor and needy.

Fasting (Roza) in the month of Ramadan or Ramzan, when the Koran was first revealed.

Haj or pilgrimate to Mecca, at least once in a lifetime.[26]

Islam does not depend upon the jugglery of words. Hence I address my Muslim brethren and say unto them; Give up sloth and indolence; open your eyes; seek to realize the glory of the great teaching 'La-ilaha-illallah'; remember the old glory of Islam and devote yourselves to the sacred task of recovering that glory; let the will of the Great God be fulfiled; let the world be again filled with the pride and glory of knowledge; let the pure spirituality of truth banish the darkness of materialism; and let all races, all sections and all religions unite together for the common benefit of Humanity. Let malice, deceit and all uncharitableness be banished for ever from the world; let Nature smile again; let the darkness of sin be removed by the pure radiance of virtue; let the name of the Holy Creator echo and re-echo from the lips of all humanity; let Truth be firmly planted in place of untruth; and let man feel in every atom of his being the play and pulsation of God's mighty force. Yea, let Islam's deep and hidden purpose be realized everywhere.

O Master of the universe, set Thy wheel rolling again so that the lost glory of Islam may be recovered; that Jews,

Christians and Hindus—perusing the ancient records of Islam —may unite again in singing her glory and praise; that the Old world and the New may testify in one voice to the deep truth and beauty of Islam; that the worship of the one true God may be established in every village, city and house-hold; that skepticism and all unfaith may be banished for ever from the world; that Asia, Europe, Africa and America may be united in a vast federation of Humanity that the nations of the earth—inspired with a feeling of Divine compassion and forgetful of malice, hatred and ill-will—may embrace one another in love and charity; that Jews, Christians, Hindu and Muslims may join together in fulfiling God's purpose towards mankind; yea, that Heaven indeed may come down on Earth. (Amen)[27]

The influence of the Upanisads on Indian Islam has not been very profound in the past. Even though Sufism, the mystical offshoot of Islam, owes much to the Upanisads, Islam as a whole, which has been generally hostile to its own offshoot as to all non-Islamic faiths, has remained largely unaffected. Prophet Mohammed was a deep lover of God and man. And he has breathed this double love into the *Koran*. Below are given a few verses taken from the English translation of the *Koran* by AlHaj Hafiz Ghulam Sarwar.

The following three verses singing the glory of God can be found repeated in any number of verses in the Vedas and the Upanisads. The opening verses of the *Koran* possess rare spiritual majesty and beauty:

(We commence) with the name of God
The most Merciful (to begin with)
The most Merciful (to the end)
All praise belongs to God,
Lord of all the worlds,
The most Merciful (to begin with),
The most Merciful (to the end).
Master of the day of Judgement.
Thee alone do we serve,
And Thee alone do we ask for help.
Guide us on the right path,
The path of those upon whom be Thy blessings,

Not of those upon whom be (Thy) wrath,
Nor of those who are lost.

In verse 255 of Chapter 2, we read about the power and glory of God:

God!
There is no deity but He,
The Ever-living,
The All-sustaining:
Slumber overtakes Him not,
Nor sleep.
To him belongs
What is in the heavens,
And what is in the earth.
Who is there to second anyone before Him
Except with His authority?
He knows what is in front of them,
And what is behind them;
And they encompass nothing of His knowledge
Except what He pleases;
And his power extends over the heavens and the earth;
And the guardianship of these tires Him not,
And He is
The Uppermost,
The Highest.

Verse 25 of Chapter 3 sings the majesty of God:

Say, 'O God! Master of the kingdom,
Thou givest the kingdom to whorn Thou pleasest,
And Thou snatchest the kingdom from whom Thou pleasest;
And Thou exaltest whom Thou pleasest,
And Thou abasest whom thou pleasest;
In thy hand is all good:
Thou art capable of doing all Thou pleasest'.

The *Koran* contains specific mention that salvation is not the monopoly of the Muslims. Verse 62 of chapter 2 says:

As to those who believe (in the *Koran*),
And the Jews,
And the Christians,
And the Sabians —
Whoever believes in God
And the future day
And does good,
For such, then, there is a reward with their Lord,
And there shall be no fear on them,
Nor shall they grieve.

The *Koran* insists that the only condition to be fulfiled to obtain divine mercy is good life and good deeds and not subscription to a creed *(ibid.,* 2,177):

There is no virtue in your turning your faces
Towards the East or the West,
But virtuous is he who believes in God,
And (in) the future day,
And (in) the messenger-spirits,
And the Book,
And the Prophets;
And he who gives his wealth, in spite of his love for it,
To the near of kin,
And the orphans,
And the needy,
And the wayfarer,
And the beggars,
And in ransoming the slaves;
And who keeps up the prayer,
And pays the stated alms;
And those who fulfil their covenants when they covenant;
And the persevering ones
In hardship,
And injury,
And in time of war;
These are the truthful,
And these! They are the reverent.

The prophet had set a high example of tolerance and respect in his dealings with non-Muslims. Verse 256 of Chapter 2 of the *Koran* upholds religious toleration and fellowship:

> Let there be no compulsion in religion,
> The right path has surely been made distinct from the wrong,
> Then whoever disbelieves in the transgressor,
> And believes in God,
> He has, then, got hold of the firm handle.
> No breaking therefore: And God is Hearing, Knowing.

Verse 135 of Chapter 4 (also verse 8 of Chapter 5) emphasizes justice and equity in inter-personal relations:

> O ye who believe!
> Be maintainers of justice,
> Witnesses for the sake of God,
> And though it be against yourselves,
> Or your parents,
> And your relations.
> Whether a person be rich or poor,
> Then God is nearer to them (than you),
> Therefore follow not (your) low desires,
> Lest you do not do justice.
> And if you distort (the evidence),
> Or keep away,
> Then, surely, God knows well what you do.

According to Prophet Mohammad (SAS), of all the gifts that parents can give to their children, the best is the gift of a liberal education. The link in the pens of students is purer and nobler then even the blood of martyrs.

The Mughal rulers who followed the early Muslim rulers had relatively greater interest in education, and hence it was in this later period that education developed more adequately. Akbar authorized the translation of many important Indian texts, including the Mahabharata, the

Ramayana, Atharveda and Lilawati into Persian. Akbar's deep interest in education is highlighted by Abul Fazals comments in the famous works "Ain-e-Akbari" to the effect that in every country, and especially in India, emphasis was laid upon imparting education in moral values. Arithmetic, political arithmetic; agriculture, medicine, logic and physical, mathematical and divine philosophy to every student.[28]

Christianity

The Christian era begins with the birth of Jesus Christ. But many scholars believe that he was born in 4 BC. According to Matthew and Luke, he was born in the little town of Bethlethem, somewhat to the south of Jerusalem. But he was brought up in Nazaret, south west of the Sea of Galilee. His mother was Mary and his father Joseph, a humble carpenter. He had a number of brothers and sisters. Christians believe that Joseph was only his foster-father, and he was really born of the Holy Ghost (Spirit).

In his famous Sermon on the Mount to his disciples, Jesus Christ gave his first address and teaching of the human values to be pursued by them.

> "How blest are those who hunger and thirst to see right prevail; they shall be satisfied.
> How blest are those who show mercy; mercy shall be shown to them.
> How blest are those whose hearts are pure; they shall see God.
> How blest are the peace makers; god shall call them his sons.
> How blest are those who have suffered persecution for the cause of right; the kingdom of Heaven is theirs" (Mathew: 5:6-10).

The specifically sacred book of the Christians is the New Testament of the Bible. It consists of twenty-seven chapters, including the Gospels of Saints Matthew, mark, Luke and John; the Acts of the Apostles; the epistles or letters of Paul and of James. Peter, John and Jude; and the Revelations.

Cardinal Concepts

The Trinity: the Father, Son and the Holy Ghost, one substance in three persons.
The Incarnation: God became man in the person of Christ.
The Fall: Adam's sin doomed mortal man to the loss of fellowship, with God.
The Virgin Birth: Jesus was born out of Mary, by way of Immaculate Conception.
The Dual Nature of Christ, at once God and Man.
The Atonement: God, as Christ: died as a man, to redeem the whole human race.
Grace: God gave man spiritual assistance to escape sin.
Resurrection: Christ, having risen from the grave, gave promise of immortality to believers.
The divine foundation of the Church.
The Second Coming: the return of Christ to judge the quick ('living') and the dead.
Eucharist
The Seven Sacraments

Views of scholars

Albert Einstein, "The religion of the future will be a cosmic religion. It should transcend a personal God and avoid dogmas and theology. Covering both the natural and the spiritual, it should be based on a religious sense arising from the experience of all things, natural and spiritual as a meaningful unity. Buddhism answers this description. . . If there is any religion that could cope with modern scientific needs it would be Buddhism."

Abraham Maslow observes—"If we want to know the possibilities of spiritual growth, value growth or moral development in human beings, then I maintain that we can learn most by studying our most moral, ethical or saintly people."

Napoleon was a great man of power and energy who used the sword to get everything done. When he was a British prisoner in the island of Saint Helena, he had time to think and assess his life. As a result, he gave the following thoughtful statement: 'There are two powers in this world—the spirit and the sword. The spirit has always vanquished the sword. Alexander, Julius Caesar, Charlemagne, and myself constructed great empires. On what did these empires depend? On the sword, and all of them have perished. Jesus alone founded an empire on the Spirit, on love. And even today, there are millions who will die for him.

Creative and happy human interactions confined to one nation is called enlightened citizenship. We consider that such citizenship is not the highest reach of human growth, even in the political and social field. It becomes highest only when it breaks down all national barriers to human neighbourliness, and becomes international and human. By opening one's windows and doors of human awareness to the whole world, national citizenship gently reaches out to world citizenship. That is why there is nothing negative in our concept of citizenship or patriotism. But it needs to be understood that a cheap and shallow cosmopolitanism is not true internationalism. Such cosmopolitans are happy wherever they get advantages, monetary or other; and they claim to be international in outlook, and rate low all national patriotisms. That is a very poor concept and attitude. Unless you are strongly rooted in your national consciousness, and discharge your citizenship responsibilities, you cannot develop a robust internationalism. Internationalism is made of sterner stuff than such cheap cosmopolitanism. The road of growth is through nationalism to internationalism—national humanism flowering into international humanism. That is India's concept of enlightened citizenship. This was highly developed in the personality of Swami Vivekananda, as revealed in his life, lectures, and letters. In his Preface to his *Life of Ramakrishna*, internationalist Roman Rolland presents Ramakrishna and Vivekananda as the splendid symphony of the Universal Soul, and presents Vivekananda, in his Life of Vivekananda, as the meeting point of East and West, and as the personification of the harmony of all human energy.

Against this spiritual and thought background, we can expect that no narrow chauvinistic nationalism can ever develop in India. India's philosophy and culture reaches out to the universal and human. We shall, and can, never say that India is always wrong. When India is wrong, it is wrong; when other nations are right, they are right. My country, right or wrong, is called chauvinism, ultra-nationalism; or, as glorification of all things military, it is also called jingoism. Nicolas Chauvin was a nineteenth century French soldier who upheld this theory: my France is always right. We have to distinguish healthy creative nationalism and citizenship from this kind of Chauvinism

India has a great mission to fulfil in the divine plan as pointed out by Prof. Arnold Toynbee, one of the greatest historians of the 20th century, in the following words:

"At this supremely dangerous moment in human history, the only way to salvation for mankind is an Indian way. The Emperor Ashoka's and Mahatma Gandhi's principle of non-violence, and Sri Ramakrishnans testimony to the harmony of religious: here we have the attitude and the spirit that can make it possible for the human race to grow together into a single family and, in the atomic age, this is the only alternative to destroying ourselves."

K.P. Misra, Senior Consultant, Cardiologist and Director, Medical Education of Apollo Hospitals, Chennai delivered the Convocation Address at the 17th convocation of Avinashilingam Institute for Home Science and Higher Education for Women, Deemed University, Chennai, on Tuesday, 8th November, 2005. He said, "Here lies the beauty of synthesizing the two apparently divergent fields called science and philosophy, with the values of a spiritual approach to life. You must in your life bring in harmony, a synthesis, between the majesty of scientific thinking with the beauty of a value system and philosophical process which will be for the benefit of you as an individual and the society and nation at large, and ultimately for the humanity. You may be a great scientist, but if you do not integrate a value system with deep sense of altruistic view of life, love, compassion and kindness, it will be a sheer waste of knowledge and talent and will be of no use to anyone. Similarly you may be a great philosopher or thinker in your own branch of specialization, but it will be only blind superstition and set of dogmatic beliefs if you do not have a scientific bent of mind and a scientific and rational approach to life and thinking. Science itself can be very abstract, dry and purposeless and philosophy can be only Utopian thinking in the realm of imagination without any application and use of life and shaping the destiny of man. Thus we have to integrate science into philosophy and philosophy into science in all our activities asking all the time not only the "why and how" of it, but also for "what purpose", for anything and everything happening in our life." Excerpts.[29]

Dr. Sarvapalli Radhakrishnan observes, "Help the students to think rightly, make them feel nobly, let them do rightly, above all let them posses the spirit of compassion, (karuna), universal love and brotherhood so that we can live together in a global village as "brothers and sisters." In this context Rigvedic wisdom says 'Let us burn our inner wisdom to remove the darkness of society. Let the noble thoughts come from all corners'. If the students are prepared on these ideals, they will not be only civilized citizen to serve the nation but also they will have the potential to save the disintegrating society. They will be able to face and overcome the challenges of terrorism, hatred, communalism and attempt to twist religion for political purpose.[30]

The Dalai Lama observes at Parliamentary Earth Summit, 92.30.1.302, "The purpose of religion is not to build beautiful churches and temples but to cultivate positive human qualities such as Tolerance, Generosity and Love. Every world religion, no matter what its philosophical view, is founded first and foremost on the precept that we must reduce our selfishness and serve others.

History bears witness to the fact that no religion can flourish merely on account of the truth it proclaims nor can the validity of a religion be judged by the popularity or the number of its adherents. The truth or otherwise of a religion too, remains a matter of academic discussion confined to the intelligent few. The vitality of a religion and its ability to influence humanity for all times really depend only upon its adherents setting their personal example of unblemished character in all walks of life by rigorously adhering in practice to the precepts of right living and persevering to enhance the quality of life by spiritual attainments and inculcation of cardinal virtues with a view to giving their best to the whole of the human race. It is by the understanding of the values of life that a scheme of right living can bring man lasting happiness and abiding peace. Perfection in being and perfection in doing is the goal by attaining which man can be true in his goodness. Let us explore the values which major religions of the world in their wisdom have prescribed for their followers as a message of righteousness in order to make them shed away their frailties and overcome their weaknesses.[31]

Mahatma Gandhi says: "I hold that it is the duty of every cultured man or woman to read sympathetically the scriptures of the world. A friendly study of the world's religions is a sacred duty."

Dr. S. Radhakrishnan observes: "We are the heirs of the heritage of the whole humanity and not merely of our nation or religion . . . we should treat all religions as friendly partners in the supreme task of nourishing the spiritual life of mankind, when they begin to fertilize one another they will supply the soul which the world is seeking."

"The living kernel of religion can be found, I believe, in almost every creed, however, much the husk may vary. And think what that means. It means that above and beneath and behind all religions there is one eternal, one universal religion. . .

Sri Ramakrishna proved the equal validity of all religions. This led him to formulate the following three fundamental principles which form the cornerstone of his harmonious approach to the phenomenon of religious plurality—

1. All religions have the same ultimate purpose, namely, God-realization; everything else in religion is secondary. Stripped of all theological trappings, every religion has for its goal the transcending of human limitations to contact the Reality beyond.
2. There is only one transcendent, ultimate Reality which manifests in various forms, with various attributes, and even as formless, and is known by various names. (This, of course, is an ancient

Indian truism. What was intuited by the Vedic sages thousands of years ago has been reconfirmed in our own times by Sri Ramakrishna through direct experience.)

3. The ultimate Reality can be realized through various ways developed by the world religions. Every religion has the inherent power to take its followers to the supreme consummation of human life.
4. In practical terms, these three principles mean that religions of the world are not contradictory or antagonistic to one another but complementary. No one need change one's religion for another or persuade others to change their religion for one's own. Every religion is equally true and authentic.[32]

Swami Vivekananda explains:

Man has an idea that there can be only one religion, that there can be only one Prophet, and that there can be only one Incarnation; but that idea is not true. By studying the lives of all these great Messengers, we find that each, as it were, was destined to play a part, and a part only; that the harmony consists in the sum total, and not in one note. . . The sum total is the great harmony.

It is this "great harmony," the sum total, that expresses itself in different ways:

That one eternal religion is applied to different planes of existence, is applied to the opinions of various minds and various races. There never was my religion or yours, my national religion or your national religion; there never existed many religions, there is only the one. One infinite religion existed all through eternity and will ever exist, and this religion is expressing itself in various countries in various ways.[33]

Conclusion

Common ethical values in different religions

Ethical and higher values in all religions and Societies

have always stood against selfishness, exploitation, killing, cheating, and degrading others by jealousy, greed, lower passions and purely individualistic, self-centered life. The Ten Commandments by Moses with the categorical imperatives of "Thou shall not kill", "Thou shall not lie", etc. form the basis of ethics of the Judeo-Semitic religions. The teachings of Christ returned to pure ethics and reduced the Ten Commandments of Moses into two central teachings of Vedanta:

> Love the Lord thy God with all thy heart and soul.
> Love thy neighbour as thyself.

Unfortunately, clanish attitude in some religions developed some respectability for the killing of non-believers. When non-believers, rationalists, materialists, or agnostics ask, "why should I love God whom I do not know?", Vedanta philosophy answers that God, the infinite excellence, holiness, bliss, knowledge and power is inside all human beings. Man, of course, loves himself. Only the finite man should love the infinite man hidden within himself, and should try to manifest the infinite excellence, knowledge, bliss within. When the utilitarians ask, "Why should I not cheat, exploit, and kill my neighbour instead of loving him, if by that process I feel happy?", the dualists say that his/her God or prophet or book has asked not to do so. The Vedantist says, "Thou cannot kill, exploit, or cheat thy neighbour, because thy neighbour is thy own self." Why does a new born baby get so much love from its human mother? Because a day earlier the two were one. All ethics, all altruistic and humanistic values as opposed to jingoistic, fundamentalist, and dogmatic values are based on the perception of this basic unity of existence.

This holistic perception of life forms the basis of ethics in all major religions. Paropakar (doing good to others) and Parahita Chinta (thinking good of others) are the first two values in Jain religion towards a joyful living. The same path of holistic living was voiced by Buddha to his intimate disciples: "Bahujana Hitaya Bahujana Sukhaya, Lokanukamapaya, Hitaya, Arthaya, Sukhaya, Devemanussanam." (For the good of many, for the happiness of many, for compassion, for bringing goodness and good things of life to all, both for common masses and the rich people.)

In Sufi mysticism of Islam, the same voice is heard in the Sufi utterance "Anal Haq" (I am God) instead of Anal ab 'd' (I am the servant of God). Jalaluddin Rumi says "Anal Haq" means—I am not, he is all; there is no being but God's. That is extreme of humility and self-abasement."

Swami Vivekananda explains the foundation of ethics and values:

Ethics is only the finding of unity.

The Utilitarian wants us to give up the struggle after the Infinite, the reaching-out for the Supersensous, as impracticable and absurd, and in the same breath, asks us to take up ethics and do good to society. Why should we do good? Doing good is a secondary consideration. We must have an ideal. Ethics itself is not the end, but the means to the end.

There are moments when every man feels that he is one with the universe, and he rushes to express it, whether he knows it or not.

This expression of oneness is what we call love and sympathy; and it is the basis of all our ethics and morality. This is summed up in the Vedanta philosophy by the celebrated aphorism: TAT TV AM ASI—'That Thou Art'. The one aim of ethics is this unity, this sameness. The highest ethical codes that mankind has discovered upto the present time know no variation.

"Love everyone as your own self, because the whole universe is one. In injuring another, I am injuring myself; in loving another, I am loving myself; from this also springs that principle, of Advaita morality which has been summed up in one word, self-abnegation. The Advaitist says: This little personalized self is the cause of all my misery. This individual self, which makes me different from all other beings, brings hatred and jealousy and misery, struggle and all other evils. He alone lives whose life is in the whole universe, and the more we concentrate our lives on limited things, the faster we go towards death.

A man of perfect ethics like Buddha and Christ, lived

every moment of their lives for the good of others. Their little individual self was dead long ago. They lived a holistic life of service to others in a holistic universe and felt all the joy and all the sorrows of humanity. "Such a man becomes a world-mover", says Vivekananda, "for whom the little self is dead, and god stands in its place."[34]

Swami Vivekananda explains:

Man has an idea that there can be only one religion, that there can be only one Prophet, and that there can be only one Incarnation; but that idea is not true. By studying the lives of all these great Messengers, we find that each, as it were, was destined to play a part, and a part only; that the harmony consists in the sum total, and not in one note. . . The sum total is the great harmony.[35]

It is this "great harmony," the sum total, that expresses itself in different ways:

That one eternal religion is applied to different planes of existence, is applied to the opinions of various minds and various races. There never was my religion or yours, my national religion of your national religion; there never existed many religions, there is only the one. One infinite religion existed all through eternity and will ever exist, and this religion is expressing itself in various countries in various ways.[36]

The modern world is marked by a widespread explosion of knowledge and tremendous achievements in Science and Technology, coupled with a general decline and reversal of human values as well as an alarming deterioration of moral and mental health both of individuals and societies. The recent spate of crimes, violence, terrorism and drug abuse makes us aware of the significance of human values, without which human life loses all meaning. It is also evident that a mere economic prosperity and material wealth cannot result in a lasting well-being of mankind. The inner strength of mankind springs from within, which seems ill-nourished now. To fill-up the void regarding human values, the richest resources are available in the texts and scriptures of all the religions of the world which have guided people in their thoughts, feelings and actions for ages. Human virtues have been propounded and preached by many great sages,

Prophets and teachers who had perceived subtle truths of human life, for the benefit of their adherents and of those who would derive benefits by studying their saying and advices. Some of their sayings were understood by people in letter and spirit, enriching and elevating them, but some others were not understood well, ending up as mere outward rituals, blind faiths, intolerance with others and hatred for other faiths. More that a century ago, Swami Vivekananda had said: "We want to lead mankind to the place where there is neither the Vedas, nor the Bible, nor the Koran, yet this has to be done by harmonizing the vedas, the Bible and the Koran. Mankind ought to be taught that religions are but the varied expression of the religion, which is oneness, so that each may choose the path that suits him best."

Study and teaching of religious literature of all religions or any religion would help the people to imbibe values which can usher an era of peace, prosperity and no enmity. All the problems in the world would vanish if people follow the values enshrined in religious literature. It hardly matters which religion you follow, but the most important fact is that people of that religion must follow the religious values of that religion. All religions teach us the values to lead a fruitful life. There is a need of constant understanding them through reading the religious literature which can keep us on right path.

Notes and References

1. V. Murabidharan Sharma, "Values" in Traditional knowledge and their implications for modern education system", in *University News*, January 20-Feb. 5, 2006, p. 39.
2. *Ibid.*, p. 40.
3. Tarulata Devi, "The Cultural impact of Vedic Education in India", *University News*, Jan. 30-Feb. 5, 2006.
4. Dr. Radhakrishna, Recovery of Faith, p. 202.
5. Swami Ranganathananda, Srimad Bhagavatan, Kolkata, Advaita Ashrama, 2006, pp. 5, 48, 49.
6. Quoted in Swami Rangnathananda, The Charm and Power of The Upanisdas, Kolkata, Advaita Ashrama, 2006, pp. 8-9.
7. *Ibid.*, p. 9.

8. H.C. Hemamalini, Values of Sustainability in the Traditions of Indigenous Indian Knowledge and their Implications in *University News*, January 30-Feb. 6, 2006, p. 64.
9. Speech delivered by Swami Rangnathananda at the Gita Jayanti Celebrations Observed under the auspices of the Ramakrishna Ashrama, Mysore, Dec. 1934.
10. *Ibid*.
11. Swami Ranganathananda, The Charm and Power of The Geeta, Kolkata, Advaita Ashrama, 2004, pp. 9-10.
12. Swami Ranganathananda, "Eternal Values for A Changing Society", Vol. I, Bharatiya Vidya Bhavan, Mumbai, 400 007, pp. 101-10, 142, 131.
13. Thikkural.
14. Harbans Kaur Sagoo, Guru Nanak and The Indian Society, New Delhi, Deep & Deep, 1992.
15. Translated by Gurbachan Singh Talib, Sri Guru Granth Sahib (In English Translation) Volume One, Patiala, Panjabi University, 2004, pp. xxii-xxiv.
16. Harbans Kaur Sagoo, Guru Nanak and the Indian Society, New Delhi, Deep & Deep.
17. Gurcharan Singh Talib, Vol. I, *op. cit.*, p. xcv.
18. Oroon Ghosh, World Religion, A Comparative Analysis, New Delhi, Minervo Press, p. 220.
19. Oroom Ghosh, *op. cit.*, pp. 84-85.
20. Samyagdarsana-jnana-caritrani moksa-margah-Umasvati: *op. cit.*
21. Surenderanath Gupta, A History of Indian Philosophy, Combridge University Press, 1969, pp. 194-95, 207.
22. M. Ahsanullah, History of Islamic World, New Delhi, Deep & Deep, 1996, p. 244.
23. Oroon Ghosh, *op. cit.*, pp. 87, 210.
24. A.T. Ariyarante in "Inspiration for Sarvodaya from the Buddhist Thought, in Prajna, Bodhgaya Temple Management Committee, Bodhgaya, pp. 60-61.
25. R.P. Dhokalia, *op. cit.*, p. 69.
26. Oroon Ghosh, *op. cit.*, pp. 51-52.
27. M. Ahsanwallah, History of the Islamic World, New Delhi, Deep & Deep, 1996, p. 256.
28. Tahseen, Bilgrami, Historical Review of Indian Education System with reference to Indian Culture, *Univesity News*, Jan. 30-Feb. 6, 2006, p. 48.
29. *University News*, Vol, 43, No. 51, Dec. 19-25, 2005, p. 17.
30. *University News*, March 28-30, 2005, p. 2.
31. R.P. Dhokalia, *op. cit.* p. 38.

32. Swami Tyagananda, Harmony of Religious in Living Wisdom, p. 126.
33. Complete Works of Swami Vivekananda, Vol. 4, pp. 120-21, 180.
34. Swami Jitatmananda, Value Education, Sri Rama Krishna Ashrama, Rajkot, 2000, pp. 42-45.
35. Complete Works of Swami Viviekanda, 1972, Vol. III, pp. 120-21.
36. *Ibid.*, p. 80.

APPENDIX I

The Global Ethics of the Parliament of World Religious 1993

A realization of this need, mentioned in the last paragraph of the preceding section, led some 250 religious readers from around the world to sign their approval to The Declaration of a Global Ethic (4th Sept., 1993). This was drafted by the Swiss-born Catholic theologian of Tubingen, Father Hans Kung. This is a fairly lengthy declaration. The main points are summarised below:

1. A common set of core values is found in the teachings of the religions and these form the basis of a global ethic.
2. We are interdependent.
3. We must treat others as we wish others to treat us.
4. We consider humankind our family.
5. We commit ourselves to a culture of non-violence, respect, justice and peace.
6. We must strive for a just social and economic order, in which everyone has an equal chance to reach full potential as a human being.
7. To change the consciousness of individuals by disciplining our minds, by meditation, by prayer, by positive thinking.
8. Belief in an Ultimate Reality and drawing of spiritual power and help therefrom.
9. A better global order cannot be created or enforced by laws, prescriptions and conventions alone.
10. There will be no better global order without a global ethic.
11. Humans must always be the subject of rights, must be ends, never mere means, never objects of commercialization and industrialization in economics, politics and media, in research institutes and industrial corporations.
12. Every form of egoism should be rejected.

13. Deal honestly and fairly.
14. The participation of all states and the authority of international organisations are needed to build just economic institutions in a socially beneficial and ecologically oriented, market economy.
15. The earth cannot be changed for the better unless we achieve a transformation in the *consciousness of individuals and in public life.* (Italics mine). The possibilities of transformation have already been glimpsed, in areas such as war and peace, economy and ecology. This transformation must also be achieved in the areas of ethics and values.

The global ethic *cannot be a static one.* It should be dynamic and take into account problems, arising out of scientific and technological advancement. This well merits a chapter to itself.

7

Legislature and Values

A great Inner revolution in just a single individual will help achieve a change in the destiny of a nation and, further, will cause a change in the destiny of humankind.

—*Daisaku Ikeda*

Legislature is one of the most important prestigious organ of the Government whose main function is to formulate policies through legislation to promote the welfare of the people after a thorough deliberation and discussion as well as review of the functioning of executive which is subordinate to legislature. Legislators through understanding the needs of people and through intellectual exercise can promulgate such legislation which can be a good pillar for good governance based on values. Legislature can do its job efficiently provided there is smooth functioning of legislature as the work is of highly intellectual nature and affects the every aspect of human life. Deliberations in the legislature require a peaceful and co-operative environment for the integration of view points of all the members. People expect the legislature to come out with solutions of the problems being faced by them in a way that solutions improve the values among the people and promote oneness of the country. In addition, the

Chart 7.1

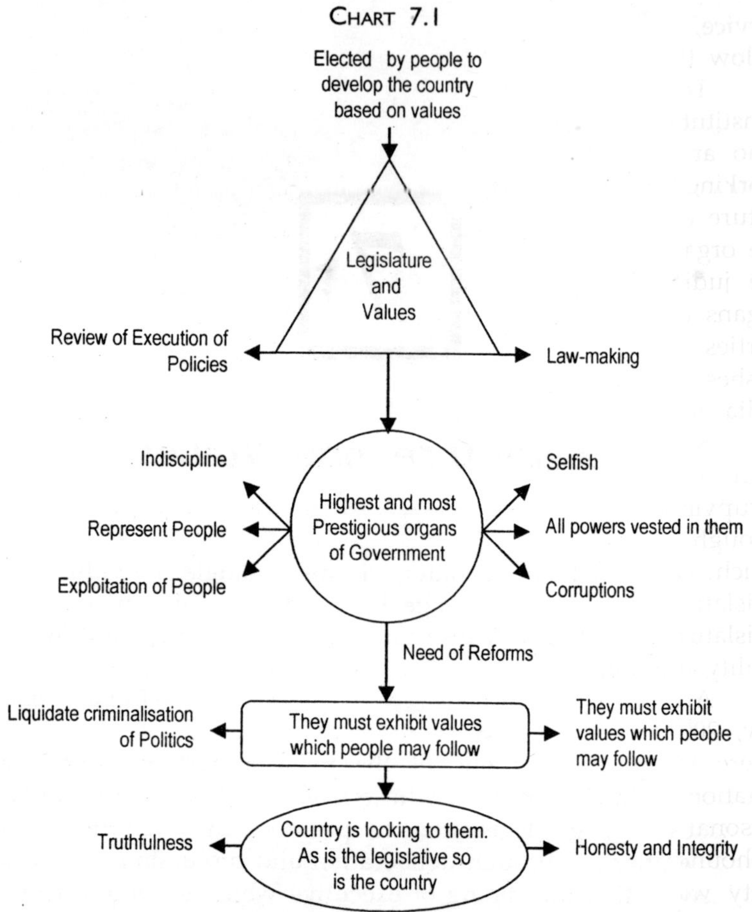

cost incurred on legislative bodies is enormous and the time wasted is money and talent wasted.

"The modern conception of legislation, which results from the growing political consciousness of the mass of the people in whose collective interest most laws are now passed, has given the legislative organ entirely new significance and at the same time raised questions as to the best means of making it do its work with the active consent of the citizens."[1]

Since legislators are elected directly by the people therefore, they must exhibit values of sincerity, selfless service, truth, integrity, honesty, etc. so that people may follow them.

To quote Dr. Ambedkar, "I feel, however good a constitution may be, it is sure to turn out bad because those who are called to work, happen to be a bad lot. . . The working of the constitution does not depend wholly upon the nature of the constitution. The constitution can provide only the organs of State such as the legislature, the executive and the judiciary. The factors on which the working of those organs of the State depend are the people and the political parties, they will set-up as their instruments to carry out their wishes and their politics. Who can say how the people of India and their parties will behave"?[2]

Recently, there has developed a tendency for persons with criminal backgrounds winning the elections and occupying the seats in the most sacred house of the nation through their muscle and money power. This is a trend which can engulf the institution and make the role of legislature insignificant. We need highly talented people in legislature. Since upon their vast knowledge depends the quality of legislation and good governance.

Arun Nehru in his Editorial in *Deccan Chronicle,* 6th July, 2007, observes that we speak of the rule of law, but where is the rule of law? We are heading for a chaotic situations, and an electoral victory is being treated as a personal licence to acquire assets and to use official agencies to hound and harass the Opposition and those within the party who complain about these excesses. The electorate is helpless till the next election. What we need are strict disclosure norms and if these are in place for all three wings of governance then we will not have these embarrassing instances. What we are witnessing is a systematic loot of public resources. The economy booms and as it grows at 8 percent plus over the years, we will see increased criminality in almost every field as effective governance and timely legal actions are missing in the system.

We are proud that our country is a democracy. Casting of ballots at periodic elections in ritualistic manner is not the *sine qua non* of democracy. We tend to forget that there cannot be a genuine democracy without an ethical content and dimension. In the wise words of Louis D. Brandeis, the great American judge: "Democracy in any sphere is a serious undertaking. It substitutes self-restraint for external restraint. It is more difficult to maintain that to achieve. It demands continuous sacrifice by the individual and more exigent obedience to the moral law than any other form of government. Success in any democratic undertaking must proceed from the individual. It is possible only where the process of perfecting the individual is pursued."

The nation today is going through a critical stage in its evolutionary growth. Divisive and destructive forces are on the increase. There is an urgent need for all peace-loving responsible citizens of India to unite in a nation-building endeavor.

Ours is the largest functioning democracy and the oldest living civilization on earth. Since our Independence in 1947 we have made great progress in science and technology, communication, transportation, agriculture, industry and a number of other fields. There is much we can be proud of. At the same time, there are also serious crises facing the nation today.

Though India had won its political freedom and had become a sovereign democratic republic way back in 1947, we Indians are yet to develop a 'citizenship' consciousness. We still continue with our 'subject' mentality, expecting the Government and political leaders to do everything for us. We are angry when the Governments do not deliver results as to our expectations. We destroy public property and disrupt public life to express our anger and disagreement.

India is counted among the poorest and most corrupt countries of the world in spite of her abundant human and material resources. More than 300 millions of Indians are still illiterate. They also continue to live in abject poverty even after 60 years of political freedom. Communal and political violence are on the increase all over the country. The disparity between the rich and the poor are ever widening. India urgently needs a 'Second Freedom Struggle' which has to be much more powerful than the first. All responsible and patriotic citizens of India must unite in this historic task.

Nation-building initiatives and efforts must come from

enlightened citizens of character and courage. When such citizens and initiatives are lacking in a country, that nation is sure to fall into corruption and moral decay. This is what is happening to India today. Responsible citizenship and duty consciousness alone can redeem India.

The responsibility for building a great new India lies with the citizens of India. The government and government servants as well as political parties and political leaders can only help the citizens in fulfiling their duties. Responsible citizenship is the basic principle and prerequisite of true democracy.

Mahatma Gandhi in a letter dated 27th January, 1948 had said: "The Congress has won political freedom, but it is yet to win economic freedom, social and moral freedom. These freedoms are harder than the political, if only because they are constructive, less exciting and not spectacular."[3]

The sight of criminals (having no faith in value system rather subverting the value systems) entering Parliament, legislative assemblies and local governmental institutions is now rather common. The National Police Commission (1997) admitted presence of the creeping evil when it observed: "The manner in which different political parties have functioned, particularly on the eve of periodic elections involves free use of muscle men and dadas (hoodlums) to influence the attitude underlined by the report submitted in the wake of Panchayat (or village council) elections in Bihar. The report painfully observed that the process demonstrated once again that there can be no sanity in Bihar as long as politics continue to be based on caste and gangsterism.[4] According to the computation made by the Election Commission 40 MPs of the last Lok Sabha and 700 MLAs were criminals and had criminal records. According to another calculation, 10 per cant of the total candidates, numbering 14000 in the 1996 elections, had criminal records. Recently (1998), a journal (Outlook) compiled a list of such shady candidates, who have criminal proceedings against them, even though it was not an exhaustive list. The process is going on unabated as the criminal politicians receive protection by the political parties of the land and even more surprisingly by the police and the state administration. As a result, even routine courtesies and norms are systematically flouted. In the Twelfth Lok Sabha, some 10 to 15 Members of Parliament are reported to be carrying fire arms on their person to parliament. In such a situation, voters are left with Hobson's choice; they have in many cases to choose between the scoundrels. Voters are not yet given the right of rejection of all candidates and saying, "None deserves my vote."[5]

As many as 10 ministers in Prime Minister Manmohan Singh's ministry and 93 Lok Sabha MPs face criminal charges ranging from murder to rape, besides extortion and even attempt to commit suicide. A study by the Bangalore-based Public Affairs Centre (PAC) says many MPs from almost all political parties are involved in crime. According to it, one out of 12 MPs have cases that could attract penalties amounting to imprisonment for one year or less while one out of two (over 50 percent) have cases that can lead to imprisonment of five or more years. There is a regional concentration in terms of criminal cases.

Bihar, Uttar Pradesh, Jharkhand and Madhya Pradesh comprise 28 percent of all MPs but account for over 50 percent of MPs with high penalty criminal cases. "A larger proportion of the less educated MPs have criminal cases against them (compared to) colleagues with higher education. Whether there is any causal connection between education, assets and criminality is not clear. Criminal cases are also found to be more among MPs in the age group 36-45."

Nani A. Palkhivala, the eminent constitutional expert observes that "I do not think India, in its entire history of five thousand years, has ever reached a lower level of degradation than it has reached now. . . . The picture that emerges is that of a great nation in a state of moral decay, of which crime, chaos and corruption are three of the several facets."

A senior parliamentarian (Prof. Hiren Mukherhee) speaking of politics generally, bemoans: It will not be far wrong to say, sorrowfully, that there never was a time in living memory when politics and politicians were, almost rightfully, as denigrated, even degraded and sometimes detested, in the eyes of our people as they are at the moment.

The work and conduct of the legislature both at the

Union and State Levels is increasingly becoming a matter of great shame for the legislators as well as the citizens who elected them. It has taken a more serious turn as citizens are viewing their performance on T.V. The legislature passes the law relating to good governance like Right to Information Act 2005, Consumers Protection Act, 1986 and other important Acts which are supposed to smoothen the life of the people. What can be the impact of the legislature when the members composing it are highly indiscipline, and possess no moral conduct and values? This is not specific to any party and individuals. The same behaviour is observed from the opposition to whatever party it may be.

Swami Vivekananda. advice to all is to attain total human excellence which can ensure real progress of the country. This idea of human excellence should be followed by legislators. To quote him (Complete Works, Vol. III, p. 1937) "Teach yourselves, teach everyone, his real nature, call upon the sleeping soul and see how it awakes. Power will come, glory will come, goodness will come, purity will come, and everything that is excellent will come, when this sleeping soul is roused to self-conscious activity."

Abhishek Singhvi, a Senior Advocate, Supreme Court of India, in his article 'Picking on nothing" in the *HT* dated 16 August, 2006 observes that on our nation's birthday, there are many things we cannot be proud of. Indeed, we have enough things to be ashamed of. This is not report card of the nation but looking at one facet alone- parliamentary democracy. A first time visitor to parliament may well be forgiven for being bewildered and disgusted with the chaos and cacophony witnessed in the two Houses. India's temple of democracy is often the hub of pettifogging, shouting and wrangling matches. Automatic opposition to anything and everything is common boycotts and interruptions reduce parliamentary time and efficiency by over 50 per cent at great cost to the nation. This excludes the more extreme examples of some state assemblies where hurling of chairs and chappals and the occasional fisticuffs is known to occur.

B.G. Varghese in an article, "Parliament below par: Serious erosion of credibility is taking place" in *The Tribune* dated 17.8.06 observes that unfortunately, both sides of the

House have been guilty of unconscionable behavior at various times. Those witness to these ugly scenes from the visitor's gallery or who watch the proceedings on television and read newspapers must increasingly fear a continuing erosion of parliamentary credibility to a point when the country will cease to take Parliament seriously.

Members of Legislators whether in the House or in Committees must come out with the solution to problems through action.

Action is the answer—not inaction. Running away from problems in cowardice—and the result of cowardice is sorrow, shame and defeat. Facing the situation is courage-and the blessings of courage are sublimity, splendor and success.

Proficiency in an individual is not creative until it transforms itself into efficiency. The means is to act—to act diligently, with your heart in your work, with a gusto to improve, a spirit to outshine, your own present abilities. This spirit of challenging yourself by yourself is the secret of self-improvement and personality unfoldment. In this subjective competition, those who succumb are the stagnant ones whose development is arrested, success foiled, achievement doomed—alas! by themselves.[6]

Parliament must set an example for good governance as this is the most powerful organ of the Government and represent the entire country. Their concern for the nation would imbibe confidence and strength among executive and judicial organs of the Government Criminalization of politics is degeneration for public life and faith in Governance.

If legislators are men and women of excellent character, they can make all the people of the country dynamic leading to overall development. The Bhagawad Geeta reveals certain definite schemes by which every individual can work out his own self-improvement. The nation is constituted of individual citizens. If the citizens are strong, efficient, industrious, self-sacrificing, then nation becomes great; if the individuals are selfish, immoral, idle and corrupt, it would be a sad nation indeed. In individual redemption lies national redemption and progress. In the Bhagawad Geeta, Philosophical theories are couched in a language of least confusion and she suggests schemes for self-improvement which are unique in their variety and effectiveness. They are most acceptable to the intelligent modern youth—as they are direct, simple, and easy-to-do—exercises for the unfoldment of personality.[7]

Several days are lost in pandemonium and forced adjournments. This costs the nation money, as running Parliament is not an inexpensive business. May be if all MPs are docked their daily allowance for every part day lost to forced adjournments, and double that on the second occasion during the same session, and so on progressively, disruptive tactics might be curbed.

Apart from legislative business, Parliament needs to have more free-wheeling debates on current issues-agriculture, the urban crisis, population, water management, the roots of Naxalism, foreign affairs, security issues, Defense, etc. In this way they can come out with mature suggestions which can take the form of policy-decisions and can become the instruments of good governance.

Parliamentary committees too could take expert advice on key issues as a means of improving legislation or formulating policy. The list could go on. At present the verdict of an old parliamentary reporter is that Parliament is functioning well below its potential.

Lord Krishna Explains:

"Whatever a great man does, that is imitated by all others. What he demonstrates by his actions, that alone people follow. We, as a generation today, do not realise how our licentious actions are leaving behind a trial for the coming generations to follow. The majority of people only imitate. They have not the originality to plan and act independently. Whatever great men do, that is followed by others."

There is an increase in the load of responsibility upon the "leaders" to live a chaste, pure and ideal life—else others will blindly follow them, and the entire community will be shattered with internal disintegration and moral dissipation. History textbooks scream the truth of this law of life in the stories of the mighty men of excesses and their times.

In short, moral beauty, cultural glory, national integrity, creative productivity, disciplined progress and such other virtues must always come from the top to the base of the social ladder. Revolution comes from the bottom to the top; evolutions proceeds from the top and seeps down to the lowest level.

"Whatever the great one (श्रेष्ठपुरुष:) demonstrates in his life, (स यत् प्रमाणं कुरुते) That alone the world follows" (लोकस्तदनुवर्तते) meaning not what the leader say, but what they do alone is demonstrative enough for the masses to follow.[8]

H.K. Dua in his article "Consensus in the way—Prime Minister must take the initiative" in *The Tribune* dated August 30, 2006 clearly states that No democracy can be run without providing plenty of space for dissent and debate on vital issues of the day. A variety of opinions gives better choices and throws up more workable policies. These can give our democracy a good government.

Democracy requires intense questioning of the executive by the citizens, a vigilant Parliament, an independent judiciary, a free Press and the unelected representatives of the people, who are being fashionably called the civil society these days. Their voice must be taken seriously and influence the policies of the government. This will make the State more responsive and give the people a sense of belonging.

Evolving a national consensus will require a capacity to look ahead, tolerance of others' points of view, willingness to give and take, and at times sacrificing personal and party interest for the well-being of the nation.

This approach to governance, in short, has the effect of reorganizing the institutional space, redefining the policy agenda, relocating rights and power and reshaping the politico-economic process. There is no doubt that a lot of rethinking on these issues is called for. The irony, however, is that this is being done in a manner which only reinforces the power of dominant interests—domestic and external—not only in complete disregard for people at the margins of survival but in many respects at the cost of their victimization. Politics is being diffused of meaning and political space is being hijacked by interests which have neither any democratic roots nor any accountability to the citizens of those countries. The need is to revitalize the political space and create possibilities of reshaping the political agenda, making it possible for it to be not only sensitive to but also inspired by people who constitute the wider society and yet continue to be marginalized under the present dispensation.[9] Thus the legislators must maintain and take care of marginalized people to improve governance.

Lord Krishna explains "Whatever a great man does, that is imitated by all others. What he demonstrates by his actions, that alone people follow. We, as a generation today, do not realize how our licentious actions are leaving behind a trial for the coming generations to follow. The majority of people only imitate. They have not the originality to plan and act independently. "Whatever great men do, that is followed by the others." (यद्यदाचरति श्रेष्ठः तत्तदेवेतरो जनः)

There is an increase in the load of responsibility upon the "leaders" to live a chaste, pure and ideal life—else others will blindly follow them, and the entire community will be shattered with internal disintegration and moral dissipation. History textbooks scream the truth of this law of life in the stories of the mighty men of excesses and their times.

In short, moral beauty, cultural glory, national integrity, creative productivity, disciplined progress and such other virtues must always come from the top to the base of the social ladder. Revolution comes from the bottom to the top; evolutions proceeds from the top and seeps down to the lowest level. "Whatever the great one (श्रेष्ठपुरुष) demonstrates in life (स यत् प्रमाणं कुरुते), that alone the world follows" (लोकस्तदनुवर्तते) —meaning not what the leader say, but what they do alone is demonstrative enough for the masses to follow.[10]

H.K. Dua in another article, "Freedom for whom?" in *The Tribune* dated 15 August, 2006 clearly mentions that the headlines in the morning's newspaper or on the television only add to the general despair. The politicians' pep talk continues to sound banal, lacking in sincerity. A Nation of over a billion people is bound to have formidable problems and there is hardly any choice for the country to tackle these problems urgently and move on. The people are ready to lend their hand in the effort but are finding that most leaders across the political spectrum are busy with their petty pursuit of power and all that goes with it. What the politicians do not realize is that neglecting concerns of the people is bound to cost them their standing among the people, who have at times shown an inclination to reject those who feed themselves at the cost of those whom they are supposed to serve. Some leaders are hopeful that India, despite its handicaps, can make it to its new destiny but they are vague about what has to go into it or the route to success. The tragedy is that those who are clear about their vision—they are only a few in numbers—are finding themselves unable to take others along; and those who can do not have the vision but only personal interest to guide them. Over the centuries the people of India have shown a tendency to live with misery and suffering with immense patience. Their tolerance threshold has been fairly high all along. But their worry about all that is happening around them is ominous. It can burst out in anger in the face of the politicians one day. The conduct of the Members of Parliament is often irresponsible and is increasingly becoming obnoxious, irrespective of who sits on Treasury Benches and who in the Opposition. When the NDA was in power the Congress party thought it fit to boycott a chunk of proceedings; now the NDA is crossing all limits of propriety in not letting Parliament function. The recent happenings in Parliament, including serious attempts to denigrate the office of the Speaker, show how MPs themselves are out to destroy what the people want them to nurture.

So busy are the politicians in petty pursuits and so trivial their concerns that they do not know that the people have begun to wonder—whether democracy in the country is really in safe hands. It is not the price of their presence in Parliament that the people grudge but the danger of degeneration of parliamentary democracy that worries most citizens.

Nearly six decades after independence, the question most people are asking across the country is: Independence and democracy are meant for whom, the elector or the elected? As discussed above, there is no doubt that even contemplation of good governance under these circumstances is totally fallacious and a wishful thinking. The legislators should follow the Saloka 48 and 62 of Chapter 2 of Srimad Bhagvad: People who become attached to senses, they cannot achieve excellence. They become slaves of their senses. They should work without having any personal interest.

The man dwelling on sense objects develops attachment for them; from attachment springs up desires, and from desire (unfulfiled) ensures anger. Sri Krisna explain Yoga as "balance of mind." When an action is motivated by desire, anxiety as to whether the desired results is going to be obtained or not will surely disturb the peace of mind of the doer. Again, when an action is inspired by self-interest, the doer is likely to lose sight of what is right or what is wrong. Even when he has chosen to do the right things with undue eagerness for obtaining the result is likely to make him swerve from the path of rectitude; whereas a doer, if he is detached towards the result, is saved from all anxiety. There is nothing to divert him from the righteous path. This teaching that we ought to discharge our obligations, social or otherwise, with a sense of responsibility, at the same time banishing from our minds all thought of obtaining personal benefit therefrom and in a spirit dedication to the Lord is what is meant by Karma-Yoga.[11]

In an article, "The Cost, in crores of Adjouranments" in *Hindustan Times* dated 30 Oct. 2006, Sutirotho Patranobis observes that at present, the cost of running the Lok Sabha is Rs. 11,22,829 per hour. The number of hours that have been lost in the Lok Sabha since 2004 is 192.91. Another disturbing, but related trend is being noticed. Due to regular interruptions, the number of the days that Parliament meets to conduct business is decreasing. This year, for example, Parliament has met for only 57 working days. If Parliament functions for all the 20 days of the coming winter session, it will still fall well short of the 100 days per year as recommended in the Speaker's Conference few years ago. "For about 10 years after Independence, Parliament used to meet for 120 days a year. It decreased to 100 after that. Now Parliament does not even meet for 100 days.

One school of thought says disruptions are necessary at times to bring focus on a burning issue and time lost during sessions is compensated when various parliamentary, standing and business advisory committees meet. "It is more than compensated by other work done by MPs. This kind of calculation is not proper", said BJPs V.K. Malhotra. The cost is escalating which can be seen from the facts below.

Congress Abhisekh Singhvi said: The situation can only be improved by a serious all-party meeting and (arriving at a) consensus to implement several rules to prevent any disruptive tactics."

Question time

1951: Rs. 6,000 per hour was the cost of running question hour in Parliament (Lok Sabha and Rajya Sabha).

1963: One sitting of Lok Sabha Cost Rs. 25,000 per hour.

1981: Average expenditure on running parliament: Rs. 48,000 per hour.

2006: It costs Rs. 11 lakh to just run Lok Sabha for an hour.

All these facts indicate that legislators themselves are abdicating their responsibilities and making the executive more powerful. This becomes the cause of bad governance. Legislators are the watchdog of the interests of the people. Their lack of seriousness cause harm to the people who have to live with bad governance. Legislature, otherwise is becoming a weak institution which is a sad reflection on good governance.

The strong positions of executive (Cabinet), according to Ramsay Muir, "has to a remarkable extent diminished the power and position of a Parliament, robbed its proceedings of significance, made it appear that Parliament exists mainly for the purpose of maintaining or of somewhat ineffectually criticizing an all good but omnipotent Cabinet and transferred the main discussion of political issues from Parliament to Platform and the members."

Regarding the decline of legislature, S.R. Maheshwari is of the view, "As compared to the executive, the legislature is a weak body not adequately equipped in terms of what is expected of it. Secondly, the legislators are people's representative and are thus essentially laymen. It is thus inevitable that an individual legislature is ordinarily no match to the institutionalized intelligence and knowledge at the command of the executive. Thirdly, the party system has further weakened the legislature *vis-à-vis* the party system, which is the mainstay of a parliamentary democracy, channelises legislators' freedom of speech, and particularly, their voting into particular pre-determined directions; and a modern executive need demand no more.[12]

Ranjit Singh Ghuman in his article, "What Ails India" in the *Sunday Tribune* dated Sept. 3, 2006 observes that India's share in world GDP around 1700 AD was about 22 per cent as against China's 23 per cent. At present, their respective share in real world GDP is 6.4 per cent and 11.1 per cent respectively. Clearly, over the period of 300 years the decline in their global position is unbelievable. The poverty incidence in China is less than 5 per cent, whereas it is 26 per cent in India!

The Political leadership, the bureaucracy and the policy-makers would have to give a new thrust and orientation to their character and intentions. The Bharat too would have to be more aware to fight for its own rights. It is often said that where the people are aware, the governments are responsive; and where the people are unaware, the governments are irresponsive. The latter scenario leads to a pathetic situation causing bad governance.

Legislature is the second Pillar of Good Governance. Let us remind ourselves the immortal address of Pandit Jawaharlal Nehru to the Indian Constituent Assembly on the eve of Independence, "Long years ago, we made a tryst with destiny, and now the time comes when we shall redeem our pledge. . . . A moment comes, which comes but rarely in history, when we step out from the old to the new, when an age ends and when the soul of a nation, long suppressed finds utterance. . ." How these words of the first Prime Minister of India can be made practical through good governance?

"Ongoing global transformation need guidance, to avoid very negative looming consequences and realize very positive potentials. Markets, civil society, etc. however important, cannot be relied upon to provide the needed guidance; normatively and realistically only governance can do so. However, in order to adequately fulfil crucial future-building tasks, politics must be revitalized, democracy must be refocused, and governance must be radically redesigned."

Assessment of Legislature Control to Promote Good Governance

Parliament powers have increasingly been usurped by the Executive and this has led to an erosion in the might and majesty of the Parliament. The decline of the power of Parliament is indeed a worldwide phenomenon, but more so in India. The rigidity of the party discipline has reduced the power of the individual member. Besides, the technicality and complexity of government have also made the individual members less powerful. In short, the powers of Parliament have passed into the hands of the Cabinet.

Laws and constitutional amendments by themselves cannot bring about a qualitative change in our thinking and regeneration of values. In this regard the vital role of the educative process cannot be over emphasised. Let me deal with another aspect. Throughout my life and my professional career I have endeavoured to uphold human rights and fundamental freedom. Our constitution in Part III rightly accords preeminence to fundamental rights. Our constitution also in Part IV-A lays down certain fundamental duties of every citizen. Some of these are the duty "to abide by the Constitution and respect its ideals and institutions"; "to cherish and follow the noble ideals which inspired our national struggle for freedom"; "to develop the scientific temper, humanism and the spirit of inquiry and reform" and "to strive towers excellence in all spheres of individual and collective activity so that the nation constantly rises to higher levels of endeavour and achievement."[13]

Parliament has neither the time nor the expertise to control the executive, especially in the financial field. Pfiffner and Presthus have rightly mentioned, "Legislatures, in sum, have neither the staff nor the expertise to exert effective control in meaningful areas. They can act expeditiously and effectively in isolated cases of notorious conduct, the official whose policy and programme controvert their will is often severely taken to task. But such haphazard expeditions are inadequate substitutes for the sustained measure of control and surveillance which official power and discretion now require." The author feels that the legislature can remain an effective instrument to promote good governance, provided its members are well read and keen in the subjects' being discussed. At present they remain busy in petty matters and never attend to study and research of the important problems being faced by the people. In this way only, they can contribute in the area of good governance.

We, thus, come to the conclusion that—

(i) Legislative Powers Ineffective

By virtue of the conduct and background of its members is not effective in formulating quality policy-making which can usher good governance and fulfil the dreams of the common-man of leading a good life. Legislative control over administration is inadequate and needs to be strengthened to maintain democratic values and spirit and promote good governance. Let us discuss some of the causes of the ineffective control and suggest remedies.

(a) The Gulf between Parliament and Executive is on the increase

There is a need of bridging the gulf. Administration is becoming highly technical and complex. Members of Parliament find it difficult to comprehend and keep pace with the latest developments. Partly, it may be because of their limited direction, and partly because of education. S.L. Shakdhar has rightly felt that Parliament must devise ways and means to exert its control in the fast-changing systems. To quote him, "The administration is becoming more complex and seriously creeping into every artery of administration. Parliamentary system must adapt itself to new environments, otherwise it may lag behind and conflicts may arise." We suggest the following to bridge this gulf:

(i) Members of Parliament may be given orientation courses in making them understand their role to make an effective contribution in the proceedings of the House for promoting good governance.

(ii) All rules and regulations need be simplified and

made available in Hindi and other languages so that members can understand them.

(iii) The reports submitted by the Government for the review and comments of the members of Parliament should be simplified, and a summary must be provided to save the time of the members.

(iv) Members may be provided secretarial assistance.

(v) Members may be encouraged to consult the Library.

(b) Members concentrate on petty issues

There is an urgent need of broadening the vision. Members of Parliament remain busy with petty issues concerning their favorites and try to extract small benefits from the administration. Under such a situation, the political executive exploits them, and they do not pursue the national objectives for which they have been elected. They should devote time and energy in reviewing the country's economic health and contribute through new ideas in improving it. If the members are alert about their rights, the executive cannot ignore them.

To be honest is to be trustworthy. Honesty is credibility. With confidence we can rely on men of honesty. Honesty is for psychic health. It is the only wealth to accompany us even after death. Blessed is the society where honest people are in plenty. Dishonesty is a psychic weakness. It is mental ill-health. It is a disastrous disease which harms others, before harming the owner. It is more dreadful than cancer, because cancer kills one but dishonesty kills many. All rules and laws whether traditional or legal are meant to check dishonesty even if they sometimes cause inconvenience to honest people.

Selfishness is at the root of all ill-will, envy, lust and greed, anger and hatred. The more we grow in pure love, the more we become unselfish. The more unselfish we are, the more loving and livable we become. We gain thereby a new power, a force, an attraction that nobody can fail to acknowledge.[14] Lord Beveridge has rightly said that democracy need not fear bureaucracy if it knows its business.

(c) Political parties are engaged in mere criticism on political grounds

There is need of generating think-tanks through research cells. Members of Parliament support or criticise any policy not on the basis of its utility but mostly from the political angle and without much examination. It is suggested that political parties must set-up their research cells to examine the implications of policies under discussion. Based upon the facts and ideas of research cells, members should contribute in the deliberation. The ruling party, in such cases, should accept the viewpoints of opposition parties, if it improves the quality of policy-making and good governance. The purpose of both ruling and opposition parties is nation-building and this can be achieved only through think-tanks and faith in honesty and integrity.

To be honest is to be trustworthy. Honesty is credibility. With confidence we can rely on men of honesty. Honesty is for psychic health. It is the only wealth to accompany us even after death. Blessed is the society where honest people are in plenty. Dishonesty is a psychic weakness. It is mental ill-health. It is a disastrous disease which harms others, before harming the owner. It is more dreadful than cancer, because cancer kills one but dishonesty kills many. All rules and laws whether traditional or level are meant to check dishonesty even if they sometimes course inconvenience to honest people.[15]

S.N. Sadasivan has rightly suggested, "In the West almost every leading political party has regularly recruited and trained personnel constituting a permanent service to undertake research and study on every leading national issue in order to appraise and advise its leaders who are the products of well-known seats of knowledge and have already achieved a fair measure of expertise in one field or another."

(d) The Increase in the Politics of Manipulation has Undermined Healthy Conventions of Impartiality

The offices of Speaker and Deputy Speaker are becoming political. They try to favour the ruling party which is already strong. The Speaker and the Deputy Speaker must imbibe confidence in members so that they can exercise their right and can help the executive in pursuing right policy. The presiding officers must be insulated from party affiliations. Besides, the personnel of the Parliament Secretariat should also perform their duties impartially. Neutrality on the part of Speaker and Deputy Speaker can promote good governance. Having been born as human beings, let us not be unethical. Every profession has certain ethics. Under no circumstances should we violate the professional ethics.

(e) Degenerates into Personalized Issues

Many a times, many members of Parliament tend to be personalized causing great harm to the process. To quote S.R. Maheshwari: Most importantly, one should take cognizance of the most serious menace to accountability. Both, the functionary called to account for his performance and the one who takes the account, being human beings, it is vital that they be motivated by purely organizational objectives in their interactions. This is critically important, for accountability runs a grave risk of becoming personalized, thus promoting privatization game at both ends. Nor should the network of accountability get tainted or polluted, an aspect needing special care and attention. In many developing countries, the formal hierarchies in many organizations, especially those involving public dealings or other kinds of patronage, have been virtually converted into integrated circuits of corruption, thereby making a nonsense of accountability. This must be avoided at all cost to promote good governance.[16]

(h) Saps the Interest of Administration

S.R. Maheshwari has rightly said that Administration, primarily is action, is doing something; and nothing ought to be done to sap the initiative and drive of those carrying programmatic responsibilities. It would be fatal for administration if the public functionaries indulge in procrastination, betray in action, or move in circles simply because accountability has overawed and benumbed them.[17]

(i) Superficial

Questions are asked superficially without reading the material causing great wastage of time. Questions must be specific, pinpointed and well prepared to pinpoint drawbacks of administration to promote good governance.

(j) Positive Aspect of Accountability Overlooked

Public accountability is not just in the negative sense of holding public servants responsible for their lapses. It has a positive connotation. This can help them to remove bottle necks suggested and promote good governance. Public servants have responsibilities to discharge which are of tremendous public significance and indeed can make all the difference between the survival and progress of the nation. To fulfil these responsibilities, a public servant needs stability of tenure and necessary administrative support. Given these pre-conditions, he must deliver the goods. If he fails, he must be held accountable. This often does not happen because of constant transfers and diffused responsibility.

The positive aspect of public accountability in terms of achieving results is far more important than the negative aspect in terms of avoiding lapses. Unfortunately the latter is often highlighted while the former is neglected. If this happens, public accountability may prove even counter-productive. Public servants would like to err on the safe side rather than take decisions which could expose them to errors and public enquiries. Public servants should have the full confidence that *bonafide* mistakes would not expose them to persecution while positive achievement would be recognized and rewarded.[18]

(l) Debates but no Results

The study leads to the conclusion that most of parliamentary procedures were, as they still remain, debate-oriented. As the outcome of the debates was and is pre-decided, they had little reality. Many times they were besides the point and not well-informed. Owing to lack of knowledge on the part of members, the Government sometimes hoodwinked them. The time at the disposal of Parliament is very insufficient and, therefore, many important matters could not be properly debated and some could not be considered at all. Generally, the debate was a post-mortem. Many times there was no relation between what was said during a debate and the vote cast in the division. In matters which were not politically live, but technical, members took so little interest that there was difficulty in maintaining a quorum.[19]

Legislature has to change its style of work through concentration on vital issues facing the people who have elected them to make Good Governance a reality in theory and practice. Good Governance is possible only provided the legislators as representatives of the people feel concerned about them and come prepared to raise the issues of people. Upon their mature wisdom, executive would implement policies for the welfare of people. It may be added that there is no need of other institutions provided the legislature the most powerful organ of the government, discharges its functions faithfully to promote good governance for the welfare of the people. Lord Beveridge has rightly said that Democracy need not fear bureaucracy if it knows its business. The legislators must study hard to find out ways and means to promote such legislation which can bring good governance to provide social, economic and political justice to the common man as enshrined in our constitution. They should not join the executive for small benefits but should guard the interest of the people who have elected them and repose their faith in them.

Tribune dated 15th Aug. observes:

In just 60 years, the language of politics has changed. Suggestions of sacrifice, struggle of the people to break out of slavery and a long slumber and the idea what freedom should mean for the "loneliest and the lost" must have seemed out of place for the ears of many who are caught in the ways of the political rat race.

Celebrations over, the politicians will now be back at the games they play in the pursuit of power and all that goes with it. They have neither time, nor inclination, to spare a thought for the idea that power ultimately is meant to serve the people, and to build a new India where freedom should mean something for the poorest of the land, where the helpless can live a life of dignity and self-respect, without fear and want.

So busy are the politicians in their wild power chase,

they don't have a moment to spare to ponder what they have done to the Constitution, one of the better charters for governing a nation of India's size and complexity. Parliament, the way it is functioning, no longer resembles the one that not long ago used to make us all feel proud.

Our Constitution did work—and worked well for the first 19 years after independence. What happened after that? I think the answer lies in this—it ceased to work well the moment politics in this country became immoral and unprincipled. We have not been able to work the Parliamentary system—we cannot work any system—unless we re-inject some degree of idealism and morality into politics.

The communalization and criminalisation of politics, endemic corruption and ineffectiveness of the governmental machinery have tarnished the image of governance and severely eroded its effectiveness.

There are many factors which have led to the continuing deterioration in the governance of our country. This writing seeks to briefly highlight the grave threat to the country's unity and integrity which arises from the politicisation of the civil, police and judicial services, which has led to nepotism, corruption, and brazen abrogation of the Rule of Law.

Instead of being constantly engaged in tackling problems and delivering programmes and services to alleviate the lot of the poor and neglected segments of our society the political parties in power in the States have remained perennially preoccupied in retaining their authority at any cost and by what ever means. The public services, including the IAS and IPS, have been used and exploited to gather huge funds through corruption and extortion and to carry out all manner of unlawful behests. The internal discipline and accountability of the administrative apparatus has been shattered; dishonest elements enjoy strong protection of the political masters who have put them in key positions.

A corrupt administration provides endless openings to anti-national elements and foreign adversary agencies to organise varied subversive activities which threaten national security. All political parties must muster courage to openly commit against exerting any kind of influence or interference in the functioning of the governmental machinery and misusing the public services for gathering funds. In turn the public services must be compelled to function strictly according to the Constitution and the law and made to face severe punishments for any deviation from the norm. To restore discipline, efficiency, accountability and credibility to the governance structures the political hierarchies in power would need to remove all criminal/corrupt elements within their own ranks and ruthlessly rid the governmental establishments of all dishonest functionaries.

According to a recent study, the present Lok Sabha has the unique distinction of having as many as 125 members with criminal background. Serious charges of murder, rape, kidnapping, extortion and the like are pending against many of them. A Media report puts their number at 139. They are all "Honourable" members. They have not been convicted yet and are not likely to be convicted in the near future. The cases against them may remain pending for years. Adjournments may follow adjournments. Witnesses may not turn up, may turn hostile or may get eliminated. Finally, the cases may somehow get dropped. Meanwhile, some of them may remain "Honourable" members and even occupy high ministerial berths. The position in our State legislatures is much worse end even more alarming.

Subhash C. Kashyap in his article, "Criminal-Politicians nexus getting stronger" in *The Tribune* dated 15th Aug. 2007 clearly mention that in the National Commission to Review the Working of the Constitution (2002-02) we examined the problem in depth and made some very potent recommendations particularly with a view to preventing "criminals" from getting into our Parliament and State Legislatures. Some of these need to be reiterated:

(i) Once charges relating to certain crimes have been framed by court against a person, he should not be permitted to contest elections unless cleared. A potential candidate against whom charges have been framed by the police may take the matter to a special electoral court. This court may decide in a time-bound manner whether there is indeed a *prima facie* case justifying the framing of charges. If yes, the person should not be allowed to contest.

(ii) Once convicted and sentenced to imprisonment, the person involved should be debarred by law from contesting elections for the entire period of the sentence plus an additional six years.

(iii) At present sitting members are not disqualified even when convicted until their appeal is decided. This provision of the RPI Act of 1951 should be deleted. If an elected representative gets convicted on charges related to specific crimes, he should be required to withdraw from the legislature for six months and if within that period he fails to get an acquittal, he should be disqualified.

(iv) Lastly and most importantly, electoral and political party reforms by law must be brought about without further delay *inter alia* for reducing the cost of elections through use of technology and stricter control mechanisms, divesting all legislators other than ministers of all executive functions and offices of profit, regulating the number and functioning of parties, audit and public scrutiny of party funds, making voting compulsory for all the adult citizens, educating the voters in regard to their citizenship responsibilities and dangers of voting criminals to public offices.

All the efforts made so far by the Supreme Court and the Election Commission like making it obligatory for candidates to disclose information about criminal cases pending against them, etc. have proved to be of no avail. In fact, after the information was made available, we have more legislators with criminal background then ever before. The question is where do we go from here?

It is not very difficult to suggest more ways and means of really unshackling public life from the strongholds of the crime world. The real problem is of implementing the suggestions. Those who can do it through peaceful constitutional means are the very law-makers who have a vested interest in the *status quo*. Why should the prime beneficiaries of a corrupt and criminalized system change it and dig their own grave? The only hope is in an awakened citizenry rising forcefully and asserting their sovereign right to change the system.

The historic Resolution passed by the Lok Sabha at the special session of Parliament on the occasion of the golden jubilee of independence, August 26 to Sept. 1, 1997 observes: "The meaningful electoral reforms be carried out so that our Parliament and other legislative bodies be balanced and effective instruments of democracy and further that political life and processes be free of the adverse impact on governance of undesirable extraneous factors including criminalization."

Dr. Rajendera Prasad on 26th Nov., 1949 while giving concluding observation in the Constituent Assembly said that "India needs to day nothing more than a set of honest men who will have the interest of the country before them. The law giver requires above all to be true to these fundamentals things of life—in one word—to have character."

Suma Varugheses in her article on Spirituality in Life Plus, July and Sept. 2004 beautifully explains that: Our ancient values can transform the existing values system. To quote her: "Let us begin by considering the concept of interconnection. One of the Buddha's great truths, as also the central truth of the Upanisads, interconnection means my welfare as linked with yours. I cannot harm you without harming myself. I cannot despoil the earth or pollute the rivers without endangering myself. I cannot exterminate species without forging my own extinction. I cannot cheat, harm or manipulate another without making the world less safe for myself. Conversely, if I spread love and goodness, goodness and love will impinge on me.

The concept of interconnection has the potential to change our outlook and therefore society radically. Politics will become a means to serve the society rather than be a naked chase for power. Economics will be guided by concern for the environment rather than for profit-making. The conflicts, whether at the level of nations, community or within the family or even with one's own self, will melt away once we experience the fact that we are all one. It all boils down to a great heaving shift in the world culture, giving birth unquestionably to the New Age.

The crux of the problem is about devising appropriate and effective mechanisms for implementing these principles. Needless to say the efficacy of any mechanism to realise and maintain ethical norms will be the innate driving force of the individuals rather than sanctions from an external disciplinary authority. Living examples of adherence to these principles by leaders in public life in various fields will be greatly conductive to implementation of these principles. Leaders should symbolize the spirit of service and sacrifice and radiate an air of honesty and decency. Unfortunately we live in times when there are no men and women to match our Himalayan peaks, when our political system has more criminals, fixers and hypocrites per capita than at any time in our history. There is crisis of confidence. There is crisis of leadership. The foremost requirement is the restoration of confidence in our institutions. This needs strong and enlightened national leadership which is able to cope with emergent problems boldly and decisively which does not seem in sight.[20]

Essential Values for Legislative Members

The scene in Parliament and State Legislature is becoming worse. It has become like a jungle with no discipline. The present Parliament saw the expulsion of eleven members who were taking money for asking questions. Can one believe it? From this very Parliament, a Member was caught at the Airport while taking a woman and his son after getting a bribe of 35 lacs. What do we expect from such Parliament and legislatures? Barring few exceptions, most of the persons seek elections for making money and promote goonda Raj. People are watching them closely. The people feel tired of such a democracy where people are exploited by the elected representatives in collision with Bureaucracy.

What is the way out? The only remedy to make them learn well established values followed in Ancient India and put them into practice to make India a super power and look after the welfare of the people.

This is my interest to orient the human mind in India in terms of the development of the people of India, for that is what is meant by freedom—freedom to build up this nation. It must become a passion in the minds of people and, particularly, in politics and in administration. We are unhappy and as the years roll by, this human value, this human factor, has been eroded. Everything else is there, power is there, money is there. But the human factor is getting eroded. Naturally the development process becomes arrested and the meaning of freedom becomes absolutely meaningless. After centuries of political subjection, we attained freedom. We have struggled hard to get this freedom. Every leader during the freedom struggle, both political and cultural and spiritual, say, men like Vivekananda or Gandhi, they always emphasized that we need freedom to shape the destiny of all our people. today we have that opportunity to build up this great nation, this immense manhood and womanhood.[21]

This is the greatest misfortune of our people who, after centuries of political subjection, got freedom, but didn't know how to use that freedom, did not know how to squeeze it to the fullest advantage of the nation. This is something amazing. What has happened to us? We have first class brains, there is no want of intellect in this country. Various other qualities are there but one quality which can trigger every other quality is missing—the concern for others. That is what is lacking throughout the nation.

A Japanese girl working in a house needs nobody to supervise her. She has got a sense of self-respect, a dignity—'I am paid, I do my work.' We have not developed that attitude in this country. If I am a free person inwardly, a work is given and I will do it to the best of my ability. I will discharge my responsibility. This is my honour, my self-respect, my dignity. There you have got the real spirit of freedom. If millions and millions of our people realise that quality of freedom, then there will be no problems here. But is has not come. We are not free inwardly.[22]

Legislative members whether in Parliament or state legislatures through their own value system can purify the Indian society which has become polluted. Indian society wants the legislators to set an example of themselves by being embodiment of values, some of which are mentioned below:

1. Legislators should try to be excellent

• Human Excellence can do wonders. Swami Vivekananda says that India is no more to be a mere geographical expression. Our ancestors conceived of India a cultural entity, the Punyabhumi. But Swami Vivekananda advances a step further and breathes life into it by making India, the symbol of the great virat. The reformers and workers bent on serving India socially, politically, or otherwise, are to be imbued with this grand idealism of the Virat, concretized in India. It is this transformation of vision with regard to our holy land which the Swami transformation of vision with regard to our holy land which the Swami teaches as one of the potent means for spiritualizing our national activities.[23]

To quote S. Radhakrishnan again, "Human nature has immeasureable potentialities and the world process has no predestined goal. The power of free choice gives us hope for the future. We can remake the world. Whatever flaws of character or deficiencies of mind we have we can remove them. If we strive to do so, the forces of the universe will assist us. We can consciously direct the process of human evolution. Nature comes to its fulfilment in the human individual, who is the bearer of the creative process. He is the unique representative of the universe in whom the unconscious creativity of nature becomes conscious creativity. The inner discord means that he can contend with the disruptive forces, conquer them and attain peace."

Indian thought asks us to liberate ourselves form bondage. We must pass from samasara, life in time subjects to discords to moksa or enlightenment or eternal life.

2. Legislators should avoid lust for wealth and follow values of Truth, Beauty and Goodness

Swami Chinmayananda observes: Materialism is wonderful, no doubt, but it burdens man with endless anxiety and craving to possess more, to acquire and aggrandise and to indulge with slavish attachment. This is natural for man seeks his fulfilment and happiness only in thoughtless intemperance, in toiling for and reaching the temporary gratification of this physical passions, mental urges, and intellectual hungers. It is not a fact that, in recent times, more people are killed by worry than by work? Man in his present misconceived civilization has learned to waste himself and his precious time in the inevitable trifles and tensions that beset his life. But to the attentive and the vigilant, life is a glorious opportunity with possibilities to reach the perfection of civilization.

3. Legislators should carry out their duties without attachment, Personal benefit or Neptoism

People who become attached to senses, they cannot achieve excellence. They become slaves of their senses. They should work without having any personal interest.

ध्यायतो विषयान् पुंसः सडक्गंस्तेषुपजायते ।
सडग्संजायते कामः कामात्क्रोधोऽभिजायते ।।

2/62 Bhagavad Gita

The man dwelling on sense objects develops attachment for them; from attachment springs up desire, and from desire (unfulfiled) ensues anger. Sri Krishna explains Yoga as 'balance of mind' (Chap. 11.48). When an action is motivated by desire, anxiety as to whether the desired result is going to be obtained or not will surely disturb the peace of mind of the doer. Again, when an action is inspired by self-interest, the doer is likely to lose sight of what is right or what is wrong. Even when he has chosen to do the right thing with undue eagerness for obtaining the result is likely to make him swerve from the path of rectitude; whereas a doer, if he is detached towards the result, is saved from all anxiety. There is nothing to divert him from the righteous path. This teaching that we ought to discharge our obligations, social or otherwise, with a sense of responsibility, at the same time banishing from our minds all thought of obtaining personal benefit therefrom and in a spirit dedication to the Lord is what is meant by Karma-Yoga."

By constantly dwelling on objects of enjoyment man develops an intensive form of attachment for them. This awakens in his mind a keen desire to obtain various forms of enjoyment. This is what is meant by attachment giving rise to desire. And when some hindrance appears in the fulfilment of this desire, he develops hatred for the cause of this hindrance, and the hatred is transformed into anger. This is what is meant by desire producing anger. Anger causes stress and poor mental status.

Neither think yourself as actor, because no actor can attempt to do anything. Discharge whatever is your duty, and remain at your ease with having done your part. (Yoga Vasistha-Utpatti-Prakarana, Book 3) If you want to secure real. happiness, then renounce all. By so renouncing you will secure happiness infinitely greater than what you could have had through your property. You can enjoy more as you will remain stress free.

Acharya Mahaprajna in his article, "Freedom of mind through spirituality" in *Deccan Herald,* dated July 6, 2007 clarifies that the conduct of a spiritual man is not a reaction. He does not compromise but behave in a magnanimous way. He does not expect returns. He acts with a sense of duty. Anyatha Vyavahara is a duty which must be done irrespective of its consequences. The man who simply reacts remains unbalanced. A balanced mind does not take sides. He is above favoritism, likes and dislikes and sweetness and bitterness. Modern ethics has considered the question of moral conduct at length. The philosopher Kant, for example, holds the view that our actions should be governed by the sense of duty rather than by the feelings of pity and compassion or by the idea of doing good to others. Action based on such feelings is not moral action. Only actions inspired by man's free will can be said to be moral. Our conduct should be on the sense of duty only.[24]

4. Honesty and Integrity

It has been rightly said in Gita that the character of the people is shaped by "leaders." As is the king, so are the subjects-our high ups in both politics and bureaucracy are highly corrupt. According to Narayan Hazare, "Corruption owes its origin to important political causes. Though at the top people preach integrity, more often than not they lack the virtue of example. Ministers are permitted to live in glaring extravagance while they make impassioned appeals for popular sacrifice. Socialism in a Rolls Royce may be eloquent but it seldom conveys an impression of sincerity. Thus, corruption, like sacrifice, starts at the top and, percolating down, colours the whole society Swami Jagadatmanada in his book, "Learn to Live", Vol. 2, Talks about honesty which is the most essential ingredient of excellence. He says that: Honesty is another essential quality like patience. Honesty is a great force. Honesty means integration of the three aspects of personality thought, speech and deed. For instance, when you give a promise to the workers, honesty demands that you act accordingly or at least make a sincere attempt to act according to the promise. Otherwise, it is dishonesty or deceit. A victim of deception does not easily forget the humiliation or shock that he has left. It explodes one day or the other in some form or the other. It doesn't explode it remains simmering within. Honesty can win the hearts of men. Though one may not be able to fulfil one's promise or keep one's word, if the effort is sincere, it has its value, it will earn respect, it will have a good effect. Legislators should dedicate their whole energy upon assuring good legislation and its review after implementation. They need work hard in this direction so that people for whom laws are legislated are benefited.

5. Selfless Service

Legislators are the representative of people and their duty is to serve the people through selfless service. However, legislators forget the people the moment they are elected.

The great secret of true success, of true happiness, then, is this; the man who asks for no return, the perfectly unselfish man, is the most successful. It seems to be a paradox. Do we not know that every man who is unselfish in life gets cheated, gets hurt? Apparently, Yes, "Christ was unselfish, and yet he was crucified." True, but we know that his unselfishness is the reason, the cause of a great victory—the crowing of millions upon millions of lives with the blessings of true success.

Swami Harshanand says that, "Ask nothing; want nothing in return. Give what you have to give; it will come back to you—but do not think of that now. It will come back multiplied a thousand-fold—but the attention must not be on that. Yet have the power to give, give, and there it ends.[25] Man is born to give not to grab, grabber pays the penalty in the form of misery"; the giver reaps the reward in the form of joy.

The resources, the bodily effort and the mental disposition becomes multiplied in the man of yajna. Such a man is never in want, always in affluence. His bounteous mind is the real Kamdhenu. Because of his frame of mind he is ever in prosperity. This is the plan and purpose of cosmos.

When the Creator said that fostered by sacrifice, the gods would surely bestow on man all the desired enjoyments unasked, he meant that, for his own part; man should go on scrupulously performing his duty. If man did not fail in the performance of his duty, there could be no doubt that fostered and nourished by his sacrifice, the gods could ever continue to supply him with all the means of leading a happy and contented life; for the gods were bound to perform their part of duty.

The essence of the spirit of service is contained in the following words of Vivekananda: "This is the gist of all worship to be pure and to do good to others. He who sees Shiva in the poor, in the weak, and in the diseased, really worships Shiva; and if he sees Shiva only in the image, his worship is but preliminary. He who has served and helped one poor man seeing Shiva in him, without thinking of his caste, or creed, or race, or anything, with him Shiva is more pleased than with the man who sees him only in the temples. He who wants to serve the father must serve the children first. He who wants to serve Shiva must serve His children must serve all creatures in the world first."[26]

The article "Religion—Ethics of Life" beautifully explains an honest attempt to probe the root cause of happiness would gradually reveal that it is within the self and not in external sources—wealth, power, fame, name, success, etc. This truth is the basis of all spiritual teaching that advocates the practice of dhrama. It also implies a disciplined life that gives peace, mental strength and inner happiness. Virtues such as patience, forgiveness, piety, honesty, sanctity, control of senses, learning, truthfulness, etc. benefit both the individual and society.

The Bhagavad Gita focuses on the ephemeral quality of life drawing the distinction between the perishable body and the immortal soul. This knowledge helps to shed attachment to worldly objects. The Lord Places great value on true devotion and promise unfailing protection to those who sincerely seek His feet. That is why it is advised that one has to pray to God with the fervency and urgency as if death were imminent. Azhwars and realized souls have felt the presence of death in every moment and pray to the Lord for liberation at the time of death since it is likely that they may be unable to remember Him then due to old age, failing Senses., etc.[27]

6. Self-Introspection and Self-understanding to make ourselves Perfect

All the elected members should also do introspection as to why are they contesting elections and for what? Most of them are engaged in money making and getting favorers.

There is a beauty shinning in the face of one whose mind has the satisfaction of contentment, the fullness of magnanimity and the purity of thoughts like that of the milky ocean in it.

The reasoning man gets released from his worldly sickness, and quits his frame which is full of diseases, as a snake cast off his time worn slough; and looks with a placid mind and clam composure upon the magic scenes of the world. Hence, the fully wise man is not subject to the misery of the imperfectly wise.

The rough and uneven pleasure of the world is but a disease to men, and stings them like a snake. It cults them as a sword, and pierces them as a spear. It binds them fast as by a rope, and burns them as with the fire, and blindfolds, their understanding as in the darkness of the night. It makes them as prostrate and dull as a slab of stone. It destroys one's prudence and lowers his position. It casts them into the pit of error, and torments them with avarice. Thus, there is almost no kind of trouble which does not betide worldly minded men.

Worldliness is as dangerous a diseases as cholera, which unless it is healed in time, is sure to trouble its patient with the torments to hell. The journey of this world is delightful to one, who after the removal of his errors and dispersion of the cloud of his ignorance has come to the knowledge of truth.

7. Good Character

Before expecting good character from people, executive machinery, judiciary the first and foremost duty of every elected person is that he should be a man of character.

All good character traits have a common denominator of social courage, usefulness, common sense besides self-acceptance and self-confidence. Men of character may not be popular, but they are respected and followed. They are true leaders of men and times. They will fight but not quarrel, differ but will not oppose or criticize, will be firm but not rigid, dogmatic, appreciate without flattery, cooperate without surrendering, self-confident but not self-important, cooperate, compromise and reconcile on non-essentials but put up a valiant, relentless fight for basic principles, act and never react.

Will power and patience are basic to personality development. Both provide fibre and tone to it. Will is the motive power, driving force and patience is the period over which this force works to develop character.

All human endeavors achievements require minimum necessary time to mature and fulfil. Impatience only wastes vital energy, tires, confuses, sickens and impairs our will power. Our personality does not register on others if we are impatient with them who can benefit or be friend you without your giving him time.[28]

Legislators have vast powers and are the custodian of the interests of the people. They are the conscience of the country. They must follow the advice of Swami Vivekananda and do their best to make India an ideal country. To quote Swami Vivekananda: Can you adduce any reason why India should lie in the ebb-tide of the Aryan nations? Is she inferior in intellect? Is she inferior in dexterity? Can you look at her art, at her mathematics, at her philosophy and answer 'Yes'? All that is needed is that she should de-hypnotize herself and wake up from her age-long sleep to take her true rank in the hierarchy of nations. . . . The national ideals of India are Renunciations and Service. Intensify her in those channels, and the rest will take care of itself.

—*Swami Vivekananda*

An article by in the *Economic Times* dated 3 July, 2007 "Changing the way life goes on" observes No, some people think a little differently. They might know that life would go on without them—they have no illusions about that—but they also know that it probably should not go on the way it was going on before. As a result, because they saw something which went against the grain of a human situation they deliberately decided to become instrumental in its change or—and here's the big difference—die trying.

Secondly, even if everything will not fall apart and life will go on without our presence, who is to say each one of us does not make a difference in our own way? It would require monumental apathy on someone's part to leave what they consider well enough alone and not do something to better it. This especially true when we consider the amount of evil doers like drug pushers, paedophiles and war-mongers who exist just to worsen it. Therefore, notwithstanding Ms. Watkins avowed good intentions in saying what she does, it's still a small responsibility for people to put the hereafter at least a little beyond their imagination.

Swami Ranganathananda in, "Democratic Administration in the Light of Practical Vedanta" portrays a poor picture of the prevailing value system in India. To quote,

India today is at the cross-roads. We are in a curious predicament. The obverse of the coin is bright, the reverse grim. We are heirs to a glorious civilization whose mighty stream has been following uninterruptedly down the millennia, enriching and ennobling all on its path. Fifty years back we have also recovered our political independence from the largest empire the world has seen, and that without firing a single shot—something unique in history. Yet chaos stalks the land. Things are falling apart. Values cherished over the centuries are getting eroded. In a country of rich natural resources the poverty of the masses is abysmal. The haves exploit the have-nots in a hundred ingenious ways. Women and the weaker sections of society reel under injustice and handicaps. Corruption is rampant. Mindless violence maims and destroys the precious lives of the innocent. The sensitive citizen finds himself asking, "Whither India."[29]

No ideal, ideology, institution or religion is self-operative. It is through human agency alone that ideals and institutions established for their realization are made operational. History bears witness to perversions, distortions and abuse or misuse of ideals and institutions for the reason that human being is essentially imperfect though he seeks perfection. It is true that perfection is not attainable by imperfect beings, however, it is always worthwhile attempting and this depends largely upon a meaningful education of man with a view to fertilizing the soil within so that the vessel may bear rich, juicy and truthful fruits.

In the words of Swami Ranganathananda, "The subject of the philosophy of service, therefore, is not meant for academic discussion in the dull philosophy courses of our universities; it should stir the minds and hearts of every section of the population. It is thus, that the nation will get the necessary strength to meet the recurring challenges that this age of revolutionary transition will throw at it. If India succeeds in responding to these challenges adequately, she will become a beacon of hope not only to herself but also to the whole of humanity. We have responded successfully to many a challenge to our national existence and integrity in our long history. And we shall face and overcome this challenge as well. With this faith in ourselves and in our national destiny, let us, from this day onwards, enter our respective fields of life and activity with hope and courage.[30]

Conclusion

In the Mahabharata you will find a beautiful discussion. Bhishma, lying on the Sarasayya addressing Yudhisthira on the subject of politics and the ethics of the State. One sentence occurs there that everything depends upon the political state. If the political state is healthy, everything else is healthy. If that is unhealthy, everything is unhealthy. How true it is today in India! Where politics and administration have gone to the dogs, everything goes to the dogs in the country. If that is clean, everything else also will be clean. Today we must realise that truth uttered by Bhishma. A large mind, a big heart, a broad attitude. In fact, that portion, the Santi parva is famous in the Mahabharata. When the war was over, for thirty six years they enjoyed the empire in Delhi. Then the old Dhrtarastra and his wife Gandhari and Vidura and Kunti, mother of the Pandavas, said they had enough of palace life, and were going to the forest. They started towards the forest. There was an outcry in the capital at these old people leaving the palace and going to the forest. They persuaded them to stay and not to go. But they were adamant. Enough of these cocktail parties everyday. Let us go and have a quiet life. They were going out of the capital of India, imagine four to five thousand years ago. Kunti had reached outside the city gate. The Pandavas came one by one to salute her, to take her blessing. When it came finally to the eldest son, i.e. Yudhishthira, the emperor of India, she blessed him and gave him a message. I wish that message enters the heart of all in India today. Looking at her son and blessing him, the emperor of India, she said:

> Nivartasva kurusrest
> Bhimasenadibhissaha,
> Dharme te Dhiyatam buddhi
> manaste mahadastu ca-

'Oh! Yudhishthira, go back to the palace, continue to rule the State along with your brothers, Bhimasena and others; (but if you want to rule the State you must develop a new attitude) let you be established in Dharma, righteousness or justice (not any particular creed or religion), and, lastly, let your heart be big'. A little heart cannot run a great State.

We have yet to develop the attitude that this is my country and these are my fellow citizens. If this attitude is

not there, all this money will be simply waste, as we are seeing every day. Crores and crores of rupees are wasted. The fruits of the crores become very much reduced by the time it reaches the people concerned. It is here that human values come in to correct the situation.

Notes and References

1. C.F. Strong, Modern Political Constitutions, 1958, *op. cit.*, p. 163.
2. Constituent Assembly Debates, Vol. XI, No. 11, November 25, 1949, p. 975, *ibid.*, p. 64.
3. Navsrushi International Trust, National Regeneration Movement, Dharma Bharti Ashram, 2001, Kerala.
4. The Second Report of the National Police Commission, GOI, 1979, p. 21.
5. The Pioneer, July, 10, 1998. Quoted in Shriram Maheswari, Political Reforms for True Governance, in T.N. Chaturvedi, Towards Good Governance, New Delhi, 1999, p. 58.
6. Swami Chinmayananda, The Art of Man-Living, Mumbai, CCT, 2002, pp. 42, 44.
7. The Art of Man-Making, *op. cit.*, p. 3.
8. *Ibid.*, pp. 42-44.
9. Dolly Arora, Governance, An Agenda the Discussion Left in T.N. Chaturvedi, ed. Towards Good Governance, New Delhi, *IJPA*, 1999, p. 132.
10. Swami Chinmayananda, The Art of Man Making CCMT, Mumbai, July 2002, pp. 118-19.
11. Swami Vijnananda, Gita on Karma Yoga, in *Yoga: Its Various Aspects*, Sri Ramakrishna Math, Madras; pp. 24-25.
12. S.R. Maheswari, Indian Administration, Orient Longman, Calcutta, 1996, p. 115.
13. Soli, J. Sorabjee, Regeneration of Ethical Values", *University News*, 16-23, July 2007, p. 23.
14. Dr. K. Subrahmanyam, Chennai, Vivekananda Kendra Prakash Turst, Apirl, 2000, p. 22.
15. *Ibid.*, p. 24.
16. S.R. Maheswari: Accountability in Public Admn., in *IJPA*, July-Sept. 1983, pp. 468-69.
17. *Ibid.*, p. 471.
18. P.R. Dubhashi, Public Accountability and Ethics in Administration, in *IJPA*, July-Sept., 1983, pp. 520-52.
19. U.N. Sukla, Parliamentary Control of Administration in India, *IJPA*, April to June 1979, p. 319.
20. Soli S. Sorabjee, Regeneration of Ethical Values, *University News*, July 16-22, 2007, p. 20.
21. Lecture delivered by Swami Ranganathananda at the Institute of Management in Govt. Barton Hill, Kerala on 15th Dec., 1983.

22. *Ibid.*, pp. 116, 120.
23. The complete works of Swami Vivekananda, Vol. IV, p. 326.
24. *Decan Herald*, July 6, 2007.
25. Swami Harshananda, "Attainment of Yoga: Maladies and Remedies" in *Yoga: Its various aspects*", Shri Ramakrishna Math, Madras, pp. 203-04.
26. Swami Jagadatmananda, Learn to Live, Vol. I, Chennai, Shri Ramakrishna Math, p. 256.
27. *The Hindu*, June 30, 2007.
28. Ram Parshad Gupta, Food for Thought, New Delhi, 1996, pp. 18-23.
29. Swami Rangunathananda, Democratic Administration in the Light of Practical Vedanta, Sri Ramakrishna Math, Chennai, 2003, p. iii.
30. *Ibid.*, p. 251.

8

Executive and Values

Government consists of three wings—the executive, the legislature and the judiciary. The executive is the strongest of the wings and runs the administration of the country. In common parlance, the executive and administration have become synonymous.

J.W. Garner writes, "In a broad and collective sense, the executive organs embraces the aggregate or totality of all the functionaries and agencies which are concerned with the execution of the will of the state as that will has been formulated and expressed in terms of law. In this sense, the term embraces not only the supreme head of the government —the chief of state, as he is called on the continent of Europe (President, King or Emperor)—but also the ministers and the whole mass of subordinate executive and administrative functionaries who constitute what in Great Britain and the United States is known as the 'civil service'. As thus understood, it comprehends the entire governmental organization, with the exception of the legislature and the judiciary and possibly the diplomatic corps. Thus tax collectors, inspectors, commissioners, policemen and perhaps officers of the army and navy are the part of the executive organisation."[1]

In a broad and collective sense, the executive organ

CHART 8.1

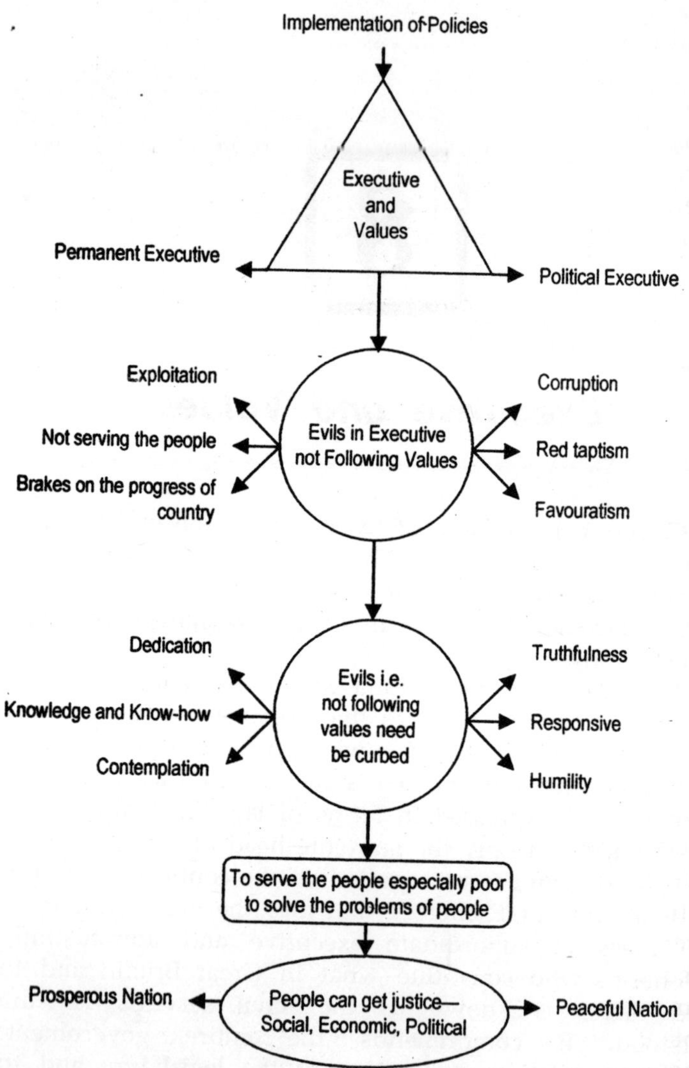

embraces the aggregate or totality of all the functionaries which are concerned with the execution of the will of the state as that will has been formulated and expressed in terms of law."[2]

The executive consists of two parts. One part comprises the elected section and is composed of ministers. In parliamentary democracy, the privilege of forming the ministry is enjoyed by the leader of the party, which is returned in majority to the legislature or which in coalition or combination with other parties or individuals can secure a majority in the legislature. In case the ministry ceases to enjoy confidence of the legislature, the ministers must quit their office. As such, there is an element of non-permanence in the elected section of the executive. The other section of the executive is comprised of civil servants. They have an element of permanence about them and are considered to be the backbone of the administration. Normally, it is the ministers who take policy decisions and set down the guidelines and general pattern of administration. The execution of those decisions and the application of policy guidelines to individual cases is, however, to be left to the civil servants. This apart civil servants of the rank of secretaries by their notings and otherwise apprise the ministers on the basis of their expertise about the various pros and cons of the proposed policy decisions and in the process express their preference. It is this role of the secretaries which often puts a strain on their relationship with the ministers. In the early years of freedom, our ministers—who were, by and large, broad-hearted persons and motivated by no extraneous considerations—welcomed frank expression of views. The situation in this respect has undergone considerable change since then.[3]

The quality of the institutions run by Government would be dependent to a great extent upon the quality of the employees engaged in their operations, Personnel move the administrative machinery. To quote Mrs. Indira Gandhi: "If government has to do more for the people, its employees must play a more dynamic and more creative role as the instrument for implementing government policies and programmes."[4] The progress of development would also depend upon the personnel in an organization. Ferrel Heady says: "The importance of administration is almost universally recognized amongst commentators on development. Visually an effective bureaucracy is coupled with a vigorous modernizing elite as prerequisite for progress."[5]

The bureaucracy, a rusted version of the steel frame, despite 60 years of freedom remains distant from the people, almost callous and indifferent and generally insensitive to their pain and despair.

The challenge of good governance would certainly require government to be reinvented, bureaucracy to be re-positioned, non government business sectors to be re-invigorated with a social motive. For all this, a shift of emphasis to the normative model of managing government would be needed. A reinvented government must have both ethical consistency and organizational flexibility to remain faithful to the goal of public service. For the sake of good governance, a reinvented government is to function in a more missionary, egalitarian and energized manner, having less machine-like and less hierarchical structure and procedures.[6]

Dr. Rajendra Prasad said at the concluding session of the Constituent Assembly, "Whatever the Constitution may or may not provide, the welfare of the country will depend upon the way in which the country is administered. That will depend upon the men who administer it. . . . It requires men of strong character, men of vision, men who will not sacrifice the interests of the country at large, for the sake of smaller groups, and areas and who rise above the prejudice which are born of these differences."

Since the minister occupies the top position in politico-administrative hierarchy, it is essential that he should have full legal and constitutional authority to administer with good governance the affairs of his department. Theoretically it is feasible but in practice, he cannot achieve much whether it is policy making or implementation or evaluation unless he gets due co-operation, help, participation, involvement of the personnel of his department. The volume of work with the Council of Ministers at the Union and the state levels is so large and the problems so complicated that it is impossible for any number of ministers to deal with all the matters themselves. The civil servants provide all the information and analysis for the guidance of the ministers and the cabinet. The channel through which a minister must operate is the secretariat. The secretariat acts as an institutionalized memory to enable the government to examine the feasibility of the proposed policy.

Sir Warren Fisher, in a memorandum to the Tomlin Commission (U.K.) defined the duties of the civil servant *vis-a-vis* the minister as follows:

Determination of policy is the function of a minister and once a policy is determined it is the unquestioned and unquestionable business of the civil servant to strive to carry out that policy with precisely the same energy and precisely the same goodwill whether he agreed with it or not. This is axiomatic and will never be in dispute. At the same time it is the traditional duty of civil servants while decisions are being formulated, to make available to their political chief all the information and experience at their disposal, and to do this without fear or favour, irrespective of whether, the advice thus tendered may accord or not with the minister's initial view. The presentation to the minister of relevant fact, the ascertainment and marshalling of which may often call into play the whole organization of a department, demands of the civil servant the greatest care. The presentation of inferences from the facts equally demand from him all the wisdom and all the detachment he can command.

The preservation of integrity, fearlessness, and independence of thought and utterance in their private communion with ministers of the experienced officials selected to fill the top posts in the service is an essential principle in enlightened government, as whether or not ministers accept the advice the frankly placed at their disposal, and acceptance or rejection of such advice is exclusively a matter for their judgement. It enables them to be assured that their decisions are reached only after the relevant facts and the various considerations have, so far as the machinery of government can secure been definitely brought before their minds.

The analysis of this definition brings out the following characteristics of Civil Services which help the ministers in promoting good governance.

(a) Civil servants can place all the facts and opinions before the minister without any fear.
(b) The civil servant is responsible for the continuity of policy.

(c) The civil servant must maintain secrecy.
(d) The civil servant remains anonymous but he has to bring creativity and excellence based upon facts.
(e) The ultimate prerogative in policy-making is of the Minister.

In India, the relationship is the same in theory but in practice many problems have crept in which have become challenging problems for god governance.

U.C. Aggarwal in his article, "Public services in India: Achievements and Disappointment" in *IJPA*, July-Sept. 2006 observe that the 5th Pay Commission, in its report of 1997 pointed that:

"There is no doubt that the productivity in government is quite low. Lack of punctuality is one reason, the five-day week and the large number of holidays another. Sufficient care has not been taken in devising a criteria for measurement of an employee's output. Most of the norms for creation of posts are outdated and need to be revised. There are no incentives for higher output and promotions are almost automatic. There is undue emphasis on rules and procedures, and not enough on output. Interference from political source creates havoc in day-to-day administration." It further observed,

"Integrity has never been a strong point of the bureaucracy in India and the situation has definitely worsened in recent years. The time is ripe for drastic steps to counter corruption, which has assumed cancerous proportion in the body politic."

V.P. Kapur in his article, "Public Services—Their performances, problems and remedies" in *IJPA*, July-Sept. 2006 observes that it has however to be accepted that despite laudable intention of the top leadership and voluminous reports submitted by various Commissions and Committees, there has hardly been perceptible change in the colonial mind-set, attitudes and style of functioning of a large majority of the public servants and, more so, at the cutting edge levels. It is commonly experienced that many such officials do not treat the common men in a humane manner and are insensitive to their problems. Generally speaking, they are not accessible to members of the public. They cause unnecessary delays, harass the common man and make him run from pillar to post primarily with a view to extort bribes. It is quite worrying that many of them succeed in circumventing even the order of the highest level of the judiciary. There are reports in the media with monotonous regularity about the bribes extorted even from the victims of extreme human tragedies and the targeted beneficiaries of vital public schemes of the government like the National Employment Guarantee Scheme, pension to freedom fighters.

1. Need of Positive Values

Hence, we must strive to find out administrators possessing the following values to ensure good governance; competence, missionary-zeal, the capacity to motivate other people, the capacity to communicate with others, the ability to get along with colleagues and the people, cultural adaptability, the capacity to organize and manage, the capacity to inspire confidence in others, patience and dignity. Besides, they must have faith in the ideal of their work, be willing to accept hardships and prepare to work in a spirit of service. Their ambition and enthusiasms should not be dampened by local conditions which may not provide them with the necessary facilities. Unfortunately, the sense of dedication has been the crassest causality of the prevailing atmosphere of cynicism bred by increasing propensity towards expediency.

Public services must also develop the normative linkages, i.e., they must develop professional values which should help them in their best performances. Values are contagious. They spread throughout an organization, a group, or a society. If an organization or group cherishes high values, the behaviour of the individual who enters it is inevitably influenced. They should not develop an excessive sense of self-importance or arrogance. As has been said in Gita, "We should pursue the path of excellence without fear or favour and work ceaselessly to achieve the objectives, i.e. service to people.

"Good organization building has to create around it a

bracing atmosphere, a prideful tradition of integrity, excellence and fellowship. Human beings breathe an ethos around them almost unconsciously, and these traditions make for that ethos.[7]

2. Promote good governance through responsiveness and accountability to people

It is widely agreed that manipulation and lack of integrity produce strong negative side-effects and reduce organizational effectiveness. With this important value commitment the organization may shift their styles and climate from one of direction, control and surveillance to one of providing help, support and instruction. Mutuality and collaboration between the leaders and the led promote self-organization. Let the newcomers strive to set-up organized society with social democracy and high human values settings up ideal societal or public management institutions and if such timely warnings are not accepted, social upsurges are bound to develop in a mild or a violent form causing damage to good governance.[8]

3. Promote good governance through value of National Integration

Employees in the public service should refrain from decisions in respect of which they have reason to believe that these are calculated to benefit any particular person, party or group at the cost of public interest. When there is any conflict between public interest and private interest they should disclose this to their superiors They should not approach politicians and outsiders in respect of service matter or private benefits and bring peer pressure. They must also not abuse their official position to obtain a benefit for themselves or for someone else financial or other form. Such attitude on the part of civil services is found to usher an era of good governance.

Every employee in the public services should recognize the integrative role of the public service in national development and resist internal and external attempts to fragment the public services and society on caste, communal and religious lines. They should not unauthorizedly release information which is not permitted by law or compromise private or business interest or the privacy of an individual when such information has been received in confidence

4. Promote good governance by infusing ethics into politics to end political degeneration and corruption

The country is passing through a terrible crisis these days. The aggravation of material greed has, as a reaction, set ablaze the fire of corruption at all levels. Through the dominant influence of the present material civilization and the ideal of enjoyment fostered by it, even the basic framework and moral fibre of the country has been affected by an internal demoralization. The heart trembles at the sight of the moral degradation practised today in the field of public administration. There is no limit to the fraud and hypocrisy that are being practised in the name of politics.

Mr. Prem Bhatia. Editor-in-Chief of *The Tribune* rightly mentioned that today's political scene is influenced by shortcuts, i.e. the urge to reap the maximum benefits with the minimum of efforts. He commented: "A large number of politicians had chosen the shortest path to power. They had bribed, cajoled and built their way to the top. The patronage of office was used by them to consolidate their positions. This had inevitably led to the spread of the short-cut system in spheres other than politics."[9]

Most of the problems in Public Administration are emanating from political corruption and interference. The credibility gap between the political and administrative leadership is on the increase causing decline of good governance. Most of the commissions, committees and the daily press have been emphasizing the gravity of the situation. No organization can progress until and unless its political leaders are above board. One of the founding fathers of the Indian Constitution, Mr. H.V. Kamath regrets that the total devaluation of moral values and ethical ideals in Public life and administration today has given rise to the present day rat race for position, power and pelf by any means, more by crook than by hook that can be done to ensure confidence of the staff and the people in the integrity of the political elite? The answer is plain and simple, i.e., the political elite must demonstrate integrity and instill faith among their subordinates about their fairness and impartiality. Faith is a contagious disease and once it is developed, it would bend the various levels of the administration into a cohesive structure.

We may follow Gandhiji's ideals, the key to making Gandhi's vision a reality and practicing his values is to persistently subvert selfish worldly pursuits with ethical livelihood. This is the immediate struggle every Indian, on an individual and collective basis, has to non-violently and passionately wage. Will the political leadership, policy-makers and administrators listen to this call and put things back on the right track? If they realize and do, it is good. The sooner the better.[10] This would promote the beginning of an era of good governance based on values.

5. Good governance need be assured through action based on knowledge rather than mere paper planning by the executive

Words, written or spoken, are of no use unless put into action. The emphasis should be more on performance rather than paper planning. Khalil Gibran has rightly said that "Believing is a fine thing, but placing those beliefs into execution is a test of strength. Many are those who talk like the roar of the sea, but their lives are shallow and stagnant, like the rotting marshes. Many are those who lift their heads above the mountain tops, but their spirit remain dormant to the obscurity of the caverns."[11]

Thus, the future of this budding developing democracy depends upon the attitudes of its political and administrative elite. There is no substitute for hard work which would be reflected in better life of the people. Nevertheless, without a concerted attempt to make the administration much more action oriented than at present, these may not yield enough results. Kalibara Ekken, the Japanese sage has nicely put it as: If by study, enquiry or thought, we have learned the truth, we should then put it into practice in both our speech and action. Let what we say be true and what we do discreet. Regulate the emotions, and suppress anger and selfish desires. Shake off evil and cling to good. Discovering our faults, let us not hesitate to correct them. Towards others let us be considerate. All this is the way of true action. . . . Without putting what we have learned into practice, it bears no fruit. Good governance thus requires sincerity and faithful action from politico-administrative leadership.

6. Promote participation of people by the executive to enhance good values among people

At present, we find a great deal of alienation between the people and the organization. This has undermined the legitimacy, effectiveness and credibility of the public administration in our country. We need to promote harmony and mutual trust among the people and public administration. The objectives of public relations should be to increase prestige and goodwill and protect the life of the organization by safeguarding it against unwarranted attacks as well as to remove the genuine complaints and grievances of the people. To improve understanding between the citizens and the personnel, public relations need to be developed in an effective manner to create favourable community opinion towards public services. This would create confidence in the minds of the people towards the competence, fairness, honesty, impartially and sincerity of the public services and thus pave the way to good governance.

Good Governance presupposes a good administrative design

Increased productivity in the developing countries depends to a great extent on the executive branch, which should pursue efficiency with greater determination. The executive branch can pursue its objectives provided the prevailing administrative system is conducive to the socio-economic system. The design of an administrative system is a basic aid to the achievement of its primary objectives; if the design is unsound, the achievement of objectives is likely to fall short of expectations. The administration can provide the means whereby the most effective use can be made of the knowledge and skills of the personnel engaged in different activities. The benefits of modern science and technology can reach the people only if such services are properly planned and effectively implemented. Without consistent and persistent efforts to achieve perfection of administration, progress in increasing efficiency/productivity is impossible.

The prevailing administrative set-up in the developing countries is in a state of crisis with regard to their management system. Its methods are inadequate and outdated. There is a need to design an integrated administrative system which may cover the planning of work programs, budget preparation, resource programming, reviewing and evaluating results and definitions of programs and aims. Besides, obsolete methods of work must be improved or replaced. Our experience during the last three decades has demonstrated that the development plans have not been satisfactorily implemented because of an outdated administrative system, entailing organizational defects, lack of co-ordination, complex and cumbersome administrative and financial procedures, etc. These defects and deficiencies need to be corrected in order to bring about a sharp reduction in the administrative obstacles to development and to bridge the gap between aspirations and performance.

The people inhabiting the developing world expect their government to pull them out of the morass of distressing under-development. This would be possible only provided the efforts of the governments are comprehensive, selective co-ordinated sustained. Besides, timely action backed by strong will and determination at all decision-making and operational levels can change the complexion of our socio-economic scene.

Public Administration in the developing countries has the potential and, can be optimized for bringing good governance in the government. The need is to enforce its reputation, prestige, credibility and viability. Public services properly recruited, rightly trained, properly motivated and given the congenial environment, can help in fulfilment of the ideals of the country. Thus, the public service would have to work hard with dedication to achieve the results.

Let us have a great ideal, an ideal that will startle us with its greatness. That is the only kind of an ideal to hold before our minds eye and to work for. Little by little our imperfections and difficulties will vanish and instead of regarding life as a drudgery, instead of shrinking from it, we shall bless this life which offers so many opportunities. We shall find joy even in the little daily tasks and wherever we are placed we shall know happiness.[12] This can fructify good governance.

The critical role of the State in the delivery of public goods and services can be realized only through an efficient, effective and responsive administration delivering quality public service. Measures for administrative reforms have, therefore, acquired an urgency, as the framework for an effective administration, capable of quality service needs to be put in place. High quality and effective public services are a vital part of a modern state as people are entitled to expect that services, which are often central to their lives, should be responsive, sensitive to their needs, easy to use, flexible and efficient.

In exercising of discretion, holders of public offices are under obligation to take into consideration the following: (i) pursue only the purposes for which the power has been conferred; (ii) there should not be any bias in observing objectivity and impartiality; (iii) only relevant factors should be taken into account; (iv) unfair discrimination should be avoided by observing the principle of equality before law; (v) maintain proper balance between any adverse effects which the decision may have on the rights, liberties and interests of persons and the purpose sought to be achieved; (vi) take decision within a time frame which is reasonable having regard to the matter at stake; and (vii) apply general administrative guidelines, if any, in a consistent manner taking into account, at the same time, particular circumstances of each case. In addition, procedural requirement of hearing, access to information, statement of reasons and indication of remedies should be followed in the interest of good administrative practice.[13]

Government is very sensitive to the expectation of the people and sincere efforts in this direction have already been initiated. Good governance is an overarching component of the agenda of our Government, which has taken measures to make administration accountable, responsive and transparent through: (a) citizen charters to signify the visible commitment for quality service and attention to grievance, (b) review of administrative laws and regulations for dismantling procedures and red tape by repeal or amendment of outdated and obsolescent laws, regulations and procedures that mystify and confuse the people, (c) creating the environment to reap the benefits of Information Technology by harnessing, Informational Technology, (d) setting up of Information and Facilitation Counters, and (e) formulation of a Freedom of Information Bill.[14]

When the British were ruling over us, our political leaders used to criticize the prevailing bureaucracy as wooden, as without imagination, and without any response to the human situation. After we gained freedom and took over the administration from the British, we soon found, to our dismay, that we were only continuing the static tradition; we could not break away from it and start a new dynamic tradition inspired of the national urges and patriotic motivation, which alone can make it responsive to the human urges and aspirations. This failure was entirely due to the dominance of this functionary attitude, the attitude of a mere careerist and job-seeker, referred to earlier, among most members of our various services.

All the functions performed by the civil services must be oriented to rebuild the country, transform its economy, instill in the people an ambition for higher standards of life and arouse in them the will and determination to work for such standards. The ambition of the greatest man of our times, Mahatma Gandhi, was to wipe out every tear from every eye. The work of civil services will not be complete until this noble objective is achieved. In a broader senses, the government through its civil servants, should ensure happiness to the people, as embodied in the following words quoted in Suriti:

All the human beings may enjoy happiness and bliss. All should be free from troubles. All should promote the welfare of others. No one should suffer from any visible cause which can be prevented by human efforts.

In a nutshell, we may keep the following commandments in mind:

- Timely, prompt service
- Minimum red tape and forms to fill
- Courteous Behaviour
- Minimum waiting time
- Good Ethical values
- Minimum visits to multiple offices
- Minimization of artibrariness
- Prompt information on delays, waiting times, etc.
- Prompt disposal of cases.

Let us explain the role of values in the context of Medicines:

On graduation, the doctor took the oath of honesty, purity, etc., which stressed all the ethical values. Later, with Western medicine becoming popular in the country, the medical students were asked to take the Hippocratic Oath, which originated in Greece. The Hindu version of such an oath has been in existence long before the Hippocratic Oath. But most Indians have not heard about it or have forgotten it. Since Independence, this practice of Oath-taking has been given up in most places.

The training of the medical students and the oath that they took on graduation fully reflected the great ethical values that were instilled into all medical students and doctors. Thus medical ethics became the bedrock of medical practice and dharmic ideals prevailed. As regards remuneration for services rendered, this always took a secondary place. The medical students and the medical profession were indoctrinated with the principle that medical treatment is based on compassion towards all beings and it is not primarily meant for earning money or for fulfiling other desires.

In Vedic India and even later for many centuries, physicians were told that medical practice was never fruitless; it always gave some benefit or other for the doctor, not necessarily material or monetary. A Sanskrit-verse describes this idea as follows:

> Sometimes punya, sometimes friendship,
> Somewhere money, somewhere else fame,

Often knowledge and experience.
Never is treatment without is fruit.[15]

Ethical or dharmic values are essential for the existence and for the progress of any society and have to be preserved and practised if human civilization has to progress. Of these values, ethics in medicine is of the greatest importance, as medicine deals with problems of life and death. To argue that the practice of values in medicine will depend on the condition of society is untenable, as the members of the medical profession belong to the elite in society and must shoulder greater responsibilities. They must have much greater concern about values than any other section of society. The doctor and the teacher-the Vaidya and the Upadhyaya—have to set a noble example to others in any civilized society.[16]

Suggestions to promote values in the executive

1. Need of Promoting the values of dramatic responsiveness to the national urges

It is in this context that the problems of administrative efficiency in our newly established democracy become urgent. That efficiency is to be measured by only one test, namely, its dynamic responsiveness to the national urges. This is achieved only by the administrative personnel, representing a cross-section of the national intelligentsia, getting trained in imaginative sympathy and national dedication. It is self-centredness and lack of concern for others that lead to corruption; and that evil is already afflicting man and society alike in India. We are not required to forego all concern for ourselves and becomes ascetics. We are only called upon to put this concern for ourselves in the context of a larger concern for others. This changes the whole aspect of our life and work. This is called enlightened self-interest in political philosophy. It is self-interest, but with a touch of spiritual enlightenment, resulting in the recognition of mutuality, inter-dependence and the spirit of service, as the truth of all healthy social process.[17]

2. Need of promoting Human Transformation of our administration through value system

It is this human transformation that must come to all in our administration, and also to all men and women in our various professions. We have a great message on this subject in a verse of one of our Upanisads, namely, the Chandogya Upanisad, only next in importance and size to the greatest among all the Upanisads, the Brhadaranayaka Upanisad. These are between three thousand and four thousand years old. What inspiring and profound ideas come out of this great literature of so ancient a period of human history. What is the source of human work-efficiency?—that is the question to which the Chandogya verse gives the following answer (1.1.10):

> Yadeva vidyaya karoti, sraddhaya, upanisada, tadeva viryavattarain bhavati

It is very simple Sanskrit utterance. Yadeva Karoti—whatever is done; vidyaya—through knowledge—what we call today the 'know-how'. The first thing to acquire is the 'know-how' of a task. Is that enough? No, says the Upanisad, and add: sraddhaya—through sraddha—faith or conviction; there must be faith in the great urges and longings of man in front of me, faith in the work I am called upon to do to fulfil those urges, and faith in myself—atma sraddha—in may capacity to rise to the occasion. Even these two are not enough. A third quality is also necessary, namely upanisada, through deep thinking and contemplation. Actions done with these three energies behind them alone become not only efficient, viryayat, but more and more efficient, viryavattaram, says the verse.[18]

3. Promoting the values of character-efficiency and work-efficiency

That the philosophy of administration as taught in the Gita, combining the energy of vision with the energy of action, and imparting to man the double energy resource of character-efficiency and work-efficiency, the heroism of saintliness with the heroism of manliness, can lead people, any people, to all round greatness, is the grand testament affirmed by the Gita itself in its luminous last verse. Our national politics and administration can do nothing more inspiring and momentous today, as much internationally as nationally, than being to check and verify that great testament in the vast modern anthropological development laboratory of our ancient country, and transform its dubious distinction of being the largest democracy into the luminous one of being the greatest democracy.

All good character traits have a common denominator of social courage, usefulness, common sense besides self-acceptance and self-confidence. Character is built in the struggle and rush of life and not in solitude. Of course, experience is toned up in solitude. A man of character has intellectual convictions, patience, willing courage, tremendous common sense and charm, promotes harmony, is socially effective impressive and inspiring. Character touches above the wills of men. It is character that purifies and develops within us a sense of discrimination.

Character is the noblest possession of an individual. It exercises a greater power than wealth and secures all the honour without the jealousies of fame. . . . Men of character are not only the conscience of society but in every well-governed state they are its best motive power. The strength, the industry and civilization of nations all depend upon individual character. Mind without heart, intelligence without conduct, cleverness without goodness, are powers in their way, but they may be powers only for mischief. We may be instructed or amused by them. But it is sometimes as difficult to admire them as it would be to admire the dexterity of a pickpocket or the horsemanship of a highway man.

Men of character may not be popular, but they are respected and followed. They are true leaders of men and times. They will fight but not quarrel, differ but will not oppose or criticize, will be firm but not rigid/dogmatic, appreciate without flattery, co-operate, compromise and reconcile on non-essentials but put up a valiant, relentless fight for basic principles, act and never react.

Swami Vivekananda says:[19]

What you want is character, strengthening of the will. Continue to exercise your will and it will take you higher.

This will is almighty. It is character that can cleave through adamantine walls of difficulties. And he proceeds to define character in this manner:

The character of any man is but the aggregate of his tendencies, the sum total of the bent of his mind. We are what our thoughts have made us. Thoughts live; they travel far. And so take care of what you think. Every work that we do, every movement of the body, every thought that we think, bears an impression on the mind-stuff. What we are, every man's character is determined by the sum total of these impressions. If good impressions prevail, the character becomes good, if bad, it becomes bad.[20]

Character is that ensemble of actualized qualities of the head and heart of an individual through the help of which he masters facts and forces of life in a creative manner and gradually reaches self-fulfilment in a way helpful to others as well.

The man of character develops upwards, the man without character slips downwards. The man of character makes history, the man without it is marred by history. The man of character is the hope, solace, well-being, peace and inspiration of mankind; the man without character causes trouble, strife, worry, and misery in society.[21]

We are now experimenting on human welfare, human development, in our country. We had never done it before on the colossal scale that we are doing today. We had the necessary philosophy and ideas; but the implementation was arrested in later centuries. Therefore, the stress today should be on practical, faster and still faster, and watching a new India, healthy and strong, rising on the horizon. This should be the great watchword of all administration in the Centre and the States, down to the zilla parishad and gram panchayati institutions, in our country.[22]

4. Change Environmental Factors, which Tactily permit Unethical Practices and are inimical to good governance

The vacuum created because of traditional and 'old fashioned' values drawn from religious sources and based on common sense being discarded in favour of materialism and selfish individualism, clearly points to the need for a code of ethics. As a matter of fact, no specific standards were left sacred against which the conduct of public officials (as well as business people) could be measured. And as clergy and religious leaders were told to keep out of the state affairs, the protective layer of public morality was left exposed to the onslaught of corruption, dishonesty, sleaziness, deception and selfish individualism. That protective layer in the body politic is needed back. For no nation or a society, irrespective of its political and religious orientation, can live in a moral vacuum. There have to be some articles of faith (drawn from the societal culture, traditions, and religions) governing our lives, which must be resurrected and strengthened. We already know that one cannot legislate honesty and good behaviour; these have to come from within. For that, one has to look to our religions where such attributes are considered sacred. But, one does not acquire such attributes by thinking alone; these have to be drilled in the thinking process of the officials. But that could be possible if their moral consciousness is raised so that they are able to fight against the forces of corruption, favoritism, and malpractice. Otherwise, they will continue to be adrift in the sea of a moralism, of which the prevailing administrative culture has come to symbolise. It is to prevent further decay that they ought to think in terms of drawing on their priceless spiritual and cultural heritage. Thus, there is a need within the secular domain of the administrative culture to seek the spiritual guidance. Only by demonstrating high standards of personal integrity, fairness, justice, and by regarding their work as Dharma, public officials may be able to arrest those insidious forces which have penetrated the foundation as well as the structure of India's administration. Such is the requisite of a moral government.[23]

Moral values, in simple terms, are the values that tell us what is the right, proper and acceptable way of behaving. Moral values are indispensable for good governance. An efficient and technologically sound administrative machinery, unless it stands on high moral pedestal, does not serve the public, but it services a self-perpetuating and exploitative system.

Unfortunately, the Indian Government sector cannot

boast of high moral standards. Superior courts have made highly critical comments on the conduct of bureaucrats, and the media is full of reports of high-handedness, corruption and other forms of inappropriate conduct of the bureaucrats. Honest and upright civil servants themselves are concerned about the low morality of the bureaucracy and have been voicing concern at various fora.

5. Understand Religious Foundations of Administrative Culture (Ethics) which can promote good governance

The Scriptures of many world religions contain pearls of wisdom about how one should behave in the public office, or what is expected of those who govern people. When scriptures were written, the world was ruled by kings; hence advice is rendered for the king and his servants. Hindu religion is no exception to this pattern; except that unlike some other religions, edicts and codes are not handed down by the rulers. The religious foundation of the duties and conduct of public officials as described in some scriptures of the Hindu religion is examined here. Let us begin by quoting Krishna in Gita:[24]

> One ought to understand what is duty
> and what is forbidden in the regulations laid down by the scriptures (Shastras).
> Knowing such rules and regulations, one should behave accordingly.
>
> (Gita, Chapter XVI, Verse 24)

Lord Krishna further says:

> O Partha ! that understanding by
> which one knows what ought to be done
> and what ought not to be done,
> what is to be feared and what is not,
> what is obligatory and what is permitted,
> leads to the righteous path.
>
> (Gita, Chapter XVIII, Verse 30)

That righteous path in Hindu religion is called Dharma.

How does one know the righteous path for specific functions or duties, Hindu scriptures (Shastras) provide guidelines. These guidelines or rules of Dharma have been prescribed by great many seers, each according to his or her wisdom.

6. Practice Ethics in Administration to inject good governance

While considering a charter of Ethics for public servants in India, there has to be a multi-dimensional approach, covering corruption, serving the Government, serving the public, solving conflict of interests, etc. Each of these attributes has an ethical connotation, and unless these are examined in depth, a holistic approach will not be visible.

Responsive and clean administration depends, *inter alia,* on adherence by the employees in public service to ethical standards and the basic principles of the Constitution such as secularism, social justice, attention to the needs of weaker sections and vulnerable groups, equality and rule of law. Both Centre and State Governments, no doubt, have notified regulations governing the conduct of employees in various services, which address the issues. However, they are more in nature of formulations of 'do's and dont's and do not represent a positive statement of values and believes that they should govern the private conduct of civil servants. In this context, Ministry of Personnel, Public Grievances and Pensions has formulated a draft code of ethics which have already been endorsed in the Chief Ministers' Conference and is at present being given a legal shape. The objective of the code is to prescribe standards of integrity and conduct in the public services. It would apply to all services, generalist and technical.

The key Public Service Regulations provide that an officer should perform with skill, care, diligence and impartiality, the duties of his office, to the best of his ability, comply with any lawful and reasonable direction given by a person having authority to give the direction, treat members of the public and other officers with courtesy and sensitivity to their rights, duties, and aspirations, avoid waste or extravagance in the use of public resources, not take improper advantage of any official information acquired as a consequence of employment, etc.

7. *Develop Ethical Traditions and Practices to keep civil servants in balance and concentrate on good governance.*

Justice R.S. Pathak has rightly sensed the need for ethical traditions. To quote him: A code of ethical principles is particularly related to each public office, but in general there are common principles applicable to all public offices. Those principles do not require enumeration, they are well known and undisputed. In large measure, continuing traditions indicate the identity and scope of ethical principles and determine the ethos controlling the exercise of all public power. And when I refer to traditions, I refer to traditions, which have been classically evolved as most appropriate for the exercise of public power. It is for that reason that it becomes necessary to educate novitiates in the ethical traditions of their office.

It is important to remember that when state power is channelised through a network of public institutions and public offices, it is intended to create a functioning system held in organic balance and unity, a system which in its holistic operation gives to the nation the intended opportunities for development and secures to the citizen his dignity and worth and the possibility of personal growth. It is vital that the constitutional system be kept in equilibrium. It may lose that organic balance and unity if its channels are clogged in consequence of the misuse or abuse or non-use of power in one or more of its constituent offices. The higher and more significant the office in the hierarchy within the system, the greater the potential for damage to the system.

8. *Love for the Citizens*

Love is the elixir of life. It has been found to have power even to cure physical and mental disorders. One who has hatred in his mind not only loses his mind, but also undermines his health and life. On the other hand, love, sympathy, and friendship not only contribute towards building one's peace of mind, but also create a balanced outlook. A man who develops these qualities will acquire serenity, joy and peace in spite of all external circumstances.

9. Need of Enthusiasm and dynamism

To make life worthwhile and fruitful, we must generate enthusiasm within ourselves. Generation of enthusiasm will take place when we discover for ourselves a goal and attach ourselves to the Altar with a spirit of dedication, reverence and love. Once we have surrendered ourselves to it, the ideal itself will provide us with the inspiration and strength. Then nothing can hinder the progress of our march towards that Goal and the ideal. The love for the ideal will overcome and vanquish all the hurdles from the ideal, and if it comes to that, life itself will be cast-off with a smile in dedication at that Altar. That was how Bhagat Singh could walk to the gallows with a smile on his face. What is important is that one should choose the right ideal . . . an ideal worthwhile even if it comes to sacrificing one's own life in the endeavour. The ideal should be inspiring, it should arouse the spring of activity in us. Thus, the discovering of the ideal is the secret of generating in ourselves Dynamism and Vitality in its fullness.[25]

10. Maximum use of time value

The statement that "Time is money" sums up the significance of time management. Though most people in Government, Public Enterprises and Private Sector understand the implications of time management, but in actual practice, we find that time is wasted and its importance is undermined. Most of the time of union and state level legislatures time is wasted in agitations, Dharans, etc. All other resources can be increased whenever required but not time as it is inelastic and therefore, we must make the best use of time. Just to illustrate the importance of time, many studies conducted revealed that person in administration hardly devote 30 to 40 per cent of their time for the activities they have been engaged for. It means that if proper use is made of time, we can provide services with the existing infrastructure two to three times more and thus, the process of development can be accelerated.

11. Effective Interpersonal relations value

Legislature consists of individuals who work in relation

to one another in different capacities to produce results. Only a coordinated effort among individuals can sustain the efficiency of legislature. Else a major effort would be wasted in misunderstandings, jealousies, etc. Today, most of the Organizations are plagued by poor interpersonal relations resulting in lack of interactions, team work, harmony and resultant low output. Only an effective interpersonal relations can lay the foundation of a sound legislature otherwise it would lead to disparate elements working in different directions causing great harm to the efficiency of the organization.

12. Selfless Service

The great secret of true success, of true happiness, then, is this; the man who asks for no return, the perfectly unselfish man, is the most successful. It seems to be a paradox. Do we not know that every man who is unselfish in life gets cheated, gets hurt? Apparently, Yes,. "Christ was unselfish, and yet he was crucified." True, but we know that his unselfishness is the reason, the cause of a great victory—the crowing of millions upon millions of lives with the blessings of true success.

Ask nothing; want nothing in return. Give what you have to give; it will come back to you—but do not think of that now. It will come back multiplied a thousand fold—but the attention must not be on that. Yet have the power to give and there it ends.[26]

"Man is born to give not to grab; grabber pays the penalty in the form of misery; the giver reaps the reward in the form of joy."

The resources, the bodily effort and the mental disposition becomes multiplied in the man of yajna. Such a man is never in want, always in affluence. His bounteous mind is the real Kamdhenu. Because of his frame of mind he is ever in prosperity. This is the plan and purpose of cosmos.

The essence of the spirit of service is contained in the following words of Vivekananda: "This is the gist of all worship—to be pure and to do good to others. He who sees Shiva in the poor, in the weak, and in the diseased, really worships Shiva; and if he sees Shiva only in the image, his worship is but preliminary. He who has served and helped one poor man seeing Shiva in him, without thinking of his caste, or creed, or race, or anything, with him Shiva is more pleased than with the man who sees Him only in the temples. He who wants to serve the father must serve the children first. He who wants to serve Shiva must serve His children, must serve all creatures in the world first.[27]

13. Faith and Reasons

67-68 GG Lord Krishna made following observations which are essential for good civil servants to imbibe leadership. (Bhagavad Gita, Chapter III, Jayadayal Goyandka, Gita Press, Gorakhpur):

1. Without performing action, man does not attain actionlessness, or perfection in Karmayoga (III. 4).
2. Merely by renouncing action, man does not attain perfection in Jnanayoga (III.4).
3. Man cannot remain totally inactive even for a moment (III.5).
4. Outwardly renouncing action and mentally dwelling on the objects of senses, is hyposcrisy (III.6).
5. He who performs action disinterestedly, controlling the mind and senses, is the best of men (III.7).
6. Action is superior to inaction (III.8).
7. Desisting from action, one cannot even maintain the body (III.8).
8. Action performed for the sake of sacrifice causes no bondage, but leads to salvaton (III.9).
9. Action has been enjoined upon man by the Creator, Brahma, and disinterested performance of action leads to the highest good (III. 10,11).
10. He who enjoys objects without performing his duty is a thief (III.12).
11. He who derives his sustenance from what is left after sacrifice, just for the sake of keeping up his body, gets absolved of all the sins (III.13).

12. He who, without performing sacrifices, cooks food only for nourishing his body is a sinner (III.13).
13. He who, abandoning his duties, hinders the operations of the wheel of creations, leads a sinful life and lives in vain (III.16).
14. Doing work without attachment, man attains God (III.19).
15. It was through action that Janaka and others reached perfection in ancient times (III.21).
16. Other men imitate what a great man does; therefore, a great man should perform action (III.21).
17. God has no duty, and yet he works with a view to maintaining the world order (III.22).
18. The wise man has no duty, and yet he should work in the interest of the world order (III.25).
19. The wise man should in no way deter men from the performance of their duty by renouncing action himself or by instructing men to do so, but should perform duties himself and get others to do the same (III.26).
20. The man of perfect knowledge should not unsettle the minds of men attached to action by instructing them to renounce their prescribed duties (III.29).

14. Performance of Duty without Attachment

तस्मादसक्त: सततं कार्यं कर्म समाचर ।
असक्तो ह्याचरन् कर्म परमाप्नोति पूरुष: ।।

3/19 AA Bhagavad Gita

Therefore, go on efficiently doing your duty without attachment. Doing work without attachment man attains the Supreme, i.e. excellence.

Renunciation of attachment implies renunciation of desire as well; for it is from attachment that desire springs up (2/62, 62). It is, therefore, that renunciation of the desire for fruit has not been separately mentioned.

Public officials who become attached to senses, they

cannot achieve excellence. They become slaves of their senses. They should work without having any personal interest.

The man dwelling on sense objects develops attachment for them; from attachment springs up desire, and from desire (unfulfiled) ensues anger.

Lord Krishna explains Yoga as 'balance of mind' (Chap. II.48).

When an action is motivated by desire, anxiety as to whether the desired result is going to be obtained or not will surely disturb the peace of mind of the doer. Again, when an action is inspired by self-interest, the doer is likely to lose sight of what is right or what is wrong. Even when he has chosen to do the right thing. Undue eagerness for obtaining the result is likely to make him swerve from the path of rectitude; whereas a doer, if he is detached towards the result, is saved from all anxiety. There is nothing to divert him from the righteous path. This teaching that we ought to discharge our obligations, social or otherwise, with a sense of responsibility, at the same time banishing from our minds all thought of obtaining personal benefit therefrom and in a spirit dedication to the Lord is what is meant by Karma-Yoga.

Neither think yourself as actor, because no actor can attempt to do anything. Discharge whatever is your duty, and remain at your ease with having done your part. Yoga-Vasistha-Utpatti-Parkarana, (Book 3).

The object of Gita is to discover a golden mean between the two ideals of action and of contemplation, preserving the merits of both. Karma-yoga is that golden mean in which the merits of both the ideals are happily integrated. It advocates a life of activity with detachment as the guiding spirit and one's spiritual unfoldment as the goal of one's activities. Thus, it discards neither ideal but integrating the spirit of renunciation of the one and the activism of the other, it purifies and elevates man. This fusion of the two ideals in Karma-yoga gives due regard to social welfare on the one hand and the other leads an individual to the fulfilment of his spiritual aspirations. Thus, the Gita ignores neither the society nor the individual. It does not advocate a life of inaction but instead recommends a life of intense action in which self is effaced in all its aspects (*Ibid.*, pp. 25.26).

Making people active and Sensitive to elect talented people

National Regeneration Movement suggest:

(a) Promoting among the citizens of the country, especially among the youth, the vision of Bharatiya Dharma Rajya, and educating them on the Fundamental Duties and Fundamental Rights of India citizens and on practical ways and means through which these Fundamental Duties and Fundamental Rights can be operationalised in the civil society.

Developing in the people of our country, especially in the youth, the noble values of tyaga and seva (sacrifice and service) though a 'skip a meal a week to feed a hungry child' programme, which will be promoted all over India as the 'common basic programme' of NRM with effect form 30th January 2007.

(b) Establishing and managing a network of 'Matru Bhavans' (homes of motherly love) in slums and villages across the country, where poor and hungry children live to make available to them with love one nourishing vegetarian meal every day and help them to become literate.

(c) Promoting 'Peace and Value Education' among the people of India, especially among the teachers and students of colleges and schools in the country, for spiritual revitalization, moral regeneration and national reconstruction of India, and establishing autonomous Dharma Bharathi Institutes of Peace and Value Education and Dharma Bharathi Schools of Study and Research for this purpose, and linking them up to form a 'Dharma Bharathi Global Open University of Peace and Value Education' in course of time.

(d) Promoting 'Gandhian Liberative Campaigns' for the economic, social and moral freedoms of India as envisaged by Mahatma Gandhi in Collaboration with all like-minded organizations and groups in the country, and educating the people of India on the liberative spirituality of NRM.

(e) Training and developing a dedicated cadre of leaders and constructive workers for moral regeneration and national reconstruction of India.

(f) Strengthening the existing organizations/ institutions/networks and creating new organizations/institutions/networks for realizing the aim and objectives of NRM.

(g) Printing and publishing literature/journals/news letters, etc. and producing audio/ visual training aids for promoting the aim and objective of NRM.

15. Lack of Sincerity and Transparency in Memo Carrying out Executive Operations

Investing in human development is, to some extent, about the provisioning of funds but merely pumping in money without addressing the subject of effective service delivery means there is tremendous wastage in human and fiscal terms. The issue is not merely how much has been provided but how it has been spent. Very often, states fail to achieve high levels of performance in human development because their systems lack accountability, are riddled with red tap and are distanced from the people. Providing good governance will ensure that the human development needs of those who are most vulnerable, will be met efficiently and effectively.

Good governance is about providing an efficient and effective administration that is committed to improving the quality of life of people. It enables a citizen-friendly, citizen-caring and responsive administration and in the process, results in the exercise of public authority for the common good. Although there are no standard indicators for good governance, a few indicators have been chosen to measure and evaluate effective implementation of programmes. These indicators include—improving service delivery; system improvement; financial management; accountability and transparency and anti-corruption measures.

Conclusion

There is more danger to the society from the immoral, improper and illegal actions committed in the name of the state than from a few cases of unethical acts by public servants. And as the state cannot perform those immoral actions without the active participation of its ministers and public servants. And as the state cannot perform those immoral actions without the active participation of its ministers and public servants, ultimately it depends upon these employees to behave morally. Given a democratic political system operating within the framework of the rule of law, an important goal of the administrative state should be to control the abuse of power and to ensure that elected representatives and responsible public servants are held accountable for the proper exercise of power. The abuse of power in the public sector can undermine public confidence and trust in government, reduce the capacity of government to fulfil its functions effectively, subvert ethical responsiveness to the citizenry, and impose unnecessary financial burden on taxpayers. The capacity of a political system to prevent, detect, punish, and control such abuses will have a direct bearing on its legitimacy and will strengthen the moral basis of its authority. The abuse of power relates not only to the commission of a crime as defined by statute but also to the omission of the use of power or non-enforcement of the law where an official is duty-bound to act but does not do so either because of refusal (*de Jure* non-enforcement), incompetence (*de facto* non-enforcement), or negligence. That is why it is very important for public servants to subscribe to the code of ethics which can guide them to resolve any ethical dilemma that they may face. It is desirable that public servant should be aware of general principles of conduct as expected of them not only by the state which employs them but also by the public. A set of such guiding principles, endorsed and enforced by the supreme political authority of the country, should be adopted both for the ministers and public servants. It should be noted that such principles and ethical guidelines may not necessarily produce a more accountable and ethical administration. However, it will assist them, as trustees of the public, to maintain a high standard of performance and to commit themselves to uphold the public good. The society looks up to them as leaders of social change and as champions of virtues and character. That is why they (but more so the ministers) should exhibit moral maturity which involves a sensitivity to questions of personal and social responsibility, and an ability to distinguish moral judgments from expressions of personal or conventional preferences. Thus, their commitment to assist the public in achieving the ideals of life in the society through the machinery of state is all the more important.[28]

What is more, administrative morality, howsoever elaborately codified and manualised, can never cover all situations encountered as well created by the civil servants. It is difficult to manualise all the possible ingredients of administrative morality. Even if this were possible, moral dilemmas would not altogether cease to beset human minds. One may, for instance, take a view, quite legitimately according to him, that a behaviour not explicitly prohibited by the code of conduct is permissible and yet there are many gray-zone cases which would be censorious in many eyes.

Nor it is possible to ascribe correct weightage to all the ingredients of administrative morality. Is punctuality to be accorded the same credit as, say integrity? Even the credits changes with the shift in the value system in the society. In a permissive age, like ours, adjectives undergo heavy depreciation and get diluted. Evaluation of moral conduct, it seems, does not remain unchanging and get diluted. Evaluation of moral conduct, it seems, does not remain unchanging over a period of time, especially in the less than dark zone, called the gray one.

But in an administration in which transgressions from norms of administrative morality are common and widespread, the culture of control and supervision is also weak and ineffectual. It would perhaps be even more correct to say that acts of moral transgressions escalate only in the absence of leadership role in the hierarchy. Coming nearer to our own times, the LIC Affairs of the early sixties implicating a civil servant (H.M. Patel) and a minister (T.T. Krishnamachari) alarmed the India society and the highest norms of political and administrative morality were enforced. Over a period of time, the incidence of deviant conduct has increased and has thus insensitised the country's public administration, especially when viewed in the context of the nineties.[29]

Japanese experience in creating a new work culture and ethos is now universally hailed as something unique. There is a pervasive perception there that nation is an extension of the organization and the organization is the extension of himself, with organizational loyalty having precedence over family loyalty. The concepts of life-time employment, guaranteeing job security, life-time education, caring for human being in all aspects and respects; emphasis on team work and group spirit than on individual excellence, giving a practical shape to this team-building faith through quality circle, have made Japanese the foremost 'productivity' prone nation. Of course, Japaneses work culture is the product of social values and culture of the people.[30]

Notes and References

1. C.F. Strong, Modern Political Constitution, Sidgwick and Jackson Limited, Land, 1952, p. 7.
2. C.F. Strong, *op. cit.*, p. 213.
3. H.R. Khanna, Judicial and Administrative Reforms—Indian Experience in *IJPA*, July-Sept. 1990, p. 51.
4. Presidential Address by Mrs. Indira Gandhi, delivered on October 22, 1971, at the Annual Meeting of I.I.P.A., New Delhi.
5. Ferrel Heady, Public Administration: A comparative perspective, Second Edition, Revised and Expanded, New York, Marcel Dekker, INC, N.Y. 1979, p. 220.
6. Ashok Mukhopadhya, Reinventing Government, For Good Governance, in T.N. Chaturvedi (ed.) Towards Good Governance", New Delhi, IIPA, 1999, p. 36.
7. A.D. Moddie: "The Brahmanical Culture and Modernity, Asia Publishing House, New York, pp. 106-14.
8. M.L. Mishra: Contemporary Management Thinkers, Associated Publishing House, New Delhi, 1980, p. 120.
9. *The Tribune*, Nov. 29, 1980: The Anatomy of a short-cut system.
10. *The Tribune*, Nov. 24, 1980.
11. Khalil Gibran: Between Night and Morn, The Philosophical Library, New York, 1972, pp. 8-9.
12. Swami Parmananda, Secret of Right Activity, Madras, Ramakrishna Math.

13. "The Lusaka Statement on Government under the Law", Zambia, October 15, 1992.
14. Prabhat Kumar, A Responsive and Effective Government, in Management in Government, January, March, 2000, p. 1.
15. Dr. B. Ramamurthi, Values in The Medical Field, in Values, p. 171.
16. *Ibid.* p. 178.
17. Swami Ranganathananda, Democratic Administration in the Light of Practical Vedanta, Sri Ramakrishna Math, Chennai, 2003, p. 21.
18. *Ibid.*, pp. 46-47.
19. Swami Vivekananda, "India and Her Problems", Advaita Ashram, Calcutta, 1976, pp. 55-56.
20. *Ibid.*
21. Swami Budhananda, How to Build Character, Advaita Ashram, Calcutta, 2002, p. 28.
22. Swami Ranganathanada, A Charter of Ethics, Reading Material For Trainees, p. 75.
23. Swami Ranjanathananda, A Character of Ethics, Reading Material For Trainees, (Some abstracts).
24. O.P. Dwivedi, Administration Theology, in *IJPA*, July-Sept. 1996, pp. 408-09.
25. Nigro Felex A., Public Administration, Readings and Documents, Rinehart and Co., New York, 1951, p. 439.
26. Swami Harshananda, Attainment of "Yoga: Maladies and Remedies", in *Yoga: Its various Aspects*, Sri Ramakrishna Math, Madras, pp. 203-04.
27. Swami Jagadhatmananda, Learn to Live, Vol. I, Chennai, Shri Ramakrishna Math, p. 256.
28. O.P. Dwivedi, "Ethics and Administrative Accountability", *IJPA*, Vol. XXIX, July-Sept. 1983, pp. 516-17.
29. Shriram Maheshwari, "Administrative Morality", *IJPA*, Vol. XXXIV, No. 2, p. 188.
30. Bata K. Dey, 'Work Culture in India—Achievements and Failure, *IJPA*, Vol. XXXIV, No. 2, April-June 1989, p. 175.

9

Judiciary and Values

According to George Washington, "The administration of justice is the first pillar of good governance." For good governance people's faith in judiciary based upon its functioning is essential. Lord Denning once said, "Justice is rooted in confidence and confidence is destroyed when the right minded go away thinking that the judge is biased. The judges should not be diverted from their duties by any extraneous influences nor by any hope of rewards, nor by any fear of penalties, nor by flattering praise, nor by indignant reproach. It is the sure knowledge of this that gives the people confidence in judges.[1] The only real source of power that the judge can tap is the respect and confidence of the people. The result of this would result in good governance.

Lord Bryce writes, "There is no better test of the excellence of a government than the efficiency of a judicial system; for nothing more clearly touches the welfare and security of the average citizen than the feeling that he can rely on the certain and prompt administration of justice."[1]

A.C. Kapur writes, The judiciary is the guardian of the rights of man and it protects these rights from all possibilities of individual and public encroachments. The feeling in an average citizen that he can rely on the certain and prompt

CHART 9.1

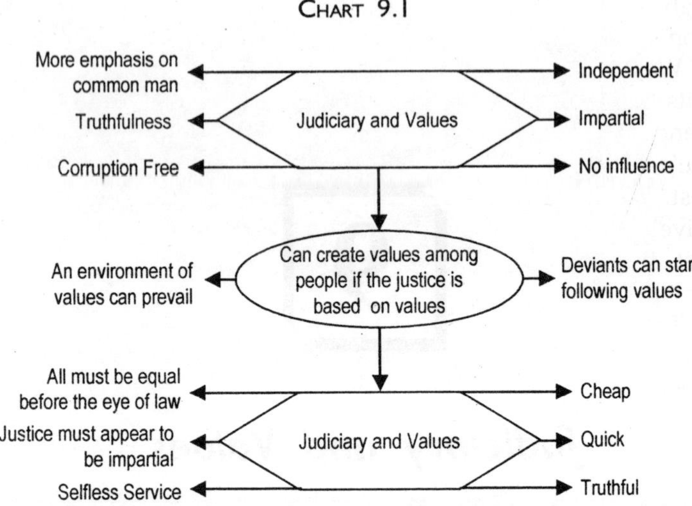

administration of justice maximizes his liberty. If there is no adequate provision for the administration of justice, the liberty of the people is jeopardized, for there is no definite means which should ascertain and decide rights, punish crimes, and protect the innocent from injury and usurpation.

Dr. A.P.J. Abdul Kalam, former President of India in his article, "Scope of Judiciary—Towards speedy dispensation of justice" in the *Sunday Tribune* dated Nov. 19, 2006 observed that as the judiciary is catching up with societal and technological evolution, the citizen of India look up to this institution with hope as the ultimate protector of human rights and the final resort for dispensation of justice. The unflinching hope the nation cherishes and looks forward to is the judiciary with its excellence and impeachable integrity. We should do everything to make the judicial systems succeed.

This casts a very heavy responsibility on the entire judicial system and participating institutions to live up to the expectations reposed in it and to maintain the sacred aura attached to it unsullied. Qualities of honesty and integrity are synonymous with each member of the judicial system.

The government has approved connecting all the 15,000 courts-from the District Courts to the Supreme Court—

through a wide Area Net-work. This is a very important step mission mode and time-bound operation.

We must ensure that legal instruments maximize the benefits for our people and nation. Laws must protect the indigenous technologies and trade to the extent they impact people's living and their welfare as well as ensure national interest. We need experts both in the Bar and the judiciary to effectively deal with the legal systems of multiple nations and protect the interest of our companies doing business and trade with these countries.

The welfare of citizens greatly depends upon speedy, timely and impartial justice. James Bryce has rightly remarked that there is no better test of the excellence of a Government than the efficiency of its judicial system. The judiciary is the guardian of the rights of people and it protects these rights from all possibilities of individual and public encroachments. "If the law be dishonestly administered" says Bryce, "the salt has lost its flavour; if it be weakly and fitfully enforced, the guarantees or order fail, for it is more by the certainty than by the severity of punishment that offenders are repressed. If the lamp of justice goes out in darkness, how great is that darkness." Thus, judiciary, if functions faithfully, is sure to promote good governance.

All the three wings of government, the three arms and instrumentalities of governance—Legislature, Executive and Judiciary—have, it seems, collaborated to set-up a joint venture in mal-governance. In our "functioning anarchy", where Legislature and Executive have conspired to sacrifice governance at the altar of political expediency, an 'activist' judiciary, in a very brief flicker of hope, seemed a saviour, but that light has also gone out, engulfing the system of governance in a thick blanket of darkness. Judicial system has also not covered itself with all glory—in Nani Palkiwal's inimitable expressions, it deals with law but does not deliver justice, resulting in a situation where amid plentiful of laws in our country, there is acute scarcity of justice. The delays, complications in legal dispensations, volumes of pendencies, the high costs, the vagaries of lawyers-all combine to make courts of justice a dreaded place, almost a prohibited area for most sufferers, where you enter to compound your sufferings.[3] How people can expect justice and good governance when even the judiciary has failed to live upto the expectation.[2]

V.N. Narayanan, the *Hindustan Times* editor, has recently observed:

I think the degeneration of politics and decline of governments every where is primarily due to the fact that the world, institutions and leaders lack the boxing ring's count often or its space-age equivalent of countdown from ten to zero. All over scams and scandals from Rajiv's Bofors to Laloo's todder via Harshad's securities and Narasimha Rao's urea are alive and unsolvable today and for eternity precisely because they do not have this count of ten firmly imposed on them. A community can be expected to respect the law only if it respects the calendar and the clock. A judiciary which has no concern for the litigants' time and money cannot deliver justice. It can only pass sentences.

He has a simple yet novel prescriptive panacea:

There ought to be a mandatory unit for MPs' speaking time in Parliament for every minute of transgression one month of his term would be cut or 10 per cent of his salary and perks slashed. Every judge who fails to decide a case in, say, six months, should be penalised with fine or imprisonment on similar terms prescribed for convicts. Ministers and bureaucrats should be punished with penal servitude when projects incur cost over-runs due to delays.

Bureaucrats, judges and politicians—the three pillars of governance—edifice do not bother about deadlines (they all want to hog headlines and bylines) because they deal in other people's money, time and morale. For the last named category, there is particularly no morals, they live in the present Raat gayee baat gayee! These three, in 'joint venture' with the other three, namely, economic-financial mafias, underworld dons and trade-union/vested interest lobbies, have made a mince-meat of good governance.

According to Jain and Jain, "It is an accepted axiom that the real kernel of democracy lies in the courts enjoying the ultimate authority to restrain the exercise of absolute and arbitrary power. Without some kind of judicial power to control administrative authorities, there is a danger that they may commit excesses and degenerate into arbitrary bodies, and such a development would be inimical to a democratic constitution and the concept of rule of law."[3]

Rai Atul Krishna in his article, "Judiciary *versus* Executive: Supreme Court has final world" in the *Sunday HT* dated Dec. 10, 2006 clearly quotes the views of Chief Justice Y.K. Sabharwal that Lok Sabha Speaker Somnath Chatterjee may insist that as a law-making body Parliament is supreme but Chief Justice of India (CJI) Y.K. Sabharwal made it emphatically clear that when it comes to interpreting the Constitution and law of the land, the final word rests with the Supreme Court. "We are final not necessarily because we are always right—no institution is infallible—but because we are final, adding that it would be improper to question the court's finality just because it may have erred on a few occasions. The CJI said the use of modern technology could go a long way in ensuring transparency in judicial functioning. "Even the marking of cases is now being done by computers", he said, adding that the use of digital signatures could help in expediting the delivery of certified copies.

Judiciary has played a great role in providing good governance to the people. Law and order is the biggest challenge for good governance as we witness daily the problems of rape, thefts, dacoity, murders, extortion, etc. The police system was governed by outdated Police Act, 1861. *Hindustan Times* editorial (Sept. 28, 2006) "Give them teeth, not fungs" rightly states a draft to a new Police Act which is being finalized by a committee set-up in September, 2005. After much nudging from the Supreme Court, which has ordered the implementation of police reforms on or before December, 31, 2006, to promote good governance, the draft is to be converted into a Bill and placed before Parliament. While reforms are likely to include the creation of separate institutions for investigation and for law and order, upgrading inter-state links to tackle inter-state crimes and incorporating modern methods to crack down on drug-trafficking, cyber-crimes and economic crimes, there is a fundamental flaw that desperately needs correction. Never bothering to rethink the colonial motive behind British India policing. Indian governments at both the Centre and states have preferred to use the police as an extension of politics.

Political interference has become norms in the Indian police system and any unwillingness to comply with the self-styled political masters have led to reprisals, harassments and humiliations. Transfers of police officials after every state government change has become a parody of musical chairs. This, above all, must stop. The Supreme Court has suggested that Director General of Police (GDP), Inspector Generals of Police (IGPs) and even Station House Officers (SHO) be given a fixed tenure. This will insulate them from being shunted around by those who believe that the police are an extension of their party cadre.

Kanwar Sandhu in his article, "Policing the impossible" in *Hindustan Times* dated Sept. 30, 2006 very rightly said that while the sweeping police reforms suggested by the Supreme Court show the apex court's concern on politicization and misuse of the uniformed police forces in the country, much will have to change in the politico-administrative system if these are to become a reality. Hearing the 10 year long petition filed by Prakash Singh (a retired IPS officer) and some others, the Bench headed by the Chief Justice of India, Justice Y.K. Sabharwal, observed that no comprehensive review of the police system had been carried out since independence, despite the recommendations of various commissions, including the National Police Commission in 1977. The reforms ordered by the SC, which are to be implemented by the year end, are based on the recommendations of various commissions that have been re-related and given practical shape. Police forces, particularly in the states, have so far been treated as a personal fief by the governments in power. It is open knowledge that false cases are often registered to serve political purposes. Tenures of field officers are at the bidding of political masters. The common man has little faith in the law and order system and even less trust in the prevailing system of investigation.

Supreme Court suggested the following reforms:

(i) Setting up of security commission to avoid political interference.

(ii) Fixed tenure for field posting preferably 2 years.

(iii) Setting up of Police Establishment Board to deal with postings and transfers of officers of the level of DSP and below.

(iv) Separating Law and order from investigation. The purpose of all reforms is to insulate law and order machinery from political interference and provide justice to common man.

B.G. Verghese in his article, "Towards Police Reforms: A Must for Cleaning up the System" in *The Tribune* dated Sept. 29, 2006 rightly observes that it is the basic duty of the state to uphold the rule of law and maintain order so that citizens may live and prosper free of fear, pressure or anxiety. This it does through the instrumentality of the police, which provides the link between law enforcement and the criminal justice system. The breakdown of the latter too has been a matter of deepening concern as it has led to increasing lawlessness and despair and given rise to sundry mafias that have come to run a parallel system of governance and street justice.

The political class as a whole, cutting across party lines, bears primary guilt for this sorry state of affairs, resulting in the criminalization of politics and the politicisation of crime. Politicians and policemen of integrity have undoubtedly tried to stem the rot but have been overwhelmed by a rising tide of venality and defiance that has created a sense of impunity among wrongdoers.

Police Commission made several practical recommendations in a series of reports submitted between 1979 and 1981. These were shelved. The same body of recommendations were reviewed and updated by the Riberio, Padmanabhaiah and Malimath Committees in 1998, 2000 and 2002, but again to no avail. Vested interests have proved too strong. Illicit control over the police has become the means of covering up wrong actions, amassing ill gotten wealth and harassing opponents.

The police reforms provide the critical framework within which other improvements can be effected to create a more independent and people-friendly police. Effecting these reforms will call for perseverance and popular vigilance.

Alok Tiku in his statement "Babus get transfer shield" in *Hindustan Times* dated Sept. 15, 2006, observes that upright civil servants who do not fall in line can stop looking over their shoulders. Chief ministers have lost the power to transfer them at the drop of a hat. In a big push to governance reforms, the Manmohan Singh government has finally notified the fixed tenure rule for All India service officers posted in the states. Now a committee headed by the chief secretary has to approve any decision to transfer a bureaucrat before his minimum tenure is over.

The notifications issued by the Centre empowers the Committee on Minimum Tenure to hear out the officer concerned *vis-à-vis* the circumstances under which the transfer was contemplated and consider "any other inputs it may have from other reliable sources." The committee shall satisfy itself regarding the inevitability of the premature transfer before making a recommendation to the government based on clear findings. The committees are also required to send quarterly reports to the Centre specifying the details of each case. The minimum tenure could vary from two to three years. Ideally, the central government wants the minimum tenure cover for all AIS officers—beginning with officers in field postings, right up to the chief secretary and director general of police.

The Supreme Court has also asked the Delhi Government for the regulation of traffic by not allowing old vehicles causing pollution to run on the roads. Supreme Court also suggested many reforms to avoid campuses from violent activities which are common during elections based on Lyngdole Committee's recommendations. These are:

(a) Students above 28 cannot participate in elections.
(b) Attendance of students taking part in elections should not have less than 75 percent.
(c) Posters and political support are prohibited.
(d) The limit of expenditure is fixed at Rs. 5000.
(e) Individuals can choose any union for its membership.

Supreme Court has also tried to solve the problems of urban development and urban life. To quote B.G. Verghese again in *The Tribune* dated Sept. 29, 2006 who clearly defines that the Supreme Court is also set to rule on demolitions and the sealing of illegal premises in Delhi. Unlawful construction and violation of zonal regulations stem from vote-bank politics, with politicians and bureaucrats turning a blind eye on master plan violations for political or monetary consideration. This is clearly wrong. But demolition and closures on a mass scale are also not practical. The court's impatience with wilful infringements of law with official connivance is understandable. A sensible via media must be found for dealing with slums, encroachment and urban building violations.

Laski states, "When we know how a nation-state dispenses justice. we know with some exactness the moral character to which it can pretend."

Justice A.S. Anand in his article "Guardians of Constitution—keep judicial activism under check" in *The Tribune* dated Oct. 9, 2006 clearly stated that Judicial review has a more technical significance particularly in countries having written constitutions. In such countries it means that courts have the power of testing the validity of the legislative as well as other governmental actions. The necessity of empowering the courts to declare a statute unconstitutional arises not because the judiciary is to be made supreme but only because a system of checks and balances between the legislature and the executive on the other hand provides the means by which mistakes committed by one are corrected by the other and *vise-versa*.

The judiciary, the last hope of the citizen with a grievance, has an occasions shown a flicker or so of conscience and dispensed justice, but seeking redress has become costly for those who need it most. What is worrying is the assiduous attempts the government's at the Centre and the State governments have been making to pack the courts for the advantage of the politicians and those who help them come to power.

The function of the judiciary is not to set itself in opposition to the policy and politics of the majority rule, but to test the validity and constitutionality of the actions of the State. The judicial institutions have a sacrosanct role to play not only for resolving *inter-se* disputes but also to act as a balancing mechanism between the conflicting pulls and pressures operating in a society. Courts of law are the products of the constitution and the instrumentalities for fulfilling the ideals of the State enshrined therein. Their function is to administer justice according to the law and in doing so, they must respond to the hopes and aspirations of the people because "We the people", in no uncertain terms, have committed ourselves to secure justice—social, economic and political—besides equality and dignity to all.

According to L.D. White, "At one extreme, the vigour of judicial control may paralyse effective administration, at the other, the result may be an offensive bureaucratic tyranny; exactly where the balance may be best struck is a major problem of judicial-administration relationship." No hard and fast principles can be laid down for judicial intervention, but the courts intervene in administrative cases on the following grounds. The powers entrusted to the executive through discretion can be misused. Judiciary in India is charged with the responsibility of ensuring Rule of Law which means that all citizens are equal in the eyes of law. The power is expressly conferred on the judiciary under Articles 32. 136 and 226. Article 32 gives the citizens power to seek the intervention of the Supreme Court through an appropriate writ in the event of any wrong done by the State in the matter of enjoyment of Fundamental Rights by them. Under Article 226 citizens can move the High Court for the same purpose. Article 136 confers on the Supreme Court a large discretionary power to entertain appeals against any judgement, decree or sentence made by any Court or Tribunal in the country. The courts can provide remedy against such abuse in the following circumstances:

1. Failure to comply discretion.
2. Abuse of discretion.
3. Non-compliance with procedural requirements.
4. Infringement of Fundamental Rights.

Evaluation

Judiciary has been doing a useful work in protecting the citizens from the wrongful acts of the Government. Lord Denning has rightly said, "that properly exercised the new powers of the executive lead to a Welfare State, but abused, they lead to a totalitarian State." Courts also keep the members of the legislature and Government machinery in their proper places. Administration is kept, through judicial decisions, in its proper place. There are remarkable achievements of judiciary in independent India in all the fields to promote good governance.

However, judiciary recently has come under a great criticism. In a special feature on judiciary, Rahul Pathak in *India Today* mentions, "As people lose faith in the integrity of the judiciary the guardians of our liberty—the very foundations of a just and lawful society are undermined." He has accused the judiciary on two counts, i.e., politicisation and corruption. Besides, he stresses the need for appointing adequate personnel to smoothen the system overloaded with work. Former Chief Justice P.N. Bhagwati says, "The judiciary is under attack. The rule of law is in danger." "If the Supreme Court exists only for the rich, what is the use of its existence? I have known judges who have sat on judgements for two years." Amar Chandel in his article, 'Make a Mess and Refer to Court' in *The Tribune,* dated 18.1.93 has also stressed the need of protecting judiciary from degeneration. To quote him, "It is a painful reality that the legislature and the executive have already become a pale, derisory shadow of their former self. The judiciary is the only arm that still has some sanctity attached to it. The Government, in its own interest, must ensure that at least this last bastion is kept hermetically sealed from the evil influence of the everyday degeneration to maintain faith of the people in Government machinery. And the judiciary, on its part, too has to take pride in the fact that the 'eye for an eye' approach is alien to its culture."

What are the reasons which are responsible for its degeneration. Let us mention some of them:

(a) Justice is very costly

It has been nicely said that justice is freely available but not free.

(b) There is too much delay in the deliverance of justice

It has been said that 'justice delayed is justice denied'. It may be because of small strength of judiciary as compared to the need. P.N. Lekhi, former President, Delhi High Court Bar Association rightly says, "India has the lowest judge-population ratio in the whole world—only two judges for every 15 lakh people."

(c) Collusion between lawyers and judges

Lawyers are working in collusion with judges to make the judicial system corrupt and unethical. Bakhtawar Lentin, former Bombay High Court Judge has mentioned, "It is the lawyers who are corrupting judges. After all, behind every fallen woman, one finds there is a fallen man." How can one think of Good governance.

(d) Unclean image

Judiciary is being polluted through the indulgence of some individuals in corrupt practices. K.K. Venugopal, a Jurist mentions, "The Contempt of Court Act, which holds that even truth is no defence, protects judges from charges of corruption?"

(e) Law of Contempt of court is not in tune with the Spirit of Good Governance

Nalini Kant Jha in an article, "The State of Justice: Urgency of Internal Reforms" in *IJPA*, Vol. XLVIII, Oct.-Dec. 2002 clearly mentions that the law of contempt in India must, therefore, be modified on the pattern of American system to enable the press to report the judicial misbehaviour. Judges must draw respect through their impartiality and competence and not with the help of any special provision as other authorities of the government such as civil servants, police and military officers, and university teachers are expected to do. After all, they too perform public functions, and it is equally important for their efficacy that public confidence in them should also be preserved. But then it has been recognized in their case that being human being they can err and also be corrupted. Therefore, the best safeguard against their degeneration is their accountability to the people for which it is essential that people should have the right to criticize them. The same applies to the judges. There is nothing special about the judiciary that warrant a law that provides that even a citizen having sufficient proof of a judge's corrupt and biased conduct and who is willing to face action for civil and criminal defamation cannot accuse them of dishonesty.

(f) Political appointments

Appointments are made by politicians without going into the merits of the proposed candidates.

(g) Unattractive conditions of service

Judges get very less salary in comparison to the earnings of an ordinary advocate. It needs to be examined in view of the current conditions and job satisfaction.

C. Lalramzauva in his article, 'Separation of Judiciary in Mizoram: Problems and Prospects' in *Administrative Review*, Vol. VI, 2001 mentioned that while emphasizing the importance of a competent independent and an impartial judiciary the Hon'ble Dr. Justice A.S. Anand, former Chief Justice of India in his inaugural address of the Golden Jubilee Celebrations of the Rajasthan High Court on 29th Aug. 1999 had quoted the speech of the first Chief Justice of the said High Court in the year 1949 which I find, is worth re-quoting here in this paper for the benefit of all of us. The same runs as follows: "Put very briefly, it means that the Judges, in the performance of their duties, should not be amendable to extraneous influences of any kind, whether those influences emanate from the Government, the people or any other quarters. The vow which a Judge takes. . . is that he will administer justice without fear or favour. He ought not to be swayed by a desire for popular applause, or by any expectation of favours from, or by the fear of the frowns of Government, or by the desire to please or oblige anybody else. . ."

R.S. Tiwari in his article, "Good Governance: Populist Democracy to Quality Democracy" in *IJPA*, Vol. XLVIII, Oct.-Dec. 2002 states that "ONGOING GLOBAL transformations need guidance, to avoid very negative looming consequences and realize very positive potentials. Markets, civil, society, etc. however important, cannot be relied upon to provide the needed guidance; normatively and realistically only governance can do so. However, in order to adequately fulfil crucial future-building tasks, politics must be revitalized, democracy must be refocused, and governance must be radically redesigned." All these are necessary to inject good governance.

It is time of appreciation that judiciary is playing an important role in providing good governance where legislature and administration are feeling hopelessness and are entrenched in poor politics of vote bank. They must understand that government is not the monopoly of any party, therefore all parties should come together to remove the irritants to citizens and make good governance a reality. In addition, judiciary must also put its house in order as we find that people are being fleeced and cheated by advocates under the very nose of judiciary. Therefore, judicial reforms is also essential which can ensure good governance in judiciary in this context. We may submit:

(a) Litigants must be provided all facilities at market price and not fleece the litigants by charging disproportionate charges.

(b) There must be some rationalization of fees charged by advocates otherwise justice would be meaningless. A survey of Chandigarh would reveal the existence of palatial buildings of advocates in all the prime sectors. The advocates must be amendable to some laws or professional standards.

(c) Judges must be transferred to places where their relatives are not practicing as this is the main cause of corrupt practices.

(d) The right to stay and reservation of judgement must be used carefully for good governance.

(e) The contempt of court should not be misused so that people can tell the truth before the court which should be ready to listen him carefully.
(f) The government has approved connecting all the 15,000 courts—from the District Courts to the Supreme Court—through a Wide Area Net-work. This is a very important step mission mode and time-bound operation.

In this way judiciary must set an example by implementing good governance within its own sphere. Charity begins at home. This would lead to appreciation of judiciary *vis-à-vis* executive and Legislature the two organs of government would welcome the steps of the judiciary to promote good governance. People would be benefited in a big way and would start feeling the atmosphere of good governance emanating from all organs of government.

Essentials

The following essentials need be there to improve the functioning of judiciary to promote good governance—

(a) Judiciary should be well equipped with required staff so that justice can be expedited and arrears may not pile up.
(b) Judiciary should ensure that citizens are not fleeced by the advocates. The fees can be reduced to make justice cheaper and within the reach of the poor people.
(c) Judges need to insulate themselves from political influences.
(d) There is need to find means to identify corrupt persons in the judicial system and do away with them.
(e) Judiciary should man the judicial infrastructure to ensure decent services to the clients—cheap typing, photostat, good canteen, public relations cell, etc.
(f) The government needs to appoint a research cell to examine judicial decisions to locate the

problems of administration, and take necessary action on such findings to avoid future recurrence.

(g) There is a need of an institution like Ombudsman as in Sweden and Finland for supervising the courts.

At present, there is no machinery to take care of the malfunctioning and maladministration in courts, resulting in many problems to the citizens. The difficulty to deal with judiciary has come to the fore recently. Donald C. Rowat, through his brilliant article, 'Should the State Ombudsman Supervise the Courts', has recommended the need of Ombudsman for judiciary and also the need of extending the jurisdiction of *Lok Ayuktas* already functioning in some states to judicial set-up in their respective states. To quote him:

"There are no provisions for remedying unintentional mistakes made by judges or officials of the courts. The debate in the legal community always seems to be about 'discipline' and codes of conduct, which are always concerned with wilful misbehaviour. But as the Ombudsman's work shows, much maladministration is unintentional, simply caused by bureaucratic bungling and delay in large organisations. Judges are only human and make mistakes, while courts are becoming large organisations, subject to the usual bureaucratic bungling. Since courts are in a hierarchy, like any other organisation, theoretically misbehaviour and mistakes are supervised by the higher levels within the court system. But like other professions and officials elsewhere, judges tend to close, ranks and 'project their own' when criticised. Their clients, knowing it is useless to complain, make few complaints. Since judges are chosen from the ranks of the lawyers, and since court lawyers want to be treated well in future by their presiding judges, they are not inclined to complain about a judge's behaviour."

The Law Commission examined the whole issue of liability of the State for the wrongs of its servants and laid down three fundamental principles on which legislation should proceed in our country. The principles are:

(1) The State should be liable, without proof of

negligence, for breach of statutory duty imposed on it or its employees which causes damage.

(2) The State should be liable if in the discharge of statutory duties imposed upon it or its employees, the employees act negligently or maliciously, whether or not discretion is involved in the exercise of such duty.

(3) The State should be liable if in the exercise of the powers conferred upon it or its employees the power is so exercised as to cause nuisance or trespass or the power is exercised negligently or maliciously causing damage."

Supreme Court has asserted that judges "should be of stern stuff and tough fibre, unbending before power, economic or political and they must uphold the core principle of the rule of law which says, "Be you ever so high, the law is above you." This is the principle of independence of judiciary which is vital for the establishment of real participatory democracy, maintenance of the rule of law as a dynamic concept and delivery of social justice to the vulnerable sections of the community. It is this principle of independence of the Judiciary which we must keep in mind while interpreting the relevant provisions of the Constitution.

Judicial activism, however, is not an unguided missile. It has to be controlled and properly channelised. Courts have to function within established parameters and constitutional bounds. Decisions should have a jurisprudential base with clearly discernible principles. Limits of jurisdiction cannot be pushed back so as to make them irrelevant. Courts have to be careful to see that they do not overstep their limits of sacred duty of guarding the constitution.

Thus, as in the case of the Legislature and the Executive, the Higher Judiciary in India is also, in a manner of speaking, at the cross-roads, but with a significant difference. At a time when public debate and scholarly discourse reflect the growing erosion of faith in the functioning of the Legislature and the Executive, the public perception of the Higher Judiciary in India is positive and that of a bulwark against arbitrary state power and self-serving legislative privileges and attitudes. Therefore, there is an undeniable case to preserve and enhance the stature and image of the Higher Judiciary without impairing its independence. That there are differences between the Higher Judiciary and the Executive over appointments to High Courts as also the manner in which questions of integrity of superior judges have been handled in recent times should serve as the context and the initiative for a review of the process of appointments to both High Court and the Supreme Court. *Hindustan Times Editorial,* "No more hiding" dated 8th December 2006 strongly feels that: The Supreme Court has done well to bring clarity into the question of prosecuting public servants. Following on the heels of the convictions of former Union Minister Shibu Soren and BJP leader Navjot Singh Sidhu, the apex court's ruling leaves no rooms for doubt that the law does not treat public servants any differently from any other citizen of India. Our political class and bureaucracy have, for far too long, hindered attempts to scrutinize their conduct and bring transparency and accountability into the working of the administration. While the state offers them enormous protection so that they may discharge their duties without undue interference, this privilege has, unfortunately, become the skirt behind which corrupt and criminal elements hide.

Concerns about the court's ruling becoming a launch-pad for political vendettas and malicious prosecution are not entirely misplaced. But the benefits of such a ruling far outweigh any real repercussions that public servants may face. Coupled with the Right To Information (RTI) Act, this judgment will have a far-reaching impact in bringing public servants to book for misconduct and unlawful activities. There is an undeniable need to improve the quality of public service in this country, especially when one takes into account India's aspiration to become an economic and political powerhouse.

Conclusion

To conclude the words of Justice H.R. Khanna in his article, "Judicial and Administrative Reforms" in *IJPA*, July-Sept. 1990.

Although there may be some civil servants, who have streaks of martyrdom and who do not hesitate to record what their conscience tells them, it is plain that the treatment meted out to them, because of this approach, causes frustration not only to them but also acts as a warning to others to desist from following such a course. This apart, the nation gets deprived of the proper benefit of services of capable civil servants because of their being put on unimportant jobs where they can hardly show their worth and make any contribution.

Question arises as to where do the courts come into the picture in the matter of administrative reforms. In this context, it is necessary to observe that a modern State has to arm itself with immense powers in order to bring about socio-economic changes and reforms. Acquisition of vast power by any human institution, including a government, which too operates through human agencies, is always fraught with the danger of abuse of power. The liberties of the citizens face real danger in insidious encroachments by men of zeal, well-meaning but lacking in due deference for the rule of law. It, therefore, has become essential that the vast powers of the administrative officers in the modern society should be cushioned with safeguards for individual's rights. Jurisdiction has consequently to be vested in some authority to ensure the protection of those rights. Jurisdiction has further to be conferred upon an authority to see that the powers which are possessed by the administrators are not abused and that those armed with such powers exercise them in accordance with the laws enacted for this purpose. According to the scheme of our Constitution, as also of that of most other free democratic countries of the world, such jurisdiction is exercised by the courts.

It is a faith and trust reposed by the farmers of the Constitution in the courts and their positions in this respect is akin to that of a trustee. When the other agencies or wings of the State overstep their limits, the aggrieved parties can always approach the courts and seek redress against such transgression. When, however, the courts themselves are guilty of such transgression, to which forum would the aggrieved parties appeal? If mankind, while passing through the successive stages of political consciousness, has done away with despotism of kings and dictators, it would be puerile to expect it to put up with despotism of judicial wing of the State. Of the different types of despotism judicial despotism is not only inexcusable, it is also most irrational.

Need of values to make judiciary impartial, independent and free from corrupt practices:

I. Truthfulness and Honesty

Truthfulness and honesty are the two pillars to sustain human existence and happiness. These imply that the persons following these values have no contradictions in thoughts and actions. An honest and fruitful person earns confidence and trust from all. He stands like a rock. Honesty is not to be proved or shown from inside rather it is a conviction from within and is as pure as God. All the religious of the world advocate the practice of Truth. Love is the religion of the universe which can keep all people united. In Sanskrit there is a beautiful verse which says, "He really lives in whose living countless people live." What is there to say about a man when even his death becomes an inspiration? He laughs at death. Death cannot destroy him. One who has fulfiled his life and has blessed and inspired many others alone can be called a successful person. He alone is proficient and he alone can be called efficient. Such is the success from which we get great happiness and the strength to face whatever situations confront us. This is where sorrow ends. Such a life is an inspiration to others.[4]

We read in the Taitiriya Upanisad that after the completion of education, the teacher advises the outgoing students. Thus, 'Speak the truth, practise dharma, never deviate from study, help the teacher though wealth in his mission of diffusion of knowledge, and become a householder and beget good progeny. Also give, give and give (sraddhaya deyam, etc.)'. Truthfulness means straight forwardness in thought, word and deed. It means to think noble, relevant thoughts only, to express them when necessary in a precise language, and act in harmony with one's thoughts. Thus, the speech of truthful has the strength of his whole personality behind it. Therefore, it cannot fail to produce its results.

Truthfulness results in fulfilment without fail, says the yoga-sutra. In fact, in realizing the highest knowledge, truthfulness occupies the highest place, 'he that speaks truth always is sitting on the lap of God, as it were,' says Sri Ramakrishna. The speech of a truthful person unfailingly produces its effect, i.e., it impresses its purport on the heart of the hearer, brings fearlessness to the speaker himself! More truths are revealed spontaneously to such a truthful man. Thus, truthfulness is a great value in education.

From truthfulness come honesty, punctuality, cleanliness, orderliness, simplicity, etc. Truthfulness is the guard against all duplicity, cunningness and hypocrisy. It saves the student from many a false step. It makes him work hard to get sound knowledge rather than putting up an appearance of it! It gives him an inner urge to confess his failures to the teachers and thus, get corrected. A true student will be humble to accept and apologize when he is in the wrong. This great quality attracts the love and solicitation from the teacher.[5]

Every successful man must have behind him somewhere tremendous integrity, tremendous sincerity, and that is the cause of his signal success in life. He may not have been perfectly unselfish; yet he was tending towards it. If he had been perfectly unselfish, his would have been as great a success as that of the Buddha or of the Christ. The degree of unselfishness marks the degree of success everywhere.

When we live thus, for a period of time, a subjective poise develops, giving us inward peace and tranquility, which, thereafter, remains unaffected by external threats and onslaughts.

2. Integrity and Character

Integrity is one of the essentials for Character-building and personality development. Integrity means to be pure in thought and action. Integrity is very easy to accept but very difficult to put in practice. A man or woman of integrity is never influenced by temptations and pressures from outside as he or she would only respond to one's conscience. In today's world, it is very difficult to adhere to integrity as every one is in material race. Swami Budhananda enumerates the qualities of character as: the man of character develops upwards, the man without character slips downwards. The man of character makes history, the man without it is marred by history. The man of character is the hope, solace, well-being peace and inspiration of mankind; the man without character causes trouble, strife, worry, and misery in society.

Character is so important for life that to have to live without it will be worse than not living at all. We may have filled the whole world with so much food that people refuse to have more. We may have succeeded in Family Planning to the extent that only adults are found sauntering around in the world. Gold bars stacked on the roadsides for people to take home at will may not be lifted. We may have industrialized the whole world to the extent of choking everybody with smog. And our established world government may have been functioning without one jarring note. Even then, for want of one thing nobody is going to know how to cope with life's new and different problems of ennui. That one thing is character.

3. Perseverance and Consistence

Sthairyam means thirata, consistency, perseverance. No work can be done in fits and starts. In order to do things consistently, a person has to be convinced about wanting to do it. To be convinced one has to do satsang and be with people who know the purpose of life. Speaking to them on how to go about with life is necessary. One has no time to lose. Before time is over, what needs to be learnt is how to reach one's destination or goal. A steady commitment in life is required to have a happy ending.

4. Selfless service

The essence of the spirit of service is contained in the following worlds of Vivekananda: "This is the gist of all worship-to be pure and to do good to others. He who sees Shiva in the poor, in the weak, and in the diseased, really worships Shiva; and if he sees Shiva only in the image, his worship is but preliminary. He who has served and helped one poor man seeking Shiva in him, without thinking of his caste, or creed, or race, or anything, with him Shiva is more pleased than with the man who sees Him only in the temples. He who wants to serve the father must serve the children first. He who wants to serve Shiva must serve His children and all creatures in the world first.[6]

5. Self-Introspection and Self-understanding to Make ourselves Perfect

We are to take care of ourselves—that much we can do—and give up attending to others; for a time. Let us perfect the means; the end will take care of itself. For the world can be good and pure, only if our lives are good and pure. It is an effect, and we are the means. Therefore, let us purify ourselves. Let us make ourselves perfect.

Besides we should always remember that we have no separate identity. We are made of the same elements as others are.

In sixth chapter of Chandogya Upanishad, a father tells his son Svetaketu with example like the rivers coming from different directions, merge with ocean loosing their identity, i.e. "the individuality has merged into sat." (Chandogya Upanishad, 6.8.1.)

The father further advises his son Svetaketu. Thus:

"Crave to know that from which all these beings take birth by which they live after being born and towards which they move and into which they merge. That is Brahman." (Chandogya Upanishad 3.1.1)

The sama view has been propounded by the Mundaka Upanishad:

"The fifteen constituencies (of the body) go back to their causes and all the senses to their respective deities, the actions and the limited intelligent self (jivatma) become one with the highest imperishable brahman which is the self of all." (Mundaka Upanishad 3.2.7)

Man, therefore, according to Vedanta philosophy, is the greatest being that is in the universe, and this world of work the best place in it, because only herein is the greatest and the best chance for him to become perfect. Angles or gods, whatever you may call them, have all to become men, if they want to become perfect. This is the great center, the wonderful poise, and the wonderful opportunity—this human life.

6. There is no one above law. However, today, we provide immunity to heads of the state. However, our ancient Sanskrit literature suggests supremacy of law.

Law is the king of kings. Nothing is superior to law. The law aided by the power of the King enables the weak to prevail over the strong.

7. As part of Rajadharma, the King was advised to appoint suitable judges and the qualities and qualifications of persons to be appointed as Judges were also indicated in Mahabharata Shanthiparva 24-18 thus:

"A person who is (i) well versed in Vyavahara (procedural laws regulating judicial proceedings) and Dharma (substantive law on all topics), (ii) a Bahushruta (profound scholar), (iii) a Pramanajna (well versed in the law of evidence), (iv) Nyayasastravalambinah (of law abiding nature), and (v) has fully studied the Vedas and Tarka (logic) should be appointed to carry on the administration of justice."

Narada Smriti also prescribed the guidelines for appointment of judges in the following words:

"Let the king appoint, as members of the Court of Justice, honourable men of tried integrity (sabhyas) who are able to bear the burden of the administration of justice and who are well versed in the sacred laws, rules of prudence, who are noble and impartial towards friends or foes."

In Sukraniti, an ancient treatise on polity, there are illuminating provisions prescribing qualification and quality of Judges. Sukraniti pages 149, 15, to 18 read:

"One who is well versed in civil and criminal law and law of procedure, spiritful, of sterling character, impartial towards friends and foes, of Dharma abiding nature, truthful, ever active and who has established control over anger, desire and greed and pleasant in speech and demeanour should be appointed as Judge irrespective of the caste to which he belongs."

"Neither father, nor a teacher, nor a friend, nor mother, nor wife, nor a son, nor a domestic priest should go unpunished for the offences committed, failure to punish amount to failure of Dharma."

8. Manu VIII 12-14 spells out the duties of Judges:

"In a case where Dharma (Justice) has been injured or made to suffer at the hands of Adharma (injustice) and still the judges fail to remove the injustice, such judges are sure to suffer for their act or omission which is adharma."

Dr. Radhakrishnan, a philosopher, no doubt, but also a person involved in public affairs, had, while seconding the Objective Resolution in the Constituent Assembly, this to say, "Much has been said that law . . . People, as well as kings, are subordinate to the Dharma, righteousness which is the king of kings—Dharmaman Kshatrasaya—it is sovereignty of this law which we have asserted." Incidentally, even Kautilya, whose Arthasastra is regarded as the classic exposion of a moral statecraft, declared, "in many matters where there is conflict between Dharmasastra and any secular transaction, the king shall decide the matter by relying on Dharma. If Shastra comes into conflict with any rational and equitable rule, then the latter shall be the deciding factor and the strict letter of the text to be nowhere."

9. The politicization of the public services has led to corruption and unaccountability. The tainted administrative and legal frameworks are inacapable of working according to the Rule of Law. Today, widespread corruption and criminalisations pose a threat to the very foundations of our policy and society and thus to the unity and integrity of our country. If effective governance is to be restored there is no more time to be lost in a cleaned-up polity ensuring that the governmental machinery, run by a totally depolitized bureaucracy, functions strictly according to the Constitution and the Rule of Law.

An independent, impartial, speedy and efficient judiciary is the very essence of civilization. Unfortunately, however, Indian judiciary, has often been accused of being ponderous, excruciatingly slow and inefficient. If these symptoms are not recognized immediately and if far-reaching judicial reforms are not initiated with a great sense of urgency and devotion, the judiciary may also fall in public esteem endangering the whole civil society with dangerous consequences for the public good.

As the saying goes, 'the charity begins at home' any agenda for judicial reform must, however, begin with the internal reforms of the judiciary. Knowledgeable people, particularly from the Bar say that for much of the problems in delivery of justice, judges are responsible. But as discussed earlier, lawyers too cannot escape the blame. It is therefore the duty of the legal fraternity to initiate reform rather than appear to be opposing whenever proposed from outside. Between lawyers and judges, a movement has to begin for reforms from within if the system has to retain its fundamentals.

Notes and References

1. Bryce, J. Modern Democracies, Vali, p. 284.
2. Bata K. Dey, Defining Good Governance, in T.N. Chaturvedi (ed). Towards Good Governance, 1999, New Delhi, *IJPA*, p. 169.
3. Jain and Jain, *op. cit.*, p. 25.
4. Right Thinking, *op. cit.*, p. 30.
5. Swami Gautamananda, Values in our Education, in *Values: The Key to a Meaningful Life*, Sri Ramakrishna Math, Madras, 1996, pp. 88-90.
6. The Complete Works of Swami Vivekananda, Vol. IV, p. 324.

10

Stress Management and Values

> Our power of life lies in thoughts. Thought is the secret key of our mental software. Human Resource Development should take us from negative thoughts (darkness) to positive thought (light), from Untruth to Truth, from Immortality to Mortality.
>
> —*Ministry of HRD*

Swami Visharananda in his book, "Human Values" beautifully states that to be happy is the universal urge of all beings and at all times. One has to be at peace with oneself to be happy. There can be no peace for a turbulent mind. Vasanas, desires, take away the peace of mind. It is only when we follow a value system that we can have a serene, contemplative mind. When mind is calm, we can turn it within to 'see' the treasure of pure consciousness. No treasure on earth is equal to a slice of that tattva. Mind has to be loosened from durvyapara (misdeeds and engaged in acquiring sadgunas (virtues). In Gita, Krsna talks about the developing human values and says that a mind which has daivisampatti (divine qualities) has santi. These values make us introspective and correct our personality.

Higher education institutes today are engulfed by materialistic values. Teachers have become salesman while the students indulge in indiscipline, take drugs, alcohol, and smoking. This scene has emerged as teachers in higher education do not take interest in the development of the personality of the youth. (See Chart 10.1)

CHART 10.1

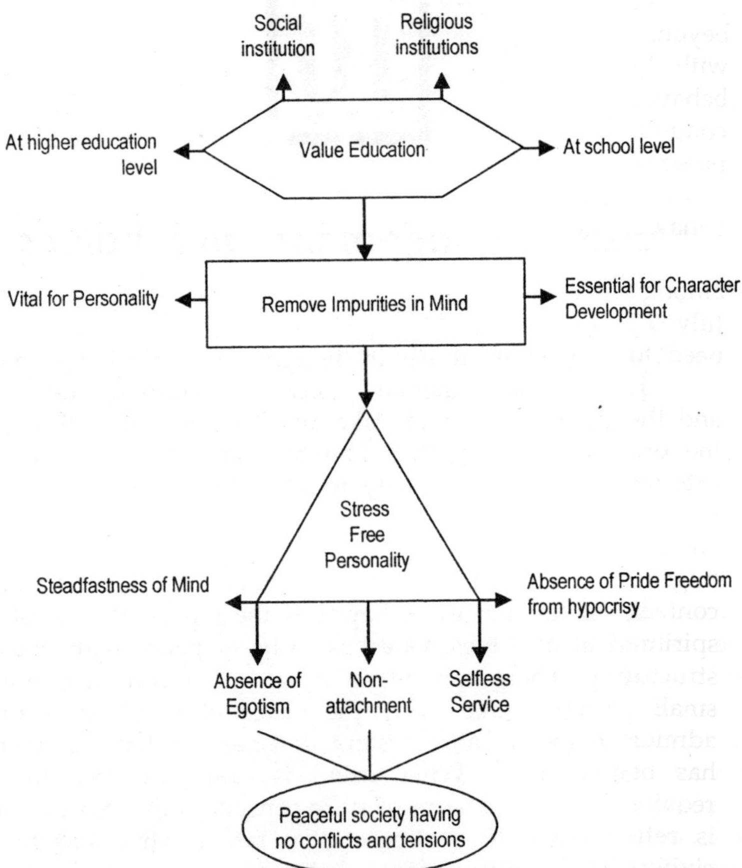

N.N. Prahallada in his Article, "Contemporary significance of Higher Education" beautifully explains the role of Moral values in Education. To quote him, "Indian Culture is rooted deeply in her spiritual values and unless these values find their way into the life of students, education will lose its significance and will not fulfil its function of endowing the students with a vision to life and by and with ideals to work for, therefore indifference to the cherished goals of democracy, socialism, humanism and secularism, it is very essential that our education system should evolve a new positive morality which could effectively be built into the school, undergraduate/Post-graduate curriculum.

Moral education involves social education but extends beyond it in so far as it covers the way the individual deals with his own powers and potentialities as well how he behaves in his relationship with other people and the community at large. It is as much concerned with striving for personal wholeness as with generating a responsible attitude towards others and an understanding of right and wrong behaviour.

Background papers New Delhi Conference on Dialogue among civilizations "Quest for New Perspectives" held on July 9-10, 2003, Vigyan Bhavan, New Delhi spells out the need for values. To quote:

Humankind is passing today through an acute crisis, and the reason behind this crisis is a disequilibrium between the progress that has been registered in recent times in the externalities of life and the progress or lack of progress in the inner realms of life. The human mind has achieved an enormous development in the building of a structure of hugeness and complexity. On the other hand, the contemporary human being has not developed enough spiritual and moral capacity to manage the hugeness of structure and its complexity. Inwardly, man has remained too small to utilize and manage the complex political, social, administrative, economic and cultural machinery. The world has become global, but man has not developed yet the required global consciousness. It is this disequalibrium, which is reflected in the great challenges that the contemporary civilizations of the world are confronting.

The necessity to develop quality education is paramount. The notion of quality education does not merely encompass aspects of educational attainment, but especially the aspects of curricula and their content focusing on peace, shared values, human rights, democracy, tolerance and

CHART 10.2

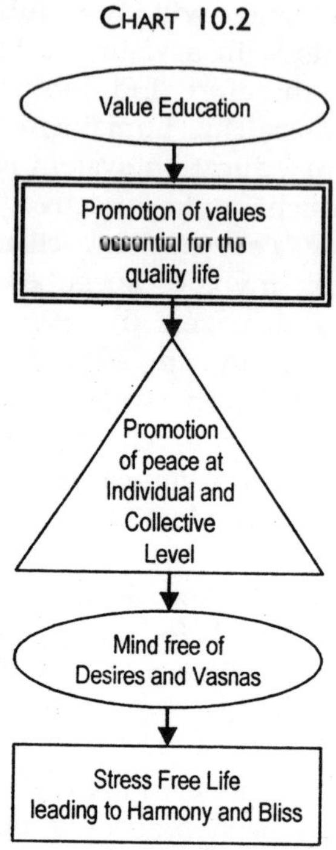

mutual understanding. Educational institutions and educational materials should serve as a vehicle for peace, dialogue and intercultural understanding, but not be instrumentalized for and used as vehicles to spread misunderstanding, intolerance and hate. For its part, UNESCO has deliberately placed programmes related to education for peace and human rights within the area of quality of education, emphasizing the importance of addressing these issues in any long-term education strategy. Such education would be antidote to individual and collective stress.

Quality education for peace and security should focus in particular on:

- Improving knowledge of cultures, civilizations, religions and traditions;
- Developing an understanding of universally shared values;

- Encouraging the development of key competencies for peace and the prevention and resolution of conflict.

There is a widespread feeling among a cross section of the people in India today that, all is not well with our body politic and that education must contribute actively and positively to find a part of the solution. The growing malaise in modern education is that it is seen and practised merely or mainly as a means of acquiring techno-informative knowledge and skills, with little or no anchoring in cultural roots of the country and its perspectives. Unless education helps the students to develop not only a personal identity (which essentially means a set of value perspectives and world views, linked to ones cultural traditions) education cannot be said to have fulfiled its essential role.

Leaders, not only in the field of education but also in other fields have tried to enhance the quality of life. Various kinds of remedies have been applied or tried but, of late, it has become, the united voice of all that Moral, Social and Human Values are the ultimate and the much-needed remedy.[1]

G. Chandrarlekka Rao in an Article; "Value Education for College Students" rightly feels that realizing this need our curriculum needs to insist on educating the young students in the art of living with values. If learning remains detached from value judgements, scholarship runs the risk of degerating into indifference. Value judgements actually enhance the accuracy of learning, teachers, therefore, should be aware of the important role they are called upon to play as professionals and citizens, as agents of development and change. They must make an effort to light a candle instead of cursing the darkness and sow the seeds of value education with a fond hope that they would diffuse their own fragrance towards the creation of a just and new society as they sprout and blossom. Can we be good role models if we are not ethical ourselves.

University education which is worthwhile should lead to the development of integrated personality and inculcate values like patriotism, spirit of national unity and a healthy appreciation of the rich variety of cultural expressions and promote a humanistic outlook. It is only in the highest education stage that the students can be enabled to acquire intellectual, democratic and aesthetic values and a deeply felt concern for the environment.

The content of value-oriented post-graduate education should include: (a) a yearning for knowledge and capacity to utilize it for the good of the society, (b) Democratic education, (c) Aesthetic education, (d) a course in ethics, (e) spiritual education, and (f) provision for activities involving values[2].

R. Satya Raju in his Article, "Human Values in University Management" suggests the following:

(a) Value education means a positive effort for bringing about a synthesis of physical, intellectual, emotional, aesthetic, moral and spiritual values in a human being;
(b) Due to total neglect in the last five decades after independence, the present focus is on revival of moral and spiritual values in education; and
(c) The government should have no reservation in introducing and funding universal religion of human values in the form, in the contents and in the methodology of education at all levels.

Let us understand three areas of education and our values; viz.

(a) "Truth" seeking through scientific and objective processes which are followed by the scientists;
(b) "beauty" creates appreciation through the processes of artistic and unique expression followed by artists; and
(c) "goodness" constructed through the processes of subjective and meaningful contracting followed by social scientists. There is danger in trespassing the boundaries of sciences to arts-to-social sciences without transforming our own respective perspective and amending the tools of analysis

> used by our own discipline areas. This has implications of prioritizing values in various disciplines and their scholars. These scholars in turn influence the value substance and methodology prescribed for institutions in a centralized model of education.[3]

All these three aspects if practiced would make students stress free. The need for value education has been stressed by all the commissions set-up for educational development from time to time,

Radhakrishnan Commission (1948)

"If we exclude spiritual training in our institutions we would be untrue to our whole historical development."

Sri Prakasa Committee on Religious and Moral Instruction

"Every effort must, therefore, be made to teach students true moral values from the earliest stages of their educational life."

Kothari Commission (1964-66)

"A serious defect in the education system is the absence of provision for education in social, moral and spiritual values. A national system of education that is related to life, needs and aspirations of the people cannot afford to ignore this purposeful force."

National Policy on Education (1986)

"The growing concern over the erosion of essential values and an increasing cynicism in society has brought to focus the need for readjustments in the curriculum in order to make education a forceful tool for the cultivation of social and moral values."[4]

Programme of Action NPE (1992)

"The framework emphasized value education as an integral part of school curriculum. It highlighted the values drawn from national goals, universal perception, ethical considerations and character building. It stressed the role of education in combating obscurantism, religious fanaticism, exploitation and injustice as well as the inculcation of values."[4]

In addition to the emphasis of commissions on moral education, persons of eminence have also advocated the cause of moral education for all round development of the youth.

Education is a powerful and pervasive agent for all round development, individual and social transformation. This alone can sustain culture and civilization. A balanced development of mind and body in harmony with the spirit is the key to the enrichment of human personality and also the key to 'true education,' which must in the ultimate analysis help humanity to rise to a higher level of consciousness. Gandhiji said: "Unless the development of mind and body goes hand in hand with a corresponding awakening of the soul, the former alone would prove to be a poor lopsided affair. By spiritual training, I mean education of the heart. A proper and all round development of the mind, therefore, can take place only when it proceeds *paripassu* with the education of the physical and spiritual faculties of the child. . . . Our children must from their infancy be taught the 'dignity of labour'. Thus the true meaning of education is harmonious development of head, heart and hand, i.e. enlighment of mind, compassion and dignity of labour." Such qualities would automatically never allow the generation of stress.

Sarvepalli Radhakrishnan said: "The three things—vital dynamism, intellectual efficiency and spiritual direction together constitute the proper aim of education. Moral and spiritual training is an essential part of education. Enfranchisement of the mind, freedom from prejudice and fanaticism, and courage are essential. What we need today is the education of the whole man—physical, vital, mental, intellectual and spiritual. . . . If education is to help us to meet the moral challenge of the age and play its part in the life of the community, it should be liberating and life giving. It must give a basic meaning to personality and existence and equip us with the power to overcome spiritual inertia and foster spiritual sensitivity. . . . Seat of learning should produce men and women who will move together to develop common ideals and purposes, love each other and co-exist to create a co-operative common wealth."

Swami Vivekananda had proclaimed: "We must have life-building, man-making, character building education." Shanker Dayal Sharma, former President of India, the scholar-educationalist had said, "The aim and objective of all education is to maintain, sustain and develop a healthy mind in a healthy body. Co-curricular and extra-curricular activities have as much place in our system as the curriculum and the syllabus. The lack of such activities is the reason for the growing evils of habitual smoking, drinking and drug-addiction fast growing amidst our student community. . . . Education is not injection or injunction. It is not indoctrination of views and ideas or just an imposition of one's views upon others. In short, education should not be an infliction. The moment education becomes such an infliction, the consequence will be student indiscipline, strikes and agitations within the campus." Pandit Nehru rightly said—"A vast responsibility. . . . rests on our universities and educational institutions and those who guide their destinies. They have to keep their lights burning and must not stray from the right path even when passion convulses the multitude and blinds many amongst those whose duty is to set an example to others."

Gurudev Rabindranath Tagore had a vision for such an education: "Education must aim at the development of moral, spiritual and ethical values and we should seek them in our own heritage as well as in other cultures and civilizations. . . . It should be such that Indians do not lose sight of their rich heritage—their thought must be rooted to the ideals set forth in the great writings and works of our sages, poets and philosophers. The noble goals and high values set forth in our precious culture must be adhered to."

Shanker Dayal Sharma had said: "Thus a teacher must succeed in conveying the larger ideals of service to the community, virtues of tolerance and respect for all faiths, the importance of character, integrity and discipline and the value of humanism to his pupils. They should also be made aware of our heritage and culture." He was a great advocate of 'developing a mature attitude towards religion'. To quote him again. . . . "Acquaintance with prayers of different religion and hymns and songs of various faiths could also, surely, help our youth to recognize the intrinsic purity, beauty and practical usefulness of different religious thoughts[5]."

Value is a "conception explicit or implicit, distinctive of an individual or characteristic of a group of those desirable traits which influence the selection from available modes and ends of action." (Wuchohn, 1957), (Rokeach, 1973) defined values as "enduring belief, a specific mode of conduct and state existence along a continuum of relative importance." Values are the criteria for determining levels of goodness, worth or beauty.

Values in our education is a hotly debated subject nowadays. This is because of the chaotic conditions observed in almost all spheres of our national life. It is conjectured, not without reason, that this chaos is mainly due to *lack of values* in the education being imparted in India. This was formulated, as is well-known, by Macaulay in 1836 more to enslave the Indian mind than to liberate it, so that Indians would remain loyal to British Raj, being alienated from their native Vedic culture, education and Sanskrit language. As planned, this gradually weaned our intellectuals away from our classical heritage and from the Sanskrit language, in which lay all our spiritual, cultural, social, and political traditions. We lost our indigenous system of education in which hearing, chanting and memorizing played a great part, assimilation of ideas took place through a well-planned life of service to teacher, contemplation and meditation, all under his guidance. Thus the educated ones in that system were men who had not only knowledge but also character. Knowledge had become a part of their life, influencing their thoughts, emotions and actions.

The Sanskrit for values is dharma or Sadâcâra. Dharma is described as 'the set of values that sustains the creation without which the very existence of it would be threatened." Sankaracharya defined dharma as the values that sustained human beings and helped them to enjoy happiness both in this as well as in the spiritual world.

Thus education in India meant not merely intellectual cramming of information into the brain but the application of them into one's life so that life became better at individual, social, secular, spiritual levels. Education was a life-transformer. That is real education which liberates.[6] Such an education would help in not allowing stress to take birth.

Eminent Journalist, Mr. V.N. Narayanan, Editor, *The Hindustan Times,* delivered the Convocation Address at the XV and XVI convocation of the Nagarjuna University. He said, "When we face problems of ethics, we tend to solve them by research, by statistics, by the use of instruments and resources rather than by moral energy. The Victorian society in Britain, the pre-Independence Congress party under Mahatma Gandhi, Abraham Lincoln's era in U.S. politics displayed this moral energy. This is not to be confused with excessive Puritanism or moralism. All it demanded of the people was the feeling that they were put on this earth in order to leave it a better place than you found it."[7]

Rationale and Philosophy of Values

A recent conference, "Dialogue among civilizations quest for new perspectives", July 9-10, 2000 elaborated the concept of values as:

Values maybe defined as those desirable ideals and goals which are intrinsic in themselves and which, when achieved or attempted to be achieved, evoke a deep sense of fulfilment to one or many or all parts of what we consider to be the highest elements of our nature. Values are norms, which hold and sustain life and society and establish a symbiotic and interdependent relationship between humankind and ecosystem. Values denote a fundamental category; in a common understanding they correspond to what we mean when it is said that Truth, Beauty and Goodness are the Supreme value of life. They occur to us whenever we try to conceive all those states of our being or becoming in which we are likely to find some kind of ultimate fulfilment.

There are, indeed, values of physical life, values of emotional life, values of mental life, but these values constantly point towards certain basic and ultimate values, which are moral and spiritual in character.

Moral and spiritual values are the foundations of the highest peaks of civilization, and since they emancipate humanity from narrow grooves of thought, they deserve to be understood more and more clearly and more and more meaningfully. Moral and spiritual values appear to be the common elements of various religions promoting everlasting peace and universal harmony; we look up to the ethical and spiritual values in our effort to rise above differences among religions. In recent times, a vast effort has been made to discover the pursuit of those values—moral and spiritual—which are to be found among all religions. And it has been rightly argued that what is most important in religions is the pursuit of ethical and spiritual values, which transcend the externalities of religious institutions.

Science, morality and spirituality are intimately intertwined and they should not be viewed as antagonistic to each other. Indeed, the survival of human race at the present critical juncture of human history will depend upon the pursuit of ethical and spiritual values. It has been rightly contended that peace is a most desirable objects of the present world and that peace cannot be achieved unless individuals and increasing masses of people contemplate and practice ethical and spiritual values such as those of unity, harmony, mutuality, friendship, faithfulness, sincerity and respect for diversity.

Spirituality is premised on universal consciousness, which can serve as the basis of the unity of humankind, and ethical systems derive their force and sustaining power from spiritual consciousness. In the field of education, ethical and spiritual values need to be encouraged, since they are directly related to the character development of students. In the latest reports of UNESCO, "learning to be" and "Learning: Treasure within", the highest ideals have been put forward. The concept of "To Be" is so defined as to mean development of the fullness of personality in all richness. And this fullness of personality involves fullness of ethical and spiritual development. The ideal of "To Be" is distinct from the ideal of "To Acquire" and "To Possess." The ideal of "To Be" refers to that direction of effort which leads the individual to look deeply within oneself and to find in his or her inner being the source and treasure of his or her potentialities and actualities, the source of a harmony of the complexity of personality, and the source of fulfilment in some kind of perfection that transcends egoism and which rests in a vast and integrated self-hood.

The National Policy on Education has laid special stress on value-education. It has said, "In our culturally plural society education should foster universal and eternal values oriented towards the unity and integration of our people. Such value education should help eliminate obscurantism, religious fanaticism, violence, superstition and fatalism. Apart from the combative role, value education has a profound positive context based on our heritage, national goals, universal perceptions. It should lay primary emphasis on this aspect."

R. Natarajan, Chairman AICTE has rightly said in his convocation address at Triputi:

When we say that a person has 'values', we imply that he has certain fundamental beliefs about what is desirable or good, and that he attempts to use these in directing his life. For beliefs of this kind to be called values, two conditions are generally held to apply:

Values are formed as a result of reflection and judgement; this they are different from desires.

- A person's values are beliefs which he sees as applicable not only to himself, but also to others; essential to the idea of value is the function of commanding.
- A person's values are beliefs which he sees as applicable not only to himself, but also to others: essential to the idea of value is the function of commanding.[8]

The Seven Sins, according to Mahatma Gandhi, are:

Politics without Principle.
Wealth without work.
Pleasure without conscience.
Knowledge without Character.
Commerce without Morality.
Science without Humanity.
Worship without Sacrifice.

If we follow these seven advices, there will be no place for stress or conflict.

To quote Anita Shetty again:

Values are those standards or codes of conduct conditioned by one's cultural tenets, guided by conscience, according to which one is supposed to conduct himself and shape his life pattern by integrating his benefits, ideas and attitudes to realize the cherished ideals and aims of life. By values we mean the criterion or basis for choosing between alternative courses of action. High values lead to objective, fair, correct decisions and actions and ensure the welfare of all concerned. Low values do exactly the opposite. Therefore, what we need more today is moral leadership focused on courage, intellectual integrity and sense of values. There is no substitute for a sense of value.

Sir Aurobindo says: "In the right view both of life and of yoga all life is either consciously or subconsciously a yoga. For we mean by this term a methodized effort towards self-perfection by the expression of the potentialities latent in the being and a union of the human individual with the universal and transcendent existence we see partially expressed in man and in the cosmos."[9]

To quote Anita Shetty, "Value is a conception, explicit or implicit, distinctive of an individual or characteristics which influences the selection, from available modes and ends of action." Wuchohn (1957), Rokeach (1973) defines values "as an enduring belief, a specific mode of conduct or end state existence along a continuum of relative importance."

Values maybe described as a system of personality traits which are in harmony with the inner nature of an individual and which are in accordance with the values approved by the society. The process of valuing is what we go through when we make judgment about things, events and people that we encounter in our day-to-day life.

Adisankaracarya has given many values which can make life beautiful. Let us mention some of them.

Yogah Karmasu Kausalam

Yoga is special skill in the performance of activities.

The skill consists in maintaining the uniformity of mind in success and failure. The person who maintains this skill performs all the works as his duty. He dedicates his mind to God.

That is knowledge:

Samacittatva is unfailing equanimity—or evenness of mind in all situations—favorable or unfavourable. The person is not elated when good things happen nor gets angry when misfortune betides. This unwavering evenness of mind is true knowledge.

That is Yoga:

That is knowledge, understanding of things like the self, acquired from the scriptures and the Preceptors. The single-pointed and striking realization of these truths, by controlling the sense organs is Yoga.

Achieve the goal:

Here in this present human life the self must be known. This is the injunction. How? If the Self is known in this birth the life's goal is achieved. This is the supreme truth. His life is fruitful. If the Self is not known in this life, that would become useless.

Experience true knowledge:

Tapah, the concentration of the physical body, the sense organs and the mind; **damah,** discontinuance from sense objects, Karma, Agnihotra, etc. rituals. One who attains holiness by means of purification of the heart through these things can get the knowledge of Brahman.

Don't speak untruth:

Not that there ever was or is in them any falsehood. Contrary to that speaking untruth is the behaviour of bad people. Can any body become free from death? and decrepitude by his falsehood. For which reason (martyah), man (sasyam iva) like corn, (Pacyate), tatters and dies and after death (punah) again; sasyam iva ajavate, (reborns like conr). Thus what one can gain in this impermanent human world by breaking his own words?

Let us discuss the role of Moral Values in education.

Role of Moral Values in Education

1. Building of Human beings with strength and power based upon our Ancient Heritage

Even during the last century Swami Vivekananda had issued the following warning, "All political and social system and organizations basically depend upon the goodness of man. Men cannot be made virtuous by an Act of Parliament. It cannot be taken for granted that if the Parliament enacts good legislation a nation becomes automatically strong. But if the people of a country become good and great, that country becomes automatically good and great. Of all forms of wealth in the world man is the most valuable.

"Acts of Parliament, Government, political administration, all these are indeed means, but they are not our final goal. Beyond them there is a goal, which is not governed by any of these factors. Christ discovered that moral fervour and purity of heart are true sources of strength. Our sages proclaimed the same truth. It is thus that religion strikes at the root of the problem, it moulds man's character.

"So every improvement in India requires first of all an upheaval in religion. Before flooding India with socialistic or political ideas, first deluge the land with spiritual ideas. The first work that demands our attention is that the most wonderful truths confined in our Upanishads, in our scriptures, in our Puranas must be brought out from the books, brought out from the monasteries, brought out from the forests, brought out from the possession of selected bodies of people, and scattered broadcast all over the land.

"The secret of achieving national spirit in our country lies in regaining our spiritual strength, which seem to have been lost. If we have to lift ourselves up, we should stop quarrelling among ourselves. Keep the motto before you— "Elevation of the masses without injuring their religion."[10]

2. Education for Peace

His Holiness The Dalai Lama in his extension lecture at

NCERT spoke of the exceptional intellectual abilities and qualities possessed by human beings, which make them superior to all other species. These qualities could be developed and nurtured through education to help man achieve higher levels of development. He referred to the rich legacy of Indian tradition, its ancient system of education, which promoted spirituality and produced great thinkers, philosophers and spiritual leaders. The inculcation of good human qualities like compassion, respect and sense of truthfulness, caring, etc. have been a part of the Indian way of life. But now when India has achieved tremendous progress, there is a decline in human values. The modern system has no place for spirituality whereas human values are essential for leading a happy life. Human values, therefore, have to be brought in the education system but without attaching them to any religion. Friendly relationships with others according to Him are essential for peace. Modern society is becoming increasingly interdependent hence learning to live together in the family, with neighbours is essential for national and world peace. Children from young age have to be made aware of the interdependence between human beings[11].

3. Promotes Efficiency

When the mind is concentrated efficiency is found to happen. Swami Purananananda rightly states[12]: The right values step up one's efficiency. In order to manage our own life at home in the world and in our professional field, the higher values are necessary, so that our reaction to the outside world, our judgement of the situation that is around us – all is totally changed. And, we will be able to, not only face the challenges in front of us, but also still discover in our minds a lot of mental energy left, which we can apply for our quantity purpose of planning the future.

Ethical virtues are the intelligent ways of reviving man's exhausted energies and fatigued spirit to live. By living these healthy values of righteous living, the individual unshackles his psychological personality from its self-made entanglements. As a contrast to this, the negative tendencies cultivated by the 'diabolically fallen' are self-made shackles that chain a man to a realm of confusions and sorrows forbidding him to grow into the ampler fields of his own inner possibility.

4. Co-ordial Relations between the teacher and students

Swami Lokeswarananda observes that according to the Indian tradition, a teacher is like a lighted lamp from which other lamps may be lighted. This underlines the fact that a teacher must himself be a highly educated man, otherwise he is not entitled to teach. Can a blind man lead another blind man?

But it will be a mistake to think that academic qualification is the only criterion of a teacher. He may have encyclopaedic knowledge, but to this must be added moral excellence of the highest order. He need not teach high moral principles, he has to live them. A teacher should be an example of what is best in man. He can inspire by what he is and not by what he knows. 'To know is to be'—runs a popular dictum in India. Knowledge is useless if it does not make a man perfect—perfect not merely in skills and abilities, but also in character.

The teacher's task is to impart knowledge but to do this, he must first enkindle in the pupil a thirst for knowledge. He must also train his pupil's body and mind, train his faculties, so that the pupil can use them to his best advantage. Mind is man's most powerful organ. A healthy mind under control is man's best friend and guide. Given such a mind and a desire to learn, a student can learn by his own efforts, with the assistance of the teacher or even without. In fact, one learns best when one learns by one's own efforts, for how much knowledge can a teacher pass on to his pupil? Also, the knowledge that the teacher imparts may turn out to be outdated, if not also wrong. The most a teacher can do is to give his pupil a sense of direction, that is, tell him what to learn and how to learn it and also how to apply that knowledge for his own good and the good of his community.

The relationship between the teacher and the taught is exactly like the relationship of the gardener and the flowers on the bush. The gardener does not create the flowers from the soil and the manure; the flowers must themselves come from the bush. The gardener can only tend its roots, water it, protect it, see that it has the correct amount of sunlight and shade—all these externals he can provide. But no mere gardener can guarantee the blossom; it can come only from the bush itself.

Similarly, the teacher's job is to nurture the student with right thoughts. The student must be given a conductive and protective environment where he or she need not overstrain to live. But the blossoming—the real fragrance and beauty of the personality—must come from within.[13]

If contemporary education is to be value-based, it can never be done without the teachers themselves understanding, appreciating and upholding the life-sustaining moral values. The teachers cannot have any excuse whatsoever. If one cannot practise these values, one should not dream of teaching as a job. In fact, teaching is not a job. It is a mission and vision for life and for posterity. Swami Vivekananda established the Ramakrishna Mission order in 1897. Now there are a number of educational institutions, administered by Ramakrishna Mission throughout the country. They are transmitting the universal values of austerity, brotherhood, compassion, dedication, empathy, faithfulness, grace, hardwork, integrity, justice, kindness, liberty, mercy, non-violence, obedience, perseverance, fortitude, rationality, selflessness, truth, unity, virtue, wisdom, yoga and zest. A unique enterprise in educational endeavour is Shri Sathya Sai Baba Institute of Higher Learning, a deemed university, for the promotion of value-based education. It is situated at Prasanti Nilayam (AP), the headquarters of Sri Sai Baba mission. There are similar institutions, run by other missions in the country. If these educational institutions can be strengthened further, of course, within the secular framework of the Indian Constitution, India will ably meet the challenges of the twenty-first century.

K. Muralidharan in his article "Value in Education: A changing concept" in *University News*, January 7-13, 2002 strongly feels that:

The Indian culture is deeply rooted in spiritual values and unless these values find their way into the life of students, education will lose its significance and will not fulfil its function of endowing the students with a vision to live by and with the ideals to work for. Therefore, in deference to the cherished goals of democracy, socialism, humanism and secularism, it is very essential that our education system should evolve a new positive morality, which could effectively be built into the school curriculum.

It is essential that, the teachers also should be exposed to the traditional values and ethics of education through training programs from time to time. They should not confine to their job to a mere matter of completing syllabus and following the curriculum. There should be a platform for teachers to deliberate on any sensitive issues or topics as and when the need arises. They should also explore the ideas of accepting modernisation, globalisation and liberalisation from the academic point of view. They should also learn while imparting their duties for which they are meant. By creating a conductive atmosphere for intellectual rigor and freedom of expression and thought, one can practice values in education.[14]

The National Commission on Teachers (1852), also known as Chattopadhyay Commission, observed:

"There has been a feeling of grievance on the part of the teachers that they do not receive the status and respect from society that their profession and role demand. It may be recalled that the Guru never demanded reverence by the Shishya, his parents and the adult community gladly and gratefully proffered it to the teacher. So must the teacher earn status through achievements. The closer the teacher the more he is able to link himself and his vocation with the mission for the nation, the more relevant he will become and more revered by students, parents and society. We underscore that the primary task of the teacher is concerned with man-making namely the making of the Indian of tomorrow. The Universal; the Guru (Teacher) is personal in relationship. The illustrious poet, Kalidasa, speaks of the Guru in the following words; "He converts darkness into light and makes the invisible God visible."

5. Value Education Promotes Personality Development and Social Cohesion

Value education helps oneself and one's relation to society. Value education makes one peaceful and by his personality, he adds peace to the society. Individual and society supplement each other.

Education is a personality building process. It has always been linked with society. It has both a personal and social dimension, and like the two sides of the same coin, these are inseparable. According to Gandhiji, real education did not consist in packing the brain with information, facts and figures, or in passing examinations by reading the prescribed number of books, but by developing the right character. At present, our education system is largely involved in preparing the younger generation for developing their cognitive domain. It is mainly based on the preponderance of public examination and excessive competitive spirit at the cost of developing the more important affective domain. Today, what is being done is to educate the heads and hands and not the hearts. Essential education must lead to internalisation of the obligation on the part of each human being to be value-conscious in word, thought and deed. Lack of value education has been an important factor in the global scenario of growing violence and terrorism, pollution and ecological imbalances. The Education Commission (1964-66) and the National Policy on Education (NPE-1986) stressed the importance of value-oriented education in our country. The Rammurthy Committee Report (1990) recommended that the imparting of value education should be an integral part of the entire educational process.[15]

6. An integral 'Vision' for National Regeneration

Value education makes the youth powerful. They contribute a great deal to the national reconstruction and national development.

An old Jewish proverb says that 'a man without a dream and a nation without a vision shall perish'. We need a great vision to build a great nation. In the multi-religious context of India, this vision has to be an inclusive one. It must be deeply rooted in the truth, goodness and beauty of our ancient culture and tradition and at the same time, it must also be in harmony with the scientific developments of the era. We are fortunate that our Constitution has been able to capture and embody this spirit of unity and harmony of cultures and religions and the scientific temperament of the modern world.

I am inspired to present to you here a vision of a great India firmly rooted in her own rich spiritual and cultural heritage and at the same time fully open to the scientific development of humankind. I have termed this great India of our vision Bharatiya Dharma Rajya or Dharma Bharathi in short.

Bharatiya Dharma Rajya is the vision of an India of love, unity and peace built on the integral concept of Dharma and on the ensuring Bharatiya Dharma as embodied in the Preamble and Article 51(A) of the Indian Constitution. This is the vision of an awakened India of political stability, social harmony and economic prosperity built on an integral vision of life and reality. It is the vision of a disciple nation of God on earth where all religions and cultures will be respected for their unique insights into Truth and valuable contributions towards human welfare, an India where all living beings will live in harmony and peace with one another as the fulfilment of our age-old dream of a Vasudhaiva Kutumbakam. This is our vision of the great India of the third millennium that will be a land and light of Dharma in humanity's quest for a culture of life, unity and peace on earth.

'Peace and Value Education for Schools/Colleges' should present and promote this noble and inter-religious vision of Bharatiya Dharma Rajya in our intuitions of learning and among our youth if it is to lead to the much needed national regeneration of India. This is a religious task more than a political task that can only be achieved through interreligious cooperative action. It will be difficult for political parties and governments to take up this task on their own, they can only support and collaborate with religious-minded and peace-loving patriotic citizens of India in this divine mission.[16]

7. Value Education will Build Character

At present, the Government of this country is striving to bring about universal education. In this context, it will be useful to consider what the purpose of education is. Great men of this land have declared that education should foster character, help the acquisition of good qualities, or seela, and eradicate vices, knowledge should also enable us to understand the truth about things. Saivite and Vaishnavite saints have proclaimed that God alone is Truth, and the rest is maya or illusion. These sages and saints endeavored to realise Truth, that is God. In Him they found their supreme joy. They looked at everything else as the sources of evil and suffering. In the Vedas, the Paramatman is spoken of as Truth. When it is declared that everything connected with this world is mithya, or false, it to so much to condemn the world as to affirm that the Paramatman alone is true.[17]

Right education should make us know that God is the Truth. Knowledge must fill one with good qualities through which alone one can realize the Truth, that is God. Therefore, the goal of knowledge is the understanding of the Ultimate Truth. The first fruit of education must be humility and self-control. Education that does not produce these qualities is useless. We find that people in countries where modern education has spread are not as virtuous as they should be. Unsophisticated illiterates, like those slaving in the tribal areas of South African jungles, are found to be more honest than those who have received the doubtful benefits of modern education. It is sad to Note that in our own schools and colleges, indiscipline is rampant nowadays. Even girls, who are by nature docile, have caught this infection of indiscipline. All these developments give rise to the question whether this kind of education is after all necessary or useful. Such education is the cause of stress among students.

From time immemorial, the necessity to acquire knowledge is being emphasized and he who has had no education is considered an animal. Vidyaa viheenah pasuh says Bhartruhari. But what is the type of education our ancients had in mind when they said: Vidyaa vinaya sampanna? A thing can be done either in the dharmic way or in the adharmic way. Good results will flow when a thing is done in the right way.[18]

8. Study of the life of Great men to learn from their practice in life

We must train our people from an early age to study the lives of great men who led an unattached life, free from debasing passions like lust, anger, greed and fear and, following their example, develop faith in God. This will help them to grow up into dutiful and honest citizens, disciplined to lead a moral and ethical life. If the government also takes sufficient interest in making provision for teaching moral and spiritual values to children, it stands to gain much. For one thing, expenditure on police and law courts will get reduced. They will also be free from the troubles arising from strikes and other forms of student indiscipline.

"The Inculcation of moral and spiritual values in the minds of the people from the early years is most desirable that provision should be made for the teaching of moral and spiritual values in educational institutions."[19]

9. Nation-building and promotion of peaceful world order

In the words of Sri Sathya Sai Baba, education is for man-making, nation-building and promotion of peaceful world order. At the dawn of the new millennium and in the changed policy framework of the Government, there is an urgent need among teachers to inculcate values among students so that they develop into integrated personalities blossoming mentally, emotionally, intellectually, ethically and spiritually (Khandelval, 2001). Teachers in higher education have to act as a role model to bring back values among students, educational institutions and in the society as a whole. They have to act as role models in terms of their honesty, sincerity, hard work and determination towards their duties and responsibilities in order to create an example before their students. The students at this stage are at the cross-road of their career and life. At this stage, normally students seek to identify with some role models for their life. Therefore, the role of teacher at this level of education is to create and recreate the values among students, in educational institutions and the society as a whole. They have a greater responsibility in shaping the destiny of future generation and the country as well. They should also come forward catering to the educational needs at primary and secondary levels in the society. They should be conscious about their social responsibilities. No external force should be required to inculcate in them a sense of dedication and responsibility. The role of teacher at the higher level is different from their counterparts at other stages on account of these teachers' greater involvement with activities related to research, publications, training and administrative responsibilities.[20]

10. Core Values Based Education Promotes Ideal Humanity

The Parliamentary Standing Committee on Human Resource Development in its Eighty-first Report on Value-based Education (1999) has highlighted that Truth (Satya), Righteous Conduct (Dharma), Peace (Shanti), Love (Prema) and Non-violence (Ahimsa) as the Core universal values, which need to be identified as the foundation stone on which the value-based education programme can be built up. All the religions of the world have also emphasized that non-violence, tolerance and peace are the fundamental components of humanity. Great philosophers and social thinkers of East as well as West have seen education as a process leading ultimately to spiritual development. UNESCO in the context of peace, refers education not only to general education acquiring cognitive capital but ability to live together.[21]

11. External and Internal Environment must act in harmony

The wonderful development of science during the past three hundred years concerns the external nature and the world outside. The study of the nature and potentialities of the human mind is of more recent origin – it has a history of about hundred years. It is true that with the help of scientific equipment, like the microscope and telescope, the scientist has understood innumerable minute details of the exterior world. But many of the scientists are realizing, though belatedly, that the nature of the mind, its constant tendency to flow outward, prevents it from getting an insight into many other aspects of the mind which can be achieved only by the practice of meditation.

Scientists have provided us with various kinds of conveniences and comforts by discovering innumerable natural laws and thus uncovering the secrets of nature. It has to be admitted that the human power of investigation has reached an all-time high; man has displayed the peak of his intellectual ability. But is it not within his power to create a beautiful world full of honesty, justice, brotherhood, mutual understanding, cooperation, peace and tolerance? Why has he not succeeded in creating such a world?

The following voice of a poet reflects the present predicament of mankind:

People fear people
Doubt reigns everywhere
Behind the curtain of peace
Martial moves the revolution
Meanness yet unheard of
Devilishness in patriotic garb
Tuskers among nations crush life apace
Not to speak of the bloody flame
Rising high on the West
Bullets are at play
Mad after martial joy
Such a situation causes stress, hatred and jealousy.

The scientist can make the five elements dance to his tune, he can transverse land, water and space at a marvelous speed, and he can drive away terrible epidemics, which threaten the human race. Can't he instill in the hearts of men, who live and thrive now, but who are liable to decay and die, a sense of brotherhood and friendship? Can't he quench the primordial fire of hatred by pouring forth the ambrosia of love?

The following is the answer to the question:

Progress is to take place in two fields. It relates to the two faces of nature:

The one is the physical nature, the nature of the external world. The other is the inner nature of man. The one is related to the world that we see. The other one is related to the inner-self of man with whose help he is able to see the world outside and investigate.

If man is able to increase his power to free himself

from the hold of the surrounding world or environment, if he increases his freedom, if he gains control over nature, we may say that the change we call development leads to progress. In this respect, the innumerable discoveries of scientists have helped us gain control over the outside nature. Undoubtedly, we are moving on the path of outward development and progress. But is there a comparable development in the regions of the mind?[22] Upon this understanding depends the solution of stress.

12. Ethical and Moral Values: The Foundation of the Quality of life

Ethical and moral values are the basis of good life as ethical culture indeed ennobles human life. Ethics, religion and spirituality have become synonymous terms in common parlance as they co-exist in the development of moral culture and of righteous and virtuous life. Moral living starts through dedication to ideal principles, maxims and human values. A righteous and virtuous life and a clear conscience provide the backbone of spiritual as well as a humane material progress of the civilized man and his society.

No ideal, ideology, institution or religion is self-operative. It is through human agency alone that ideals and institutions established for their realization are made operational. History bears witness to perversions, distortions and abuse or misuse of ideals and institutions for the reason that human being is essentially imperfect though he seeks perfection. It is true that perfection is not attainable by imperfect beings, however, it is always worthwhile attempting and this depends largely upon a meaningful education of man with a view to fertilizing the soil within so that the vessel may bear rich, juicy and truthful fruits. Sustenance of human values, ethics and morals in human society and spiritual enlightenment of man seem to be decidedly more effective and meaningful goals of educational philosophy to follow. It is principally inadequate appreciation of the essentially spiritual nature of man and prevailing disrespectful attitude towards the role of true religion or spiritualism in protecting and promoting the spiritual core of human beings which accounts for the crisis of our times.

Ever since the dawn of human civilization, conscious efforts have been made by man to cultivate values in order to humanize himself by conquering his animal instincts and ennobling his life by harmonious development of all the faculties. When one realizes that one's actions affect the entire society, the value system that we live by and the choices that we make acquire paramount importance. Living a life based on noble values enables human beings to refine their character which is called culture. The culture of a people or a nation is based upon the values that those constituting it live and uphold in their lives. When the cultural values deteriorate, civilization declines but when these are promoted civilization flourishes. Whenever higher ideals are abandoned and fundamental cultural values of the society are totally ignored, civilizations have disappeared. If perversions of man's desires and natural urges transgress the control and limits set by nature, it results in the loss of culture which is his internal aspect. When his culture declines, it eventually results in withering away of civilization which essentially manifests external aspect of man's social life.

The modern world is marked by a widespread explosion of knowledge and tremendous achievements in Science and Technology, coupled with a general decline and reversal of human values as well as an alarming deterioration of moral and mental health both of individuals and societies. The recent spate of crimes, violence, terrorism, and drug abuse makes us aware of the significance of human values, without which human life loses all meaning. It is also evident that a mere economic prosperity and material wealth cannot result in a lasting well-being of mankind. The inner strength of mankind springs from within, which seems ill-nourished now. To fill up the void regarding human values, the richest resources are available in the texts and scriptures of all the religions of the world which have guided people in their thoughts, feelings and actions for ages. Human virtues have been propounded and preached by many great sages, Prophets and teachers who had perceived subtle truths of human life, for the benefit of their adherents and for those who would derive benefits by studying their sayings and advices. Some of their sayings were understood by people in letter and spirit, enriching and elevating them, but some others were not understood well, ending up as mere outward rituals, blind faiths, intolerance with others and hatred for other faiths. More than a century ago, Swami Vivekananda had said: "We want to lead mankind to the place where there is neither the Vedas, nor the Bible, nor the Koran, yet this has to be done by harmonizing the Vedas, the Bible and the Koran. Man ought to be taught that religions are but the varied expression of the religion, which is oneness, so that each may choose the path that suits him best."[23]

13. Growth in Spiritual status

One of our noblest duties in life is to grow. This is the screaming cry of all evolution. Growth in the biological apparatus was the command in the lower stages of evolution. After having attained manhood, the demand is to grow our moral stature, in our spiritual worth, in our cultural dignity. This is where study of the scriptures, regular and continuous, and sadhana, constant and sincere, come to serve us. The study clearly points out the goal and the way—the sadhana yields to us the energy and vitality to walk the path and explode into the goal. These we must.

14. Harmony and Peace

In the world today, we are living through an age of confusions and tensions, both within and without us. The external challenges persecute us and render our lives unhappy and sorrow ridden. The intelligent philosophy of the Rishis advises man 'to live in harmony' with the situations in life and steadily work on to meet them with discretion and constant application. When we live thus for a period of time, a subjective poise develops, giving us inward peace and tranquillity, which, thereafter, remains unaffected by external threats and onslaughts.

Revered Shri Vethatheri, Maharishisays 'has beautifully written that Harmony is a precious treasure of human life'. Real success and satisfaction, happiness are the different facets of harmony. If one is to enjoy the benefits of life to the fullest, it is necessary to develop and maintain harmony; and for this understanding the philosophy of nature is required.

Harmony should be maintained in all spheres of life, and these are:

- Between body and life;
- Between wisdom and habits;
- Between self and society;
- Between the purpose of life and the method of living; and
- Between will and nature.

The more one understands life, the more one will achieve harmony; and success will be proportionate to that. No doubt harmonizing life is a difficult task, but it is worth all the striving, for it is the only way to equip oneself to enjoy life to the fullest extent and to reach the goal of life, which is the perfection of consciousness. By the development of knowledge man comes to understand the cause and effect system which is the law of nature.

15. Values of Devotion and Dedication

Of the innumerable techniques prescribed by the rishis for self-development, the most popular ones are the path of selfless dedicated service (karma yoga), the path of discriminative knowledge (jnana yoga), and the mystic path of self-development through disciplined contemplation (raja yoga).

According to Sage Narada, true devotion for the Lord is superior and nobler to all these, because devotion is the final outcome of all other methods of self-development.

This supreme devotion is indeed, as a technique, even superior to the path of action, the path of knowledge, and the path of disciplined contemplation. (Narada Bhakti Sutra II:I:25)

All the other paths are the means that take the seekers to the final goal of spiritual experience, but in devotion there is very little difference in essence between the means and the end, between the way and the goal. Love alone is love's own end and fulfilment. Devotion is both the means and the end. As long as residual vasanas (inherent tendencies) are still lingering in the devotee's personality, so long is devotion only the path. But when, as a result of his love for the Lord, his vasanas disappear totally, a stage comes when his supreme love itself becomes the Lord of love Supreme.

Than all other paths, devotion is the one most readily available and most easily attainable. (Narada Bhakti Sutra VI:1:58)

Having dedicated all activities unto Him, the devotee should turn all desire, anger, pride, and so forth toward Him alone (Narada Bhakti Sutra VI:2:65).

Having gained this supreme devotion, the devotee attains perfection and immortality and becomes extremely satisfied. (Narada Bhakti Sutra I:1:4)

Acharya Vinoba Bhave says: Knowledge, love, and constant effort are the three legs on which life stands. If one of the legs of a tripod is broken, it cannot stand, since all three legs are needed. This is also the condition of life. Even if we logically distinguish between devotion (bhakti), knowledge (jnana), and action (karma), we cannot divide them in experience. The three together make up one great entity.

Conclusion

The worst days of a serious threat to Indian society are over. Under foreign domination and western influence we had developed the foolish notion of degrading everything, morals, ethics and spirituality and were easily swept off our feet by the glamour and glitter of the exotic. The wonderful phenomenon that is taking place now is that we are returning to these things which have lent stability and strength to our culture over the centuries. Because the various educational programmes launched by the NCERT, UGC and other organizations (such as Sri Sathya Sai Organization) ranging all the way from nursery to post-graduate level, are bringing into proper focus the valuable ingredients of our culture. By far the most important aspect of these programmes is that besides giving a theoretical and conceptual base in the curriculum they also seek to transform the quality of life through inculcation of human values of peace, love, truth, spirituality, right conduct, ahimsa and, above all, national character which, in effect, represent the highest and the noblest in our culture system.[24]

About ethical or approved conduct Apastamba-Dharma-Sutra (22.14) enjoins:

Absence of anger, elation, indignation, avarice, delusion, vanity and enmity; speaking truth; moderation in eating; refraining from exposing others' weak points; freedom from jealousy; sharing one's good things with others; sacrifice; straightforwardness; gentleness; quietude; self-control; friendliness with also beings; absence of cruelty; contentment —these form the approved conduct for men of all stations of life. By observing them duly one becomes universally benevolent.

Suresh Prasad Singh in his Article "Emerging values in modern Education" suggests an integrated vision to promote value education. To quote him:

The power of modern education can be better realized by achieving a happy integration of utility and value, integration of body and mind, emotions and ideas, individual and society, and the world. The vision of progress must not be devoid of human element, the aspect of vision which makes the progress meaningful and purposeful. The progress that is aimed at the desired, is an assertion of the powers of human imagination, and soothe fruits of this progress must be realized with the ends of humanity in mind. The tools of change are powerful but their application must be human and they must be employed for pious purposes.

In the wake of the phenomenal developments on the educational front, re-orientation of values in the post-modernist education assumes special significance. Here are certain concrete recommendations for tempering utilitarian pursuit of together education with desirable ideals and visions of human happiness:

(a) Education must promote rational outlook on life and scientific approach to issues confronting the real life situations;
(b) An imaginatively farmed course in fundamental freedom and human rights must constitute of our degree level curriculum;
(c) Power that education generates must be employed for constructive human purposes;

(d) Education must develop sensitivity to environment and must foster human ethos for the enjoyment of the fruits of progress;

(e) Humanism should be the central concern of education in all circumstances, and it must promote quality concern for corporate behaviour and corporate life; and

(f) Education must be able to develop a working mechanism to fight the evil of consumerism and acquisitive culture so that environment may be protected and development may remain sustainable.

In New Delhi Conference on "Quest for New Perspectives", held on July 9-10, 2003 feels that:

As we reflect today on the theme of dialogue of civilizations, it seems imperative that education should be so developed that a new mentality is created which spontaneously turns to dialogue rather than to conflict, which spontaneously responds to the call of interchange, and which is spontaneously eager to see problems from various points of view and which is capable of synthesizing different points of view without sacrificing uniqueness of various truths that are synthesized. We have to develop particularly a new curriculum that aims at explaining the basic theme of human progress as a mighty expression of an adventure of continuous self-exceeding. This curriculum should inspire students to work for unity even while rejecting uniformity; this curriculum should also encourage students to respect cultural diversity. Finally, this curriculum should develop a new science and art of living together which necessitates adherence to the law of mutuality rather than conflict and the law of variety of expressions rather than any uniform monotone. It may also be urged that since science and technology characterize a large part of modern civilization, we should develop a new curriculum where by a fresh impetus is given to scientific studies that are in harmony with the study of values. There is, today, an increasing awareness that unless science and value are blended together, humanity will have to face a great peril, the peril of inner human suffering even in the midst of increase of knowledge and increase of material comforts. It is in the hands of educationists today to develop a new dimension in education so that education can not only build the defences of peace in the minds and hearts of people but also build bridges between the past and the future, and serve the great ends of the dialogue among civilizations.

To conclude in the world of Honorable Minister of HRD, Govt. of India, Prof. Murali Manohar Joshi: what is now needed is a concerted action at the development of a curriculum that can bring home to the students three important lessons, namely, (i) that the entire humanity shares one basic impulse towards progress and by sharing this impulse humanity can be seen as one vast surge of adventure which aims at continuous self-exceeding; (ii) that humanity, in its mature developments, tends to reject uniformity and adopts the law of unity that permits and respects cultural diversities; and (iii) that the future progress of humankind is bound up with the development of a new science and art of living together which necessitates adherence to the law of mutuality rather than conflict and the law of varied expressions rather than any uniform monotone. Education should aim at strengthening democratic and universal human values and respect for human rights. Education is the most powerful instrument for preparing a mind which can promote the culture of dialogue.

Notes and References

1. Anita Shetty and K. Pushpanadham, Valuing Values, *University News*, Dec. 29, 1997, pp. 7-8.
2. H. Venkataiah, Value Education, Curriculum for Graduates and Postgraduates in *University News*, June 22, 1998.
3. R.S atya Rajiv, Human Values in University Management, in AIU, Value Education in India, New Delhi, 2001, pp. 86-87.
4. Quoted in Anita Shetty *et. al.*, Value Education: Need of the present generation in *University News*, Oct. 13, 1997, p. 12.
5. Quoted in N.P. Sinha, Towards inculcating values in Education, in *University News*, Oct. 22-28, 2001, pp. 1-2.
6. Swami Gautamananda, Values in our Education, in *Values: The Key to A Meaningful Life*, Ramakrishna Math, Madras, India, pp. 83-85.

7. *University News*, Dec. 9, 1996, p. 22.
8. R. Natarajan, *University News*, July 21-27, 2003, p. 16.
9. Şri Aurobindo, The Synthesis of Yoga, 1976, Sixth Edition, Sri Aurobindo Ashram, Pondicherry, p. 2.
10. Swami Jagadatmananda, Learn to Live, Vol. 2, Ramakrishan Math, Chennai; India, 2000, pp. 154-57.
11. H.H. The Dalai Lama, Education for Peace, in *Journal of Value Education*, Vol. 2, No. 1, January 2002, p. 1.
12. Swami Purnananda, Making Life Valuable by Imbiding values, in *Journal of Value Education*, Vol. 2, No. 1, January 2002, pp. 30-31, (NCERT).
13. *Ibid.*, p. 15.
14. P. Dhannavel. Importance of value based teachers, in *University News*, May 1, 2000, p. 2.
15. Hemanta K. Khandai, Value Oriented Approach from Primary to University Education, *University News*, March 31 to April 6, 2003, pp. 9-10.
16. Swami Sachidananda, Vision and values for National Regeneration, *Journal of Value Education*, Vol. 2, No. 1, January 2002 (NCERT), pp. 70-71.
17. H.H. Jagadguru's Madras Discourse Acharya Call, Part III, Peetam Kanchipuram, 1998, pp. 66-67.
18. *Ibid.*, p. 192.
19. *Ibid.*
20. Nageshwar Rao and R.P. Das, Bringing values back: The Role of Teachers in Higher Education in *Journal of Value Education*, Vol. 2, No. 1, January 2002, p. 89.
21. J.S. Rajput, Symphony of Human Values in Education, NCERT, December 2001, New Delhi.
20. Learn to Live, Vol. I, *op. cit.*, pp. 139-41.
23. R.D. Dhokalia, External Human Values and World Religions, NCERT, New Delhi, 2001, pp. 10, 13, 24.
24. Girijesh Kunal, How to inculcate value education through teacher education, *Journal of Value Education*, *op. cit.*, pp. 118-19.

Appendix 10.1

Given below are the five verses from Bhagavad Gita (Chapter XIII, from 7th to 11th) enumerating the important values. The original Sanskrit test is followed by the transliteration and the meaning:

अमानित्वमदम्भित्वमहिंसा क्षान्तिरार्जवम् ।
आचार्योपासनं शौचं स्थैर्यमात्मविनिग्रह : ।।

13/7 (Srimad Bhagavad Gita)

Amanitvamadambhitvamahimsa ksantirarjavam
Acaryopasanam saucam sthairyamatmavinigrahah.

Absence of pride, freedom from hypocrisy, non-violence, forbearance, straightness of body, speech and mind, devout service of the preceptor, internal and external purity, steadfastness of mind and control of body, mind and the senses.

इन्द्रियार्थेषु वैराग्यमनहंकार एव च ।
जन्ममृत्युजराव्याधिदुःखदोषानुदर्शनम् ।।

13/8 (Srimad Bhagavad Gita)

Indriyarthesu vairagyamanahankara eva ca,
Janmamrtyujaravyadhidukhadosanudarsanam

Dispassion towards the objects of enjoyment of this world and the next, and also absence of egotism, pondering again and again on the pain and evils inherent in birth, death, old age and disease.

असक्तिरनभिषवङंग: पुत्रदारगृहादिषु ।
नित्य च समचित्ततवमिष्टानि ष्टोपपत्तिषु ।।

13/9 (Srimad Bhagavad Gita)

Asaktiranabhisvangah putradaragrhadisu
Nityam ca samacittatvamistanistopapattisu

Absence of attachment and the feeling of mineness in respect of son, wife, home, etc. and constant equipoise of mind both in favourable and unfavourable circumstances.

मयि चानन्ययोगेन भक्तिरव्यभिचारिणी ।
विविक्तदेशसेवित्वमरतिर्जनसंसदि ।।
13/10 (Srimad Bhagavad Gita)

Mayi cananyayogena bhaktiravyabhicarini
Viviktadesasevitvamaratirjanasamasadi

Unflinching devotion to Me through exclusive attachement, living in secluded and holy places, and finding no enjoyment in the company of men.

अध्यात्मज्ञाननित्यत्वं तत्त्वज्ञानार्थदर्शनम् ।
एतज्ज्ञानमिति प्रोक्तमज्ञानं यदतोन्यथा ।।
13/11 (Srimad Bhagavad Gita)

Adhyatmajnananityatvam tattvajnanarthadarsanam,
Etajjnanamiti proktamajnanam yadatonatha.

Fixity in self-knowledge and seeing God as the object of true knowledge; all this is declared as knowledge; and what is other than this is called ignorance.

ANNEXURE 10.2

Role of UGC in Human Value in Higher Education

1. A scheme for promoting ethics and human values in Higher Education

The National Policy on Education has laid considerable emphasis on Value Education by highlighting the need to make education a forceful tool for cultivation of social and moral values. The policy has stated that in our culturally plural society education should factor universal and eternal values oriented towards the unity and integration of our people.

In the present times of unprecedented changes dislocating traditional values and creating conflict between traditional and new values there is a universal concern in respect of erosion of values, promoting values and culture which fit in with the needs of the modern times. This concern is universal but is more acute for our country which has lead its distinct culture, worked view and a living value tradition. The process of developing into a modern nation with new social, political and economic institutions, and with emphasis on science and technology has thrown up many new values— challenges in all areas of our national life. It is important that we examine these challenges and prepare our youth to face and resolve them.

2. Objectives of the Scheme

(i) To create awareness, conviction and commitment to values for improving the quality of life through education, and for advancing social and human well-being

(ii) To encouraging universities and colleges to undertake academic and other activities pertaining to teaching, research and extension programmes in respect of values and culture like extramural lectures, seminar, conferences, workshops and orientation programmes for teachers and students.

(iii) To encourage universities to undertake preparation and production of requisite material including books, handbooks, journals, teaching materials, video and films relating to values.

3. Eligibility/Target

All eligible Universities colleges which are included under section 2(f) and 12(b) of the UGC Act are covered under the scheme.

4. Nature of Assistance

The different activities for which support will be provided are as under: (i) Research, (ii) Teaching, (iii) Organisation of Conferences/Seminars, (iv) Awareness/ Sensitization/Programme, (v) Human Enrichment/integrated personality development! Character Building Workshops.

The nature of research projects under this scheme would be different from the usual Ph.D. oriented academic research. They would be aimed at understanding and clarifying value issues of contemporary; concern in the public and professional, and to suggest possible ways of resolving these value problems. The research could be a combination of conceptual and empirical investigations. Some of the likely areas of the research projects could be:

Value Issues in:

(i) Core values of human life with reference to the individual, family Community, nation and Human society,
(ii) Values relating to Democratic polity and the Rule of Law,
(iii) Professional values, like of engineering, medicine, law, teaching, public service, management, business, etc.,
(iv) Values of good governance, administration, and of judiciary,
(v) Values relating to environment, science and technology, and sustainable development,
(vi) Strategies of transmission of value through formal/ informal/ non-formal/Education, and
(vii) The role of the films and the Multi-media in respect of Value transmission and the potentials of multi-media learning to promote awareness and understanding of human values.

The theme should be developed in the light of Indian ethos, aspirations and social realities. The outcome of this research should be in the form of book, monograph, research papers, report. The support provided would be by way of seed money which could be utilized for the purpose of contingency, books and journals, travel, stationary, typing and hiring, etc. The duration of the research project would be ordinarily two years.

5. Teaching

Support under this head would be provided for encouraging and facilitating introduction of new courses on value related themes like human values, professional ethics, environmental ethics, science, technology, parliamentary democracy civil society and the rules of law and human values, etc. Financial assistance would be provided by way of:

(i) Grant to teachers teaching such courses for books, preparation of teaching material, travel grant to consult libraries elsewhere, to attend conference lectures themes related to the subject matter, preparation of manuscript for writing books, etc.

(ii) Grant to university/ college, department for paying honorarium to retired teachers visiting Professors to teach such courses.

6. Organisation of Conference/Seminars

These could be of two types:

(i) Aimed at generating new ideas related to themes of ethics and human values.

(ii) To provide a platform to teachers engaged in teaching value-related courses to share ideas and experiences.

The conference should be properly focused and their proceedings should be published.

Financial support would be provided to meet expenses on TA/DA. boarding and lodging expenses, local transport, publication of report, secretarial assistance, etc.

7. Awareness/Sensitisation Programmes

These could be in a form of lectures. Workshops for a day or two, aimed at specific groups, like teachers, research scholars and students of a particular discipline academic administrators, non-teaching staff, etc.

Support would be provided for meeting expenses of the programme including TA/DA for one or two persons from outside the institution.

Human enrichment/integrated personality—development/character-building workshops.

These workshops could be very effective non-formal means of seeking a positive change in the value-temper of students and teachers. They could be organized during vacations or after the working hours. They could include presentations and discussions on different themes like spiritual, moral, aesthetic, societal, cultural, environmental values, values of democracy, scientific temper, communication skills, problems of youth, career choices, etc. Some of these workshops could also be for groups from outside the university, like school teachers, NGOs, government officials, corporate executives, etc. As far as possible these external workshops should be self-financing.

The support provided for this activity would be by way of TA/DA and honorarium for resource persons, contingency amount for preparation of reading material, field trips, postage, office assistance, etc., payment to part time organizing assistants, etc.

One time grant will be provided to take up activities described above, Maximum ceiling of financial support will be Rs. 5.00 Lakhs. Maximum ceiling does not mean that each College/University will get this grant. It will depend on type of activities that will be undertaken by them.

Bibliography

A Guide to the Protection of Human Rights Act, 1993.

Abhigyana Shakuntala, trans. C.R. Devdhar, N.G. Saru and S.S. Sadri, Bombay, 1946.

Agarwal, Arun K. (1998), Developing Self-Confidence, New Delhi; Hind Pocket Books.

Agarwal, H.O. (1999), Human Rights, Central Law Publications, Allahabad.

Agarwal, H.O. (1983), Implementation of Human Rights Covenants with Special Reference to India, Kitab Mahal, Allahabad.

Agarwal, R.S. (1974), Human Rights in the Modern World, Chetana Publication, New Delhi.

Aggarwal, J.C. (1985), Theory and Principles of Education, Philosophical and Sociological Bases of Education, Vikas Publishing House Pvt. Ltd., New Delhi.

Ahlawat, S, June-December, 1991), Human Rights and Education, Vol. 111, No. 2-4, *NCTE Bulletin*, NCERT, New Delhi.

Ahmad, A. (1973), A Study of Relationship between Values and Modernity with Special Reference to College Girls, Ph.D., Psy., P. at V., Second Survey of Research in Education, NCERT, New Delhi.

Ahmedabad 1939 reseted. Bombay, 1954.

Aitareya Upanisad Ed. Sharhyanda, Swami Ramakrishna Math, Madras, 1927.

Altekar, A.S., Education in Ancient India, Banaras.

Altekar, A.S., Methods of Teaching and Study in Ancient India, Gopal Krishnamacharya Corom., Vol. 1942.

Altekar, A.S., State and Government in Ancient India.

Altekar, A.S., The Position of Women in Hindu Civilization, Banaras, 1936.

Ammal, O.K., Anantalakshmi, Studies in the Upanisada, JOR 3-4.

Ancient India, trans. J.W. MacCrindle Chakravarty and Chatterjee, Calcutta, 1926.

Anitha Shetty, (December 1997), Valuing Values, Vol. 35, No. 52, *University News,* Association of Indian Universities, New Delhi.

Apasthumba Dharma Sutra ed. G. Buhler, Bombay, Sanskrit Series, Bombay, 3rd ed., 1932.

Apte, Y.M., Social and Religious Life in the Garhys Sutras.

Arjun Dev (Ed.) (2003), A Handbook of Human Rights, Creative Learning Series, NBI, New Delhi.

Asian Educationists Conference in Human Rights and Values, Achieving the Goals of UN Decade for Human Rights Education (1995-2004), June 22 to 25, 1997 Organised by Prajapati Brahma Kumaris Ishwariya Vishwavidyalaya International Headquarters, Mount Abu, *Education in Asia*, 17(2), 1997, pp. 142-44.

Asthana, D.K. and Asthana Meera (1998), Environment Problems and Solutions, S. Chand and Company Ltd., Ram Nagar, New Delhi.

Asthdyayi of Panini trans. S.S. Vasa, Motilal Banarsidass, Delhi, 1962, 2 volumes.

Atharva-Veda Samhita, trans. Griffth R.T.H., Vol. 2, Banaras, 1916.

Attareya Upanisad, Kalpaka 30, 1935.

Aurobindo, System of National Education: Some Preliminary Ideas, Pondicherry, Sri Aurobindo Ashram, 1970.

Baba, S.S., Spiritual Basis of Value Education, Santhana Sarathi, October 1977, pp. 269-72.

Bader, C., Women in Ancient India, London, 1923.

Bajwa, G.S. (1995), Human Rights in India: Implementation and Violation, Anmol Publications, New Delhi.

Bake, Arnold A., Different Aspects of Indian Music: Indian Art and Letters, London, 1934.

Banara, 1949, Altekar, A.S., Yajnopavita, JBORS, June, 1934.

Bandopadhyaya, N.C., Economic Rift and Progress in Ancient India, Calcutta, 1944.

Banerji, R.D., Pre-historic Ancient and Hindu India, Blackie and Sons, 1950.

Bantock, G.H., Education and Values: Essays in the Theory of Education, London, Faber and Faber, 1967.

Basham, A.L., The Wonder that was India, Sidwick and Jackson, London, 1954.

Basu, D.D. (1994), Human Rights in Constitutional Law, Prentice Hall of India Pvt. Ltd, New Delhi.

Baxi, Upendra (Ed.) (1987), The Right to be Human, Lancer International, New Delhi.

Beck John, Morality and Citizenship Education, London, Willington House, 1998.

Bell (1976), The International Encyclopaedia of Education, Vol. 9, Pergamon Press, Oxford.

Benerjee, P.K. (1980), A Study in the Appreciation of Prose and Poetry of Secondary School Children, Ph.D. Edu., Kal. U., Third Survey of Research in Education, NCERT, New Delhi.

Bernard Mayo (1967), What are Human Rights, Political Theory and the Right of Man, Ed. By Raphael, D.D. McMillan, p. 68.

Bertend Russell (1961), Education and the Social Order, George Allen and Unwin Ltd., London.

Bhatnagar, I. (1984), A Study of Some Family Characteristics as Related to Secondary School Student Activism, Values, Adjustment and School Learning, Ph.D. Edu., Meerut University, Fourth Survey of Research in Education, NCERT, New Delhi.

Billing, J.C., Teaching Values by Example, *Illinois School Board Journal*, 58, 1990, pp. 28-29.

Bloom Field, The Religion of the Vedas, New York, 1908. Bhagavaddatta, History of Vedic Literature: Hindi. Day Sk. Grantha 10, Lahore, 1935.

Brightman, E.S. (1978), Personality and Reality, Ronad, New York.

Buddhist Birth Stories. Rhys-Davids, T.W. George, Routledge and: Sons, London, 1878.

Budhananda, Swami, How to Build Character: A Primer?, New Delhi, Ramakrishna Mission, 1983.

Burgess, Jas, Buddhist Art in India, Bernard Quaitch, London, 1901.

Burrow, L. (1987), Group Singing—The Power of Music. In Sathya Sai Education in Human Values, Handbook for Teachers Part-II, Sri Sathya Sai Bal-Vikas Education Trust, Prasanthi Nilayam (A.P.), pp. 105-06, 140.

Buzzelu, C.A., Young Children's Moral Understanding: Learning Right and Wrong, *Young Children*, 47(6), 1992, pp. 47-53.

Cairn, S. Jo; Lawton, Denis; Gardner, Roy, Eds. Value, Culture and Education: World Year-Book on Education, 2001, London, Kogan Page, 2001.

Caland, W., Relative Chronology of some Ritualistic Sutras, AO 9, 1930.

Carr, D., Moral Values and the Teacher: Beyond the Paternal and the Permissive, *Journal of Philosophy of Education*, 27, 1993, pp. 193-207.

Central BMrd of Secondary Education, Value Education a Handbook for Teachers, New Delhi, The Author, 1997.

Central Board of Secondary Education Value Education: A Handbook for Teachers, New Delhi, The Author, 1997.

Chakladar, H.C., Social Life in Ancient India, Sushil Gupta, Calcutta, 1954.

Chakrabarti, Mohit, (1997), Value Education Changing Perspective, Kanishka Publishers, New Delhi.

Chakravarty, Chandra, Pragmatic Philosophy, Vijaya Krishna Bros., Calcutta.

Challenges of Education—A Policy Perspective—A Status paper, (1985), MHRD, Government of India, New Delhi.

Chandgyopanisad Ed. *JHA*, Ganganatha. OBA, Poona, 1942.

Chandna, R.C. (1998), Environmental Awareness, Kalyani Publishers, Ludhiana.

Chandra Lekha, R.S. (December 1995), Value Education for College Students, *University News*, Association of Indian Universities, New Delhi.

Chandra Sekharaih, B.K. (1964), An Investigation into the Basic Vocabulary of Elementary School Children of Standard I to VII of Mysore State, Educational Research Bureau, Bangalore.

Chattopadhyaya, S., Early History of North India, Progressive Publishers, Calcutta, 1958.

Chaudhari, L.S. (1977), A Critical Evaluation of School Textbook Improvement Programmes in India, Ph.D., Education, Punjab University, Second Survey of Research in Education, NCERT, New Delhi.

Chaudhary, S. (1985), Silent-sitting. In Report on the Orientation course-*cum*-Workshop on Human Values. Department of Education, Government of Himachal Pradesh, Shimla, p. 48.

Childe, V.G., New Light on the most Ancient East, Groves Press Inc., New York (V.D.)

Chittibabu, S.V., Value-orientation in Higher Education, *Progressive Educational Herald*, 2(2), 1988.

Chittybabu, S.V. (May 1997), Convocation Address at Annamalai University, Vol. 35, No. 8, *University News*, New Delhi.

Choudhary, K. (1996), Value Education in India: The Social-ideological Dimensions, Indian Journal of Social Research, Vol. 37(i), p. 1526.

Chullavagga (Ed) J., "Kashyapa Nalanda-Dt'llanagar, Pall Granthalaya (Pali).

Corwin Press, 1998, Development, Early Education and Development; Special Issue on: Early Education for Moral Development, 11(1), Jan. 2000.

Cragg, A.W., Moral Education in the School: The Hidden Values Argument, Interchange, 10(1), 1978, pp. 12-19.

Cronbach, (1995), The Encyclopaedia of Education Research, Fourth Edition, The Macmillan Company, Collier, Macmillan Ltd., London.

Cuber, M.S. (1963), Sociology: A Synopsis of Principles, Appleton Century Craft.

Cummings, Rhoda; Harlow, Steve, Constructivist Roots of Moral Education, *The Educational Forum*, 64(4), 2000, pp. 300-07.

Cutt, Early Hindu Civilization, R.P. Mitra & Co., Calcutta, 1927.

Dackawish, S.J. (1959), An Analysis of Values of Modern Age, Midwestern Community, Sociology and Social Research, 44(i).

Dale and Chall (1948), The International Encyclopaedia of Education, Vol. 9, Pargamon Press, Oxford.

Daniel, J.T.K. (1990), Value Education Today, AIACHE, New Delhi.

Das, A.C., Rigvedic Culture, Calcutta, 1925.

Das, R.C., Study of the methods adopted by selected Secondary Schools in India for development of moral and ethical values and measurement of value judgment of students of class IX of these schools, Bhubaneswar, Regional College of Education, 1991.

Das, S.K., The Educational System of the Ancient Hindus, Calcutta, 1930.

Dave, Indu, Concept of Value Education, *Rajasthan Board Journal of Education*, 27(23), 1991, pp. 1-6.

Davidson, Scott (1993), Human Rights, Philadelphia, Open University Press, USA.

DeRoche, Edward F., Williams, Mary M., Educating Hearts and Minds: Comprehensive Character Education Framework, California.

Dev, Arjun and Indira Arjun Dev and Supta Das, (Ed.), (1996), Human Rights: A Source Book, NCERT, New Delhi.

Dewey John and Dewey Evenly, Schools of Tomorrow, N.D., London, J.M. Dent and: Sons.

Dewey John, Moral Principles in Education, 1909, Boston Houghtan Mifflin Co.

Dewey John, My Peda, Logic Creed, 1987, Washington, Progressive Education Association.

Dewey John, Problems of Men, 1946, New York, Philosophical Library.

Dewey John, School and Society, University of Chicago Press, Chicago, 1915.

Dewey, John, A Common Faith, 1947, New-Haven (London), Yale University Press.

Dewey, John, Child and the Curriculum and the School and Society, Chicago, University of Chicago Press.

Dewey, John, Democracy and Education: An Introduction to the Philosophy of Education, Macmillan, 1916.

Dewey, John, Education Today, Vietnam, 1940.

Dewey, John, Experience and Education, MacMillan, 1947.

Dewey, John, Freedom and Culture, 1952, Bombay.

Dewey, John, Individualism Old and New, Allen and Unwin, 1931.

Dewey, John, Philosophy of John Dewey, ed. Key, Schilpp, Paul Arthur, 2nd ed., 1951, New York, Tudar Publishing Co.

Dhaliwal, G.S. *et. al.* (1996), Fundamentals of Environmental Science, Kalyani Publishers, New Delhi.

Dhameja, S.K. (2002), Environmental Engineering and Management, S.K. Kataria and Sons, Nai Sarak, Delhi.

Dhar, P.L., (November, 2000), How can Values be Taught?, *Journal of Value Education*, NCERT New Delhi.

Dhokalia, R.P. (1948), Democracy and Education, McMillan Co., New York.

Dhokalia, R.P. (2001), Eternal Human Values and World Religions, NCERT, New Delhi.

Dictionary of Education (1959), McGraw Hill, Inc, New York.

Digumarti, B.R. (Ed.) (2004), Methods of Teaching: Environmental Science, Discovery Publishing House, New Delhi.

Diwedi, C.B. (1983), An Investigation into the Changing Social Values and their Educational Implications, Ph.D., Edu. Gor. Uni., Fourth Survey of Research and Studies, Vol. 9, Pergamon Press, Oxford.

Ediger Marlow, Values and Curriculum, New Frontiers in Education, 12(3), 1982.

Education for Values Development, Chapter 5. In National Curriculum Framework for School Education, New Delhi, NCERT, 2000, pp. 117-19.

Edwars, J., Pogelman, K., Developing Citizenship in the Curriculum, London, Fulton, 1993.

Erricker, Clivei, Erricker, Janė, Reconstructing Religious, Spiritual and Moral Education, New York, Routledge Falmer, 2000.

Fawcett, J.E.S. (1968), The Law of Nations, Allen Lane Penguin Press, London, p. 151.

Gaikwad, Shashi, Role of Women in Education for Human Rights and Values, *Education in Asia*, 17(2), 1997, pp. 128-29.

Gandhi, M.K. January-March, 1974), Gandhiji on Education, Compiled by Rita Roy, Vol. IV, No. 2, New Frontiers in Education, AIACHE, New Delhi.

Garlatt, G.T., The Legacy of India, Oxford University Press, 1951.

Gaur, R.S. (1975), A Study of Values and Perceptions of High School Students of the State of Rajasthan and their Relation to Learning, Ph.D. Edu.; Rajasthan University, Second Survey of Research in Education, NCERT, New Delhi.

Gautama Dharma Sutra, English Tr. G. Bihler in SBE, Vol. II ended, Oxford, 1896.

Gautama Dharma Sutra with Maskari-Bhaya: Ed. Srinivasacarya, Mysore, 1917.

Ghanta, Ramesh and Rao, D.B. (1998), Environment Education: Problems and Prospects. Discovery Publishing House, New Delhi.

Ghose, Aurobindo, Hymns of the Atris, Arya 2-3-4, Pondicherry; 1915-16-17.

Ghose, Aurobindo, Life Value of Indian Philosophy, CR 63, May, 1937.

Ginsberg Morris, Swami Vivekananda on Universal Ethics and Moral Conduct, India, Ministry of Education, 1965.

Glen Langford and Cornor, D.J. (1973), New Essays in the Philosophy of Education, Routledge and Kegan Paul Ltd., London and Boston.

Goel, A. and Goel, S.L. (2005), Human Values and Education, Deep & Deep Publications Pvt. Ltd., New Delhi.

Gokak, V.K. (1973), A Value Orientation to Our System of Education, M.M. Gulab and Sons, Gulab Bhawan, New Delhi.

Gokak, V.K. (1975), Sri Sathya Sai Baba: The Man and the Avatar, Shakti Malik Abhinav Publications, New Delhi, pp. 24-26.

Gokak, V.K. (1981), Stories for Children—Part II. Sri Sathya Sai Books and Publications Trust, Prasanthi Nilayam (A.P.).

Gokak, V.K. (1981), The Syllabus for the Education in Human Values Course. In V.K. Gokak and S.R. Rohidekar (Eds.). Teacher Handbook for the Course in Human Values. Sri Sathya Sai Bal Vikas Education Trust, Prasanthi Nilayam, (A.P.), pp. 52-53.

Gokak, V.K. (1985), Human Values, Higher Education and the

Six Aspects of Reality. In Seminar on Education Human Values. Sri Sathya Sa; Education Human Values Trust in Co-operation with Government of (A.P.), pp. 18-19.

Gokhale, B.G., Ancient India, Asia Publishing House, Bombay, 1952.

Gopaliah, G. Oanuary-1981), A Study of Moral Judgement in Children, Vol. VIII, No. 11, Experiments in Education, New Delhi.

Gosh, N.G. (1977), Distribution of Four Social Values Among Certain Selected trata of Youths and Prediction of Good Citizenship with the Help Values, Ph.D., Education; Kal. University; Third Survey of Research of Education, NCERT, New Delhi.

Goudie, A.S. (1992), Environmental Change: On Temporary Problems in Geography, Clarendon Press, Oxford.

Goudie, A.S. (1993), The Human Impact on Environment, Blackwell, Oxford.

Goyal, B.R. (1979), Document on Social, Moral and Spiritual Values in Education, NCERT, New Delhi.

Greeley, A.M. and Gockel, G.L. (1971), Encyclopaedia of Educational Research, Fourth Volume, Fifth Edition, the Free Press, A Division of MacMillan Publishing Company, Inc., New York.

Griffith, .R.T.H., The Hymns of the Rigveda, English Translation, E.J. Lazarus and Co., Banaras, 1920-26.

Gupta, N.L. (1986), Value Education: Theory and Practice, Krishna Brothers, Ajmer.

Gupta, Ltd., Calcutta, 1958.

Gupta, Vinay K. (Ed.) (1996), Perspectives on Human Rights, Vikas Publishing House Pvt. Ltd., New Delhi.

Halstead, J.M. and M.J. Tayler, Liberal Values and Liberal Education, In Values in Education and Education in Values, ed. by London, Falmer Press, 1996.

Heaman, John, Cornerstone Values—A Value Education Curriculum, New Zealand Foundation for Values Education, 1996.

Hebalkar, I. (1985), Group-activities in Report on the Orientation Course-cum-Workshop on Education in Human Value. Deptt. Of Education, Govt. of H.P. Shimla, p. 58.

Heritage of India, P. Max Muller, published by S. Gupta, Calcutta, 1951, Hedmann, Betty, Plurality, Polarity and Unity in Hindu Thought: A Doxographical Study, BSOS 9, 1939.

Higgins (1980), Hand Book of Research of Training, Third Edition, p. 925, American Educational Research Association, Macmillan Publishing Company, Inc., New York.

Hilton, Ernest, (1969), The Encyclopaedia of Educational Research, Fourth Edition, The Macmillan Company, Collier, Macmillan Ltd., London.

Hingurani, R.C. (1985), Human Rights in India, Oxford and IBH Publishing Co., New Delhi

http:// www.ncte.in.org.

http:// www.pulseplanet.com/

Huck, (1965), The International Encyclopaedia of Education Research and Studies, Vol. 9, Page 1471, Pergamon Press, Oxford. Isavasyopanisad, Kalpaka 31, 1936.

Isha Upanishad, Ed. Ghose, Aurobindo, Arya Publishing House, Calcutta, 1941.

Iyengar, P.T.S., Life in Ancient India, Madras, 1912.

Jaila, H.L. and Kushal (1998), Parents and Value Education, Mumbai; D.A.V. Centre for Creative Education.

Jain, J.C., Life in Ancient India, New Book Co., Bombay, 1947.

James William, Pragratism a new name from some old ways of thinking, 1946.

John W. Best (1982), Research in Education, Fourth Edition, Prentice Hall of India Private Ltd., New Delhi.

John, W. Best, (1982), Research in Education, Fourth Edition, Prentice Hall of India Private Ltd., New Delhi.

Jois, M. Rana, (1998), Human Rights and Indian Values, NCTE, New Delhi.

Joshi, Kireet, (1976), Education for Personality Development, New Delhi, NCERT, (NIE Lecture Series).

Jumsai, A.A. (1987), Silent-sitting (Meditation or Tuning in). In Sathya Sai Education in Human Values, Sri Sathya Sai Foundation of Thailand, Bangkok, p. 53.

Jumsai, A.A. (1991), Prayers. In Sathya Sai Education in Human Values Handbook for Teachers, Sri Sathya Sai Foundation of Thailand, Bangkok, p. 98.

Kalia S., (1970), Ego Ideals and Values of Students, Ph.D., Psy., Agra University; First Survey of Research in Education, NCERT, New Delhi.

Kalra, R.M. (2002), Teaching of Science with Focus on Values, Vikas Publishers, New Delhi.

Kalra, R.M. (2002), Value Oriented Education in Schools, New Delhi, Shipra Publications.

Kalra, R.M. (2002), Value Oriented Education in Schools, Shipra Publications, New Delhi.

Kalra, R.M., Curriculum Development with a Focus on Values, Ambala: International Book Agencies, 1977.

Kalra, R.M., Teaching of Science with Focus on Values, New Delhi: Vikas Publishers, 2002.

Kamasutra (Vatsyayana) trans. Upadhyaya, B.O.S., Tarapurwala Sons and Co., Bombay.

Kane, P.V., History of Dharma Sastras, Vols. I-V, Poona, 1930-57.

Kathakopanisad. An 557, Poona, 1935.

Kathardekar, C.N. (1982), A Study of Basic Vocabulary of Students Studying in Standard VII, Ph.D., Edu., Poona Uni., Third Survey of Research in Education, NCERT, New Delhi.

Keay, F.E., Ancient Indian Education, London, 1915.

Keith, A.B., The Religion and Philosophy of the Vedas and the Upanisads, Harvard Oriental Series, Vols. 31 and 32; Cambridge, Massachusetts, 1925.

Kena or Talavakara Upanisad, Kalpaka 31, 1936 (English trans.)

Khan, S. (2004), Human Rights in India (Protection and Violence), Devika Publication, New Delhi.

Khanna, N. (1995), Story-Telling. In S. Saraf (Ed.), Education in Human Values Programme Implementation, Apeejay Education Foundation, New Delhi, pp. 124, 128, 130.

Khanna, N. (2000), Concept and Programmes of Education in Human Values, Sri Sathya Sai Books and Publications Trust Prasanthi Nilayam, India (A.P.).

Khoshoo, T.N. (1984), Environmental Concerns and Strategies, India Environmental Society.

Kishore, Lalit (1990), Value Oriented Education: Foundation and frontiers-World Overview, Doaba House, Delhi.

Kluckhohn (1951), The International Encyclopaedia of the Social Sciences, Vol. 16, The Macmillan Company and the Free Press, New York, Collier, Macmillan Publishers, London,

Kluckhohn, C., Values and Values Orientation in the Theory of Action: An Exploration in Definition and Classification, In Towards a General Theory of Social Action, Co. by T. Parson and E.A. Shill, Cambridge, Harvard University Press, 1951.

Kluckhohn, C.F. (1959), The Scientific Study of Values, University of Toronto Press, Toronto.

Kothan, D.S. (1966), Report of Education Commission, Ministry of Education and Youth Services, Govt. of India, New Delhi.

Kumar, A. (2004), A Text Book of Environmental Science, A.P.H. Co., New Delhi.

Lataka Storit: Ed. E.B. Cowel, Vols. I-V.

Linda and Richard Eyre (1995), "Teaching your Children Values, Teaching your Children" Sensitivity, New York, Rockefeller Center. Mahabharata (Vol. 6) trans. Shastri, R.D., Gita Press, Gorakhpur (Hindi).

Louis B. Sohn (1982), The New International Law: Protection of the Rights of Individuals Rather than States, Thomas, Buergenthal and Dinah Shelton, Supra No. 50, pp. 9-17.

Louis P. Pojman (2000), Global Environmental Ethics, May Field Publishing Company.

Mahabharata, Rajagopalachari, C. Chakravarti, Vidya Bhavan, Bombay, 1958.

Maharashtra State Bureau of Textbook Production and Curriculum Research, MSBTPCR (1974), State Wide Survey of Use of Text-books, Third Survey of Research in Education, NCERT, New Delhi.

Maitrayana Brahmana Upanisad, Kalpaka 35-26, 1940-41 (English trans.) Maitri or Maitrayaniya Upanisad, with commentary of Ramatirtha, Ed. Cowell, E.D. BI, Calcutta, 1935.

Majumdar, R.C., Co-operate Life in Ancient India, Calcutta, 1922.

Majumdar, R.C., Vedic Age, London, 1951.

Mandukya Upanisad, Ed. Sharvananda, Swami, Ramakrishna Math, Madras, 1939.

Manu Smriti (Ed.), C.N. Jha, Eng. trans., Vols. I-VII, Calcutta, 1921-29.

Margenau (1959), Education for Human Values, Compiled by Asha Sharma and Ahluwalia, S.P., p. 84, *Journal of Education and Allied Sciences*, New Delhi.

Mascarenhas, M.M. (1983), Family Life Education-Value Education, AIACHE and CREST, New Delhi.

Mishra, R. (1968), Ecology Work Book, Oxford and IBH, New Delhi.

Mitra, Dr. Veda, Education in Ancient India, Arya Book Depot, New Delhi, 1964.

Mitra, Shib K. (1994), Value Education and Habits, NCERT, New Delhi.

Mohanty, J., Ed. (2000), Human Rights Education, Deep and Deep Publications Pvt. Ltd., New Delhi.

Mookerii, R.K., Ancient Indian Education, MacMillan, 1951.

Mookerii, R.K., Glimpses of Ancient India, Bharatiya Vidya Bhawan, Bombay, 1961.

Mookerii, Radha Kumud, Practical Aspects of Education in Ancient India, JUPHS 14, 1941.

Morris, C. (1956), Varieties of Human Value, University of Chicago Press, Chicago.

Mrichchakatika, trans., S.K. University of Calcutta.

Mudaliyar, L.S. (1953), Report of the Secondary Education Commission, Ministry of Education, Govt. of India, Delhi.

Mukeriee, S.N., History of Education in India, Baroda.

Mukerii, R.K., Education in Ancient India, London, 1936.

Mukerii, R.K., Hindu Civilization, London, 1936.

Mukherjee, R.K. (1964), Social Structure of Values, McMillan and Co. Ltd., London.

Mukherjee, Rama (2002), Environmental Management and Awareness Issues. Sterling Publishers Private Limited, New Delhi.

Mundaka Upanisad, Kalpaka 33, 1938 (English trans.).

Munshi, K.M. and Niyyar, N.C., Indian Inheritance, Bhartiya Vidya Bhawan, Bombay, 1955.

Muthukumaran, S. (1991), Issues in Higher Education, Science and Technology, Published by Mrs. M. Ratan Vathi, Madras.

Mundakopanisad (Ed.), Chose, Aurobindo, Arya VII, Pondicherry, 1920.

Nagaraja Rao, P. (1986), Value in Changing World, Bangalore: Indian Institute of World Culture.

Nanda, R.T., Contemporary Approaches to Value Education in India, New Delhi, Regency, 1997.

National Policy on Education (1986), Ministry of Human Resource Development, The Challenge of Education Policy Perspective, Govt. of India, New Delhi.

National Policy on Education (1986), Ministry of Human Resource Development, The Challenge of Education Policy Perspective, Govt. of India, New Delhi.

NCERT (1980), Environmental Studies: Teachers' Guide, New Delhi.

NCERT (1981). Environmental Education at the School Level, NCERT, New Delhi.

NCERT (1988), National Curriculum for Elementary and Secondary Education: A Framework (Revised Version), NCERT, New Delhi.

NCERT (2000), Education for Values Development, Chapter 5, In National Curriculum Framework for School Education, New Delhi, pp. 117-19.

NCERT (2000), National Curriculum Framework for School Education, NCERT, New Delhi.

NCERT (2001), Guidelines and Syllabi for Primary Stage, Upper Primary Stage, Secondary Stage and Higher Secondary Stage, NCERT, New Delhi.

Nehru, J.L., The Discovery of India, Meridian Books, London, 1956. Nurullqh, S. and Naik, J.P., History of Education in India, Pillai, C.K., Vedic India, Kitabistan, 1959.

Nicholas, R. (1969), Introduction to Value Theory. Prentice Hall, New Jersey.

NIEPA, Environmental Education Handbook for Education Planners, New Delhi.

O.U.B.

Odum, E.P. (1971), Fundamentals of Ecology, W.B. Saunders, Philadelphia.

Pagels, Elaine (1979), "The Roots and Origins of Human Rights", Human Dignity-The Internationalization of Human Rights, Ed. by Alince H. Hanbin.

Pal, B.P. (1981), National Policy on Environment, Department of Environment, Government of India, New Delhi, p. 15.

Pandey, R.B., Hindu Samskaras, Banaras, 1949.

Pandya, A.R.C. (1959), Measurement of Modern Educational Values from Different Stand Points, Ph.D., Education, Bombay University; First Survey of Research in Education, NCERT, New Delhi.

Panneerselvam, A. and Ramakrishman, Mohan (1996), Environmental Science Education, Sterling Publishers, New Delhi.

Pargiter, F.E., Ancient Historical Traditions, Motilal Banarasidass, Delhi, 1962.

Park, C.C. (1980), Ecology and Environmental Management, Bitterworths, London.

Parker, D.A., The Philosophy of Values: An Arbor, University of Michigan.

Parliament of India, Rajya Sabha (January, 1999). Eighty-first Report on Value-based Education, Rajya Sabha Secretariat, New Delhi.

Passi, B.K. (1991), Value Education, National Psychological Press, Agra.

Patel, M.G. (1981), A Study of the Prevalent Value System of the Students of South Gujarat Studying in Standards X and XI, Ph.D. Education, S.G. University, Fourth Survey of Research in Education, NCERT, New Delhi.

Paul, P.V. (1986), A Study of Value Orientations of Adolescent Boys and Girls, Ph.D., Psy.; M.S. University; Fourth Survey of Research in Education, NCERT, New Delhi.

Paul, R.C. (2000), Protection of Human Rights, Commonwealth, New Delhi.

Paul, W. Tayler, Respect for Nature, Princeton University Press, Princeton, New Jersey, USA, 1994.

Pepper (1958), The International Encyclopaedia of the Social Sciences, Vol. 16, The Macmillan Company and the Free Press, New York, Collier, Macmillan Publishers, London.

Pepper, S.C. (1958), The Sources of Values, University of California, Berkley.

Pillai, C.K., Vedic India, Kitabistan, 1959.

Pingle, V.S. (1972), A Critical Evaluation of Marathi Text Books for Standard V, Ph.D., Education; Aurangabad University, The Survey of Research in Education, NCERT, New Delhi.

Poole, M., Belief and Values in Science Education, Buckingham, Open University Press, 1995.

Prabhavathy, G. (1974), Study on Education Values in Children's Literature, Ph.D. Education, Thesis submitted to Nagarjuna University, Andhra Pradesh.

Prakash, B., Studies in Indian History and Civilization, Shiva Lal Aggrawal, Agra, 1962.

Pranjpa, V.G. (Edited by Peterson), Hymns from the Rigveda, BSPs 58, Poona, 1939.

Puri, B.N., India in the Times of Patanjali, Bhartiya Vidya Bhawan.

Radhakrishan, S., Brahma-Sutra, the Philosophy of Spiritual Life, 1960, London,, George Allen and Unwin.

Radhakrishan, S. (Chairman Editorial Board), History of Philosophy, Eastern and Western, Volume II, London, George Allen and Union, 1953.

Radhakrishan, S. (Ed.), Principal Upanisads, 1963, London, Allen and Unwin.

Radhakrishnan, S., Eastern Religious and Western Thought, Oxford Univ. Press, London, 1939.

Radhakrishnan, S., Dharma-pada, English Translation, 1950, London,

Radhakrishnan, S. (1965), Convocational Address, As Cited in Vol. XL, No.5, The Progress of Education, Delhi.

Ragozin, Z.A., Vedic India, Munshiram Manoharlal, Delhi, 1961.

Rajput, J.S. (2001), Symphony of Human Values in Education, NCERT, New Delhi.

Ramji, M.T. (1986), Value-Oriented School Education, NCERT, New Delhi.

Rao, M. Srinivasa, Mandtlkya-Upanisad, QIMS 22-23, 1930, 31-32.

Raphael, D.O. (1967), Human Rights Old and New, Political Theory and the Rights of Man, ed. By Raphael, McMillan.

Rathakrishna, S., Regional and Society, London, George Allen and Unwin, 1959.

Raths, L., Harinin, M.; Simon, S., Values and Teaching: Working with Values in the Classroom, Columbus D.H., Merril, 1996.

Reddy, Y.N.K. (1976), Education as a Medium of Integration of Value and Effective Value Changes, Osmania University, Second Survey of Research in Education, NCERT, New Delhi.

Renon, Louis, The Civilization of Ancient India. trans. Philip Spratt, Sushil Gupta, Calcutta, 1954.

Report of Core Group on Value Orientation of Education, (1992), Planning Commission, Govt. of India, New Delhi.

Report of the Kothari Commission (1964-66), Ministry of Education, Government of India, New Delhi.

Report of the Religious and Moral Instruction (1959), Ministry of Education, Government of India, New Delhi.

Report of the Secondary Education Commission, (1953), Ministry of Education, Government of India, Delhi.

Report of the University Education Commission (1948-49), Ministry of Education, Government of India, New Delhi.

Report, Inculcation of Ethical and Social Values in Education, Sri Ramakrishna Mission Vidyalaya, Coimbatore.

Report, Seminar on Gandhian Concept of Human Values, Citizenship Development Society, New Delhi.

Reynolds (1979), Encyclopaedia of Educational Research, Fourth Volume, The Free Press, Macmillan Publishing Company, Inc., New York.

Rgveda (Ed.), A.B. Kaith, Cambridge, 1920, Rgveda Samhita (Ed.), F. Max Muller, 1980-92.

Rhys-Davids, T.W., Buddhist India, Shushil Gupta, Calcutta, 1950.

Riley, Sue Spayth, How to Generate Values in Young Children, Washington, National Association for the Education of Young Children, 1989.

Ritchie, D.G., Natural Rights, Allen and Unwin, London.

Rizvi, S.A.H. (1986), A Study of Attitudes towards Religious Education in Relation to Certain Value Orientations,

Ph.D., PSYi A.M. Urn., Fourth Survey of Research in Education, NCERT, New Delhi.

Roer (Mitra and Cowell), Twelve Principal Upanisads, Theosophical Publishing House, Madras, 1931-32.

Rohtdekar, S.R. *et. al.* (Ed.)(1982), Education in Human Values: Handbook for Teachers, Part-II, Sri Sathya Sai Bal Vikas Education Trust, Prashanti.

Rokeach (Dec., 1997), Valuing Values, Compiled by Anitha Shetty, Vol. 35, No. 52, *University News*, New Delhi, Ruhela, S.P. (1986), Human Values and Education, Sterling Publishers Private Limited, New Delhi.

Rokeach, M. (1973), The Nature of Human Values, McMillan, Free Press, New York.

Rowe, D., Newton, J. eds., You, Me, Us: A New Approach to Moral and Social Education for Primary Schools, London, Citizenship Foundation, 1994.

Ruhel, S.P. (1996), Education in Human Values, Regency Publication, New Delhi.

Ruhela, S.P. (1986), Human Values and Education, Sterling Publishers Private Limited, New Delhi.

Sai Leela, K. (1996), Realisation of Educational Values in the Ancient Sathakas, Ph.D., Edu. Thesis submitted to Nagarjuna University, Andhra Pradesh.

Sankalia, H.D., The University of Nalanda, Paul and Company, Madras, 1934.

Saraf, S. (1995), Education in Human Values: Programme Implementation. Apeejay Education Foundation, New Delhi, pp. 40-42.

Sarala Kumari, K.L.S. (1996), A Study of the Values Related to Women in the Secondary School Telugu Textbooks in Andhra Pradesh, Ph.D. Edu. Thesis submitted to S.P.M. University, Tirupati, A.P.

Saroj Bansal (April 1981), Values, Foundation of Curriculum, Vol. LXXXVII, No. 4, *The Educational Review*, New Delhi.

Satyavathy, G. (1995), Study of Educational Values in Telugu Novels, Ph.D. Edu. Thesis submitted to Nagarjuna University, Andhra Pradesh.

Saxena, A.B. (1996), Education for the Environmental Concerns, Radha Publications, New Delhi, p. 112.

Schuhler (1980), Hand Book of Research on Teaching, Third Edition, p. 925, A Project of the American Educational Research Association, Macmillan Publishing Company, Inc., New York.

Science in the Vedas (Ed.), Hans Raj, Ludhiana, 1936.

Seetha Ramu, A.S. (1974), An Experimental Study of the Problem of Moral Instruction in Upper Primary Schools, Ph.D. Edu., Mysore University, Second Survey of Research in Education, NCERT, New Delhi.

Selby, David (1987), Human Rights, Cambridge University Press, Cambridge.

Sen, A.N. (2002), Human Rights, Sri Sai Law Publications, Faridabad, Haryana.

Sen, D.N., The Upanisads in Relation to Practical Life, IV Ind. Phil. Congfig., Madras, 1928.

Seshadri, C. (1992), Education in Values: A Source Book, Sri Aurobindo Marg, NCERT, New Delhi, p. 23.

Sharma, B.K. (1996), An Introduction to Environmental Pollution, Goel Publishing House, Meerut.

Sharma, B.L. and Maheshwari, V.K., Education for Values, Environment and Human Rights, R. Lall Book Depot, Meerut.

Sharma, B.R. (1997), Environment and Pollution Awareness, Sathya Prakashan, New Delhi.

Sharma, D.P. (1997), Value Education in Action, University Book House, Jaipur.

Sharma, P.D. (1990), Ecology and Environment, Rastogi Publishers, Meerut.

Sharma, R.A. (2003), Environmental Education, Surya Publication, Meerut.

Sharma, R.C. (1981), Environmental Education, Metropolitan Book Co., New Delhi.

Sharma, S. and P.P. Singh (2004). Teaching of Environment: New Trends and Innovations. Deep & Deep Publications Pvt. Ltd., New Delhi.

Sheila Kaul (July-1983), Objectives of the Teaching Profession, Vol. XIII, No. 3, New Frontiers of Education, New Delhi.

Shetty, Anita (December, 1997), Valuing Values, Vol. 35(52), *University News,* Association of Indian Universities, New Delhi.

Shrimali, K.L., Search for Value in Indian Education, Delhi, Vikas, 1971.

Simon, S.B., Howe, I.W., Kirschenbaum, R., Values Clarification: A Handbook of Practical Strategies for Teachers and Students, New Delhi.

Singh, A.K. (1980), Political Attitudes of College Students in Relation to Some Socio-Psychological Variables, Ph.D., Psy.; Manglore University, Fourth Survey of Research in Education, New Delhi.

Singh, Joginder (1996), Text Book of Environmental Education and Pollution Control, Kalyani Publishers, New Delhi.

Singh, L.C. and Singh, R. (1986), Effectiveness of Value Clarifying Strategies in Value Orientation of B.Ed. Students, NCERT, New Delhi.

Singh, Nagendra (1981), Human Rights and the Future of Mankind, Vanity Books, Delhi.

Singh, R.P. (1960), Democracy and Higher Secondary Education in Uttar Pradesh, Ph.D., Education; Lucknow University, First Survey of Research in Education, New Delhi.

Singh, Ranjan R.K. (2000), Global Environmental Concerns, Rajesh Publications, New Delhi.

Singh, S.K. (2004), Dictionary of Ecology and Environment, Commonwealth Publishers, New Delhi.

Sirohi, S.S., Environmental Education Publications, Ludhiana.

Spaulding, I.A. (1963), Of Human Values Social Research, 47(2).

Smith, V.A., Early History of India.

Solmon, M. (1978), Encyclopaedia of Educational Research, Fourth Volume, Fifth Edition, The Free Press, A Division of Macmillan Publishing Company, Inc., New York.

Sree Prakasa Committee on Religious and Moral Instruction, (1959), Report of the Secondary Education Commission, Government of India, New Delhi.

Sutaria, M.C. (1990), The Role of Values Education in Environmental Education: The Resource Book on Environmental Education; Paris, UNESCO, pp. 189-202.

Svetasvatra Upanisad, Kalpaka 34, 1939.

Swami Vivekananda: Complete Work, Calcutta, Advaita Ashram, 1992, Vol. I, p. 389.

Syed, Muhammed Hafiz, The Aryan View of Life, KKT X(3): March, 1944.

Symonds, P.M. (1964), What Education has to learn from Psychology, New York; Teacher's College, Columbia University, Taithiriya Upanisad, Gita Press, Gorakhpur, 1920.

Taittiriya Upanisad (Ed.), Sharvananda, Swami, Ramakrishna Math, Madras, 1942.

Talesra, Hemlata, Pancholy, Nalini and Nagda, Mangilal (2000), Human Rights Education: A Global Perspective, Regency Publications, New Delhi.

Talyor, P.W. (1986), Respect for Nature, Princeton University Press, New Jersey.

Tamhankar, D.K., Essays on the Rigveda and other Topics, Poona, 1932.

Tandon, B.K. (1967), A Study of Attitudes towards Religion of Higher Secondary School Students in U.P., Ph.D., Edu., Agra University, First Survey of Research in Education, NCERT, New Delhi.

Taneja (1986), Inculcation of Human Values. In S.P. Ruhela (Ed.), Human Values and Education, Sterling Publishers Private Limited, New Delhi.

Tarlok Singh (January 1983), Educational Values of Life Rate and Illiterate Adults Belongings to Scheduled and Non-Scheduled Castes, Vol. 19, No. 3, *Journal of Educational Research and Extension*, New Delhi.

Tarrow Bernstein, Norma (1987), Human Rights and Education, Pergamon Press, USA.

Taylor, M.J. ed., Values Education in Europe: A Comparative Overview of a Survey of 26 Countries in 1993 Dundee, SCCC for UNESCO/CIDREE, 1994, Teacher Training Authority, 1997.

The International Conference on Environmental Education (1977), Referred in Source Book for Environmental Education, Living in the Environment (Ed.) Sytnik, K.M. (1985).

The Thirteen Principal Upanishads, Oxford University Press, 1958.

The Travel Account of Hiollen, Thsang (Volumes 1-4) trans. Bed, S. Sushi I.

Thinkers, *Journal of Values Education*, November, 2000.

Thirty Minor Upanisads (Ed.), Aiyar, K. Narayanaswami, Madras, 1914.

Thomas Lickona, Education for Character: How Our Schools can Teach Respect and Responsibility, Bantam Books, 1992.

Thomas Lickona, Education for Character: The School's Highest Calling, Georgia Humanities Council, 1992 (Lecture).

Travels of Fa-Haiten, Gilas, H.K., Routledge and Kogan Paul, London, 1923.

Tripathi, R.S., History of Ancient India, Motialal Banarasidass, Delhi, 1960.

UGC (1998), IXth Plan Approach to Promotion of Human Rights Education (HRE) in Universities and Colleges, New Delhi.

UNDP (1996), Human Development Report India, Oxford University Press, New Delhi.

UNESCO Report (1976), World in Classroom, Ministry of Education and Social Welfare, New Delhi.

UNESCO (1989), Teaching Human Rights, New York.

UNESCO (1990), International Environmental Education Programme United Nations.

UNESCO (1991), The State of the World Population, United Nations Population Fund (UNPF), New York.

UNESCO (1996) Earth Summit, Agenda 21, The United Nations Programme for Actions from Rio, United Nations Publication, E 931.11.

UNESCO (1996). World Resources, 1996-97: A Guide to Global Environment, World Resources Institute *et al.* Oxford University Press, New Delhi.

UNESCO, UNEP (2002), Youth X Change: Towards Sustainable Life-Style: The Guide, Paris.

Upanisads (Twenty-eight) (Ed.), Wasudeva and Sastri, Bombay, 1918.

Urban, W.N. (1949), Fundamentals of Ethics, Henry Holt and Co., New York.

Vaikhanasa Grhya Sutra (Ed. and translated), W. Caland in Bib. Indi., Calcutta, 1927.

Valdya, C.V., History of Sanskrit Literature (Vedic Period), Poona, 1930.

Vasak, Karel, "Human Rights a Legal Reality", The International Dimensions of Human Rights, Vol. 1, English Ed. By Philip Alston, UNESCO, pp. 4-10.

Vasistha Dharma Suo'a; English translation by C. Biihler in SIBE, Vol XIV, Oxford, 1882.

Vedantatirtha, Vanamali, Glhyasutras of Gobhile, Calcutta, S.K. Series 28, Calcutta, 1941.

Velankal, H.D., Meters and Music, PO VIII, (3-4), Oct.-Dec. 1943.

Venkataiah, N. (1998), Value Education, APH Publishing Corporation, Ansari Road, New Delhi.

Verma, N.K. and Sood, R.K. (1997), Environment Awareness, S.K. Kathri and Sons, Guru Nanak Market, Main Nai Sarak, Delhi.

Verma, P.S. (1986), The Values of Human Values. In S.R. Ruhela (Ed.) Human Values and Education, Sterling Publishers Pvt. Ltd., New Delhi, p. 29.

Vincent, R.J. (1986), Human Rights and International Relations, Cambridge University Press, New York.

W.H.O. (1995), The World Health Report, Bridging the Gaps, p. 41.

Walia, K. (November, 2000), Value-based Teacher Education Views of Modem Indian Thinkers, *Journal of Values Education*, NCERT.

Web site used:

West Sylvia, Educational Values for School Leadership, London, Kogan Page, 1993.

Wildon John, India: Three Thousand Years Ago, Indological Book House, Varanasai, VA.

Wilson, H., Rigveda (English Translation), Bangalore, 1925, 28.

World Commission on Environment and Development, (1989), Our Common Future, O.U.P.

World Health Organization (1997), Young People and their Families: A Cross Cultural Study of Parenti Adolescent Discord, in Cote d'Ivoire, India and Nigeria, Geneva, Switzerland.

World Health Organization: Health Hazards of the Human Environment, W.H.O., Geneva, 1972.

World Health Organization Atmospheric Pollutants, W.H.O. Technical Report Series No. 271, 1964.

World Health Organization European Standards for Drinking Water, Second Edition, W.H.O., 1963.

World Health Organization Air Pollution, W.H.O., 1961.

World Health Organizations: International Standards for Drinking Water, Second Edition, W.H.O.,1963.

Yajurveda (White), Ed. Ralph, T.H. Criffth, Banaras, 1957.

Yogasikha-Upanisad, Kalpaka, 29-30, 1934-35.

Zaleznik, A. and David, D. (1964), The Dynamic of Interpersonal Behaviour, John Wiley and Sons, Inc., New York.

Index